1970

SOCIETY FOR NEW TESTAMENT STUDIES
MONOGRAPH SERIES

GENERAL EDITOR
MATTHEW BLACK, D.D., F.B.A.

5

GREEK WORDS AND HEBREW MEANINGS:
STUDIES IN THE SEMANTICS OF
SOTERIOLOGICAL TERMS

GREEK WORDS AND HEBREW MEANINGS:

STUDIES IN THE SEMANTICS OF SOTERIOLOGICAL TERMS

BY

DAVID HILL

Department of Biblical History and Literature
The University of Sheffield

CAMBRIDGE

AT THE UNIVERSITY PRESS

1967

Published by the Syndics of the Cambridge University Press
Bentley House, 200 Euston Road, London, N.W. 1
American Branch: 32 East 57th Street, New York, N.Y. 10022

Library of Congress Catalogue Card Number: 67–21959

Printed in Great Britain
at the University Printing House, Cambridge
(Brooke Crutchley, University Printer)

To my Mother and Father

CONTENTS

CONTENTS

PREFACE

The appearance of a book containing New Testament word-studies which follow, to a large extent, the methods adopted in the *Theologisches Wörterbuch zum Neuen Testament* probably requires some explanation. In recent years the legitimacy of studying biblical words has been called in question and the methodology of the *Wörterbuch* severely criticised. No writer may proceed as though these views had never been expressed. The first section of this book submits them to detailed investigation, and, at this point, I content myself with stating the conclusions which emerge from that discussion and which guide the subsequent studies. First, the study of the background and semantics of theological words in the New Testament is a valid and necessary enterprise: valid, because such words are markers for different fields of meaning, pointers to recognised areas of thought and experience; necessary, because they have become, in many cases, technical terms whose special connotations cannot be appreciated without knowledge of their use and meaning outside the Greek New Testament. Secondly, although arguments and interpretations put forward in some of the studies of theological words in the *Wörterbuch* are open to criticism on linguistic grounds, the methodology on which the whole work is based is not thereby invalidated: the general approach can still be used and used fruitfully in laying the foundations for biblical theology, provided those who employ it exercise caution and common sense and are acquainted with the scope and procedures of modern linguistic science.

If the method of word-study found in the *Wörterbuch* is sound, why then are the studies in this book being presented at this time? The *Wörterbuch* is not only still available, but is also currently being translated into English in order that its riches may be more widely accessible to students of the New Testament. This observation evokes two comments. In the first place, the claim that the methodology of the *Wörterbuch* is defensible does not mean that every contribution is being judged adequate and unassailable. It is hoped that the studies published here do not perpetuate the linguistic errors and mistaken interpretations which can be found in some of their predecessors. I must add, however, that the words I have investigated were not chosen because I considered the articles devoted to them in the *Wörterbuch* to be especially weak or ill-informed: they were chosen because they are all relevant to New Testament soteriology and because, to some extent, they are representative of the ways in which aspects of that theme were expressed by the main New Testament witnesses. In the second place, it must be pointed out that the English translation of the volumes of the *Wörterbuch* presents the articles without revision (by contributors who are still alive), without editing and without any attempt to bring the bibliographies up to date. This is in no way intended as a criticism of a gigantic piece of translation work for which every English-speaking New Testament student will be grateful: it is a simple statement of fact which makes a fresh investigation of some of the words desirable and useful. The *Wörterbuch* articles on four of the words studied in this book were written between twenty and thirty years ago: the amount of material touching on the interpretation of those terms which has appeared in that time is very great. To obtain, read and assess all of it would be virtually impossible, but much of it that is significant has been allowed to contribute to my investigations and interpretations, but without taking away from the independence of my conclusions.

In an earlier form this work was submitted to the University of St Andrews for the degree of Doctor of Philosophy, and that degree was granted in June 1964. It is a pleasure to record here my thanks to the supervisors of my research, the Rev. Principal Matthew Black, D.D., F.B.A., and the Rev. Dr R. McL. Wilson: their interest in my work, at all stages of its preparation, has been a source of encouragement and enrichment. I would also like to thank the administrators of Mrs Honyman-Gillespie's Trust for the scholarship by which I was supported during my research-studentship. Staff and fellow-students in St Mary's College, St Andrews, colleagues in the University of Sheffield and several other friends have contributed to these studies through conversation and discussion. My thanks are due to them, as they are to the staffs of the University libraries where I have worked.

Finally, I must express my gratitude to Principal Black and

other members of the Editorial Board of the Society for New Testament Studies for accepting this book into the Monograph series, and to the officers and staff of the Cambridge University Press for their courtesy and help in all stages of its publication.

D.H.

The University
Sheffield
December 1966

ABBREVIATIONS

AJT	*American Journal of Theology.*
BASOR	*Bulletin of the American School of Oriental Research.*
BDB	*A Hebrew and English Lexicon of the Old Testament,* by F. Brown, S. R. Driver and C. A. Briggs: Oxford University Press, 1907, reprinted 1959.
BJRL	Bulletin of the John Rylands Library, Manchester.
ET	*The Expository Times.*
FRLANT	Forschungen zur Religion und Literatur des Alten und Neuen Testament.
HDB	*Hasting's Dictionary of the Bible,* 5th edition, Edinburgh, T. T. Clark, 1906, and revised edition (ed. H. H. Rowley), Edinburgh, 1963.
HTR	*The Harvard Theological Review.*
ICC	The International Critical Commentary.
IDB	*The Interpreter's Dictionary of the Bible,* 4 vols., Abingdon Press: New York and Nashville, 1962.
JBL	*Journal of Biblical Literature.*
JJS	*Journal of Jewish Studies.*
JQR	*Jewish Quarterly Review.*
JSS	*Journal of Semitic Studies.*
JTS	*Journal of Theological Studies.*
KB	*Lexicon in veteris testamenti libros,* L. Koehler and W. Baumgartner, Leiden, 1953.
LS	*A Greek–English Lexicon,* by H. G. Liddell and R. Scott; revised edition by H. S. Jones and R. McKenzie, Oxford, 1940.
MNTC	Moffatt New Testament Commentary.
NEB	The New English Bible.
NT	*Novum Testamentum.*
NTS	*New Testament Studies.*
PTR	*Princeton Theological Review.*
RB	*Revue Biblique.*
RQ	*Revue de Qumran.*
RSV	The Revised Standard Version of the Bible.
SB	*Kommentar zum Neuen Testament aus Talmud und Midrasch,* by H. L. Strack and P. Billerbeck, Munich, 1922–8.
SJT	*Scottish Journal of Theology.*
ST	*Studia Theologica.*
TBlätt	*Theologische Blätter.*

TLZ	*Theologische Literaturzeitung.*
TWNT	*Theologisches Wörterbuch zum Neuen Testament,* ed. G. Kittel and G. Friedrich, Stuttgart, from 1933.
TZ	*Theologische Zeitschrift.*
VGT	*Vocabulary of the Greek Testament,* ed. J. H. Moulton and G. Milligan, London: 1914–29.
VT	*Vetus Testamentum.*
ZAW	*Zeitschrift für die alttestamentliche Wissenschaft.*
ZNW	*Zeitschrift für die neutestamentliche Wissenschaft.*
ZTK	*Zeitschrift für Theologie und Kirche.*

The abbreviation LXX refers to the Septuagint translation of the Old Testament. The edition used is *Septuaginta,* ed. A. Rahlfs (Stuttgart, 1933).

The commonly accepted abbreviations for the Dead Sea Scrolls are used.

CD	The Damascus Document (Fragments of a Zadokite Work).
1QM	War of the Sons of Light with the Sons of Darkness.
1QH	The Hymns of Thanksgiving.
1QS	The Manual of Discipline.
1Qpsr Hab.	The Habakkuk Commentary.
4Qpsr Ps.	Fragments of Commentary on Psalms from Cave 4.

The scriptural and rabbinic abbreviations are customary and self-explanatory. The commonly accepted abbreviations for the names of authors and their works in the classical Greek and Intertestamental literatures are used throughout the work.

The abbreviations for Philo's works used by H. A. Wolfson (*Philo,* 2 vols., Harvard University Press, 1947) have been adopted.

Abr.	*De Abrahamo.*
Aet.	*De Aeternitate Mundi.*
Agr.	*De Agricultura.*
Cher.	*De Cherubim.*
Conf.	*De Confusione Linguarum.*
Congr.	*De Congressu Eruditionis Gratia.*
Cont.	*De Vita Contemplativa.*
Decal.	*De Decalogo.*
Deter.	*Quod Deterius Potiori Insidiari Soleat.*
Ebr.	*De Ebrietate.*
Flacc.	*In Flaccum.*
Fug.	*De Fuga et Inventione.*
Gig.	*De Gigantibus.*

Heres	*Quis Rerum Divinarum Heres.*
Hypoth.	*Hypothetica.*
Immut.	*Quod Deus Sit Immutabilis.*
Jos.	*De Josepho.*
Leg. All.	*Legum Allegoria.*
Legat.	*Legatio ad Gaium.*
Migr.	*De Migratione Abrahami.*
Mos.	*De Vita Mosis.*
Mut.	*De Mutatione Nominum.*
Opif.	*De Opificio Mundi.*
Plant.	*De Plantatione.*
Post.	*De Posteritate Caini.*
Praem.	*De Praemiis et Poenis.*
Probus	*Quod Omnis Probus Liber Sit.*
Provid.	*De Providentia.*
Qu. in Exod.	*Quaestiones et Solutiones in Exodum.*
Qu. in Gen.	*Quaestiones et Solutiones in Genesin.*
Sacr.	*De Sacrificiis Abelis et Caini.*
Sobr.	*De Sobrietate.*
Somn.	*De Somniis.*
Spec.	*De Specialibus Legibus.*
Virt.	*De Virtutibus.*

CHAPTER I

AN APPROACH TO NEW TESTAMENT WORD-STUDY

The studies presented in this work are directed towards ascertaining the meaning with which certain important words were used by the writers of the New Testament documents. Absolute certainty on this is admittedly impossible to obtain, but nevertheless the attempt to determine this meaning must be continued if we are to begin to understand the message of Scripture, and that attempt must proceed in accordance with sound linguistic and exegetical methods. Now it has to be admitted that there has been a conspicuous lack of serious interest in the problems and discussions of linguistic meaning on the part of those who seek to interpret what is expressed in the ancient languages of Scripture.[1] Recently the attention of biblical scholars has been drawn to this situation by Professor James Barr in his book *The Semantics of Biblical Language*,[2] a volume which courageously reveals the misleading methods and erroneous conclusions in exegesis which ignorance or neglect of the basic principles of linguistic semantics has allowed to gain acceptance within the movement for biblical theology.[3] It must be emphasised that

[1] The blame for this state of affairs does not lie solely with the theologians, although their education in biblical languages and approach to biblical texts is directed towards the assessing of literary content rather than towards systematic description of a language and analysis of its structure: the linguists, on their part, have failed to inform the theologians, in any appropriate way, of the methods and findings of their science, and seem to neglect discussion of the special character of the language of a religious tradition.

[2] Oxford University Press, 1961. See also his 'Hypostatisation of Linguistic Phenomena in Modern Theological Interpretation', *JSS*, VII (1962), 85–94, which carries further the author's criticism of the practice of extracting linguistic phenomena from the syntactical environment in which their linguistic functioning takes place. In his more cautious study *Biblical Words for Time* (London, SCM, 1962) Barr treats of the interpretation of these words in the writings of John Marsh, J. A. T. Robinson and Oscar Cullmann.

[3] 'Biblical theology' may be understood either as a solely descriptive discipline revealing the theology (or theologies) contained in the Bible, or as

Barr is not concerned to criticise the prevailing conclusions of this 'school' of theology, but the insecure, if not definitely unsound, linguistic methods and assumptions which characterise the writings of some of its most outstanding exponents. One of the basic presuppositions of this biblical theology is that a vast difference in views of reality existed between the biblical and Greek worlds, the one characterised by 'Hebraic' modes of conception, the other by 'Graeco-Hellenistic'. The major differences between these are thought to consist of the contrast between dynamic and static ways of thinking and expression, the contrast between abstract and concrete, and the contrast in the conceptions of time and of man. Barr claims that the purpose of his book is not to question the validity of these contrasts, but rather to expose the faulty linguistic basis on which they are established, especially by Th. Boman.[1] He and other writers claim that these particular features of Hebrew thinking are built into the Hebrew language and that the examination of Hebrew as a linguistic phenomenon will therefore point directly to the mental patterns behind it. Now it is clear that this kind of argument has been developed with a complete disregard of the discipline of linguistic semantics, and Barr is not slow to point out its many weaknesses.[2]

a kind of dogmatics with the Bible as its only source of authority. See G. Ebeling, 'The Meaning of Biblical Theology', *JTS* (n.s.), VI (1955), 210–25, and P. S. Watson, 'The Nature and Function of Biblical Theology' *ET*, LXXIII (1962), 195–200. But much that may be included under the name tries to unite both understandings, and to be descriptive and dogmatic at the same time. In attempting to do this, it proceeds from a contrast drawn between Hebrew and Greek thinking to a synthetic view of the biblical material in terms of dominant Hebraic thought-patterns. It is of the methods of this intermediate kind of biblical theology that Barr is most critical. See also in this connection, 'Biblical Theology: Past and Future', by D. H. Wallace, *TZ*, XIX (1963), 88–105.

[1] *Hebrew Thought compared with Greek* (SCM, London, 1960). See also his contribution to *Current Issues in New Testament Interpretation*, ed. W. Klassen and G. F. Snyder (SCM, London, 1962), pp. 1–22, entitled, 'Hebrew and Greek Thought-Forms in the New Testament'. Barr is aware of the value of this contrast, but observes that its existence and use are not dependent on its extension into a contrast of linguistic phenomena. Boman's article (just mentioned) would tend to bear this out: he there discusses thought-forms without recourse to argument from linguistic facts.

[2] The failure to engage in a comprehensive study of the Hebrew verb-system has permitted the claim that Hebrew thinking is 'dynamic' because

Professor Barr observes that the idea of a correlation between language and thought has led to a number of abuses at the level of vocabulary studies. There is what he calls *the adding of significances*. This means that where several Hebrew words are found translating one English term the significance of each of these words is regarded as an aspect of the total reality in the thought-structure, and then these various aspects are brought together to form, as it were, the reality for theological interpretation.[1] This kind of procedure ignores the existence of synonyms and the theory behind it ignores the phenomenon of polysemy, that is, the fact that one word can have more than one sense. Linguistic material is being subjected to a systematising method. Then Barr discusses *the dependence on etymologies*, where the original meaning of a word is regarded as an authoritative guide to its meaning in subsequent usage and as necessarily present in all proper usage. Moreover, it is often assumed that an appeal to etymology will lead to the right sense in the interpretation of difficult or ambiguous words. In opposition to this view, Barr emphasises that etymology is no sure guide to the semantic value of words in their current usage, but that such value has to be determined from the current usage itself and not from derivation. The etymology of a word, he maintains, is not a statement about its meaning, but about its history, and the historical past of a word is not a reliable guide to its present meaning. No reasonable person will question this claim; yet no reasonable person will wish to maintain that

the verb in Hebrew always expresses movement and activity: whereas, in fact, there are many stative, intransitive verbs in Hebrew which do not express action, and the forms יֵשׁ ('there is') and אַיִן or אֵין ('there is not') may come near to possessing the significance of absolute existence or non-existence in certain contexts. The domination of assumed modes of thinking over the investigation of linguistic peculiarities has caused a sharp distinction to be drawn between the 'aspectual' system of the Hebrew verb (as an index to the Hebrew understanding of time) and the 'tense' system of the Indo-European verb: yet, in Greek, for example, an 'aspect' system for verbs is strongly represented. Furthermore, can it be seriously maintained that the Hebrew language discloses the distinctiveness of Israelite theological thinking when it is recalled that, structurally, Hebrew is no more than a Semitic language and shares many of its features with the whole Semitic family of languages?

[1] See Barr's strictures (in *Semantics*, pp. 144 ff.) on E. Jacob's statement on the nature of man, which is based and built on the meaning of the four Hebrew words which may be roughly translated into English as 'man'.

1-2

the original or etymological meaning of a word (when it is discoverable) cannot, in any circumstances, assist our understanding of its present semantic value.[1] The past history of a word (and etymological study involves historical study)[2] *may* be valuable in helping us to grasp the fulness of its present meaning, and, on occasion, etymology may enable us to understand why an author selected certain words in preference to others in order to express his thoughts. Bad examples of etymologising—and there are many[3]—do not vitiate its careful and correct use. In short, there *is* a scientific use of etymology, helpful in the recognition of homonyms and in elucidation of the problems of change, loss and addition of meaning.[4]

The underlying cause of these errors in vocabulary studies is the failure to interpret words in their contexts. The semantics of words in their actual usages is not investigated; their interpretation is taken directly from the dictionary and not from the texts in which they appear, and the question of what the writer meant when he used a particular word is not raised. In contrast to this type of procedure, Barr maintains, in what is the only really positive solution to the problem which his book offers, that

[1] Barr himself says of the identification of cognates for some Hebrew words in Arabic and Accadian, 'the etymological recognition may be used in conjunction with the context of the Hebrew word to give a good semantic indication for its occurrence' (*Semantics*, p. 158).

[2] On this, see Y. Malkiel, 'The Place of Etymology in Linguistic Research', *Bulletin of Hispanic Studies*, XXXI (1954), 78–90.

[3] One may mention here what Barr calls 'the root fallacy'—the assumption that the 'root meaning' (which is supposed to provide the original meaning and to express the concept or idea) is a basic part of the actual semantic value of any word or form which can be assigned to an identifiable root, and that any word may be presumed to contain some suggestion of other words formed from the same root. But, as Barr points out, the 'meaning' of a root is not necessarily part of the meaning of a derived form, and two words having the same root need not suggest one another, e.g. לֶחֶם = 'bread', and מִלְחָמָה = 'war'. The distinction between grammatical variations of a root form and fresh word-formation must be kept in mind.

[4] On the scientific approach to etymology, see S. Ullmann, *Semantics: An Introduction to the Science of Meaning* (Oxford, 1962), chs. 4 and 8: also Y. Malkiel, *loc. cit.* This article contrasts modern etymological study with the bizarre conjecturing—based on sound resemblances or on some seductive affinity of meaning—that it was during the pre-scientific era of language study.

4

a 'better way to approach biblical language in its relation to theology' will be 'at the level of the larger linguistic complexes, such as the sentences'. And he continues, 'it is the sentence (and of course the still larger literary complex, such as the complete speech or poem) which is the linguistic bearer of the usual theological statement, and not the word (the lexical unit) or the morphological and syntactical connection'.[1] The uniqueness of the religious structure (either of ancient Israel or of the Christian preaching) did not consist primarily (if at all) in the issuing of new words, new word-concepts or of new conceptual content for old words: rather, its newness, says Barr, 'consisted in new combinations of words, in which it was often possible for the semantic value of the words to be changed only slightly or not at all, and for the new or distinctive concept to be indicated by the word-combination'.[2]

The failure to realise that distinctive (theological) meaning belongs to the word-combination or sentence (treated in context) rather that to individual words is, in Barr's opinion, the basic misconception underlying the construction of the monumental *Theologisches Wörterbuch zum Neuen Testament*, ed. G. Kittel and G. Friedrich. This work purports to be a dictionary of Greek *words*, but in it 'external lexicography', that is, the listing of word-occurrences with word-substitutes in another language which provide guidance on the semantic contribution of the word to the sentences in which it is used—this is presupposed or given the briefest treatment, whereas 'inner lexicography', which attempts to penetrate the field of thought with which the words are related and which therefore stresses religious, philosophical and theological usage, is emphasised. This, according to Barr, is an improper methodology. Lexicography, if it is to be true to its name, cannot pass from linguistic material to the inner world of thought, without making the false assumption that the *word*, rather than the word-combination, indicates the concept. Moreover, according to Barr, the study of the varied semantic value of words in their contexts tends to be subordinated in the *Wörterbuch* to the attempt to build up 'general concepts', especially those associated with the *Heilsgeschichte*, or history of salvation. These 'general concepts' may be valid and useful categories for theological systematisation, but seldom do all

---

[1] *Semantics*, p. 263.   [2] Barr, *loc. cit.*

instances of a word's usage fit into them, and consequently those which can be connected with such categories are assumed to be the important and regulative ones. In this way, interest in theological themes is permitted to assume dominance over adequate semantic description and investigation. While Barr commends some of the articles in the Kittel *Wörterbuch* and observes that it may be better (even as a whole) than the principles on which it was planned, he nevertheless feels that the general conception of the work must be criticised.

It cannot be doubted that Professor Barr has rendered a valuable service to biblical scholarship by exposing the careless linguistic methods upon which imposing theological statements have been content to rest: nevertheless, his zeal to warn students of the Bible of the errors into which they may fall has allowed him to be over-critical of some authors and to over-simplify some of the issues.[1]

As pointed out earlier, Barr insists that it is at the level of the sentence or larger linguistic complex, and not the word, that semantic distinctiveness is clarified and theological thought communicated. This affirmation gives rise to two questions: one concerning the adequacy of the context suggested for interpretation; the other concerning the autonomy of the word in linguistic study. It is true that the contextual analysis of meaning is possibly the most influential single fact in the growth of twentieth-century semantics, but the context of interpretation is not regarded as being simply verbal: it is now increasingly realised that the non-verbal elements of a situation and the wider influence of social setting and cultural background are also of direct relevance to the complete understanding of a communication event.[2] Indeed, the context must be regarded as comprehending all the conventions and presuppositions accepted in a society in which the participants live, in so far as these are relevant to the understanding of what is said, or written, in

---

[1] Of the published reviews of *Semantics* the following are the most valuable: B. S. Childs in *JBL*, LXXX (Dec. 1961), 374–7; Th. Boman in *TLZ*, LXXXVII (April 1962), 262–5 and in *SJT*, XV (1962), 319 ff.; R. McL. Wilson in *NTS*, VIII (1962), 282–3; G. E. Wright in *Union Seminary Quarterly Review*, XVII (May 1962), 350–3; and L. Alonso-Schökel in *Biblica*, XLIII (1962), 217–23.

[2] See J. R. Firth, *Papers in Linguistics* (Oxford, 1957), ch. 3, and esp. p. 32.

communication.[1] Part of what is then involved in 'context' is covered by W. M. Urban's conception of the 'universe of discourse'.[2] Urban developed this theme in order to provide theoretical foundation for his conviction that propositions other than those containing terms denoting entities in the physical world may yet have meaning—propositions such as those concerning the supernatural and ethics; and in any linguistic theory of meaning it seems right and important to incorporate this notion of context as 'universe of discourse'. The cultural context builds up from this 'universe of discourse', taking into itself all that is relevant from what is said or written and what is happening. Now this understanding of the context for interpretation is very much wider than Barr seems to allow,[3] and carries with it the necessity of treating themes and ideas from a historical standpoint in order to place statements and words in the appropriate 'universe of discourse'. A historical perspective is needed to provide an adequate context of meaning. The importance of this point is clarified through discussion of the second matter which Barr's affirmation raises. His affirmation implies that *words* are not the bearers of meaning and are therefore not a proper object of semantic analysis. It is obvious that the contextual theory of meaning constitutes a direct threat to the relative independence of the word as a unit of meaning. Nevertheless the exponents of the theory do not think that it is incompatible with a certain measure of word-autonomy,[4] and even Barr himself, at two points in his book, is prepared to concede to the lexical unit such autonomy. 'It is true...that a word may be used in such a way as to suggest *some wide area of recognised thought* which can be somehow connected with the word but which goes beyond its normal signification.'[5] Barr goes on to claim (and rightly) that we cannot assume that this is always happening,

[1] A particular instance of this is that the context of a sentence in a written work must be understood to include the conventions governing the literary genre of which the work is an example.

[2] Urban, *Language and Reality* (London, 1939), pp. 128 ff., 195 ff., 203.

[3] But see note 1 on p. 217 of *Semantics*.

[4] Cf. S. Ullmann, *Principles of Semantics* (2nd ed., Oxford, 1957), pp. 60 ff. Lexicography demonstrates the existence of a measure of word-autonomy: 'no dictionary could exist without an element of permanence, a core or inner fortress within the area of meaning' (Ullmann, *op. cit.* p. 67).

[5] *Semantics*, p. 217 (italics mine).

7

but it is important to notice his preparedness to admit that a word may be used to suggest an *idea*, for what can 'some wide area of recognised thought' mean, if not an 'idea'? Again, when Barr modifies his statement that the semantic value of the words in a new word-combination may be changed only slightly or not at all, his words imply the rightfulness of investigating the lexical unit as a unit of meaning.

It is true of course that the use of a word might come in due course to be specially stamped by its frequent *recurrence in sentences of a particular kind*, and so to undergo semantic change...But...such semantic change is not at all to be related in its extent proportionately to the degree of newness or originality of the statements in which it occurs. And it has to be related to other factors, such as the degree of *specialization of the word in earlier usage*, and the degree to which it becomes completely *technical in its use* in the new statements.[1]

To what kind of word in biblical usage can the phrases—earlier specialised usage, technical use, recurrent use in sentences of a particular kind (left undefined!)—be applied? It is surely very reasonable to suggest that many of those words which are items in the theological vocabulary of the Bible are such. On the basis of these two observations we may say that words which were, or were to become significant theologically came to the biblical authors with their own particular content and associations, and as semantic markers of a concept: therefore the investigation of their historical and traditional usage is a necessary preliminary to discovering the extent of indebtedness or uniqueness in their use by a writer within a specific context. In this connection, the elucidation of the original, or earliest discoverable, context of meaning (within the life of ancient Israel, or of the early Church) will provide valuable assistance in understanding the choice of a word by a writer and the nature of its development up to the time of and within his use. Knowledge of the scope and the change of meaning depends on a broad historical perspective.

Throughout Barr's book one is constantly aware of his rejection of the theory that the basic lineaments of a culture are traceable in the vocabulary, grammar and syntax of a language—a theory which underlies many attempts to draw distinctions and parallels between Greek and Hebrew views of life, and which strongly

---

[1] *Semantics*, p. 263 (italics mine).

influences Boman's work. Barr expresses his own attitude to this theory in these words:

In this view [i.e. that linguistic structure reflects or corresponds to the thought structure] there are very great difficulties, and though it may be possible to maintain it in some greatly modified sense, the way in which it is at present used in theology may well be regarded as wholly outmoded and a survival from the time before the scientific study of language began.[1]

But criticism of the current use made of a theory is not a substitute for the discussion of the validity of the theory itself: and Barr does not adequately deal with the Humboldtian theory. Whatever dangers the view that linguistic structure reflects thought structure may have for linguistics and for theologians who embrace it (and these dangers are real), it nevertheless forms (as Barr knows) the basis of a significant school of language study in Europe and in America. Humboldt's ideas underlie the work of such distinguished linguists as J. Trier and L. Weisgerber in their exposition of the fruitful theory of 'semantic fields'.[2] In America, they are basic to the well-known Sapir–Whorf hypothesis on the influence of language on thought.[3] This hypothesis has been developed in the main by anthropologists on the basis of research into American-Indian languages, and has been subjected to searching debate.[4] Linguists are critical of many of the details of the hypothesis and of the generalisations built upon it, and they observe that it lays too great emphasis on languages which have no historical dimension and give no scope for studying the role of language in the higher reaches of culture and thought: nevertheless, they are appreciative of its main principle. For instance, S. Ullmann can say:

It is becoming increasingly clear that there is some kind of reciprocity between language and thought: language not only expresses our

[1] *Semantics*, p. 33: see also pp. 294–5.

[2] See H. Basilius, 'Neo-Humboldtian Ethnolinguistics', *Word*, vIII (1952), 95–105, and S. Öhman, 'Theories of the "Linguistic Field"', *Word*, IX (1953), 123–34.

[3] See B. L. Whorf, *Four Articles on Metalinguistics* (Washington, 1952) and *Language, Thought and Reality*, ed. J. B. Carroll (New York, 1956).

[4] Cf. *Language in Culture*, ed. H. Hoijer (Chicago, 1954) and *Language, Thought and Culture*, ed. P. Henle (Ann Arbor, 1958).

thoughts, but, to some extent, conditions and predetermines them: it furnishes the speaker with a ready-made system of categories and scale of values and directs his thinking into certain channels.[1]

This might appear to some as a too rigid statement of the relation, and it may well be that some modification might be made in the direction of suggesting that language predisposes to, rather than determines, a way of thinking.[2] But within the framework of this general approach, most linguists agree that vocabulary provides some kind of index to cultural emphases and reflects environment and mental set as well: but there is not the same general agreement with reference to grammar and sentence construction.[3]

Sufficient has been said on this topic of language structure and thought structure to indicate its importance and the need for testing the hypothesis, especially on the level of semantic study. Barr's negative attitude to the Humboldtian position reflects his attitude both to language and to philosophy in general. In his definition of 'linguistics' (on page 2, note 1) and throughout his entire discussion, Barr excludes almost entirely the psychological and sociological viewpoints in the science of language. The result is that a mechanistic approach dominates which is concerned with the laws of language and usage, not with the processes of the mind. But this formalistic branch of semantics (with which Barr identifies himself) is not the only one which merits the name of science.[4] In the second place, Barr is sceptical of the Humboldtian theory because it rests on an idealist type of philosophy: indeed, all exponents of the mechanistic approach to language

[1] From Ullmann's review of the Hoijer volume (mentioned in preceding note) in *Romance Philology*, x (1956–7), 225.

[2] For this approach, see J. W. Swanson, 'Linguistic Relativity and Translation', *Philosophy and Phenomenological Research*, xxii (Dec. 1961), 185–92.

[3] Cf. Henle's own contribution to *Language, Thought and Culture*, pp. 1–24.

[4] Cf. Ullmann, *Semantics: An Introduction*, pp. 58 ff. H. Kronasser's conception of semantics in the *Handbuch der Semasiologie* (Heidelberg, 1952) to which Barr often refers, has a broader extension than Barr's, including the psychological aspects of meaning, and even criticising the formalistic branch of semantics to which Barr belongs: page 61, sect. 34. W. Porzig, *Das Wunder der Sprache* (Bern, 1950, pp. 93–108) assesses the advantages and limitations of all the major schools of linguistic thought, and declares that no one of them, by itself, is entirely or uniquely valid and right.

are deeply suspicious of and opposed to Idealism. The philo-
sophic outlook within which it flourishes is that of Positivism,[1]
and Th. Boman and L. Alonso-Schökel have even suggested in
their reviews of his book that Barr seems prepared to align
himself (unconsciously) with this standpoint by reason of his
logicism which reduces philosophy to matters of logic and word-
usage. It is true that this impression is created by Barr's general
approach, but it must be admitted that two passages clearly
contradict it. 'To the word "truth" there may presumably
correspond a mental or psychological reality or "concept" of
truth. To the sentence "God is truth" there also corresponds a
mental or psychological reality. But these are different kinds of
thing.'[2] And a little later, in the exposition of this difference:

Modern biblical theology in its fear and dislike of the 'proposition' as
the basis of religious truth has often simply adopted in its place the
smaller linguistic unit of the word, and has been forced to overload
the word with meaning in order to relate it to the 'inner world of
thought'. Likewise in its reserved attitude to any psychological
treatment of religious thought it has paid insufficient attention to
that frontier of linguistics and psychology which is seen in the relation
between any word and the mental reality or concept corresponding to
it; and from this neglect is forced either into the attempt to relate the
words directly to the divinely or theologically existing realities, or else
into a normative interpretation of words, for example by etymolo-
gizing.[3]

Has Barr himself paid sufficient attention to the frontier he
mentions? Biblical theology may often be guilty of confusing
'word' and 'concept', but too often Barr gives the impression
that there is no connection between the two, that the meaning of

[1] Humboldt's philosophy of language (being, in large measure, an application of the Kantian critique of Reason in the linguistic sphere) was
ineffective in the second half of the nineteenth century when a positivist
interpretation dominated in the science of language: when philosophical
positivism was overcome by neo-Kantianism in Germany, then interest in
Humboldt's work revived. Cf. the remark of R. E. Longacre, *Language*,
xxxii (1956), 299: 'The mechanistic-behaviouristic slant given to descriptive
linguistics by Bloomfield has undoubtedly created in some quarters a certain
prejudice against anything savouring of idealism, and a pre-disposition
towards logical positivism.' Barr himself seems to be aware that the formalistic linguistic method of the late nineteenth century was a consequence of
the prevailing positivistic philosophy, *Biblical Words for Time*, p. 94.
[2] Barr, *Semantics*, p. 245.   [3] Barr, *op. cit.* p. 246.

words can be discovered solely on the basis of their use, without reference to any non-empirical realities[1]—a view which would have most serious consequences for any theology! But, in fact, the meaning of biblical language (indeed of all religious language) can be grasped only by penetrating beyond the words and matters of usage to an understanding of the religious experience or perception of truth which they attempt to express or to which they point. This pointing or directing character of language is usefully described by M. Sandmann:

> ...a linguistic sign always refers to a world thought of as lying 'opposite' both speaker and listener—even should this world exist only in imagination—and subjected to their attention, and the role of the sign is precisely that of directing the listener's attention towards that goal. A linguistic sign is a directing as well as directed sign, and the ultimate goal of that direction is the 'thing meant'.[2]

In this connection, we must stress the fact that the *word* may be such a directing sign: it directs the reader (or listener) towards the area of experience or sphere of interest it symbolises: it *introduces* him to a segment of the 'universe of discourse' with reference to which meaning can be established.

This approach to word-meaning is important in view of Barr's criticisms of the Kittel *Wörterbuch*. Much of what he has to say on this work is fair and right: the articles vary in quality, and the whole project has deficiencies, as its second editor admits.[3] But the whole undertaking cannot be considered invalid on the grounds Barr seems to indicate it is, namely, that a dictionary cannot pass from detailed linguistic material to the inner world of thought, for by so doing, it assumes that the word indicates the concept. But this is not a wrong assumption! Apart altogether from the fact that the word, and not the formulation, is ordinarily the basic tool of the lexicographer, we must stress our conviction that every word is a semantic marker for a field of meaning, a

---

[1] He is not altogether consistent on this matter, and (it should be noted) he does not need to associate himself in any way with positivism (in linguistic or philosophical study) in order to point out and avoid the errors made by many biblical theologians.

[2] M. Sandmann, *Subject and Predicate* (Edinburgh, 1954), p. 61.

[3] G. Friedrich, 'Die Problematik eines theologischen Wörterbuchs zum NT', *Studia Evangelica*, ed. K. Aland (Berlin, 1959), pp. 483 ff., and in particular the closing paragraph of the article.

pointer to what Barr calls 'a wide area of recognised thought' (p. 217), connected with it and going beyond its normal signification. Whether this be termed 'idea' or 'concept', the interpreter must be acquainted with it, if he is to assess the total meaning of the word. Therefore a dictionary must begin at a linguistic point with an adequate word-history, but it cannot claim to have completed its task until it attempts to enter the field of meaning for which the word is a semantic marker. Semantics is surely concerned with something more than the non-theological when it is engaged in the explication of theological terms and contexts. Where else but in a *theological* word-book (as the *Wörterbuch* most avowedly is) would one expect to find pointed out and discussed the semantic variations which accompany the appearance of a word within different contexts and situations of thought? It is the use made of the *Wörterbuch* and the authority attributed to it by scholars which are at fault, rather than the work itself. The *Wörterbuch* attempts to set before the scholar the range of possible meanings belonging to a term: admittedly these are sometimes too neatly synthesised to look like a homogeneous essay on a biblical conception: nevertheless, the range is presented: the onus of responsibility lies on the interpreter of a particular passage to choose the correct (or most nearly correct) meaning in the context with which he is dealing.

One further point: without giving the reason why (but, in our opinion, because he rejects the Humboldtian hypothesis on the relation of language and thought or culture), Barr associates himself with those semanticists who appear to minimise the problem of translating one language into another. While there is an admission that 'there is likely to be some loss in translation' (p. 266), the implication seems to be that anything can be translated into another language without fundamental loss, if linguistic laws are strictly and carefully followed. It is doubtful if this view would evoke wide agreement among the various schools of semantic study. Because each word has a history and individual development of meaning within a language, the particular area of reality which it articulates (within a particular world-view) may overlap, but will not exactly coincide with that expressed in another language. Within the study of biblical languages, the problem of the relation of many Greek words in

the New Testament to their Hebrew counterparts is of fundamental importance.[1]

This brings us to the discussion of the language of the New
Testament. Consistently with his general theory, Barr maintains
that the impress of the Hebraic-Old Testament background on
the New Testament is to be found at the level of the things which
the various authors said—sentences, word-combinations, themes,
subject-matter—and not of the words they used to say them.
These words often retained (in his view) the same semantic value
as they normally had in the usage of Hellenistic speakers, and
this value was not greatly deepened even when words were
technically overprinted with a Jewish reference.[2] This is not an
adequate statement of the position. Not only word-meanings
in the New Testament, but also the structure and syntax of New
Testament language bear the impress of a special Hebraic
influence channelled, *for the most part*, through the Septuagint.
Because of the importance of this matter, it seems proper to
devote some attention to it.

THE GREEK OF THE NEW TESTAMENT[3]

Until recent years it would have been very widely agreed among
biblical scholars that the language of the New Testament writers
belonged to what is known as Koine (Greek), a kind of average
Greek in which many dialects shared (though Attic was the
foundation) and which developed with the spread of Hellenistic
Greek culture to become the 'common language' of the entire
Mediterranean world. The early exponents of this view were of
the opinion, however, that it was not with the rather artificial

[1] For ancient statements regarding the 'untranslatability' of Hebrew into
Greek, see R. McL. Wilson's review of Barr's book in *NTS*, viii, 282.

[2] See *Semantics*, p. 250.

[3] Among recent studies are: 'The Language of the New Testament', by
N. Turner in the *Peake's Commentary* (rev. ed. edited by Black and Rowley:
Nelson, 1962), pp. 659–62: 'An Introduction to the Lexicon of the Greek
NT' in *A Greek–English Lexicon of the New Testament*, ed. Bauer, trans.
W. F. Arndt and F. W. Gingrich (Chicago and Cambridge, 1957), pp. ix–
xxv; B. M. Metzger, 'The Language of the NT' in *The Interpreter's Bible*
(Nashville, 1951–7), vol. 7, 43–59; and E. C. Colwell, 'The Greek Lan-
guage' in the *Interpreter's Dictionary of the Bible* (Nashville, 1962), vol. 2,
479–87.

language found in the literature of this period that most of the
New Testament writings appeared to reveal close affinities, but
with its colloquial forms, and especially with the language of the
non-literary papyri, ostraca and inscriptions discovered in
Egypt.[1] This language was vigorous and fresh, but lacked much
of the subtlety of classical Greek: it was characterised by simplifi-
cation of the verb system, less involved syntax, an increasing
frequency of prepositions and compound verbs and by a tendency to disregard the rules of concord. Here it seemed to the
early enthusiasts was a type of Greek which was almost exactly
that of the New Testament. Even at the present time, few would
deny that some parts of the New Testament (particularly in
Mark's Gospel) are written in the ordinary vernacular Greek of
the period and that the papyri have made a useful, though
limited, contribution to New Testament linguistic studies;
nevertheless, modification of this general viewpoint has taken
place over the years. The first shift of opinion was in the direction
of stressing the likeness between the language of some New
Testament authors and that of *literary* Hellenistic Greek.[2]
E. K. Simpson's *Words Worth Weighing in the Greek New Testament*[3]
studies a number of significant words on which the papyri shed
no light at all, but which receive clarification from their usage in
literary Hellenistic texts. But even this more balanced view has
left many scholars dissatisfied, and another approach to the
problem of the nature of the Greek of the New Testament has
been taking shape.

Taking as its starting-point the fact that the New Testament is
religious literature, this approach seeks illumination on its
language from the only extensive religious work written in
Koine, the Greek translation of the Old Testament scriptures,
commonly called the Septuagint (LXX).[4] The very fact that

[1] The chief contenders for this view were A. Deissmann, Grenfell and
Hunt, and with rather less enthusiasm, J. H. Moulton and G. Milligan, in
Vocabulary of the Greek Testament (London, 1914–29). Recently N. Turner has
discussed the history and limitations of this position in 'Second Thoughts—
VII. Papyrus Finds', *ET*, LXXVI (Nov. 1964), 44–8.
[2] Cf. G. Milligan's final preface (1929) to the *Vocabulary of the Greek
Testament*. [3] London, Tyndale Press, 1946.
[4] This does not mean that the only literary activity of pre-Christian
Greek-speaking Judaism was confined to the LXX. The translation (and
redaction) of such works as Enoch and the Testaments of the Twelve

many of the quotations from the Old Testament found in the New reflect the LXX, rather than the Hebrew, proves that this Greek version—perhaps in the various stages of its establishment[1]—was familiar to and used by at least some of the early Christian writers. But the extent of the influence is not limited to the provision of quotations. Because the same general themes (sacred themes) characterise both Testaments, the vocabularies of the Greek Old Testament and the Greek New Testament have a great measure of similarity: and research into the syntax of the Greek of the LXX has revealed its remarkable likeness to that of the New Testament.[2] 'When the LXX was established', says Turner, 'its idioms powerfully influenced free compositions of Biblical Greek. The idiosyncrasies of Biblical Greek syntax are shared in varying degrees by almost all the NT writers, whether they were translating or not.'[3] On account of these similarities in vocabulary and syntax, the emphasis in investigation of New Testament Greek has been directed more and more towards clarifying the character of LXX Greek. On the basis of his researches in this field, H. S. Gehman claims that, while the Greek of the Old Testament is undoubtedly Koine, it differs from other Koine Greek in having a distinctive Hebraic cast.[4] This Hebraic

Patriarchs—though in their final form they underwent much Christian re-editing—probably also predate the Christian era.

[1] The complexities of Septuagint study are great: for discussion of some of the problems (e.g. date(s), redactions, methods of translation) we refer to H. M. Orlinsky, 'Current Progress and Problems in LXX Research' in *The Study of the Bible Today and Tomorrow*, ed. H. R. Willoughby (Chicago, 1947), pp. 144–61; P. Katz, 'Septuagintal Studies in the Mid-Century', in *The Background of the New Testament and its Eschatology* (Cambridge, 1954), pp. 176–208; and B. J. Roberts, *The Old Testament Texts and Versions* (Cardiff, 1951), part 2, esp. pp. 172–87. One is aware of great oversimplification in referring to 'the LXX': but the dependence on the Greek Old Testament in this work is on patterns and methods of translation which are witnessed to throughout the entire Testament, even though it be the work of many translators.

[2] Cf. N. Turner, 'The Unique Character of Biblical Greek', *VT*, v (1955), 208–13. Though Gehman's work (see below) is helpful, one is always aware of the lack of a full study of the syntax of the Greek Old Testament: the volume by H. St J. Thackeray on syntax was never written. On New Testament Greek syntax we now have Turner's volume, completing Moulton's *Grammar of New Testament Greek:* vol. III: *Syntax* (Edinburgh, 1963).

[3] Turner, *Syntax*, pp. 4–5.

[4] Gehman, 'The Hebraic Character of LXX Greek', *VT*, I (1951), 81–90.

influence he finds demonstrated at the level of idiom, of syntax (in the use of conjunctions, prepositions and pronouns, and in the frequency of the optative mood) and of vocabulary.[1] 'Certain Greek words', he says, 'had to be adapted to OT usage and in this way they received a meaning not found in classical or ordinary Hellenistic Greek.'[2] Gehman admits that many of the Semitic idioms in LXX Greek may be due to a literalistic rendering of the Hebrew, but he goes on to suggest that if the translation actually made sense to Hellenistic Jews (as one expects it did) then it was because it corresponded to an already familiar way of expression. Consequently he is prepared to posit the existence of a special Greek with a pronounced Semitic cast, used and understood in religious circles—a Jewish Greek—a vernacular 'Jews' Greek' which may still have been current among Jews in New Testament times.[3] It is in terms of this Jewish Greek, as a probable vernacular and as it finds literary expression in the LXX, that we should understand the language of the New Testament.

It is not our concern here to discuss in detail the relation of this hypothesis to the question of Aramaic sources for the Gospels and other New Testament books,[4] save to say that the Greek of those

---

[1] Gehman has shown (*VT*, IV [1954], 337–48) that the word 'holy' (ἅγιος) can, on some occasions in the Greek Old Testament, be understood only if one is conversant with the Hebrew text. For the importance of the study of the LXX and the underlying Hebrew in the task of determining the meaning of certain New Testament words, see C. H. Dodd, *The Bible and the Greeks* (London, 1935), part I.   [2] Gehman, *VT*, I, 87.

[3] See Gehman, *loc. cit.*, and Turner in *New Peake*, p. 660. In the introduction to his volume on *Syntax* in Moulton's *Grammar*, Turner claims that biblical Greek, as a whole, 'is a unique language with a unity and character of its own' (p. 4), and that that unique quality was imparted to it by Semitic influences, first on the LXX translators, and then on New Testament authors whose style was moulded by the LXX, though they themselves may have been unacquainted with Semitic speech or idiom. He is also inclined to approve the theory of the existence of a literary and unliterary or spoken type of Jewish Greek influencing the New Testament. For a careful statement of this general position, see M. Black, 'Second Thoughts—IX. The Semitic Element in the New Testament', *ET*, LXXVII (October 1965), 20–3: 'we are led to look...to the language of the Greek-speaking synagogue, possibly itself a spoken "koiné" Greek, as the *matrix* of New Testament Greek' (p. 23).

[4] On this, see M. Black, *An Aramaic Approach to the Gospels and Acts* (2nd ed., Oxford, 1954) and the article cited above. In the case of the tradition of

books which have Aramaic sources lying behind them will reveal the Semitic character to an especial degree: what we are concerned to affirm is that the language of the New Testament, apart altogether from the source materials of the books, reveals in its syntax[1] and—more important for our work—in its *vocabulary*, a strong Semitic cast, due in large measure to its indebtedness to the Jewish biblical Greek of the Septuagint.[2] The studies which form the main part of this work are, to some extent, both the test and the proof of this affirmation. Greek *words* changed their meaning, or added a new meaning, in Jewish and Christian usage, and the change was due to the influence of the Greek version of the Old Testament scriptures.

THE METHOD OF WORD-STUDY

It is now time to indicate the linguistic and exegetical procedures we have sought to follow in the subsequent word-studies.

(1) We have indicated our conviction that the word itself is a proper object of semantic enquiry, since the word is a semantic marker, a pointer to a concept or field of meaning which must be clarified and understood. Together with this acceptance of a measure of word-autonomy, we emphasise the importance of the *immediate context* in which the word appears for the interpretation of its meaning. By 'immediate context' we mean the sentence in which the word occurs and the larger surrounding literary complex, the paragraph or pericope.[3] This context must be kept in mind when we investigate each separate occurrence of the word lest we miss any new development in its semantic value, or erroneously read into the word a meaning belonging to another occurrence or another author, the latter being what Barr calls 'illegitimate totality transfer'.[4]

the sayings and teachings of Jesus, the majority of the Semiticisms are translation phenomena (from Aramaic). On the linguistic phenomena of Acts, see M. Wilcox, *The Semitisms of Acts* (Oxford, 1965).

[1] Cf. K. Beyer, *Semitische Syntax im Neuen Testament*, Band I, Teil 1, Satzlehre (Göttingen, 1961), which demonstrates the Semitic sentence structure in the Synoptic Gospels, the Johannine writings and the Epistle of James.

[2] 'Septuagintal study...is the clue to Christian exegesis, exposing the catalyst which produced the great words concerning salvation and Christian living', N. Turner, *ET*, LXXVI, 47.

[3] See our approach to δίκαιος, etc., in the Synoptic Gospels.

[4] *Semantics*, p. 218.

(2) Advancing upon this first principle, we pay regard to what we will call *historical context*. This involves the realisation that each of the theological terms discussed possessed special content and associations which it had developed in the course of its history and through its use in the Greek of the LXX. These the New Testament authors either accepted, modified or rejected. If they pursued either of the latter two courses, then the investigation of the word's historical usage is essential to discovering the extent of the uniqueness of its meaning in their work: if they accepted the content which the word possessed at the time of their writing or that which belonged to it at some earlier stage of its development, then the study of historical use is necessary if we are to discover the place and measure of their indebtedness. For this reason, no study of a word in the New Testament is adequate without investigation of its use and meaning in the literature of Classical Greek and of later pre-New Testament Greek, especially the Septuagint. Within this process of contextualisation in history and culture we include the attempt to ascertain the original (or earliest discoverable) life-situation within which a word was used and possessed meaning. This is to be found in the institutions and thought of ancient Israel, or in some aspect of the life and experience of the early Christian Church. This search will shed light sometimes on the reasons for the choice of a particular word by an author: and the original life-situation (when discovered) will provide a point of reference for the tracing of semantic development. The influence of this approach underlies our attempt to locate the situation or thought-reference within which our terms (and especially the Hebrew words) originated,[1] and thereafter to pursue as far as possible a chronological study.

(3) It is clear that the discussion of the semantics of New Testament words and word-families requires us to deal with *the meaning of their Old Testament Hebrew equivalents*. The language of the New Testament is a special kind of Jewish biblical Greek (both in the syntax and in the thought-forms it expresses) and the LXX translation plays a very important role in locating the area of Hebrew meaning which has contributed to the meaning of

---

[1] This has proved to be of significance in the case of roots צדק and גאל/פדה which are the common Hebrew equivalents of the δικαιοσύνη and λύτρον complexes respectively.

New Testament words. Consequently, in our studies we give a section to the examination of the LXX translators' use of the term we discuss. We have also found it profitable (especially in the λύτρον complex) to find out and discuss not only any Hebrew words other than the usual equivalent which are rendered by our Greek term, but also any other Greek words used to translate the main Hebrew equivalent. In this way we extend our knowledge of the translators' understanding of both the Greek words they used and the Hebrew terms which formed their background.[1]

(4) We cannot assume, however, that the Old Testament provides the only source of Jewish influence on the thought and language of the New Testament. It seems to have been the main source, but we have also to remember that the Hebrew terms of the Old Testament developed in meaning, and their later significations may have contributed to, or at least may illumine, New Testament usage. For this reason we have included a study of the various relevant Hebrew terms in the Qumran literature, which is the source for our understanding one strand of Jewish thought immediately prior to and during the birth of Christianity. We have also added surveys of the rabbinic teaching on the themes indicated by the words.[2] Extreme caution is required in postulating rabbinic influence upon the New Testament because of the uncertainty which prevails in the dating of the various traditions: but, in these studies, we have not tried to show precise areas of dependence; rather, we have sought to suggest the state of Jewish thinking, or (more correctly) the directions in which it was moving in relation to the themes we discuss, which directions the New Testament writers might share or reject.

(5) Because Hebraic ideas were associated with the Greek vocabulary of the New Testament writers, we must reckon with the possibility that, while these ideas communicated themselves to Jewish minds, they may not have registered with Gentile hearers and readers, who would understand the words in their

---

[1] Great care must be exercised in assessing the importance of the unusual translations of the Hebrew words. In his discussion of the ἱλάσκεσθαι words, C. H. Dodd has allowed the unusual translation to dictate the meaning of the whole complex: see below, p. 26.

[2] The relevance of rabbinic teaching for the understanding of the New Testament has been disclosed by such scholars as W. D. Davies and David Daube.

normal Hellenistic sense.[1] But this difference between the meaning intended and the meaning taken up can be exaggerated. The words were heard (or read), even by Gentiles, not in isolation, but in a context within which, even to them, the Hebraic meaning was probably suggested. This is certainly the case with a dominant theological term like δικαιοσύνη, though it may not have been so with the word λύτρον. However, it must be affirmed that our concern is with the meaning intended by the authors, not with the interpretations or misinterpretations of their readers.

(6) In our discussion of Barr's criticisms of the Kittel *Wörterbuch* we have indicated general support for its lexicographical approach to the interpretation of theological words. It is not necessary therefore to present further arguments here in support of a methodology which is, in many ways, like that of the *Wörterbuch*. Nevertheless, we have tried to avoid the errors of practice which characterise some of its articles. We allow context its rightful place in matters of interpretation: we discuss all the occasions on which a word appears (even if the degree of detail differs) and not only those which will fit into a neat pattern or theological scheme: we have tried to avoid a false emphasis on etymology, as well as the error of interpreting a word primarily from its most pregnant sense: and we have endeavoured not to allow theological presuppositions to dominate exegetical interpretation. Furthermore, by treating the data historically, we have permitted (as not all the *TWNT* articles do) each biblical writer his own voice, not attempting to assemble them into a harmonising chorus. The danger of a too great concern for theological synthesis is that some aspects of meaning which do not easily conform are entirely neglected or inadequately presented. Finally, we have not allowed the distinction between Greek and Hebrew thinking to obtrude itself unnecessarily upon our arguments or to prejudice our use of evidence.

In short, we hope that the studies here presented are not open to the criticism of being 'a series of theological essays on the doctrines associated at certain points with the words studied'.[2] We have not set out to write theological essays, not even essays

---

[1] The Bauer/Arndt–Gingrich Lexicon, preface p. xxi, reminds us of this possibility.

[2] This is Barr's verdict on the *Wörterbuch*, *Semantics*, p. 262.

in biblical theology: we investigate words and their meanings: but since we are dealing with theological words and theological contexts, we are obliged to use theological expressions and ideas. Our approach is, however, descriptive, not dogmatic, and that is surely the proper approach for the biblical interpreter. 'The task of biblical studies, even of biblical theology', says Krister Stendahl, 'is to *describe*, to relive and relate, in the terms and presuppositions of the period of the texts, what they meant to their authors and their contemporaries.'[1]

The words selected for study here are representative of the vocabulary of New Testament soteriology. The terms ἱλαστήριον and λύτρον indicate two understandings of the place of Christ and of his death in bringing about the possibility of salvation. The study of δικαιοσύνη discloses the Pauline understanding of the nature of the salvation won and the character of the 'saved' life. The use and meaning of ζωὴ αἰώνιος is discussed because, to a considerable extent, it represents the Johannine equivalent of Paul's idea of δικαιοσύνη. We end with the examination of the word πνεῦμα which, within the complexity of its meanings, expresses the New Testament understanding of the power of God in the life of the Saviour and in the life of his followers. This selection will make possible, we believe, the fulfilment of our aim, which is to illustrate the distinctive ways of expressing a New Testament theme which are characteristic of the various New Testament writers. It is only as this discipline is pursued and its scope extended that we have a right foundation on which to construct valid statements in biblical theology.

[1] K. Stendahl, 'Implications of Form-Criticism and Tradition-Criticism for Biblical Interpretation', *JBL*, LXXVII (1958), 38. The author goes on to claim that the task of relating this description to the present belongs to systematic theology and that the principles which guide this process of relating are called 'hermeneutics'.

CHAPTER II

THE INTERPRETATION OF ΙΛΑΣΚΕΣΘΑΙ AND RELATED WORDS IN THE SEPTUAGINT AND IN THE NEW TESTAMENT

The terms 'propitiation' and 'expiation' are so closely related that they are often regarded as interchangeable in religious contexts. This is due also to the fact that there is no difference in the actions performed to bring about expiation or propitiation. Nevertheless, it is of some importance that the distinction between the meanings of the two words should be indicated and remembered. It is a distinction which stems from a difference in interest or intention. The action of propitiation is primarily and directly orientated towards the deity or offended person. The purpose which underlies it is that of making the deity favourable, of causing his attitude to be changed from anger and displeasure to good-will and favour. There may also be included within the scope of 'propitiation' (though in a somewhat weakened sense) such action as is designed to maintain the favourable inclination, after conciliation of wrath has been effected. Expiation is also concerned with the relation of the subject of the action to the deity, but in this case the initial thought is less directly and immediately oriented towards the offended party: there is an intermediate concern. Expiation is directed towards that which has caused the breakdown in relationship; it deals with sin and guilt; it is concerned with the performance of compensatory rites or with making reparation for the offence.[1] By recognising the cause of displeasure and dealing with it (often at the command of the deity), the subject of the expiatory action is made more acceptable and the way is opened for the restoration of good relations.

This difference in emphasis or intention is scarcely discernible

---

[1] Cf. J. Barr, *HDB* (rev. ed., 1963), 810, 'The difference is in the directing of the verbal action towards a person or an offence'.

in the actual action performed: consequently, if we wish to decide whether a specific act is propitiatory or expiatory, we must try to penetrate to the motive which prompted and the purpose which carried through the action. We must try to detect, either from the narrative or from our understanding of the situation itself (in so far as we can enter into it), whether the action was intended to deal with sins, to make adequate reparation for wrong done so that reconciliation might proceed, or whether the primary concern was to appease wrath by direct means, to render and retain the deity favourably-inclined. Considerations of a purely grammatical kind—the voice of verbs, the cases which follow verbs and the nature of their objects, i.e. thing or person—may be helpful guides to interpretation, but they do not exhaust the evidence which must be taken into account. The fact that C. H. Dodd limited his discussion of ἱλάσκεσθαι and related words in the LXX to matters of grammar and translation equivalence partly explains its inadequacy.[1]

It is generally agreed that in the overwhelming majority of those passages in pagan writers where ἱλάσκεσθαι and its cognates are used, the word means 'propitiation' or 'appeasement'.[2] Dodd admits this, but claims that the usage of the LXX is so completely different that practically no vestige of this meaning remains. 'Hellenistic Judaism, as represented by the LXX, does not regard the cultus as a means of pacifying the displeasure of the Deity, but as a means of delivering man from sin.'[3] In so far as Dodd is concerned to maintain that ideas of celestial bribery and of capricious, vindictive anger on the part of Yahweh are absent from the Old Testament, his work com-

---

[1] The study appeared first in *JTS*, xxxii (1931), 352–60. It was reprinted without alteration in *The Bible and the Greeks* (London, 1935), pp. 82–95. Quotations are from the former.

[2] The use of ἐξιλάσκεσθαι to mean 'expiate' is probable in the late Men Tyrannus inscription (Dittenberger, *Syll.*, 3rd ed., 1042). The context of Plato Leg. 862c suggests (*pace* Dodd) that the verb is used to mean 'propitiate': so Büchsel, *TWNT*, vol. 3, p. 317. According to Moulton and Milligan, *VGT*, *sub* ἱλάσκομαι, the word group in Hellenistic Greek, as in Classical, refers to placating wrath. They interpret ἱλάσκομαι (with acc. of the person) as 'render propitious to oneself', and go on to note 'a similar use of the compound ἐξιλάσκομαι which extends to the LXX'.

[3] Dodd, *op. cit.* p. 359.

mands grateful agreement. But this must not be taken to mean that all ideas of divine wrath are foreign to the Old Testament. In actual fact the idea of the 'wrath of God' is deeply embedded there, but it is a responsible anger, a holy reaction caused only, but inevitably, by sin and wrong-doing. That this idea is present in many, if not all, of those passages in which the LXX uses ἱλάσκεσθαι and related words is the thesis of Leon Morris's study of the term in *The Apostolic Preaching of the Cross*.[1] 'The averting of anger', he claims, 'seems to represent a stubborn substratum of meaning from which all the usages can be naturally explained, even those with God as subject, for while the OT is emphatic about the reality and seriousness of the wrath of God, the removal of that wrath is due in the last resort to God himself.'[2] On some occasions Morris appears to force evidence to support his argument,[3] but, in general, he convincingly demonstrates the truth of his claim. In the majority of passages where ἱλάσκεσθαι and related words occur, the context contains clear reference to the anger of God: many in fact express the desire that God should turn from his wrath,[4] and so suggest that the meaning of ἱλάσκεσθαι is closely related to the idea of rendering God favourable. Dodd omitted all discussion of contexts from his study and thereby deprived himself of an important guide to interpretation.

This is not the only criticism which may be made of Dodd's investigation. The first part of his discussion is summarised as follows:

Where the LXX translators do not render כִּפֶּר and its derivatives by words of the ἱλάσκεσθαι class, they render it by words which give the meaning 'to sanctify', 'purify' persons or objects of ritual, or 'to cancel', 'purge away', 'forgive' sins. We should therefore expect to find that they regard the ἱλάσκεσθαι class as conveying similar ideas.[5]

Three observations on this are pertinent. First, the meanings of those words (other than ἱλάσκομαι) which translate כִּפֶּר vary so greatly (from 'sanctify' to 'cancel') that they cannot offer any

[1] Tyndale Press (London), 1955.   [2] *Op. cit.* p. 155.
[3] The opinion that divine wrath is envisaged in Ps. 25: 11 and Ps. 65: 4 depends on Morris's own judgment as to what constituted signs of the anger of God. (All Psalms references retain the numbers of the Hebrew text.)
[4] For example, Exod. 32: 12–14 and Dan. 9: 16.
[5] Dodd, *op. cit.* p. 353.

precise guide to the meaning of the ἱλάσκομαι-group. In the
second place, the method of argumentation is itself open to
criticism. It may be true that כִּפֶּר and ἐξιλάσκομαι mean nearly
the same thing; but we cannot then conclude that every other
Greek word which translates כִּפֶּר must bear a similar significance
to ἐξιλάσκεσθαι, any more than we can assume that every
other Hebrew word rendered by ἐξιλάσκεσθαι is closely related
in meaning to כִּפֶּר. Considerations of context must be given their
proper place in every interpretation. Moreover, some shades of
meaning which belong to the semantic breadth of a term may
require translation by a word significantly different from that
used to render the main sense of the term. At most, translation
variants—if they possess a *single theme of meaning*—may provide
a *guide* to the sense of the regular translation terms. Thirdly,
Dodd appears to assume that the translation-variants clearly
indicate the sphere of meaning within which the meaning of the
regular translation word, ἐξιλάσκεσθαι, is to be found. It would
have been more satisfactory if the meaning of the latter had been
established first and confirmation then sought from the other
translation-words.

The second main point in Dodd's article is that, in almost all
cases where ἱλάσκεσθαι, etc., do not render כִּפֶּר and its derivatives, 'they render words which fall into one or other of two
classes: (i) with human subject, "to cleanse from sin or defilement", "to expiate"; (ii) with divine subject, "to be gracious",
"to have mercy", "to forgive"'.[1] Hence, the meaning of
ἱλάσκεσθαι, both in these cases and generally, is not 'to propitiate'. As well as being exposed to the second and third of the
criticisms listed above, this argument is built on the assumption
that if we know or can discover the meaning of a Hebrew word,
then we know the meaning, not only of the Greek word which
usually renders it in the LXX, but of any Greek word which
translates it, however infrequently. The first part of this assumption may be partially justifiable: the second part is of very
doubtful validity. When we seek the meaning of a Greek word
the meaning of the Hebrew word it renders on many occasions
in the LXX is an important *guide*, but the meaning of the
Hebrew words it translates on a very few occasions is a much less
reliable clue. The LXX translators may have had good reasons

[1] *JTS*, xxxii, p. 356.

for using the particular Greek word in an unusual place: not all of them seem to have regarded translation as a process of mechanically inserting equivalents. The ideas expressed in the context, rather than the presence of a particular Hebrew term, may have influenced their choice of translation words. For instance, why was וְלֹא־אָבָה יהוה לִסְלֹחַ in 2 Kings 24: 4 translated οὐκ ἠθέλησεν Κύριος ἱλασθῆναι, when the root סלח could have been rendered adequately and more simply by ἀφιέναι, ἀφαιρεῖν, or καθαρίʒειν? The context here (as at Dan. 9: 19 and Lam. 3: 42, where the construction is similar) expresses the necessity of avoiding the divine wrath and therefore suggests the idea of propitiation: it may be that the passive of the Greek verb successfully expresses this idea, 'the Lord refused to be placated'. The same may be said of Exod. 32: 14 where 'the Lord repented' (root נחם) is rendered by καὶ ἱλάσθη Κύριος. By the intercession of Moses (not by sacrifice) the fierceness of the divine wrath was turned away from Israel: is the Greek giving expression to this thought (present in the context) in the words 'the Lord was placated', using ἱλάσθη because propitiatory ideas belonged to it? There are cases, however, in which uncertainty does not prevail. At Zech. 7: 2; 8: 22 and Mal. 1: 9 ἐξιλάσκεσθαι translates חָלָה, a verb whose range of meanings includes 'to mollify', 'to appease', 'to entreat the favour of' and 'to approach (in worship)'. Dodd admits that these are 'unmistakeable examples of the ordinary classical and Hellenistic sense of ἐξιλάσκεσθαι, "propitiate"',[1] but by arguing that the translators deliberately used the word with a note of contempt for its standard meaning or because it referred to the attitude not of Israelites but of pagans, he allows these three examples little or no significance in the report of his findings: they are exceptional cases. Nevertheless, he has had to admit that on three occasions ἐξιλάσκεσθαι in the LXX means 'to propitiate': the context, the grammatical construction and probably the Hebrew word which is being translated (and which is usually rendered δεῖσθαι) support the interpretation of the Greek verb in terms of its normal meaning.

More interesting is the single occasion (Ps. 106: 30) where ἐξιλάσκεσθαι renders פָּלַל, a verb which means 'pray' or 'intercede'. The incidence referred to in the Psalm is described in Num. 25 and Dodd acknowledges that the story is 'one of

---

[1] *Ibid.* p. 355.

"propitiation" in the crudest sense'.[1] He suggests that it is possible that the translator had the Numbers passage in mind and meant us to interpret, 'Phineas stood up and placated (the Lord)': but he does not in fact think that this is the case, and adds '...it would be a curiosity of translation if a sense of ἐξιλάσκεσθαι, which is elsewhere carefully avoided...were gratuitously introduced in this single passage, where there is nothing in the Hebrew to suggest it'.[2] Can the matter be disposed of so easily? In the first place, although there is nothing in the verb פִּלֵּל to suggest 'propitiation', we must reckon with the possibility that the LXX translator had a reason for introducing the idea here. Secondly, is this sense of ἐξιλάσκεσθαι so carefully avoided elsewhere and introduced only here? It is present in the three passages Zech. 7: 2; 8: 22 and Mal. 1: 9, whether or not we give them significance. Thirdly, the fact that פִּלֵּל is rendered by ἐξιλάσατο and not by one of the usual terms, εὔχεσθαι, προσεύχεσθαι, seems to be best accounted for by the suggestion that the translator of the Psalm had the Numbers passage in mind or knew its content. Furthermore, from this 'propitiatory' narrative Dodd quotes v. 11 but nowhere does he mention v. 13 which speaks thus of Phineas: ἐξήλωσεν τῷ θεῷ αὐτοῦ καὶ ἐξιλάσατο περὶ τῶν υἱῶν 'Ισραηλ, the Hebrew being וַיְכַפֵּר, and ἐξιλάσατο being used without an object, as in Ps. 106: 30. On Dodd's own admission concerning the character of this story ἐξιλάσατο bears the meaning 'propitiate' or 'make propitiation' in Num. 25: 13. The same is true, we submit, at Ps. 106: 30, and also in Ecclus. 45: 23 where the incident of Phineas is again referred to in the words ἐξιλάσατο περὶ τοῦ 'Ισραηλ.

On one occasion, 1 Sam. 6: 3, the LXX has ἐξιλασθήσεται where the Hebrew has נוֹדַע. Perhaps this translation rests on a misunderstanding of the Hebrew or on a different (and now lost) reading, but does the passage shed no light on the meaning of the Greek word, as both Dodd and Morris[3] claim? The sentence, as it stands, in Greek is coherent, makes good sense and is worth examining. The context describes how the Philistines have been smitten with plague because of the Ark in their midst: they want to send it back, but their diviners warn them that they should not send it back empty, but with a guilt-offering, for then (they say),

---

[1] *JTS*, xxxii, p. 355. [2] *Ibid.* p. 356.
[3] *The Apostolic Preaching of the Cross*, p. 152 note 1.

'You will be healed and (MT) it will be known to you why his hand does not turn away from you'. The Greek version is: 'You will be healed καὶ ἐξιλασθήσεται ὑμῖν μὴ οὐκ ἀποστῇ ἡ χεὶρ αὐτοῦ ἀφ' ὑμῶν.' Since the immediate concern of the Philistines was the getting rid of the plague (the manifestation of divine displeasure) it is plausible to suggest that the thought of propitiating a deity was present in their minds, cf. *v.* 5. The Greek translator may have perceived the propitiatory significance of the action and conveyed it by the use of ἐξιλασθήσεται in his rendering which may be interpreted, '... and propitiation will be made for you lest his hand turn not away from you'.

The appearance of ἐξιλάσκεσθαι as the translation of אָשֵׁם at Hab. 1: 11 is difficult to interpret.[1] Various emendations of the Hebrew have been proposed. Since the discovery of the Qumran Habakkuk commentary it is certain that the most satisfactory of these is the reading וישם, though the mention of בית אשמ(ה) in the Pesher (col. 4, 10–11) seems to imply acquaintance with the reading וְאָשֵׁם. Now this latter reading (וְאָשֵׁם) may have been in the text very early and the LXX translators of Habakkuk (if they found it) appear to have considered that the idea of guilt or guilt-offering could be expressed by ἐξιλάσεται, but the Greek sentence fails to make sense: τότε μεταβαλεῖ τὸ πνεῦμα καὶ διελεύσεται καὶ ἐξιλάσεται.

The preceding paragraphs reveal weaknesses in Dodd's semantic investigation of ἐξιλάσκεσθαι, etc., when they do not render the Hebrew term כִּפֶּר. In approaching these *unexpected* appearances of the Greek word we must not be governed always and solely by the meaning of the Hebrew word which lies behind the translation. The Greek is worthy of investigation in its own right, and the theme expressed in a context may guide us to the reason for which and the meaning with which the LXX translators adopted the word ἐξιλάσκεσθαι. Having followed these lines of approach, we now claim that the LXX uses ἱλάσκεσθαι

---

[1] Amos 8: 14 speaks of 'those who swear by the אשמה of Samaria'. This means either a Samaritan goddess, Ashimah (cf. 2 Kings 17: 30) or the *guilt* of worshipping the calf at Bethel (cf. Hos. 10: 8). The LXX has οἱ ὀμνύοντες κατὰ τοῦ ἱλασμοῦ Σαμαρ., which R. S. Cripps, *Commentary on Amos* (London, 1929, p. 316) interprets, 'by propitiation of Samaria'. The root אשם is nowhere else rendered by the ἱλάσκεσθαι words: one wonders if the peculiarity of translation points to a single translator of Habakkuk and Amos.

with a propitiatory meaning in Ps. 106: 30; Ecclus. 45: 23; Zech. 7: 2; 8: 22 and Mal. 1: 9, and very probably also in 2 Kings 24: 4; Exod. 32: 14 and 1 Sam. 6: 3. The significance of this evidence, or any part of it, should not be underestimated or explained away in assessing how the LXX uses the word.

We turn now to the usual word rendered by our terms. In eighty-three out of the 105 occasions where it is used in the LXX ἐξιλάσκεσθαι renders the root כפר, and other Hebrew roots only eleven times. These figures suggest that the translators regarded the two words as very closely related in meaning, and therefore investigation of כפר in the Old Testament may provide significant guidance on the meaning of ἐξιλάσκεσθαι.[1] The conclusion reached by Dodd on this matter is that 'the LXX translators did not regard כִּפֶּר (when used as a religious term) as conveying the sense of propitiating the deity, but the sense of performing an act whereby guilt or defilement is removed, and accordingly rendered it by ἱλάσκεσθαι in this sense'.[2]

Much controversy has raged through the years about the meaning of the root כפר. The main division has been between those who advocate the view that it means 'to cover' (Arab. kaphara) and those who claim that the original significance is 'to wipe away' (Babyl. kuppuru). Investigation into this matter is interesting and valuable, but there are two reasons why we do not stop to review the literature and opinions offered. First, and on the general level, it is easy to overestimate the importance of etymology and to assume that the root-meaning (when discovered) is applicable in almost any context in which the word appears. This procedure ignores the semantic principle that, in the course of time, the meaning of words changes through being conventionalised and formalised, as well as through the application of the words to new situations. When we are seeking to establish the meaning of a word, knowledge of its root-value may be helpful, but it is usage which is ultimately decisive.[3] Secondly, the difference between the two root-meanings suggested for כפר

[1] This approach is not in conflict with our earlier criticism of Dodd for interpreting solely from the Hebrew. He failed to do justice to the unexpectedness of some appearances of ἐξιλάσκεσθαι. Here it is a matter of doing justice to a consistent practice in translation.

[2] *JTS*, xxxii, p. 359.

[3] Cf. J. Barr, *Semantics*, ch. 6, pp. 107–60.

is not great: both may well be associated with the words. In any case, the establishment of the root-meaning of כפר does not assist us in knowing whether the intention of the action so described was expiatory or propitiatory. While it is true that the meaning 'to cover' would most naturally refer to the covering of the face of the angry or wronged person (i.e. propitiation), it could also connote the covering of the sin, in the sense of making it without further effect on the person who committed the fault or on the wronged party (i.e. expiation). On the other hand, if 'to wipe away' is the original significance,[1] this could refer to the removal of wrath (propitiation) or of the cause of wrath, the sin[2] (expiation).

The usage of root כפר in the Old Testament divides naturally into two sections according as atonement is viewed as coming by *cultic* action or by *non-cultic* means. By far the most common is the use in connection with the cult, but the other group is logically of greater significance for our purpose, since it enables us to understand what the verb meant in ordinary usage and to assess what made it specially fitted for use in connection with the cult.[3] That the non-cultic use is fundamental was noticed by S. H. Langdon[4] and more recently by J. Herrmann,[5] but Dodd seems to miss its importance. He admits that ἐξιλάσκεσθαι means 'to appease' or 'placate' when used to translate כִּפֶּר in Gen. 32: 20 and Prov. 16: 14, but adds, 'this use...does not strictly belong to our present subject, since ἐξιλάσκεσθαι is not here a religious term'.[6] Presumably then כִּפֶּר is not here a religious term either and its meaning irrelevant. But it may well be that it is precisely where the term is not a religious and conventionalised cult-word that we can discern its basic meaning. Now at Gen. 32: 21 (which is listed by KB as an example of the oldest usage of the verb, belonging to the E stratum) Jacob thinks that his present will appease Esau's wrath and the LXX renders the words literally, ἐξιλάσομαι τὸ πρόσωπον αὐτοῦ ἐν τοῖς δώροις. The gift was primarily a means of turning away anger so that reconciliation

---

[1] Cf. G. R. Driver, *JTS*, xxxiv (1933), 34 ff.

[2] So Th. Vriezen, *An Outline of Old Testament Theology* (1958), p. 287.

[3] It is probable, as Morris suggests (*op. cit.* p. 142), that in the case of כפר a word familiar in connection with ordinary affairs was adapted to, and its meaning conventionalised within cultic use.

[4] *ET*, xxii (1910–11), 323.   [5] *TWNT*, iii, 302.

[6] *Op. cit.* p. 358.

could proceed, and only secondarily a partial paying off of Jacob's debt. The idea of propitiation is strongly present in both the Hebrew and the Greek terms. The same is true of Prov. 16: 14, 'The wrath of a king is as a message of death, but a wise man will appease it' (LXX ἐξιλάσεται). Another example from the E stratum is Exod. 32: 30, where Moses says to the people, 'You have sinned a great sin: and now I will go up to the Lord; perhaps I can make atonement (כפר) for your sin', and the proffered means of atonement is the offering of Moses' own life for the people's (v. 32). The divine anger is expressed in the passage (vv. 22 and 35) and the thought of propitiation is probably present and conveyed by the LXX in ἐξιλάσωμαι: Moses is concerned to turn away the divine wrath, even if it means the sacrifice of his own life, as well as to offer an equivalent to make amends for his people's sin. An instructive example for the understanding of כִּפֶּר is 2 Sam. 21: 1–14 which describes an attempt to get rid of a famine in Israel, the cause of which is traced back to Saul's treatment of the Gibeonites. David asks them, 'What shall I do for you? Wherewith shall I make atonement (וּבַמָּה אֲכַפֵּר, LXX ἐν τίνι ἐξιλάσομαι;) that you may bless the heritage of the Lord?' They demanded that seven sons of Saul should be hanged. Once again, the idea of propitiating anger, as well as of making compensation, seems to be present in the passage: the favour of the Gibeonites had to be won, even at the price of the destruction of life.

On the basis of his examination of the entire non-cultic use of כפר Leon Morris affirms that the idea of providing a 'ransom' (כֹּפֶר) in money or in life to turn away wrath is so strongly present that the verb should be interpreted as a denominative, 'to give or pay a כֹּפֶר'.[1] Some of his arguments to support this may be rather forced (for example on Ps. 65: 4 and Dan. 9: 24) but adequate grounds are given for doubting the legitimacy of the claim that all ideas of propitiating wrath are absent from כפר, when used in non-cultic contexts, and accordingly from ἐξιλά-σκεσθαι which so frequently translates it.[2]

---

[1] *The Apostolic Preaching of the Cross*, p. 148. *BDB* also suggest that the verb is denominative.

[2] In addition to the passages discussed above, the idea of propitiation may possibly be present in Jer. 18: 23, where Jeremiah prays against his enemies, 'Forgive not (אַל־תְּכַפֵּר) their iniquity nor blot out their sin...deal with

When we turn to consider the cultic use of כִּפֶּר we find Morris insisting that the relationship indicated between the noun (כֹּפֶר) and the verb form provides the key to the understanding of the term. He maintains that the general impression produced by the sacrificial system is that an offering of a propitiatory character is being made: the verb כִּפֶּר carries with it the implication of a turning away of divine wrath by the offering of a כֹּפֶר.[1] In this view, too much is built on the hypothesis of the denominative character of the verb and insufficient importance is attached to the conventionalising of the meaning within the cult. Even if (as we would maintain) ideas of propitiation were present in the original usage of the word in non-cultic connections, it does not follow that they were *always* there, nor that they were necessarily present in the later cultic usage.[2] In many of the cultic appearances of כִּפֶּר in sacrificial contexts and in particular in Leviticus and Ezekiel, we cannot distinguish whether ideas of propitiation are foremost,[3] and we should therefore be content to render the word in terms of 'atonement', 'reconciliation' and 'forgiveness', words which include aspects of both ideas.[4] We might say of such

them in the time of thine anger'. In this passage, 'expiation' would be entirely meaningless. The willingness to be propitiated lies in the free resolution of God, and the meaning inclines towards 'to forgive'—a point recognised by the LXX which translates by μὴ ἀθῳώσῃς.

[1] *The Apostolic Preaching of the Cross*, pp. 151–2.

[2] Cf. G. B. Gray, *Sacrifice in the Old Testament* (Oxford, 1925), ch. 5, pp. 67–81.

[3] Commenting on such passages as Num. 16: 46; 25: 9–11, J. Barr (*HDB*, rev. ed., p. 282) draws attention to the apotropaic sense and 'the awareness that the anger of God follows closely on the offence done and will not be turned away until proper expiation is made. In such cases, it may be that no absolute distinction can be made between expiation and propitiation as the general purpose of the action as whole.'

[4] This is the case with the use of כפר in the Dead Sea Scrolls, where it generally means 'to make atonement', e.g. 1QH 4. 37, 17. 12—God atones for (not, expiates) sin. 1QM 2. 5 uses the verb in a context where the idea of propitiation or appeasement is present. More significant is the expression in the Qumran documents of a doctrine of vicarious atonement. 1QS 5. 6 ff.; 8. 4–10; 9. 3 ff. attribute atoning efficacy to the life and work of the community, or of a group within the community. In 1QS 3. 6 ff. and CD 2. 5; 3. 18 it is implied that the individual makes atonement for sins by a renewed and complete obedience to the Law. See the recent work by Bertil Gärtner, *The Temple and the Community in Qumran and the New Testament* (Cambridge, 1965), pp. 123 ff.: he claims that this atonement in Qumran doctrine is centred on the idea of the cult of the new Temple constituted in the community.

occurrences that, while the ritual of sacrifice was performed as a means of expiation, the whole action was regarded as propitiatory, because the consequences due to sin in the divine wrath were averted.[1]

The idea of propitiation is witnessed to in other words and actions in the Old Testament. For instance, in Job 42: 8 the friends of Job are commanded by God to offer a burnt-offering, and 'Job shall pray for you, for I will accept his prayer not to deal with you according to your folly'. That the prayer of Job is such as to turn away divine wrath from his detractors illustrates the thought of propitiation. Again, David's words to Saul (1 Sam. 26: 19), 'If it is the Lord who has stirred you up against me, may he accept (lit. smell) an offering', are clearly an expression of a propitiatory purpose. This passage leads to the consideration of the burnt-, gift- and thank-offerings described in Lev. 1–3. The use of the word כִּפֶּר, so frequent in the sin- and guilt-offering ritual, does not appear here:[2] these offerings are said to be performed לְרֵיחַ נִיחֹחַ לַיהוה, that is, to provide a rest-giving or soothing smell which quiets Yahweh's anger or placates him, cf. Gen. 8: 21.[3] Most scholars would admit that the literal sense of this expression suggests propitiation, but they think that such an idea passed out of currency at an early date, and that the phrase came to mean to the Hebrews what it meant to the Greek translators when they rendered it ὀσμὴ εὐωδίας, 'a smell of sweetness, of pleasure', referring presumably to Yahweh's pleasure in the due discharge of his service.[4] It may be true that לְרֵיחַ נִיחֹחַ did lose its original force, but it seems to us that the general motive behind these offerings was still, to some extent, propitiatory. They were not made in order to atone for sins: they were gifts offered to renew and maintain a favourable attitude on the part of Yahweh towards the faithful. We would submit that a purpose of that kind belongs to the realm of ideas suggested

---

[1] Cf. the statement of J. Barr, quoted in note 3, p. 33, above.

[2] The one exception is Lev. 1: 4. This may be an introductory formula to the description of the cult and probably means 'atonement' in the general sense of renewing the relation with God: cf. Vriezen, *An Outline of Old Testament Theology*, pp. 286–7.

[3] Cf. Ezek. 5: 13, where הֲנִחֹתִי חֲמָתִי must mean 'I soothe my fury'.

[4] Cf. G. B. Gray, *Sacrifice in the Old Testament*, pp. 77–80; J. Barr, HDB (rev. ed.), p. 810.

by the term 'propitiation' (even with a weakened force), rather than to the realm of 'expiation'.[1]

Sufficient evidence has now been brought forward to demonstrate that the idea of propitiation is not entirely absent from the Old Testament. It belongs to the earliest non-cultic use of כִּפֶּר, though we would not go so far as Morris in claiming that it belongs to the entire cultic use of the word as well. It seems more likely that the term became formalised in meaning within the sacrificial system and signified then, as now, 'atonement'. When it was used in this sense, we cannot easily decide whether the emphasis lay on expiation or propitiation: both ideas were probably present. Nevertheless, on the positive side, we have indicated some passages where the thought of propitiation within the cult is clear, and we have also suggested that the idea (albeit modified) also belongs to those parts of the sacrificial system which were not directly concerned with sins.

Before leaving this discussion of the Old Testament idea of sacrifice, it is necessary to assess the significance of our findings for the interpretation of ἐξιλάσκεσθαι. We begin by recalling Dodd's claim that 'the LXX translators did not regard כִּפֶּר (when used as a religious term) as conveying the sense of propitiating the deity...'.[2] Now the distinction to be drawn in the use of כִּפֶּר should not be between the religious and the non-religious, but between cultic and non-cultic use. In the latter use, ideas of propitiation are present, and we may presume that the LXX translators conveyed them by the use of the word ἐξιλάσκεσθαι which had, as its regular meaning in both classical and Koine Greek, the sense 'to placate' or 'to propitiate'. In cultic contexts, the matter is less clear, but it would appear logical to assume that just as the Hebrew texts continued to use כִּפֶּר in a formalised

---

[1] Vriezen (*An Outline of Old Testament Theology*, p. 290) says of the burnt- and gift-offerings, 'These offerings were sacrificed particularly to *propitiate Yahweh*, just for instance as presents were used to please the king'. Also L. Koehler, *Old Testament Theology* (London, 1957, p. 187) observes that the idea contained in the term 'sweet savour' is that the offering appeases God's wrath. On the basis of the use of רֵיחַ נִיחֹחַ at Lev. 4: 31, Koehler includes the sin-offering (of which כִּפֶּר is used) among these soothing sacrifices. This is the only occasion on which the phrase is applied to the sin-offering and Vriezen (*op. cit.* p. 288 note 1) considers it (probably correctly) to be a secondary text.

[2] *JTS*, xxxii, p. 359.

sense which included ideas of expiation *and* propitiation within one act of atonement, so the LXX translators, for reasons of consistency, chose to retain the same word ἱλάσκεσθαι, which probably, in the course of its association with the Hebrew term, underwent a shift in semantic emphasis towards a meaning which is peculiar to biblical Greek, 'to atone'. At an earlier stage in this study we suggested that, with reference to the meaning of ἱλάσκεσθαι when it renders words other than כִּפֶּר, Dodd's arguments against the interpretation in terms of propitiation are not persuasive: now, with reference to the appearance of the word-group to translate כִּפֶּר, we submit that his case against the presence of any thought of propitiation there requires modification.

THE NEW TESTAMENT USAGE

The verb ἱλάσκεσθαι and related words are not frequently found in the New Testament. The prayer of the publican recorded at Luke 18: 13 is ὁ θεὸς ἱλάσθητί μοι τῷ ἁμαρτωλῷ. The divine wrath does not find expression in the passage, but the holy reaction of God to sin is implied. The publican's approach to God is direct; there is no idea of expiating sins; his plea is that God may be gracious or favourable to him, and, although mercy or forgiveness is the content of the desired attitude,[1] a trace of the ideas connected with propitiation surely lingers in the background: God is asked to be favourably-disposed or propitious towards the sinner. In Heb. 9: 5 τὸ ἱλαστήριον means 'the mercy-seat'. This is the familiar LXX rendering of כַּפֹּרֶת, the lid of the Ark or mercy seat, where the cultic act of כִּפֶּר was carried out. Since this word belongs to the cultic terminology it is impossible to decide definitely whether the emphasis lies on the purpose of expiation or propitiation: both are included in the one sacrificial act of atonement. The mercy-seat is the place (or means) of atonement *and* reconciliation.

The noun ἱλασμός occurs only in the First Epistle of John, at 2: 2 and 4: 10. The first passage declares that 'If any man sin, we have an advocate with the Father, Jesus Christ the righteous, καὶ αὐτὸς ἱλασμός ἐστι περὶ τῶν ἁμαρτιῶν ἡμῶν': while the

---

[1] Cf. the later use of כִּפֶּר. In Heb. 8: 12 (ἵλεως ἔσομαι ταῖς ἀδικίαις αὐτῶν) the favourable or propitious attitude of God is again that of mercy and forgiveness.

second describes the nature of God's love, 'Herein is love, not that we loved God, but that he loved us and sent his Son to be ἱλασμὸν περὶ τῶν ἁμαρτιῶν'. Dodd rejects the traditional rendering 'propitiation' in favour of 'sin-offering', which he characterises as 'a divinely supplied means of cancelling guilt and purifying the sinner'.[1] Nevertheless, there are signs that the meaning 'propitiation' should be retained. In the case of 1 John 2: 2 the immediate context (which Dodd elsewhere admits might make it possible that the sense 'propitiation' is in place at this point)[2] refers to an advocate; and as Morris says,

...if we sinners need an advocate with God, then obviously we are in no good case; our misdeeds prevail against us, we are about to feel the hostility of God to all that is sinful. Under these circumstances we may well speak of Christ turning away the wrath of God, and thus ἱλασμός is a natural word in the context.[3]

In the LXX the word ἱλασμός is used frequently in connection with the sacrifices of the Day of Atonement in which ideas of expiation and propitiation probably overlap; and it is found in Dan. 9: 9 (Theod.) with the meaning 'forgiveness' in a context where the presence of divine wrath is expressed. It is clearly used in a propitiatory sense at 2 Macc. 3: 33, where it is applied to the offering made by Onias to deliver Heliodorus from further chastisement. It would appear therefore that the LXX does not use the word in the simple sense of 'expiation' (either means or activity): it means 'atonement', 'forgiveness' or 'propitiation', and always within the context of the turning away of divine wrath. Only the first and third of these meanings are suitable in 1 John 2: 2 and 4: 10. If we choose the rendering 'atonement', it should be remembered that the idea of propitiation belongs to the total meaning of that term in its cultic usage. If, on the other hand, the meaning 'propitiation' is accepted, we rightly emphasise the personal nature of the breach with God caused by sin, and we have, in Morris's words, 'one of those resounding paradoxes which mean so much for the understanding of the

---

[1] *JTS*, xxxii, p. 360.
[2] *The Johannine Epistles* (MNTC, London, 1946), p. 26.
[3] *The Apostolic Preaching of the Cross*, pp. 178–9. The NEB renders the word by 'remedy for the defilement of sins'. This is a theological interpretation, not a translation of the Greek word.

Christian view of sacrifice',[1] namely that from God's love comes the means of averting the consequences of sin.

The verb ἱλάσκεσθαι occurs in Heb. 2: 17, but the context provides no reference to the wrath of God. The verb is followed by the accusative (referring to sin)—εἰς τὸ ἱλάσκεσθαι τὰς ἁμαρτίας τοῦ λαοῦ—and it is urged that this construction indicates that 'to expiate' is the meaning of the term here. Morris again prefers the traditional rendering and translates, 'to make propitiation with regard to the sins of the people',[2] treating τὰς ἁμαρτίας as an accusative of general respect. In support of his thesis he marshals the following arguments: (i) that Christ is said to be a 'merciful High Priest' implies the possibility of God punishing in wrath; (ii) the phrase τὰ πρὸς τὸν θεόν directs the mind to the Godward, rather than the manward aspect of atonement, and the former, when expressed by ἱλάσκεσθαι, is likely to include ideas of propitiation; (iii) the few occurrences of the accusative of sin after the verb seem to imply the thought of propitiation; (iv) the variant reading, ταῖς ἁμαρτίαις, arose probably because the accusative was felt to be difficult after ἱλάσκεσθαι, and this would indicate that 'expiate' was not the accepted meaning of the verb in those circles in which the variant arose. Although Ecclus. 5: 6 and 34: 19 (which Morris does not mention) might support the third argument, one is left with the impression that Morris is here making a virtue out of necessity. The passage moves in the realm of cultic ideas and terminology, and, on that account, it is doubtful whether it is correct to press for the interpretation of the verb exclusively in terms of propitiation. It is more likely that the general cultic usage of the verb to mean 'atonement' is the dominant influence here, a usage which includes ideas of forgiveness,[3] as well as of expiation and propitiation.

We come now to the much-debated word ἱλαστήριον in Romans 3: 25. Since this term appears in one of the most important sections of the Epistle, it demands careful and comprehensive examination. Dodd's comment says:

Here it is unnecessary for our present purpose to decide whether ἱλαστήριον is an adjective in the accusative singular masculine or a

---

[1] *The Apostolic Preaching of the Cross*, p. 179.   [2] *Ibid.* p. 176.
[3] This seems to be the simplest rendering of ἐξιλάσκεσθαι with the acc. (referring to sin) in Dan. 9: 24 and Ecclesiasticus.

neuter substantive. In any case, the meaning conveyed (in accordance with LXX usage, which is constantly determinative for Paul) is that of expiation, not propitiation.[1]

Now we agree that the meaning of ἱλάσκεσθαι, etc., in biblical Greek will be the best guide to Paul's use of the related word here, but on the basis of the preceding discussion we cannot support the implication that the LXX uses the words solely with the meaning 'expiation'. The idea of propitiation is unmistakeably present in ἐξιλάσκεσθαι at Zech. 7: 2; 8: 22; Mal. 1: 9, often when it renders כִּפֶּר in non-cultic contexts, as well as at Ps. 106: 30; Ecclus. 45: 23; 1 Sam. 6: 3, and probable also at 2 Kings 24: 4 and Exod. 32: 14. The idea of propitiation cannot be dismissed simply on the basis of LXX usage. Are there any other guides to the meaning of ἱλαστήριον in Romans? The immediate context does not offer any help but when we consider the general argument of the Epistle to this point we find that the opening chapters have a single, dominating purpose, namely, to demonstrate that all men lie under the condemnation and wrath of God. The wrath of God is first described at 1: 18 as being 'continually revealed from heaven upon all impiety and unrighteousness of men', and it is never out of sight as Paul builds up his argument that Gentiles and chosen people alike are sinners and therefore under the condemnation of God, ending with that powerful catena of Old Testament passages which leaves 'no man sinless before God'. But now, Paul declares, a new factor has entered the situation: now, quite apart from the law, there is a righteousness of God revealed, a righteousness leading to the justification of the sinner through the work of Christ, ὅν προέθετο ὁ θεὸς ἱλαστήριον διὰ πίστεως ἐν τῷ αὐτοῦ αἵματι, εἰς ἔνδειξιν τῆς δικαιοσύνης αὐτοῦ. In a context so dominated by the themes of judgement and wrath it seems plausible to find a trace of the idea of propitiation in the meaning of the term we are discussing. Other expressions in vv. 21–6 may be regarded as dealing with God's judgement on sinners: there is nothing but this word to express the turning away of divine wrath.

The word itself directs the mind to the LXX use of ἱλαστήριον to translate the Hebrew כַּפֹּרֶת, or 'mercy seat',[2] the gold

---

[1] *JTS*, xxxii, p. 360.
[2] In twenty of the twenty-seven times ἱλαστήριον is found in the LXX it renders כַּפֹּרֶת.

slab on top of the Ark in the Holy of Holies, which was regarded as the special location of God's presence and which was sprinkled with blood on the Day of Atonement. T. W. Manson accepted this connection and regarded it as being reinforced by the fact that ἱλαστήριον is often used of places.[1] He considered that the word in Rom. 3: 25 means either 'an expiatory place or object' or more probably in Jewish–Christian usage, 'the place where God shows mercy to man',[2] and this view is supported by the claim that the background of Paul's expression lies in the ceremonies of the Day of Atonement, when the mercy of God was supremely manifested at the mercy-seat. This is an attractive interpretation, but it has not won universal assent. Leon Morris has disagreed, claiming that while it is difficult to give final proof either way, 'it is to be contended that the balance of probability is strongly in the direction of seeing in ἱλαστήριον in Rom. 3 a general reference to the removal of the wrath of God, rather than a specific reference either to the mercy-seat or to the Day of Atonement ceremonies'.[3] He prefers to translate the word as 'means of propitiation'. His arguments are cogent and may be summarised as follows: (i) when ἱλαστήριον means 'mercy-seat', it is used always with the definite article (cf. Heb. 9: 5), save once, Exod. 25: 17, and there the addition of ἐπίθεμα has the effect of removing ἱλαστήριον from the realm of the general (any propitiating thing) to the particular (a specific object); (ii) the appearances of ἱλαστήριον which Manson regards as referring to places are not conclusively so: they refer rather to the propitiatory nature and purpose of the object (sanctuary, church, ark); (iii) the suggestion that Rom. 3: 21 ff. should be interpreted in terms of the Day of Atonement ritual, with chapters 1–3 representing an 'elaborate confession of sin for all mankind' (Manson) is not convincing; the epistle to the Romans does not move in the sphere of Levitical symbolism, and a single unexplained reference to one part of the tabernacle furnishings is unlikely;[4] moreover, the opening chapters of the

---

[1] As well as translating כַּפֹּרֶת, ἱλαστήριον renders עֲזָרָה (a part of the great altar) five times in Ezekiel. It is used for the altar (in Hesychius and Cyril), Noah's ark (Symmachus) and even for a church and a monastery.

[2] *JTS*, XLVI (1945), 4.

[3] 'The Meaning of ἱλαστήριον in Rom. 3: 25', *NTS*, II (1955–6), 33–43. The quotation is from p. 43.

[4] Cf. A. Deissmann, *Bible Studies* (Edinburgh, 1901), p. 132.

letter are clearly a condemnation, not a confession of sin; (iv) it is doubtful whether the προ in προέθετο is strong enough to admit of Manson's interpretation 'to set forth *publicly*',[1] and it is questionable whether the αὐτοῦ is to be stressed in the phrase ἐν τῷ αὐτοῦ αἵματι in the interests of a contrast with the mercy-seat which was sprinkled with the blood of sacrifices; (v) it is harsh and complicated to make Christ, at one and the same time, priest, victim and place of sprinkling. In the light of Morris's examination some uncertainty must still attach to Manson's interpretation of ἱλαστήριον as 'mercy-seat' or 'place where mercy is shown to man', and also to his affirmation that the early chapters of Romans and especially 3: 21 ff. are to be understood in the light of the Day of Atonement ceremonies.[2]

The form[3] and the grammatical function[4] of the word ἱλαστήριον do not assist us much towards an interpretation. There remains, however, one other occurrence of the term (as an adjective) in a passage not denoting a cultic object. It is 4 Macc. 17: 22 where the death of the seven brothers is referred to thus: 'they having become as it were a ransom for the sins of the nation; and through the blood of these righteous men and their propitiatory death (τοῦ ἱλαστηρίου θανάτου)[5] the divine providence delivered (διέσωσεν) Israel which had hitherto suffered evil...'. Here the thought of the passage

---

[1] Moulton and Milligan (*VGT*, p. 536) prefer the meaning 'offered' or 'provided'. Deissmann (*op. cit.*) and Sanday and Headlam (ICC, *Romans*, 5th ed., Edinburgh, 1902, p. 87) accept the rendering 'set forth publicly'.

[2] W. D. Davies, *Paul and Rabbinic Judaism* (London, 1948), pp. 241 f., will not endorse Manson's detailed application of the ritual to Rom. 1–3, but does accept the view that the background of 3: 25 is the Day of Atonement idea.

[3] J. Jeremias (*ZNW*, XLII [1949], 197 note 8) regards the word as formed after the analogy of σωτήριον (Dankopfer), χαριστήριον and καθάρσιον and therefore as meaning 'Sühnopfer'.

[4] The adjectival form does occur, and it must be considered as a possibility that the word in 3: 25 stands relatively with ὅν: the meaning would then be that Christ is the 'propitiatory' agent or object. The use of the word as a noun is more common. But if Paul had wanted a masculine noun, then ἱλαστής was available. It is more likely therefore that it is a neuter noun here.

[5] The reading of ℵ—τοῦ ἱλαστηρίου τοῦ θανάτου—is possibly secondary. Fourth Maccabees is usually regarded as a Hellenistic-Greek document rather than as a Hebrew work: but its community of thought in respect of this incident with the earlier books of Maccabees makes the expression worthy of consideration.

requires that the word ἱλαστήριος be given a propitiatory significance[1] and that in turn suggests that ἱλαστήριον may have the same significance in Rom. 3: 25. This is as far as the parallel would be taken generally, but the similarities between the two passages (most of which are noticed by Morris in the discussion cited) are such as to invite comment. (i) Both contexts declare that the wrath of God has been active. (ii) Both refer to the shedding of blood and the surrender of life. (iii) The death in both cases deals with sin. (iv) 4 Maccabees regards the deaths as the means of bringing about deliverance, and Rom. 3 declares that the death of Christ effects a liberating redemption. (v) Both passages interpret death as being vicarious.[2] (vi) In both cases, it is God who provides the means of atonement or propitiation. This is clear in the 4 Maccabees passage which says, ἡ θεία πρόνοια (divine providence)...διέσωσεν. Now in Rom. 3 the verb προέθετο (usually rendered 'set forth') may be interpreted as 'provided',[3] since the noun πρόθεσις and the verb appear several times in the New Testament in contexts where the idea of the divine purpose or intention is clearly present.[4] But however the word is translated, the initiative belongs to God.

The remarkable community of thought between 4 Macc. 17: 22 and Rom. 3: 21 ff. creates a strong presumption that ἱλαστή-

---

[1] With regard to this very incident 2 Maccabees speaks thus: 'We are suffering for our own sins, and though our living God is angry for a little in order to rebuke and chasten us, he will again be reconciled (καταλλαγή-σεται) to his own servants...I, like my brothers, give up body and soul for our fathers' laws, calling on God to show favour (ἵλεως γένεσθαι) to our nation soon...and to let the Almighty's wrath, justly fallen on the whole of our nation, end in me and in my brothers' (7: 33, 37, 38). The character of the sacrifice is interpreted as propitiatory, as well as expiatory, in this passage. The significance of this passage and others, which are concerned with martyrdom, will be treated later in this work.

[2] Of this event Büchsel says, 'Only through substitutionary suffering, through personal self-offering, is the community atoned' (*TWNT*, III, 323). Cf. the words of Eliezer: 'Be merciful to thy people, being pleased to accept our punishment on their behalf: make my blood a means of cleansing (atonement) for them and take my life as a substitute for theirs' (4 Macc. 6: 28–9).

[3] So Moulton and Milligan, *VGT*, p. 536.

[4] Cf. Rom. 8: 28; 9: 11; Eph. 1: 9, 11. Patristic exegesis supports this interpretation, but the construction (with two accusatives, if ἱλαστήριον is a noun) presents difficulty. However, the related word προορίζω has that construction at Rom. 8: 29 and Eph. 1: 5.

ριον in the latter is used, as in the former, with 'propitiatory' significance. Morris thinks that it is not necessary to assume the dependence of the Romans verses on 4 Maccabees, but as long ago as 1919 Hastings Rashdall regarded it as 'highly probable' that the 4 Maccabees passage was the source of Paul's thought and expression.[1] This study concludes with a discussion of this possibility.

We deal first with the question of the dating of the two works. There is wide agreement that Paul composed the letter to the Romans during his three-month stay in Greece (probably at Corinth) mentioned at Acts 20: 2 f. The date of this visit cannot be fixed with certainty but it took place in winter, some time between late A.D. 55 and early 59, and probably just after the completion of the Corinthian correspondence. A definite date for 4 Maccabees cannot be provided. The fact that the Temple and its services appear to be still in existence places the book before A.D. 70. M. Hadas has recently claimed that the title given to Apollonius, στρατηγὸς Συρίας τε καὶ Φοινίκης καὶ Κιλικίας, reflects the state of affairs at the time of writing and not during the Maccabean period: if so, then the time of writing must have been between A.D. 20 and 54, since it was only in those years that Cilicia was associated with Syria for administrative purposes.[2] Because there are references in the book to a state of peace being enjoyed by the nation, Hadas dates the work to the middle or end of Caligula's reign (37–41) before the persecution linked with his name.[3] Therefore no impediment exists on the basis of date to the suggestion of dependence. The probable Alexandrian origin of 4 Maccabees and its dependence on Greek philosophical ideas do not necessarily militate against the theory that Paul knew and was influenced by the work.

We must go on to ask whether it is likely or even possible that Paul could have shared or used the dominant theme expressed in 4 Maccabees. This work is one of the finest expressions of the

---

[1] *The Idea of Atonement in Christian Theology* (London, 1919), p. 132.

[2] *The Third and Fourth Books of Maccabees*, ed. M. Hadas (New York, 1953).

[3] Many commentators date the book to this time. J. Jeremias, *Heiligengräber in Jesu Umwelt* (Göttingen, 1958) dates it to *c*. A.D. 35, and E. Lohse, *Märtyrer und Gottesknecht*, FRLANT, 46 (Göttingen, 1955, p. 66 note 2) places it before A.D. 50. Dupont-Sommer, *Le Quatrième Livre des Macchabées* (Paris, 1939) dates it much later, but is followed by no one else.

glory and worth of martyrdom. Around this theme there had grown up in Judaism a theology within which the sufferings of righteous men and the deaths of martyrs were regarded (i) as examples of supreme obedience to the demands of God, (ii) as having atoning significance, and (iii) as creating merit which availed for others.[1] Such views concerning the value of suffering were very old in Judaism and found clear expression in the rabbinic writings which contain many reports of martyrdoms to which vicarious atoning power is ascribed.[2] The same ideas are hinted at in such works as the Assumption of Moses, the Psalms of Solomon (10: 2), parts of the Testaments of XII (Benj. 3: 8), and are clearly presented in the works commemorative of the Maccabees. If we are to claim that the language and thought of one profound statement of this Jewish belief influenced Rom. 3, we must seek to discover whether or not the ideas expressed there are witnessed to elsewhere in Paul. In this connection, it is noteworthy that recent scholarship has been asserting the influence of the righteous-martyr theology on New Testament Christology and soteriology. C. K. Barrett allows it prominence in his discussion of Mark 10: 45;[3] it is powerfully present to the thought of E. Schweizer when he interprets Jesus' life and death in terms of the fate of the 'Suffering Righteous' of Wisdom 3–4;[4] H. J. Schoeps asserts that it foreshadows Pauline soteriology,[5] and W. D. Davies regards it as a pattern of thought familiar to and used by the Apostle Paul. Dr Davies indicates that the idea of the righteous obedience of the martyr appears at Rom. 5: 13–18 and Phil. 2: 8, that the notion of the atoning significance of

[1] Cf. W. H. C. Frend, *Martyrdom and Persecution in the Early Church* (Oxford, 1965), pp. 31–68.

[2] Cf. Gen. R. 44 on Ch. 5: 15; Ex. R. 35. 4. Moses, David, Ezekiel, Job, Jonah and Isaac were thought of as suffering vicariously for the sins of the people.

[3] *New Testament Essays*, in memory of T. W. Manson, ed. A. J. B. Higgins (Manchester, 1959), pp. 1–18.

[4] As in his book, *Lordship and Discipleship* (S.C.M., London, 1960); also *NTS*, II (1955–6), 88.

[5] *Paul: The Theology of the Apostle in the light of Jewish religious History* (ET, London, 1961), p. 128. He thinks that the 'binding of Isaac' which belongs to this general theme, is the ultimate pattern of thought behind Paul's theology of Atonement; but references to it in Paul are hard to establish. In 4 Macc. 7: 14; 13: 12; 16: 20, Isaac is considered a prototype for the martyrs.

suffering underlies Rom. 5:6–8, 17–19, and that the idea of the merits of the righteous is basic to Rom. 5 and suggested in Rom. 9:5 and 11:28.[1] Since this martyr-theology, which is a well-defined element in the religious milieu out of which Paul came, seems therefore to have contributed to Paul's soteriology and to Romans in particular, it is reasonable to suggest that we should interpret Rom. 3:21 ff. in terms of the atoning value of the death of the righteous martyr and especially the Maccabean statement of that theme,[2] rather than in terms of the Levitical ritual and the Day of Atonement. As to the method by which the value or validity of the death is made available Paul leaves us in no doubt: it is διὰ πίστεως ('Ιησοῦ Χριστοῦ). This is his unique Christian contribution to the theme.[3]

The possibility of a community of ideas between Romans and 4 Maccabees leads to a further point. Indications derived from the latter suggest that the book was not a mere literary exercise, but an address given to an audience[4] on a set occasion (κατὰ τοῦτον τὸν καιρόν, 1:10). If our text does not record the actual address, it is probably a later revision and extension of it. But for what occasion was the address composed? Was there any festival at which the Maccabean martyrs were remembered? Many years ago, B. W. Bacon examined with great acuteness the leading features of the Feast of the Dedication with special reference to 4 Maccabees.[5] It is well known that this festival, beginning on Chisleu 25 and known as the Feast of Hanukkah or 'Εγκαινία ('Illumination', or more probably 'Renewal') commemorated the rededication of the Temple in 165 B.C., but Bacon claims that the remembrance of the martyrs who prepared

---

[1] *Paul and Rabbinic Judaism*, pp. 265–73. He notes that the terms 'redemption', 'justification' and 'atonement' are the words most often found in the rabbinic literature to describe the effects of the merits of the righteous (p. 273).

[2] This point of view has been advanced recently by E. Lohse, *Märtyrer und Gottesknecht*.

[3] It is interesting that Bultmann (*Theology of the New Testament*, ET, London, 1952, I, 46–7) and E. Käsemann (*ZNW*, XLIII [1950–1], 150–4) and others who regard Rom. 3:25 as a pre-Pauline tradition concerning the death of Jesus, claim that he added to it the all-important words διὰ πίστεως.

[4] Cf. the use of the 2nd person throughout, especially 1:10, 12.

[5] 'The Festival of Lives given for the Nation in Jewish and Christian Faith', *Hibbert Journal*, xv (1917), 256–78.

the way for its recovery from Antiochus was a significant feature
of the festival for a long time after its inauguration.[1] This aspect
of the festival's content and purpose was largely forgotten by
Pharisaic Judaism, probably because of the unworthy record of
the successors of the Maccabeans in the Sadducean priest-
nobility; but Hellenistic Judaism made up for the ingratitude
of the Palestinian synagogue and preserved the books of
Maccabees, glorying in the memory of the great deliverers. At
a later date there was a cult of the martyrs' graves at Antioch
in which even Christians for a time shared.[2] It is therefore quite
probable that 4 Maccabees (or part of it) is, in Bacon's phrase,
'a Memorial Day Address' composed for and repeated on the
occasion of the Feast of Dedication.

Now if the 4 Maccabees statement concerning the martyrdom
of the seven brothers influenced Paul's thought and language in
Rom. 3 and if, as seems likely, the remembrance of their deaths
was associated with the Feast of Dedication, then we may be
able to find more convincing traces of the influence of the Jewish
festivals on Paul's correspondence with Corinth and Rome than
those suggested by T. W. Manson.[3] It may be recalled that

[1] The possibility that Hanukkah derived from an earlier (pagan) feast an
interest in renewal and revival would make it a fitting festival for the
remembrance of men whose faithfulness won them 'resurrection'. Again,
2 Maccabees (which also commemorates the martyrdoms) gives directions
for the due observance of the Feast of Dedication (chs. 1–2). A late piyyut
commemorating the seven brothers and their mother is designed for the
Sabbath of Hanukkah (see L. Zunz, *Die Gottesdienstlichen Vorträge* [Berlin,
1832], p. 124). J. Freudenthal, *Die Flavius Josephus beigelegte Schrift: Über die
Herrschaft der Vernunft (IV Makk.)* (Breslau, 1869, p. 106), suggested that
4 Maccabees presents a sermon (or expansion of a sermon) given during the
Hanukkah festival: cf. also H. Gressmann, *The Tower of Babel*, ed. J. Obermann (New York, 1928), p. 73 note 30. The Ninth of Ab was another
occasion on which the Maccabees were remembered: see J. Obermann,
'The Sepulchre of the Maccabean Martyrs', *JBL*, L (1931), 250–65.

[2] Cf. E. Bammel, 'Zum jüdischen Märtyrerkult', *TLZ*, LXXVIII (1953),
119 ff. and H. A. Fischel, 'Prophet and Martyr', *JQR* (n.s.), XXXVII (1947),
265 ff. and 363 ff.

[3] *JTS*, XLVI (1945), 1 ff. Manson does not give the precise year in which
he thinks the correspondence took place. Uncertainty prevails on this
matter; but, in any case, neither Manson's argument nor the view presented
here requires any special year: any one of those suggested (54–9) can sustain
the position. What is necessary is that Romans should have been written
soon after the Corinthian correspondence and in the winter season: and both
these points are widely accepted.

Manson claimed that 1 Corinthians was written around the Passover season and that that ritual was present to Paul's thought (cf. 5: 7ff.); that 2 Cor. 1–9 (written in the autumn) contains themes associated with Tabernacles (cf. ch. 5) and the New Year (since the giving of the Law is compared with the promulgation of the Gospel). He goes on to suggest that the thought of Romans, particularly in ch. 3, was partially inspired by the ritual of the Day of Atonement of the same year. But would that not place the writing of Romans too close to the completion of the Corinthian correspondence? The Day of Atonement falls less than two weeks after the festival of the New Year. It is more probable that if the occurrence of a festival turned Paul's mind to a certain theme in his writing of Romans (or of part of it), then that festival was the Feast of Dedication. It began on Chisleu 25 (i.e. two and a half months after the New Year) and thus was a winter festival, and Paul is usually regarded as having written Romans in the winter season (Acts 20: 2ff.). The epistle bears traces of the influence of the martyr-theology, and one of the supreme expressions of that theology (4 Maccabees) was associated with the death of the seven heroes who may well have been commemorated at the Feast of Dedication. Was the language and thought of propitiatory, atoning death given to Paul as he wrote Romans by the remembrance of the Maccabean martyrdoms celebrated in the Feast of Hanukkah? We cannot of course prove this hypothesis, but it is a fascinating conjecture that the sequence of Jewish festivals may at certain points have influenced Paul's presentation of the Gospel.

This investigation has revealed throughout the importance of the study of context for the interpretation of word-meanings. In the case of the ἱλάσκεσθαι words, the frequent references to divine wrath and its turning aside which are found in their contexts suggest that the idea of propitiation belongs to the terms. The work also demonstrates that the meaning of a Hebrew word is not a reliable guide to the meaning of every Greek word which may render it. In assessing the meaning of Greek terms, the Greek of the LXX is worthy of consideration in its own right. It is necessary to ask why and with what meaning the LXX translators used a particular word, especially when it is an unusual rendering of the Hebrew. When we are confronted by a regular translation method which does offer guidance on the interpretation of the Greek word (as, for example, כִּפֶּר and (ἐξ)ιλάσκεσθαι), we must do justice to the history and development of meaning in the Hebrew term[1] if we are rightly to determine the Greek meaning with reference to it. The attempt to discover the general background of an author's thought has proved valuable in allowing us to postulate the idea that Paul was influenced in the writing of Romans, and in particular chapter 3, not by the recollection of the cultic ritual of the Day of Atonement, but of the passage from 4 Maccabees. Furthermore this recollection may have been prompted (we suggest tentatively) by an occurrence of the Feast of Dedication at which the seven Maccabean martyrs were commemorated.

[1] In the case of כִּפֶּר this development is from an original non-cultic usage, in which the idea of propitiation was strong, to a later cultic usage in which ideas of expiation and propitiation were present to a system of atonement.

CHAPTER III

THE BACKGROUND AND USAGE OF ΛΥΤΡΟΝ AND COGNATE WORDS IN BIBLICAL GREEK

The group of words associated with the term λύτρον in the Greek of the New Testament is the usual, but not the exclusive means of expressing the idea of redemption.[1] The following survey of the linguistic usage of the λύτρον-words is an attempt to penetrate the meaning which the terms had for the writers of the New Testament documents, and, as such, is a necessary preliminary to any statement or interpretation of the Christian doctrine of Redemption.

CLASSICAL GREEK USAGE

The word λύτρον and its derivatives go back to the verb λύειν, which has the general meaning 'to loose'. Among the varied extensions of its use, this verb, when applied to persons, commonly means 'to release, set free from bonds, danger or difficulty'. It developed a particular usage with reference to the freeing of prisoners when a ransom was supplied as the condition of release, and so came to signify 'to release on receipt of a ransom, to hold to ransom' (active) and 'to secure release by payment of a ransom' (middle).[2] Now the suffix—τρον (contracted from—τήριον) denotes the instrument or means by which the action of the verb is accomplished, so that λύτρον will signify 'the means of releasing': or, if Debrunner is correct in suggesting a stage at which the suffix denoted payment,[3] it will mean 'the price of releasing'. This is the basic significance of the word according to LS, which lists the various senses in which it is used:

[1] The verbs ἀγοράζω, ἐξαγοράζω and περιποιέομαι express the same idea.

[2] Cf. LS, λύω under 2 c, for examples of this from Homer onwards.

[3] A. Debrunner, *Griechische Wortbildungslehre* (Heidelberg, 1917), pp. 176 ff. Also P. Chantraine, *La Formation des Noms en grec ancien* (Paris, 1933), p. 332.

4　　　　　　　　　　　　49　　　　　　　　　　HGW

(i) To mean (almost always in the plural form) 'ransom' or 'ransom money': when bearing this sense the word is often used with such verbs as λαβεῖν, ἀποδιδόναι and καταθεῖναι. It would appear to be as a special application of this sense that the word (in the plural) is used in inscriptions and papyri to mean 'the sum paid' for the manumission of slaves (P. Oxy. 48 *b*, 49 and 722, from first century A.D.) or for the redemption of a pledge (P. Bad. 3, 4, from second century B.C.).[1]

(ii) To connote a means of expiation or atonement: this infrequently found sense applies in Aesch. *Choeph.* 48 (reading Canter's emendation) and possibly in Lucian, *Dial. Deorum* 4. 2.[2]

(iii) Very rarely in the general sense of 'recompense', e.g. Pindar, *Isth.* 8. 1 and *Ol.* 7. 77.

The process of word-formation which began with λύτρον continued and created a new verb λυτροῦν, λυτροῦσθαι. Throughout the whole history of profane Greek literature this verb seems to have maintained unbrokenly the sense 'to ransom'. In the active voice (according to LS) it means 'to release on receipt of a ransom' or 'to hold to ransom', of which meaning 'to redeem a pledge' (P. Oxy. 530, 14 from second century A.D.) is a special application: in the middle voice, the sense is 'to release by payment of a ransom', and in the passive, 'to be ransomed'. The suggestion that in this verb and especially in the middle voice the λύτρον-idea may be neglected and the meaning regarded merely as 'to deliver'[3] cannot be validated from classical Greek sources. The only three passages where the active or middle form appears (apart from inscriptions and papyri) are Plato, *Theat.* 165 *e*, Polybius 18. 6. 1 and Plut. *Cimon* 9, and all these expressly mention a price paid in the exchange.[4] The noun λύτρωσις is rare in non-biblical Greek and the lexicons cite only three occurrences: Plut. *Aratus* 11 (in which we read of money being needed for the ransoming of prisoners); P. Teb. 120, 41 (first century) where the word is used

---

[1] See A. Deissmann, *Light from the Ancient East* (transl. of 4th German ed., London, 1927), pp. 327–8 for details.

[2] F. Steinleitner, *Die Beicht im Zusammenhange mit der sakralen Rechtspflege in der Antike* (Leipzig, 1913), pp. 36 ff., interprets λύτρον in this expiatory sense in two late inscriptions from Lydia.

[3] So Th. Zahn, *Römerbrief* (1st ed., Leipzig, 1910), pp. 179–81.

[4] LS observes that in a third-century B.C. papyrus (Eleph. 19. 8) the passive of λυτρόω is used in the sense of 'to be released from obligation'.

in the sense of 'redemption of a pledge'; and P. Oxy. 1130, 20 (fifth century A.D.) where it means 'release or discharge from an obligation'.

The compound verb ἀπολυτρόω occurs seven times in non-biblical Greek: four times in the active voice,[1] in two very late passages in the middle[2] and once only in the passive.[3] In each of these cases the price of liberation is indicated and the verb plainly bears the meaning 'to release on receipt of, or by paying a ransom'. The noun ἀπολύτρωσις is also a rare word, but since it is the characteristic New Testament word for 'redemption' its extra-biblical use requires careful examination. In *Pompey* 24, 2, Plutarch says that 'seizings of the persons of officers and ransomings of captive cities (πόλεων αἰχμαλώτων ἀπολυτρώσεις) were a reproach to the Roman governorship': here the word means 'holding to ransom', the action of the active voice. Josephus, *Ant.* 12. 2. 3 tells how Aristaeus agreed to pay more than 400 talents to soldiers as the ransom for their prisoners: here ἀπολύτρωσις means 'price of release'. In the Epistle of Aristeas the word occurs twice (12, 33) with reference to the release of prisoners of war, and the ransom price is stated in section 22 as being 20 drachmae per person. At Diod. Fragm. 37. 5. 3 we read about a slave who had agreed with his masters for the purchase of his freedom but before the manumission could be carried out, Scaevola 'anticipating the ransoming... crucified him'. Here ἀπολύτρωσις probably means 'release on payment of a ransom'. The word appears in an inscription (second or first century B.C.) from Cos[4] which deals with the liberation of a slave. It is suggested by Deissmann[5] and Zahn[6] that 'deliverance' is the meaning here, since the term ἀπελευθέρωσις describes the same transaction elsewhere in the inscription. But Warfield[7] and Morris[8] claim that ἀπολύτρωσις

---

[1] Epist. (Phil.) *apud* Demos. 12, 3, p. 159; Plato, *Laws* 11, 919a; Polybius 2. 6, 6 and 22. 21, 8.

[2] Pantaenus, *Strategemata* 5, 40; Julian, *Imp. Grat.* VI (Teubner, vol. 1, p. 253). For details, see B. B. Warfield, 'The New Testament Terminology of Redemption', *PTR*, xv (1917), 211–12.

[3] Plutarch, *Pompey* 24. 4.

[4] W. R. Paton and E. L. Hicks, *The Inscriptions of Cos* (Oxford, 1891), no. 29.   [5] *Light from the Ancient East*, p. 327 note 6 and p. 321.

[6] *Römerbrief*, p. 180 note 51.   [7] *PTR*, xv (1917), 214.

[8] *The Apostolic Preaching of the Cross*, p. 25.

defines more precisely the kind of liberation involved; it is a liberation by the paying of a ransom. Another occurrence of the word which may cause some difficulty in interpretation is Philo, *Probus* 114, a passage which tells of a captive Laconian boy who 'judged death a happier lot than his present valueless life, and despairing of ransoming (ἀπογνοὺς ἀπολύτρωσιν), gladly put an end to himself'. It could be argued that here the meaning is simply 'deliverance', but the context, with its reference to slavery, suggests that the idea of a ransom price to gain freedom is implied.

There is some uncertainty as to whether the noun ἀπολύτρω- σις expresses the action of the active or of the middle voice of the verb from which it is formed, that is, whether the meaning is to be found in terms of 'holding to ransom' or of 'paying a ransom'. Both Warfield and Morris, while admitting the difficulty in choosing, prefer to interpret it in the sense of the middle: but T. K. Abbott[1] examines the passages and claims that 'as far as usage goes, it would seem that if we are to attach to ἀπολύτρωσις the idea of ransom, the word will mean "holding to ransom" or "release on receipt of a ransom", not "payment of a ransom"'. While this interpretation may be correct in some of the passages (e.g. Plut. *Pompey* 24. 2), it cannot be correct in them all, and the passage from Philo is clearly against it. In fact, the noun may take the sense of either voice of the verb from which it is derived.[2] With reference to Abbott's implied question concerning the rightness of attaching the idea of 'ransom' to ἀπολύτρωσις, it would seem that this application is generally correct: in most passages where the word occurs, the price of release is clearly stated, and where it is not expressed, the context suggests it, with the possible exception of the Cos inscription. In the case of the verbs λυτρόω and ἀπολυτρόω and of the nouns λύτρον and λύτρωσις, the contexts in which they appear repeatedly make explicit the notion of price, thus giving precision of meaning. In short, our survey has shown that in the use of the word λύτρον and its derivatives in profane Greek literature there is a marked consistency in the retention and expression of the ransom idea.[3]

---

[1] *Ephesians and Colossians* (ICC, Edinburgh, 1897), p. 12.

[2] So Zahn, *op. cit.* pp. 179–81.

[3] The only exception which LS notes among all derived forms is ἐκλυτ- ροῦσθαι meaning 'to deliver', Schol. on Homer, *Ody.* 4. 35. The text, 'we must look to Zeus henceforth to keep us safe from harm' is explained in

THE USAGE OF THE SEPTUAGINT AND ITS OLD TESTAMENT BACKGROUND: THE DEAD SEA SCROLLS AND PHILO

When we examine the use of the λύτρον-words in the LXX, we find that the verb λυτροῦν, λυτροῦσθαι occurs ninety-nine times in the Old Testament books, and in these cases it represents the Hebrew root גאל forty-five times and פדה forty-three times.[1] The fact that the translators (or group of translators) working independently, and sometimes at great intervals of time from one another, should have confined, almost entirely, their use of the Greek verb to the rendering of these Hebrew words suggests that there was a large measure of semantic overlap between their meanings, and consequently makes the study of the Hebrew terms significant for our purpose.

The actions described in the Pentateuch by the verb גָּאַל are closely associated with the sphere of family relationships.[2] The word expresses the action of 'standing up for' a relative (i) where blood has been shed: thus the avenger of blood (גֹּאֵל) makes good the family honour (Num. 35; Deut. 19: 6, 12; Josh. 20: 3, 5, 9; 2 Sam. 14: 11); (ii) where the family name is in danger of dying out: this is illustrated by the process of levirate marriage (Ruth 3: 13); (iii) when land falls into the possession of strangers: here גָּאַל means 'reclaim' (Lev. 25: 26, 33); (iv) when a member of the family has become a slave, and גָּאַל means 'buy back' (Lev. 25: 48ff.). From its association with these actions it is generally assumed that the basic idea inherent in the root גאל is that of 'acting as a kinsman', of doing one's duty within the family group by recovering what has been lost.[3] The association

terms of the hope that 'after these things he (Zeus) may deliver (ἐκλυτρώσηται) us from the impending disaster'. There is no suggestion of ransoming here.

[1] λυτροῦν translates the root פרק on four occasions and a few other verbs once each. These will be investigated later.

[2] See further, the study of the terms גָּאַל and פָּדָה in *Erlösen und Vergeben im AT*, J. J. Stamm (Bern, 1940).

[3] In his article, 'The Primary Meaning of √גאל' (*VT*, Suppl. 1 [1953], 67–77) A. R. Johnson suggests that the single common principle which underlies all the actions expressed by the verb is that of 'protection'. R. de Vaux, *Ancient Israel: Its Life and Institutions* (ET, London, 1961), p. 21, agrees that this is the fundamental meaning of the verb.

of the words with the action of reclaiming property led to their being used to express the process of redeeming (through adding one-fifth to the valuation) by the original owner of something he had sanctified to the Lord (Lev. 27: 13, 15, 19, etc.).

The verb גָּאַל occurs forty times with Yahweh as subject. This usage suggests that Yahweh is the great Kinsman or Protector of his people, who would succour them in times of distress and rescue them in times of disaster. Accordingly, the word is frequently used of the deliverance from Egypt[1] and of the rescue from Babylon.[2] Moreover, Yahweh is spoken of thirteen times in Isaiah 40–66 as גֹּאֵל and his people may be referred to as the 'redeemed (גְּאוּלִים) of the Lord'.[3] However, the action of Yahweh described by the verb גָּאַל is not confined to occasions of national liberation: it may be the deliverance of an individual from evil[4] or the constant redemption of the saints (Prov. 23: 11).

Since Yahweh did not pay to the Egyptian or Babylonian oppressors any price for the release of his people, it may be said that the verb גָּאַל (with Yahweh as subject) means 'to set free, to liberate, to emancipate', and that the idea of strict ransoming has fallen into the background, if not entirely disappeared. Nevertheless, many writers wish to retain it and point out that the deliverances effected by Yahweh are not effortless performances: the cost in terms of his strength and power is frequently stressed (e.g. Exod. 6: 6; Ps. 77: 16). For instance, B. F. Westcott says: '. . . the idea of the exertion of a mighty force, the idea that the redemption costs much, is everywhere present. The force may be represented by divine might, or love, or self-sacrifice, which become finally identical.'[5] However, it seems a very doubtful claim that the idea of the exertion of divine power keeps alive in גאל the notion of paying a ransom price. An apologetic interest seems to dominate in this interpretation, and in the attempt to make the meaning conform to a presupposition a significant case of semantic development is neglected. This we shall explain after we have looked at the root פדה.

---

[1] E.g. Exod. 6: 6; 15: 13; Ps. 77: 16; 78: 35; 106: 10.

[2] E.g. Isa. 43: 1; 44: 22, 23; 48: 20; 52: 3, 9; 63: 9; Hos. 13: 14 (metaphorical); Mic. 4: 10.

[3] Ps. 107: 2; Isa. 35: 9; 51: 10, etc.

[4] Cf. Gen. 48: 16; Ps. 69: 19; 103: 4; 119: 154.

[5] *Commentary on the Epistle to the Hebrews* (3rd ed., London, 1903), p. 296.

If the verb גָּאַל has its roots in the realm of family or civil law, פָּדָה appears to be related to the sphere of commercial transaction, in which there is no obligation arising from ties of kinship. The word refers to the action of taking a thing or person out of the possession or ownership of another into one's own possession and ownership by giving a ransom as an equivalent or substitute for it. Examples of this may be found in the 'redemption of the first-born' (Exod. 13: 12ff.; Num. 18: 15ff.), the 'redemption' at five shekels each of the Israelites who were in excess of the number of Levites whom God accepted instead of the first-born (Num. 3: 40ff.). In accordance with this usage, the word is applied to the redemption of a slave-concubine: Exod. 21: 8 'If she does not please her master...then he shall let her be redeemed (וְהֶפְדָּהּ)', presumably by her father.[1]

Like גָּאַל, the verb פָּדָה is used frequently (thirty-three times) with Yahweh as subject. While the deliverance from Egypt is often so described,[2] Yahweh's act in 'redeeming' from the Exile is not often represented by this verb.[3] Sometimes the word refers to Israel's deliverance without mention of a specific occasion.[4] Moreover, the deliverance described by פָּדָה may be from iniquity or trouble (Ps. 25: 22; 130: 8) and frequently refers, not to the nation, but to the individual.[5] Of this use of פָּדָה (as with גָּאַל) we may fairly say that 'deliverance' is the dominant theme and that the idea of ransom falls into the background. To stress the costliness of the deliverance in terms of Yahweh's strength and activity in order to keep alive the notion of ransom price (cf. Neh. 1: 10 and 2 Sam. 7: 23) would be to place an undue strain on the evidence: wherever there is need to emphasise the exercise of Yahweh's power in saving his people, it is stated explicitly in the context. We have no right to read it into every occurrence of the verb in order to make the word retain a

---

[1] The interpretation of the word as 'he shall release her' is made unlikely by the statement that, if this or other means of giving freedom are not employed, 'she shall go out for nothing, without money' (v. 11). Both D. M. Stalker, *New Peake*: Exod. para. 194b and de Vaux, *Ancient Israel*, p. 86, think that the action of the verb involves the paying of a price.

[2] 2 Sam. 7: 23; Deut. 7: 8; 9: 26; 13: 5; 15: 15; 24: 18; 1 Chron. 17: 21; Ps. 78: 42.

[3] Only at Isa. 35: 10 and 51: 11.

[4] Deut. 21: 8; Neh. 1: 10; Hos. 7: 13; Zech. 10: 8.

[5] E.g. 2 Sam. 4: 9; 1 Kings 1: 29, and often in Psalms.

presumed original and single unchanging sense. The meanings of words are seldom static and semantic development is often influenced by the events of history. It seems probable that the words גָּאַל and פָּדָה, which had a close association with the idea of releasing slaves and of reclaiming persons and things,[1] were taken up into the vocabulary of Israel's writers as the most suitable terms to describe the liberation from slavery of those whom Egypt and Babylon had conquered, and the reclaiming by Yahweh into his rightful ownership of 'the people of his possession'.[2] This semantic development does no more than extend and emphasise what was already the essential theme of גָּאַל and פָּדָה in their specialised use, namely that of bringing persons into freedom.

The semantic development suggested receives confirmation, in the case of פדה, from the usage of the Dead Sea Scrolls. The verb is used four times in 1QH and on each occasion the meaning is 'to release, save or deliver', usually of divine deliverance from association with false worshippers (1QH 2. 32, 35; 3. 19; 17. 20). The same meaning is borne by the verb at 4Qpsr Ps. 37 vv. 14–15. At CD 16. 8 root פדה is used with reference to the impossibility of redeeming an oath even at the price of death. The idea is similar to the Old Testament 'redemption of a pledge' and the notion of price is present in the phrase עד מחיר מות. The ransom

[1] Whether this was the only and original use of the words is an open question, for גָּאַל and פָּדָה are found in early material with the straightforward sense of 'deliver', Hos. 13: 14; Mic. 4: 10; Gen. 48: 16 (J or E stratum). The ransom idea may therefore not belong to the earliest meaning of the words, but may be dependent on their particular use in social and legal codes.

[2] In his book *The New Testament and Rabbinic Judaism* (London, 1956, pp. 268 ff.) D. Daube thinks that this application of the words illustrates the development of the concept of redemption. (Note that concept-history is here based on word-study.) He suggests that primitive social laws (like those in the Pentateuch) governing the recovery of persons and property determined the way in which the Exodus was thought of and described: p. 279, 'Deliverance by God is "recovery". The notion goes back to ancient social legislation. It was transferred to the Exodus which, in turn, gave a new impetus to the social laws. It was applied to later deeds of God for his people. It was also applied to the rescue by God of the faithful individual and to the final salvation of his own at the end of days. In the New Testament it is applied to the redemption through Jesus.' See also the same author's *Studies in Biblical Law* (Cambridge, 1947), pp. 39 ff., and more recently, *The Exodus Pattern in the Bible* (London, 1964).

content of the verb is guaranteed here, as in Old Testament legal passages, by the clear expression of price in the context. The noun פדות occurs several times in 1QM,[1] but never with a ransom significance: it usually refers to the hoped-for eschatological deliverance *by God* of his faithful saints. The use of the root גאל seems to have been avoided by the writers of the Scrolls: it appears once only, in a passage reconstructed by Schechter (CD 14. 6), in the noun form meaning 'kinsman or protector'.

If the use of the root גאל to describe God's deliverance of his people is avoided in the Qumran documents, it is quite otherwise in the rabbinic literature where גאל is often used of the Exodus deliverance, whereas פדה, commonly found in the Scrolls referring to God's past and future deliverances, never bears this sense in the Mishnah.[2] Both words are frequently found to describe legal and cultic 'redemption',[3] and in these passages the ideas which belong to the use of the words in the Pentateuch are dominant. But Tractate Pesahim (Feast of Passover) is rich in examples of גאל being used of the Exodus deliverance (10. 5–6), but in none of them is there present the notion of ransom price in terms of the exertion of Yahweh's power. This is the natural continuation of the Old Testament use of the term to describe God's saving action. The fact that in the Old Testament and rabbinic literature גאל is the leading term to describe this action suggests that the ideas of relationship and recovery which are implied in that verb are the main themes in the Jewish understanding of 'redemption'. In the rabbinic literature גאל is frequently applied to Israel's future deliverance when all her afflictions will be ended. An example of this use is found in the Seventh of the Eighteen Benedictions, a petition whose origin may be in the Maccabean era:[4] 'Look upon our afflictions and plead our cause and redeem us (וּגְאָלֵנוּ) speedily for thy name's sake; for thou art a mighty redeemer (גּוֹאֵל). Blessed art thou,

---

[1] 1QM 1. 12 (*bis*); 11. 9; 13. 14; 14. 5; 15. 1; 17. 6; 18. 11.

[2] Was the use of פדה at Qumran a protest by the sectarians against the common practice of Judaism?

[3] The root גאל refers to the 'redemption' of property (Arak. 9: 1–4) and of things dedicated to the Lord (Arak. 7: 3–5): פדה to the 'redemption' of standing corn (Peah 4: 7), dough (Hallah 3: 3), dedicated produce (Terum. 6: 5; Pes. 2: 5), captive slaves (Ketub. 1: 2, 4; 3: 1), persons from Gentile ownership (Git. 4: 9).

[4] Cf. H. J. Hertz, *The Authorised Daily Prayer Book* (1959), p. 140.

O Lord, the redeemer of Israel.' Leon Morris suggests that in this prayer the idea of cost in the expenditure of mighty power may be discerned, but admits that this use of the term tended to be conventionalised, so that it is not always possible to insist upon this.[1] It is this kind of conventionalising of use that is important in the history of meaning. The regular use of גָּאַל and פָּדָה to describe God's deliverances placed the emphasis on 'release' rather than on the ransoming process. The noun גּוֹאֵל is frequently applied by the rabbis to the coming Messiah, the great Redeemer of the glorious future. This use of the noun was probably derived from the use of גאל in connection with the Exodus, and therefore the Messiah was thought of as a Moses-like deliverer.[2]

Can we claim that the development of meaning which we have traced in גָּאַל and פָּדָה in the Old Testament and the Scrolls applies to the Greek word λυτρόω by which they are usually translated? The facts of translation on which we must base our judgment are these: on eighteen of the forty-five occasions it renders גָּאַל, λυτρόω clearly connotes the paying of a ransom price, within the context of legal processes; these occurrences are confined to Lev. 25 and 27, and in each of them the verb has a human subject: the other twenty-seven occurrences of the verb have reference to God's deliverance of Israel and of individuals, and are found mainly in Deutero-Isaiah and Psalms. Likewise, on ten of the forty-three occasions on which λυτρόω translates פדה, the reference is to strict ransoming by individuals through provision of a substitute, and these ten occurrences are all in the Pentateuch, whereas the remaining thirty-three refer to God's deliverance of his people and are found in Deuteronomy, Psalms and occasionally in the prophets. It would appear then that in the legal codes of the Old Testament where the price of restitution or freedom is stated or clearly implied, the verb λυτρόω (like the Hebrew words it translates) connotes strict ransoming by payment, as in its profane usage:[3] but it is plausible

---

[1] *The Apostolic Preaching of the Cross*, p. 20.

[2] For a survey of the Moses–Messiah motif see, *Moïse: L'Homme de l'alliance*, by H. Cazelles and others (Paris, 1955), sections I–III. Traces of the idea may be found at several points in New Testament Christology.

[3] It is perhaps significant that the examples of late Greek usage cited by Deissmann (*op. cit.*) and Moulton and Milligan (*VGT, ad loc.*) as guides to

to suggest that the use of λυτρόω to render גָּאַל and פָּדָה in passages which refer to divine deliverance influenced its biblical Greek meaning, in these and similar contexts, towards 'release' or 'deliver' and away from emphasis on price and payment.

Support for this suggested semantic development may be drawn from the use of the verb λυτρόω in the Intertestamental literature. The Wisdom of ben Sirach employs the verb five times: four of these occurrences refer to the action of God in delivering Israel or an individual,[1] and one to the action of the Twelve prophets in delivering Jacob by the confidence of hope (49: 10).[2] In none of these places is the idea of ransoming expressed, implied or suitable: the verb clearly connotes release or deliverance. This is true also of 1 Macc. 4: 11 where Judas Maccabeus rallies his followers with the recollection of the Red Sea deliverance and bids them call on the divine assistance that 'all the Gentiles may know that there is one who delivers and saves Israel (ὁ λυτρούμενος καὶ σῴζων τὸν 'Ισραηλ)'. The context and the verbal parallelism make the introduction of the ransom idea impossible. Morris finds 'an interesting use of the ransom idea'[3] in Enoch 98: 10, 'Wherefore do not hope to live, ye sinners; but ye shall depart and die, for ye know no ransom': and he suggests that the passage is reminiscent of Ps. 49: 8–9. The words of the Psalm are quite clear in their import: the rich man's wealth cannot buy freedom from the experience of death; therefore the ransom idea is certainly present. The Enoch passage, however, does not have the same precision and λύτρον may denote simply 'way of deliverance'. In any case, the emphasis in the meaning of the λύτρον-words in the Palestinian Apocryphal writings appears to be on the theme of deliverance rather than on the particular method of gaining release.

Further confirmation of this semantic emphasis is given in

the meaning of λύτρον in the New Testament are almost all taken from legal transactions which state or imply the theme of purchase. Commerce and the slave-market were the spheres in which this connotation was kept alive.

[1] Ch. 48: 20, 'The Holy One delivered (ἐλυτρώσατο) the people of Jerusalem by the hand of Isaiah'; 50: 24, 'Let God deliver us (λυτρωσάσθω) in his time'; 51: 2, 'Thou didst deliver my body from destruction...Thou didst deliver me according to the abundance of thy mercy (ἐλυτρώσω)'.

[2] Here and at 48: 20 the Hebrew text was ישׁע ('save', 'deliver'): R. Smend, Die Weisheit des Jesus Sirach (Berlin, 1906).

[3] The Apostolic Preaching of the Cross, p. 21.

Philo's usage. Even though the λύτρον terms do not refer to divine action, they are frequently *interpreted* by Philo as connoting 'release' or 'deliverance'. The procedure he adopts is this: he finds the words in his biblical texts and quotes them in his work with the ransom significance which their contexts in legal codes required; when he explains the *meaning* of the passages, the strict ransom sense is missing and the idea of freedom is dominant. For example, at *Sac.* 114 Philo quotes Exod. 13: 3 'Every firstling of an ass you shall redeem (λυτρώσῃ) with a lamb', and in his explanation of this says that the word 'ransom' suggests that 'you shall free (ἐλευθερῶσαι) your soul from care', cf. *Heres* 186. Later in the same work (117 ff.) Philo interprets the ransoming of the first-born by the Levites in terms of homage to God which rescues (ἀπαλλάσσω) the soul from cruel task-masters and delivers it into liberty (ἐξαίρεται εἰς ἐλευθερίαν), cf. *Heres* 124. Again, the ransoming for ever of the Levite cities is explained as the eternal freedom (αἰώνιος ἐλευθερία) which the worshipper of God achieves. Philo's procedure is clearly illustrated in *Spec.* 1. 77 where he says that the first-fruit contributions to the Temple revenue are λύτρα since 'they are expected to gain release from slavery, healing of diseases, to secure freedom and preservation from danger'.

As well as passages which quote Old Testament legal usage (e.g. *Spec.* 2. 116, 121, 122), there are in Philo other passages which use the verb λυτρόω with the meaning 'ransom by payment of money' (*Spec.* 1. 135; 2. 95; 3. 145; *Heres* 44). In these cases, the price paid for release is stated or implied in the context. What is of significance is that when Philo explains the meaning of the action involved he does so in terms of the general notion of deliverance. The noun ἀπολύτρωσις appears twice in Philo. We have already noticed that at *Probus* 114 the word probably contains the idea of paying a ransom to win freedom from slavery, but it would be difficult to justify the claim that the notion is present in *Congr.* 109. There Philo says that the ten righteous men for whose sake God was willing to spare Sodom formed τελευταία ἀπολύτρωσις. There is no idea of ransoming here: the phrase means 'the final possibility or means of deliverance'. The verb ἀπολυτρόω is used once in the course of an allegorical interpretation of the Jacob–Laban story (*Leg. All.* 3. 21) with the meaning 'to free'—'the understanding is freed from vices and passions' by subduing all sensual claims. In summarising the significance of Philo's usage, we may say that his interpretations of the Old Testament ransom passages in terms of the general idea of freedom or deliverance and his use, on occasion, of the λύτρον-words without their having any ransom significance indicate a development in the semantic value of the words in the direction of stressing the central idea of deliverance rather than the ransom method of achieving it.[1]

In the LXX of the Old Testament books the noun λύτρον, usually in the plural form, occurs nineteen times. It renders כֹּפֶר six times,[2] פִּדְיוֹן seven times,[3] גְּאֻלָּה five times,[4] and מְחִיר ('price') once (Isa. 45: 13). In the sixteen of these passages which belong to legal sections of the Old Testament, and in the verse from Isaiah, λύτρον conveys, in accordance with its use in Greek, the meaning required by the Hebrew original, namely, 'ransom price'. In the two Proverbs passages the Hebrew term may be open to a wider interpretation. In Prov. 6: 35 כֹּפֶר may mean 'compensation' with reference to the outrage committed by an adulterer, while at Prov. 13: 8 a man's wealth is regarded as 'the ransom of his life', i.e. as the means of securing him against oppression. It may be that the meaning of the term כֹּפֶר developed from being a *terminus technicus* for the ransom exacted towards a more general sense, retaining the idea of exchange, but connoting mainly the means by which some particular freedom was gained.[5] If the translator of Proverbs is not to be thought of as rather mechanically inserting the usual translation word where כֹּפֶר appeared, it is possible that he used λύτρον to refer to any

---

[1] Morris (*The Apostolic Preaching of the Cross*, p. 21) supports the view that the λύτρον-words retained their essential significance by reference to the usage of Josephus, where the noun λύτρον is used for the ransom paid for prisoners in time of war (*Ant.* 12: 28, 33, 46, etc.). Here the contexts and the clear implication of payment give to the noun its precision of meaning.

[2] Exod. 21: 30; 30: 12; Num. 35: 31, 32; Prov. 6: 35; 13: 8.

[3] Num. 3: 46, 48, 49, 51; 18: 15; Exod. 21: 30; Lev. 19: 20.

[4] Lev. 25: 24, 26, 51, 52; 27: 31.

[5] This development is witnessed to in the rabbinic literature where כֹּפֶר is used to refer to a fine or indemnity paid to atone for one's own offence (cf. B. Kam. 4. 5 and 5. 3) and also to denote something much wider. The idea of the vicarious power of a כֹּפֶר underlies the recurring expression, 'May I be an atonement for you' (cf. Neg. 2: 1), by which a man declares his readiness to suffer that another person may be free.

means by which deliverance was achieved, and not just to the price paid in the process of ransoming. The adjective λυτρωτός (Lev. 25: 31, 32) and the compound noun ἐκλύτρωσις (Num. 3: 49), though not occurring in the New Testament, witness to the retention of the ransom idea in the meaning of the word-group in the LXX of the Pentateuch, The noun λύτρωσις occurs eight times, representing words derived from the roots גאל and פדה, each four times.[1] In four of these occurrences, in the Pentateuch, it is employed in the straightforward literal sense of 'a process of ransoming or redeeming by payment', as the contexts make clear (Lev. 25: 29 bis, 48; Num. 18: 16). Outside the Pentateuch, however, the notion of price is not obvious. At Ps. 49: 9, פִּדְיוֹן is translated τιμή τῆς λυτρώσεως: the presence of τιμή suggests that, for the translator, λύτρωσις by itself did not necessarily include the idea of payment. In Ps. 111: 9 and 130: 8, where the λύτρωσις is the gift of Yahweh, the implication of a process of ransoming is not present. The same is true of Isa. 63: 4, 'The day of vengeance was in my heart and my year of redemption has come (λύτρωσις)': this year is the same as that announced in 61: 2 as 'the year of the Lord's favour', a time of general release and salvation. The noun denoting the agent, λυτρωτής occurs twice, being applied to God and translating גּוֹאֵל (Ps. 19: 15 and 78: 35) with the meaning 'deliverer' or possibly 'protector', but without any suggestion of his having paid a price for his people's release.

In view of the fact that some scholars insist that the idea of ransom-price (in terms of the costly exertion of divine power) must adhere to λυτρόω, even when used of Yahweh's acts of deliverance, it is important to observe two other facts. First, the other Greek words which are used to translate גאל and פדה contain no suggestion of the ransom idea, but express simply the action of Yahweh in rescuing or releasing men.[2] This suggests

---

[1] At Judges 1: 15 it appears in a mistranslation of גֻּלֹּת מָיִם, through confusion of גאל and גלל.

[2] The verb σώζω renders פָּדָה at Job 33: 28 and Isa. 1: 27; ῥύεσθαι translates גָּאַל at Gen. 48: 16 and eleven times in Isa. 40–66, and represents פָּדָה in Job 5: 20; 6: 23; Hos. 13: 14; Ps. 69: 19 and Isa. 50: 2; ἐκλύειν renders גָּאַל in Job 19: 25. The unity of meaning in these translation-variants is important. The variants do not prove that λυτρόω means 'deliver', but they may offer confirmation of what has already been proved likely. Dodd wrongly

that this aspect of the meaning of λυτρόω is dominant when that verb is used to translate the same Hebrew words and to describe the action of Yahweh. The second fact is that when λυτρόω occasionally represents words derived from roots other than גאל and פדה (and פרק which we investigate separately) neither those Hebrew words nor their contexts suggest the idea of ransoming, by payment of a price: they refer usually to rescuing, delivering, protecting, saving, but for the LXX translators these meanings could be represented adequately (though admittedly occasionally) by λυτρόω.[1]

The use of λυτρόω to translate פָּרַק is of interest. The basic meaning of this Hebrew verb is 'tear away' or 'break off', as in Gen. 27: 40, 'Thou shall break off (פָרַקְתָּ) his yoke from your neck', where the LXX translates by ἐκλύω. Semantic development appears to have led in two directions: (i) to the meaning 'break up' or 'crush', as in Ps. 7: 3, '. . .lest like a lion they rend me, crushing me with no one to deliver (פֹּרֵק וְאֵין מַצִּיל)'. Here the LXX has μὴ ὄντος λυτρουμένου μηδὲ σῴζοντος,[2] where λυτρόω is clearly drawn into the sphere of meaning of 'rescue' or 'deliver', the idea of ransom not being in the context; (ii) towards the meaning 'break away, break free, rescue, deliver'. This was the connotation of the root in the Targums and in Syriac, where pūrḳānā means 'salvation'. The Old Testament examples of this meaning are Ps. 136: 24 and Lam. 5: 8 where the LXX translates by λυτρόω. There is no suggestion of paying a ransom expressed in the context, and the Greek word may be

assumes that the translation-variants of כפר (see above, p. 25 f.) provide the meaning to which the interpretation of ἱλάσκεσθαι (the usual translation) may be conformed: and in that case there is no clear unity of meaning in the variants.

[1] λυτρόω translates the Piel of שָׂגַב = 'protect, set in security' at Ps. 59: 2: it renders the Piel part. מְשֵׁיזִב ('rescue, deliver') in Dan. 6: 28: and it represents פָּצָה ('tear away, save, deliver') at Ps. 144: 10. At Exod. 15: 16 LXX (A) used ἐλυτρώσω (all other texts have ἐκτήσω) for קָנִיתָ, where the idea of purchase may be present. At Exod. 13: 13 a confusion has resulted in ערף being rendered by λυτρόω: even the error in translation of Ps. 32: 7 reveals that λυτρόω has been drawn into the meaning 'deliver'—'songs of deliverance (רָנֵּי פַלֵּט) encompass me' appears as τὸ ἀγαλλίαμα μοῦ λύτρωσαι με.

[2] The LXX reading has led many scholars to suggest that the original Hebrew reading was וְאֵין פֹּרֵק וְאֵין מַצִּיל, i.e. 'no one to rescue (see under (ii) above), no one to help'.

interpreted in terms of the general meaning 'deliver'. At Dan. 4: 24 (E.V. 27) the verb פְּרַק is used in the course of Daniel's counsels to Nebuchadnezzar, 'Break off (פְּרֻק) your sins by (practising) righteousness'. The LXX here translates by λύτρωσαι. There is no apparent justification in the context for this rendering, but it may reflect knowledge of the Aramaic use of פרק to mean 'redeem', although it is difficult to understand what 'to redeem sins' could mean.[1] To claim that the practice of righteousness is the ransom-price paid by the king for his deliverance[2] is to give to the interpretation of the value of Nebuchadnezzar's changed attitude a precision which the words ἐν ἐλεημοσύναις λύτρωσαι will scarcely sustain. A few verses later (Dan. 4: 34, LXX only) there occurs the only instance of the use of ἀπολύτρωσις in the LXX: 'at the end of the seven years the time of my ἀπολύτρωσις came, and my sins and ignorance were fulfilled in the sight of the God of heaven', where the word refers to Nebuchadnezzar's deliverance or release from the consequences of his self-glorification.[3] Both Morris and War-field admit that the emphasis here lies on the deliverance achieved, but they wish to retain for the noun some suggestion of price, in terms of their interpretation of λύτρωσαι in *v.* 24. This view insists on explaining the process by which release was accomplished, but it is very doubtful if the context will justify either the attempt or the conclusion.

The verb ἀπολυτρόω occurs twice in the LXX, at Exod. 21 : 8 and Zeph. 3 : 1. The Exodus passage is a legal one in which, as we have seen, the idea of purchasing freedom is present. The verb וְהֶפְדָּהּ ('he shall let her be redeemed') is translated ἀπο-λυτρώσει αὐτήν, which probably means 'he shall release her on receipt of a ransom'. At Zeph. 3: 1 (3) the phrase ἐπιφανὴς καὶ ἀπολελυτρωμένη (πόλις) renders מוֹרְאָה וְנִגְאָלָה הָעִיר. The Hebrew means 'rebellious and defiled city', the second participle being derived from the root גאל meaning 'stain, defile'.[4] The

---

[1] J. Barr, *New Peake*, p. 595, para. 522*e*, suggests that the verb may mean 'commute, exchange' and notes that 'righteousness' could have the later sense of 'almsgiving'.

[2] So Warfield, *PTR*, xv (1917), pp. 218–19 and Morris, *The Apostolic Preaching of the Cross*, pp. 11 and 39 note 3.

[3] So Büchsel, *TWNT*, IV, 354.

[4] A. R. Johnson (*VT*, Suppl. 1 [1953], 67–77) reduces the two roots גאל ('redeem') and גאל ('defile') to one with the general meaning

64

Greek translator has rendered the form as if it were derived from גאל = 'to protect, reclaim, redeem', for which the usual translation word was λυτρόω, but there is nothing in the context which implies that the idea of ransoming adheres to the Greek verb.

Before proceeding to the discussion of the λύτρον-words in the New Testament, our attention must be given to one further aspect of the background of thought against which the terms are to be understood: this is the connection in Palestinian Jewish thought between suffering (and particularly death) and atonement.[1] Traditionally, atonement was regarded as coming through the cult and the ceremonies of the Day of Atonement, but after the destruction of the Temple and the cessation of sacrifice it was considered as being accomplished by the life of obedience, through suffering and particularly through death.[2] While the idea that a man's death atones for his *own* sins is not traceable in pre-Christian Judaism, the theme of a *representative* atoning power is pre-Christian.[3] Thus Test. Benjamin 3. 8 reads,[4] 'In thee shall be fulfilled the prophecy of heaven (Isa. 53) that a blameless one shall be delivered up for lawless men and a sinless shall die for ungodly men'. The old Jewish tradition concerning the Binding (Akedah) of Isaac, which some scholars regard as having been

'cover'. To 'cover' with a mantle (Ruth 3: 9) is the action of a kinsman; but 'to cover' may also develop towards the meaning 'to coat over, stain, defile'. This is an instance of what Johnson calls 'semantic polarisation', in which one root came to be associated with (i) protecting from harm and degradation, and (ii) suffering and causing degradation.

[1] Already hinted at in our note on the rabbinic use of כֹּפֶר, p. 61 note 5.

[2] See A. Büchler, *Studies in Sin and Atonement* (London, 1928), pp. 175–89; G. F. Moore, *Judaism* (Oxford, 1927), I, 546–52; S. Schechter, *Some Aspects of Rabbinic Theology* (London, 1909), pp. 307–11.

[3] See R. H. Charles, *The Testaments of the Twelve Patriarchs* (London, 1908), p. 202, and E. Lohse, *Märtyrer und Gottesknecht*, Teil 1: Sühnetod im Spätjudentum. It should be noted, however, that the Qumran materials do not suggest that the sufferings of the community or of its leader, the Teacher of Righteousness, had atoning effect: cf. J. Carmignac, 'Les citations de l'AT et spécialement des Poèmes du Serviteur dans les Hymnes de Qumran', *RQ*, II (1959–60), 384 ff. It is just possible that the idea can be traced behind 1QpHab. 5. 4 f. and a few texts in the Hodayot, but scholarly opinion is not agreed on this matter.

[4] The form quoted is probably pre-Christian: the Christian additions are absent from the Armenian version.

influential on the Pauline doctrine of the Atonement,[1] reveals also the representative value of suffering. The whole theme may have owed much to the content of Isa. 53 and its interpretation. According to Pesik. 27, 174 *b* it is to be learned from 2 Sam. 21 : 14 where, after the deaths of Saul and Jonathan, God is said to have been entreated for the land. Examples of this doctrine are found in the traditions concerning the Maccabean martyrs, especially in the passages quoted in our first study, namely 2 Macc. 7: 37[2] and 4 Macc. 6: 28, which reads 'Be merciful to thy people and let my punishment be sufficient for their sake. Make my blood an expiation for them and take my life as a substitute (ἀντίψυχον) for theirs', and 4 Macc. 17: 21–2, which sums up the achievement of the seven brothers—'They having become as it were a ransom (ὥσπερ ἀντίψυχον) for the sins of the nation, and through the blood of these righteous ones and their propitiatory death, the divine providence delivered Israel which had hitherto suffered evil.' No clearer or more profound statement of vicarious atonement can be found in Judaism,[3] and it may well be of some significance (as we have suggested elsewhere in this work) for the understanding of the New Testament statements concerning the death of Jesus.

THE λύτρον-WORDS IN THE NEW TESTAMENT

By way of introduction to this part of our study we may recall two points from our earlier discussions. The conclusion we reached on the special Jewish–biblical character of New Testament Greek is of significance for the interpretation of this word-complex. If the papyrological finds of Egypt—which are predominantly fragments of legal and commercial transactions

---

[1] Cf. H. J. Schoeps, *Paul: The Theology of the Apostle in the light of Jewish Religious History*, ch. 4. G. Vermès has made a full study of the theme in *Scripture and Tradition in Judaism* (Brill: Leiden, 1961), pp. 193–227: this work provides a full bibliography on the subject and argues both for the ancientness and the importance of the theme in Jewish thought.

[2] This book is dated to *c.* 120 B.C. by F. M. Abel, *Les Livres des Maccabées* (Paris, 1949), p. xliii. E. Lohse, *op. cit.* p. 66 note 2, dates it to about the time of Christ's birth, but this seems too late.

[3] Cf. A. R. C. Leaney, 'The Eschatological Significance of Human Suffering in the Old Testament and the Dead Sea Scrolls', *SJT*, xvi (1963), 286–96.

66

—were to be taken as the clue to the nature of New Testament Greek, then Deissmann would have been correct in his contention that ἀπολύτρωσις, λύτρον, etc., must be interpreted in terms of the manumission of slaves, with emphasis on the idea of payment in order to gain freedom.[1] But if biblical Greek provides a better source from which to investigate the words, then our survey of the LXX and Jewish usage reveals that the interpretation of their meaning is neither so straightforward nor so simple: themes and ideas other than those related to commerce and the slave-market provide the background of meaning, the most important of these being the theme of Israel's deliverance. The second point is that, since the New Testament writers were using this peculiar biblical Greek, we must allow for the possibility (though we must not exaggerate it) that the first-century readers of the documents interpreted the λύτρον-words along the lines of the familiar Greek of the market-place. Such a procedure would involve a significant narrowing of the reference of the terms and would affect the interpretation of redemption.

We now turn to the consideration of the New Testament passages. The noun λύτρωσις occurs three times in the New Testament. There can be no doubt that when Zechariah exclaimed (Luke 1: 68), 'Blessed be the Lord God of Israel for he has visited and redeemed (ἐποίησεν λύτρωσιν) his people, and has raised up a horn of salvation for us from the house of David', and when Anna spoke about Jesus to 'all who were looking for the deliverance (λύτρωσιν) of Jerusalem' (Luke 2: 38), the word is being used in the sense of the long-awaited intervention by God to save and deliver his people into freedom and blessing. This applies also to the remark by the Emmaus-road pilgrims (Luke 24: 21), 'We had hoped that he was the one to deliver Israel (ὁ μέλλων λυτροῦσθαι Ἰσραήλ)'. In these cases there is no idea of ransoming or purchasing: the usage is in accord with that of פָּדָה and גָּאַל in the Old Testament and Jewish sources to describe God's deliverance of his people. Morris claims that these occurrences of the terms are not of great importance for 'clearly a redemption rendered impossible by the cross can tell us little about the redemption effected by the cross'.[2] But the word λύτρωσις is used for both and it is the meaning of that word

---

[1] Deissmann, *Light from the Ancient East*, pp. 319 ff.
[2] *The Apostolic Preaching of the Cross*, p. 35.

which is his concern, and ours, not the doctrinal meaning of redemption!

The third instance of λύτρωσις is Heb. 9: 12, where Christ is portrayed as a High Priest who 'not through the blood of goats and calves, but through his own blood, entered in, once for all, to the holy place, having obtained eternal redemption (αἰωνίαν λύτρωσιν εὑράμενος)'. The background of thought here is obviously the ritual of the Day of Atonement through which, year by year, the High Priest made atonement (כפר) for his own sins and those of his house and of all the people. It is important to note that the animal sacrifices of that ceremony did not bring about atonement because they were accepted as a *ransom* for the life of the people:[1] they did not form a sacrificial gift to win Yahweh's favour since they were not brought to the altar. It was the blood of the sacrificed animals, brought within the Holy of Holies, which was the means of taking away the sin that lay between Yahweh and his people: 'blood makes expiation for a life (or by reason of the life that is in it)' Lev. 17: 11. The background of ideas, therefore, is against the interpretation of λύτρωσις in terms of ransoming. Furthermore, to interpret λύτρωσις thus requires that διὰ τοῦ ἰδίου αἵματος should be understood as 'at the price (cost) of his own blood'[2] and this is most improbable. Occasionally in the New Testament the preposition ἐν (with dat.) may express price (literally rendering the *beth pretii*),[3] but never in Classical, LXX or Koine Greek is διά with the gen. used to express cost: it means 'through' or 'by means of' (instrumental). To say that Jesus secured freedom 'at the price of his blood' implies a rationale of the Atonement process which is not implied when we say 'Jesus secured freedom by means of his blood'. It is worth remembering, in any case, that the phrases δι' αἵματος...διὰ δὲ τοῦ ἰδίου αἵματος may be taken with εἰσῆλθεν and may therefore simply mean 'he entered...*with* his own blood', cf. the parallel ἐν αἵματι, *v.* 25.[4]

---

[1] Even the scapegoat on which the people's sins were placed (but which is not alluded to in Hebrews) was not strictly a ransom paid to gain freedom: it was neither a sacrificial gift to Yahweh nor a bribe to Azazēl, the desert demon.

[2] Morris, *The Apostolic Preaching of the Cross*, p. 36.

[3] See N. Turner, *Grammar of N.T. Greek*: vol. III: *Syntax*, p. 253; also C. F. D. Moule, *Idiom Book of New Testament Greek* (2nd ed., Cambridge, 1959), p. 77.

[4] On διά of attendant circumstances, cf. Moule, *op. cit.* p. 57.

A third reason for opposing the claim that λύτρωσις in 9: 12 suggests the idea of ransom and for advancing the interpretation 'deliverance' lies in the context of the chapter as a whole. When in *vv.* 25–6 the author restates the argument of *vv.* 11 ff., he says that the sacrifice of Christ was the means of 'putting away' sin (εἰς ἀθέτησιν τῆς ἁμαρτίας), cf. *v.* 28: and at *v.* 22 he declares that the purpose of his death was to win remission—'without (χωρὶς) the shedding of blood, there is no remission of sins', cf. Lev. 17: 11. Consequently, when the author says that 'by means of the blood of Christ eternal redemption (λύτρωσις) was secured', that 'redemption' is equivalent to 'forgiveness' and to the putting away of sin: therefore it must be interpreted as 'eternal deliverance' from sin, without any notion of ransoming being present. As the blood of bulls and goats in the Day of Atonement ceremony cleansed and freed the assembly of Israel from sin for one year, the blood of the great High Priest himself is the means (not the price) of bringing deliverance from sin and a renewed relationship with God (*v.* 14) to all men for ever.

At this point in our discussion we may consider Heb. 9: 15 which speaks of Christ's death as having taken place εἰς ἀπολύτρωσιν τῶν ἐπὶ τῇ πρώτῃ διαθήκῃ παραβάσεων. The expression 'redemption of (or from) transgressions' is unusual, but the meaning of ἀπολύτρωσις is clearly very close to that of ἄφεσις in *v.* 22. The idea of 'ransoming sins' is quite inappropriate: the author means that the death of Christ is the divinely-appointed means by which atoning deliverance from sin (or forgiveness) is brought about. The occurrences of λύτρωσις and ἀπολύτρωσις in connection with Christ's blood and death ought not to be interpreted in terms of paying a ransom-price without careful consideration of their contexts and without assessment of the theory of Old Testament sacrifice which such an interpretation implies. In saying this we do not deny that the death of Christ and our deliverance from sin were costly: they were costly to Christ in terms of suffering and self-surrender: we are only concerned to deny that a particular theory of Atonement can be based on the occurrences and meaning of the λύτρον-words.[1]

Returning to the New Testament use of λυτρόω, we find that,

[1] Cf. C. Spicq, *L'Épître aux Hébreux* (Paris, 1952), I, 306, who says that the accent, in Heb. 9: 12, 15, is on the idea of liberation rather than on price. But see also II, 257 on 9: 12, 'le sang est le prix du rachat'!

in addition to Luke 24: 21, the verb occurs at Titus 2: 14 and
1 Pet. 1: 18. The passage in Titus says of Jesus, 'He gave himself
for us (ὑπὲρ ἡμῶν) in order that he might redeem us (λυτρώση-
ται) from all iniquity and purify for himself a people for his
possession (λαὸν περιούσιον)'. The verse recalls Ps. 130: 8,
'He shall redeem Israel from all his iniquities', where in the LXX
λυτρόω connotes 'deliverance'. If we stress the indebtedness to
the language of the Psalm we will render the verb as 'deliver', as
does the NEB. Morris, however, speaks of 'the specific mention
of the ransom price ("gave himself")'.[1] But is the action of self-
surrender the same as the process of ransoming? A ransom is a
price *exacted* and *paid* (often unwillingly): self-surrender, even of
a substitutionary nature, is an offering *given* and *accepted*. The
self-oblation of Christ, referred to in the verse, is therefore not
the price paid to ransom men from sin, but the means of delivering
them, and the verb should be translated as 'rescue' or 'free'.
The phrase 'a people for his possession' recalls the gathering of
the chosen people on the basis of the Exodus deliverance. The
remaining passage, 1 Pet. 1: 18–19, probably contains the idea of
purchase: 'You know that you were redeemed (ἐλυτρώθητε)
from the futility of your traditional ways, not with perishable
things like gold and silver, but with the precious blood of Christ,
as of a lamb without blemish and without spot.' The realm of
thought is that of the Passover sacrifice and Exodus: and whether
or not the author thought of sacrifice in general as having the
character of a ransom payment, the notion of a price paid for
deliverance seems to be present in the context.[2] The RSV
translates the verb by 'ransom' and the NEB speaks of 'freedom
bought'. But the importance we attach to this one probable

[1] *The Apostolic Preaching of the Cross*, p. 35.
[2] F. W. Beare, *The First Epistle of Peter* (Oxford, 1947), p. 78, finds in the
passage reference to the cost of redemption but draws attention to the fact
that the author 'does not use for this the gen. of price (cf. 1 Cor. 6: 20) which
would be the normal way of indicating the amount of the ransom, but the
dative, which is not used at all of price (at least not without a preposition)
and seems therefore better taken as *instrumental*'. E. G. Selwyn, *The First
Epistle of Peter* (London, 1947), p. 144, claims that the use of the dative for
redemption-price instead of the gen., is an indication of LXX background
(cf. Exod. 34: 20; Lev. 19: 20; 27: 31; Num. 18: 15). In their discussions of
the dative case neither Turner (*Grammar of N.T. Greek: Syntax*) nor Moule
(*An Idiom Book of New Testament Greek*) list as one of its functions the
expression of price, but both refer to its instrumental use.

reference to the process of ransoming will depend on the presence
or absence of the theme elsewhere in the New Testament.

The noun λυτρωτής is found once, Acts 7: 35, and describes
Moses as the deliverer of God's people from the bondage of
Egypt. Since the context is the New Moses Christological state-
ment in which Jesus is both likened to and contrasted with
Moses, as the greater to the lesser, it is implied that Jesus, as
Messiah, has the role of a Moses-like deliverer or saviour
(cf. Acts 5: 31).

A noteworthy feature of New Testament usage is the comparative frequency of the compound noun ἀπολύτρωσις. We have
pointed out that it is a rare word in non-biblical Greek, appearing
only once (Dan. 4: 34) in the LXX in a passage for which there
is no corresponding Hebrew in the Massoretic Text. While the
non-biblical texts give some support to the view that ἀπολύτρωσις implies the payment of a price for redemption, the single
LXX occurrence is quite satisfactorily translated by 'deliverance'. Now this rare word appears seven times in the letters of
Paul, twice in the letter to the Hebrews and once in Luke's
gospel. It is obviously an important term in the New Testament
salvation vocabulary and merits careful study. The structure of
the word might be taken to suggest the thought of a 'ransoming
away' (ἀπό = away from), with emphasis on the resulting
deliverance rather than on the method of redemption.[1] This,
however, would be to place undue emphasis on word-form in the
matter of interpretation: investigation of each occurrence in its
context must be the guide to the measure of truth in the claim.

The appearance of the word at Heb. 9: 15 has already been
discussed. The second occurrence in that letter is at 11: 35 which
says, with reference to times of persecution: 'Women received
their dead by resurrection: some were tortured not accepting the
deliverance (τὴν ἀπολύτρωσιν) that they might have a better
resurrection', that is, to the life of the Age to come. The allusion
is most probably to the Maccabean martyrs under Antiochus
Epiphanes and therefore the correct interpretation of ἀπολύτρωσις will be 'deliverance' or 'release'. The lives of the martyrs

[1] This is what Chrysostom meant in his comment on Rom. 3: 23, 'and he
said not simply λύτρωσις but ἀπολύτρωσις so that we come not again into
the same bondage'. What interests Chrysostom is the result of the action
(freedom) not the process.

71

would have been spared if they had agreed to forswear their faith, but apostasy cannot be considered as the *price* of freedom, save in a vague metaphorical sense.

There are three occurrences of ἀπολύτρωσις in passages of an eschatological character:

(i) Luke 21:28: Now when these things begin to take place, look up and raise your heads because your redemption (ἡ ἀπολύτρωσις ὑμῶν) draws near.

(ii) Rom. 8:23: ...but ourselves also, which have the first-fruits of the Spirit, even we ourselves groan within ourselves, waiting for our adoption, namely the *redemption* of our body.

(iii) Eph. 4:30: Grieve not the Holy Spirit of God in whom you were sealed unto the day of redemption (ἀπολυτρώσεως).

The Lucan passage clearly refers to the *deliverance* of the saints at the coming of the Son of Man. Rom. 8:23 implies (i) that acceptance into God's family (υἱοθεσία) is synonymous with the redemption of the body, and (ii) that the desire for this adoption and freedom is at one with a universal longing described in *v.* 21, 'The creation will be set free from its bondage to decay and obtain the glorious liberty (ἐλευθερία) of the children of God'. The contents of the hopes are parallel: the adoption of Christians is their entering into 'the glorious liberty of children' and the redemption of their bodies is their being set free from bondage at the Resurrection (cf. 1 Cor. 15:45-9). If this is the correct interpretation of the passage, ἀπολύτρωσις clearly means 'liberation' or 'deliverance from all the ills to which the flesh is heir'.[1] Eph. 4:30 refers to the day of final deliverance, the future consummation of faith and Christian living, guaranteed by the presence of the Spirit and bringing with it emancipation from the power of evil in all its forms. There is no idea of price attaching to these occurrences of ἀπολύτρωσις. It is very difficult to accept the view which keeps alive the notion of ransom in these passages by interpreting them as referring to the ultimate effects, or consummation, of the ransoming wrought by Jesus in his death, and not to some new or further action of God. 'There is no specifically eschatological sense of ἀπολύτρωσις, there is only an eschatological application of the ransoming which has been wrought by

---

[1] W. Sanday and A. C. Headlam, *Commentary on Romans* (ICC, Edinburgh, 1902), p. 209.

Christ's gift of himself.'[1] It is true that, in Christian faith, final redemption is related to the work of Calvary, but their relation is based on the fact that they are both divinely-initiated acts bringing deliverance to men, and not on their sharing, in some way, the ransom method of winning or providing freedom. Warfield is guilty of assuming that he can legitimately import into his interpretation of the word ἀπολύτρωσις in an eschatological context the ideas which he thinks are central to its meaning in a different (atonement) context.

We come now to Eph. 1: 7—'In Him (Christ) we have the redemption through his blood (τὴν ἀπολύτρωσιν διὰ τοῦ αἵματος αὐτοῦ), the forgiveness of our trespasses'. With this verse we may consider Col. 1: 14, 'In whom we have redemption, the forgiveness of sins'. Recently F. F. Bruce commented thus on Eph. 1: 7:

The word [i.e. ἀπολύτρωσις] implies that our former existence was one of slavery from which we required to be ransomed. The ransom price is expressly mentioned (as it is not in the best-authenticated texts of the parallel passage in Col. 1: 14): it was a price of immeasurable costliness, nothing less than the blood of Christ. If, even under the shadowy economy of the Levitical ritual, sacrificial blood was accepted for the worshipper's atonement 'by reason of the life' (Lev. 17: 11), then the price at which our emancipation was purchased was the infinitely more acceptable life of the Incarnate Son.[2]

The claim that ἀπολύτρωσις possesses a ransom content is here based on the interpretation of δι' αἵματος as 'at the price of blood'. Confidence in this interpretation, however, is shaken by the fact that neither in Classical, Koine, nor LXX Greek is διά + gen. used to express cost: the preposition means 'through' or 'by means of' (instrumental). Moreover, even in a context expressing sacrificial ideas, the shedding of blood is hardly to be regarded as the price paid for the release from sins;[3] neither in

[1] Warfield, *PTR*, xv (1917), 239–40, note 71. Cf. Morris, *The Apostolic Preaching of the Cross*, pp. 43f.
[2] *Epistle to the Ephesians* (London, 1962), p. 31. Cf. Morris, *op. cit.* p. 43.
[3] The use of 'blood' in the New Testament probably implies more than death: it has the active connotation of living power as well, based possibly on the view of the life-force set free in sacrifice in order that it may be effective for the benefit of others, to expiate sins or to communicate the

Old Testament thought nor in modern discussion[1] is sacrifice interpreted in terms of ransom: even the rationale of sacrifice in Lev. 17: 11 (which Bruce quotes) offers, not a ransom theory, but possibly a substitutionary theory. In any case, in the verse under discussion, the explanation of 'redemption through his blood' by 'the forgiveness of sins' suggests that the author is concerned to stress the releasing nature and effects of the atoning death, not its ransom significance. At Col. 1: 14 the noun ἀπολύτρωσις is again virtually equated with forgiveness of sins. The verse follows the declaration that 'He (God) has delivered us (ἐρρύσατο) from the dominion of darkness and transferred us to the Kingdom of his beloved Son', and it seems likely that the two terms, redemption and forgiveness, make more explicit the theme of that verse: ἀπολύτρωσις is the emancipation from the powers of darkness, and ἄφεσις describes the nature of the deliverance, a freeing from sin.[2] Consideration of the context therefore suggests that it is not correct to assume that the idea of ransom-price is expressed or implied in the use of ἀπολύτρωσις at Eph. 1: 7 and Col. 1: 14.

At Eph. 1: 14 we find the strange phrase, '... the Holy Spirit, which is the guarantee of our inheritance εἰς ἀπολύτρωσιν τῆς περιποιήσεως'. The RSV interprets this as 'until we acquire possession of it', thus referring περιποίησις to *our* possession of the inheritance. The NEB offers a better rendering, 'until God has redeemed what is his own', the word περιποίησις thus connoting our lives as *God's* possession. The eschatological reference in the verse recalls Rom. 8: 23 and it is probable that

divine blessing to men. Cf. W. D. Davies, *Paul and Rabbinic Judaism*, p. 234; V. Taylor, *Jesus and his Sacrifice* (London, 1937), p. 54, and W. O. E. Oesterley, *Sacrifices in Ancient Israel* (London, 1937), p. 224. For the view that 'blood' means only death, see J. Behm, *TWNT*, I, 173; Morris, *The Apostolic Preaching of the Cross*, pp. 108 ff. and *JTS* (n.s.), III (Oct. 1952), 216–27.

[1] Cf. de Vaux, *Ancient Israel*, pp. 418 ff., 451 ff. and 507 ff.; H. H. Rowley, 'The Meaning of Sacrifice in the Old Testament', *BJRL*, XXIII (1950–1), 74–110; R. J. Johnson, *Sacrifice and Penitence in Israel* (Brill: Leiden, 1964).

[2] The definition of the redemption or emancipation as 'the forgiveness of sins' may have been offered in order to counter some doctrine of the Colossian false teachers, such as the possibility of an escape into immortality without a change in moral character: cf. C. F. D. Moule, *Colossians and Philemon* (Cambridge, 1957), p. 58.

ἀπολύτρωσις is to be understood here, as there, of the final deliverance of God's people into the fullness of the life to come.

At 1 Cor. 1: 30 Paul declares that Christ has become for us the 'wisdom of God' and that this wisdom is not characterised by intellectual knowledge but by 'righteousness, sanctification and redemption (ἀπολύτρωσις)'. Whether we regard these terms as describing the three consequences of the death of Christ (i.e. the setting right of man with God, sanctification through union with him, and redemption as the deliverance from sin), or as referring to the progress in Christian living (i.e. initial justification, the process of sanctification and the final deliverance into life to come), there is nothing in the verse which requires that the word ἀπολύτρωσις be understood as 'ransoming'.

The context surrounding the appearance of ἀπολύτρωσις in Rom. 3: 24 presents many problems for the exegete, not the least of which is the interpretation of ἱλαστήριον in v. 25. We have already suggested the possibility of interpreting this word in terms of the atoning and propitiatory value of the deaths of the martyrs, rather than in terms of the ritual of the Day of Atonement. Does this approach assist us in explaining the word ἀπολύτρωσις: 'Being justified as a free gift by his grace through the redemption which is in Christ Jesus, whom God set forth (or provided) as a means of atonement (propitiation)...' The summary statement on the death of the seven brothers which effected the release of Israel refers to it as ὥσπερ ἀντίψυχον (4 Macc. 17: 21, cf. 6: 29). Some translators render this word as 'ransom' and this would support the claim that ἀπολύτρωσις in Rom. 3 (still assuming the influence of the Maccabees passage and ideas) means 'deliverance by the payment of a ransom price'. But is 'ransom' an accurate translation of ἀντίψυχον? Ch. 6: 29 suggests that the better rendering is 'substitute': 'Take my life as a substitute for theirs.' May we interpret ἀντίψυχον... τῆς τοῦ ἔθνους ἁμαρτίας (4 Macc. 17: 21) in the same way? It would be senseless to regard this as meaning 'a substitute for the sins of the people', but H. W. Robinson may be right in explaining it as 'a substitute for the life forfeited by the sin of the people'.[1] The people's sin deserved the penalty of death, but the brothers became their substitute. If this is the correct interpretation of

[1] *The Cross of the Servant* (London, 1926), pp. 58 ff.

ἀντίψῦχον, then (still assuming the influence of 4 Macc. 17: 21 f. on Rom. 3) the term ἀπολύτρωσις will connote deliverance through the *substitutionary* death of Jesus, the emphasis being all the time on liberation.

If this hypothesis concerning the background of Rom. 3 does not commend itself, what shall we say of the meaning of ἀπο-λύτρωσις? T. W. Manson speaks of 'emancipation' and 'restoration to true ownership',[1] thus suggesting the Exodus-character of the deliverance in Christ: C. H. Dodd sees the word as a metaphor taken from the institution of slavery (that of 'justification' being taken from the law-courts, and that of 'expiation' from the sacrificial ritual),[2] but emphasises the freedom secured by God for men, not the transactional element involved in ransoming. Dodd's suggestion recalls Deissmann's stress on the indebtedness of Paul to the language associated with the manumission of slaves, and it must be admitted that the notion of payment (without which manumission was not granted) would readily come to the minds of readers familiar with current usage of the term. However, in seeking the meaning intended by Paul himself, we take seriously the biblical character of his Greek and therefore emphasise the theme of the deliverance of Israel from captivity by the power of God, their recovery into God's rightful ownership, without a ransom price. The two approaches to Paul's language at this point—that it suggests the manumission procedure or that it recalls the Exodus pattern—do not lead to two opposing interpretations. The central idea provided by both approaches is that of liberation effected by Christ's death, freedom from the state of slavery into which our sins brought us; but the second (and preferable) path to interpretation makes it very doubtful that Paul intended to imply the precise theory of release by ransom when he used the word ἀπολύτρωσις.

The word ἀντίλυτρον occurs once in the New Testament, in 1 Tim. 2: 6 which describes Christ as him 'who gave himself ἀντίλυτρον ὑπὲρ πάντων'. The word λύτρον in biblical Greek means 'the ransom paid to gain freedom' or 'the means by which release is achieved': the prepositional prefix emphasises the

---

[1] *New Peake:* Romans, para. 819a, p. 943.

[2] *Epistle to the Romans* (MNTC, London, 1932), p. 56, 'God takes the part...of the benefactor who secures freedom for the slave'.

notion of substitution and Morris claims that it is a 'substitute-ransom' which is signified.[1] In view of our discussion up to this point, we may find it difficult to assume such precision of meaning.[2] The verse closely resembles Mark 10: 45 and the words may be a citation or a reminiscence of a primitive credal formula. To the consideration of the Markan verse we now turn, with the expectation that our understanding of 1 Tim. 2: 6 will be clarified by it. Mark 10: 45: 'The Son of Man came not to be ministered unto but to minister and to give his life a ransom for many (λύτρον ἀντὶ πολλῶν).' The problems of this verse fall under three heads: (i) the genuineness of the saying, (ii) the meaning of the words used, and (iii) the background of interpretation.

(i) The authenticity of the saying has been assailed (a) on the grounds that the critical words about ransom are absent from the parallel passage in Luke 22: 26–7: Luke, however, is dealing with a *similar*, not the same incident as Mark; and although the language of the narratives is closely akin, Luke's verse 27 may be an independent saying altogether, whereas Mark 10: 45 is integral to its context, and the Semitic form and structure argues for its genuineness in the tradition of Jesus' words; (b) because it looks like an addition due to Pauline influence: we would observe however that Paul never uses the word λύτρον, although related words are found in his (and the deutero-Pauline) vocabulary of redemption: moreover, we ought to remember Vincent Taylor's remark that 'Paulinism was rooted in primitive Christianity';[3] (c) because the λύτρον idea is absent from the Gospels elsewhere and is out of harmony with its context in Mark 10: but the unusualness of the theme in the Gospels may mean no more than that it was not the central point in Jesus' teaching about his death; while the claim that the idea of sacrificing life itself on behalf of others is out of harmony with the

---

[1] Morris, *The Apostolic Preaching of the Cross*, p. 48.
[2] The NEB renders, 'Christ sacrificed himself to win freedom for all mankind'.
[3] *The Gospel according to St Mark* (London, 1952), p. 446. Lagrange pertinently asks: 'Jésus a-t-il fourni le thème aux développements de Paul, ou Mc. a-t-il condensé en un mot la théologie de Paul pour la prêter à Jésus?'; and he replies, 'La première hypothèse est la seule vraisemblable', *Évangile selon S. Marc* (6th ed., Paris, 1942), p. 283.

theme of service indicates a very strange logic: self-sacrifice is the crown of service to others. It is certainly true that we cannot prove beyond all doubt the authenticity of any word which tradition has ascribed to Jesus, but there is no sufficient reason, in our view, to doubt that Jesus, who saw his work as fraught with critical significance for his people, could have referred to his death in the terms of this saying of Mark 10: 45.[1]

(ii) What do the terms used mean? In both biblical and non-biblical usage the prevailing idea behind the word λύτρον is that of the price paid as a ransom in return for which liberation is won, that is, something given in order to gain or regain freedom. The word is seldom used with ἀντί, and this preposition (meaning 'instead of' or 'in place of') stresses the substitutionary character of the λύτρον.[2] The use of πολλῶν (a non-Pauline idiom to describe the efficacy of Christ's death) contrasts the sacrifice of the *one* with the others for whom it is made and is here tantamount to 'all'. It is not possible to find the meaning of λύτρον in this verse without taking it in conjunction with ἀντὶ πολλῶν: these words give to the term a definite substitutionary content. For a full understanding of the phrase, however, we must inquire into the background of thought to which the verse points.

(iii) Many commentators on Mark 10: 45 have assumed that the background of thought is to be found in the great Suffering Servant passage, Isa. 52: 13—53: 12. C. K. Barrett has subjected this claim to careful scrutiny, and from his study of the *language* employed in the passages he concludes that 'it would be difficult indeed, on the basis of it (i.e. the language) to claim that Mark's words point clearly to Isaiah 53 rather than to any other part of the OT and Jewish literature'.[3] One of the strongest points of his

[1] See W. Manson's discussion in *Jesus the Messiah* (London, 1943), pp. 131–4.

[2] The words ἀντὶ πολλῶν depends on λύτρον, not on δοῦναι. That the substitutionary emphasis belongs to the phrase λύτρον ἀντί can be demonstrated from Jos. *Ant.* 14. 107 which describes the attempt made (in 54 B.C.), by Eleazar to buy off Crassus: 'He gave him a bar of gold λύτρον ἀντὶ πάντων', i.e. in the hope that he would take it instead of all the other things he might have taken. What was offered was *given* as a substitute, not exacted as a ransom price.

[3] 'The Background of Mark 10: 45', *New Testament Essays for T. W. Manson* (Manchester, 1959), pp. 1–18: quotation from p. 7. Cf. also M. D. Hooker, *Jesus and the Servant* (London, 1959), pp. 74 ff.

argument is that the terms λύτρον and אָשָׁם (Isa. 53: 10), which it is supposed to represent, are not equivalents: λύτρον and its cognates never represent אָשָׁם, and אָשָׁם is never rendered in the LXX by any of the λύτρον-words: in fact the ideas represented by the words are quite different, for λύτρον involves the idea of equivalence, while אָשָׁם does not, since it was not a compensation.[1] Barrett's critique of the *linguistic* evidence for the dependence of the saying on Isaiah is convincing, but we must add that even if the language of the logion does not recall the exact words of Isa. 53, the *ideas* expressed in the Suffering Servant passage are echoed in the Markan verse.[2] It would be unwise to claim that there is nothing common to the Servant song and Mark 10: 45 because the words used are not the same. It is our opinion that the background of thought of the Markan logion is to be found in a theme at once wider than but including that of the Servant, namely, the Jewish theme of the suffering righteous, described in Wisdom 2–5 and earlier in many Psalms.[3] The various strands of this theme—righteousness, obedience, suffering, vindication, exaltation—are present in the picture of the Isaianic Servant, with a significant addition: the sufferings of the Servant (Israel or a remnant within Israel) are vicarious. The expression of this aspect of suffering within the Servant songs probably contributed to the development, within our general theme, of the idea of the representative, atoning value of the sufferings and death of the righteous, and particularly of martyrs. We have already drawn attention to the profound statement of this theme in the Books of Maccabees, in which the self-sacrifice of the seven brothers is

---

[1] This is true, in general: the act of restitution was distinguished from the אָשָׁם sacrifice (Lev. 5: 14–26). But at Num. 5: 7–8 אָשָׁם is used for 'restitution' of what is wrongly possessed, a sense found nowhere else in the Old Testament.

[2] Cf. C. E. B. Cranfield, *The Gospel according to St Mark* (CGT: reprint 1963), p. 486, argues that the word διακονεῖν sums up in a word the whole picture of the service of men which the Servant is to render. He thinks that behind the evangelist's use of the verb lies the creative reflection of Jesus on the Servant passages. Cf. further, p. 487 of the same work.

[3] Cf. E. Schweizer, *Lordship and Discipleship* (London, 1960). Schweizer has drawn attention to this background of the Son of Man concept in 'Der Menschensohn', *ZNW*, L (1959), 185 ff., and in 'The Son of Man', *JBL*, LXXIX (1960), 119 ff., but he does not accept Mark 10: 45 as an authentic word of Jesus. Cf. also M. Black, 'The Son of Man Problem in recent Research and Debate', *BJRL*, XLV (1962–3), 305 ff.

described as a means of atonement for Israel, an instrument of blessing bringing mercy and deliverance.[1]

Some scholars in the past have appealed to the idea of martyrdom as providing the correct understanding of Mark 10: 45, because the context speaks of service, διακονία.[2] But according to Morris, 'such interpretation seems to lean too heavily on the context' and 'the context of a saying, while undoubtedly important, can indicate only in a general way the drift of a saying; it cannot finally determine its meaning in detail'.[3] But 'meaning in detail' can only be arrived at by penetrating to the background of thought and the realm of ideas in which the writer is rooted: and the context is a definite guide to that. Service of a kind which disciples may share (though perhaps not to the same degree) is what is in view in this paragraph: but the background is not *any* martyrdom, but martyrdom of the kind extolled in the old Jewish theme. Long ago C. G. Montefiore saw this when he said, 'It is true that to give your life for others is the highest possible service, but the word *lutron* seems to imply something more': and then, after drawing attention to the passages from Maccabees, he goes on, 'God somehow makes the death of Jesus help in the salvation of others. It is in this more special sense that Jesus gives his own life for the sake of many lives'.[4] The special sense is the possibility of the righteous life atoning for and thus delivering others.

If then the background of Mark 10: 45 is to be found in the Jewish belief in the atoning suffering of the righteous, how are we to understand the word λύτρον? In the first place, it is not the אָשָׁם of Isa. 53: 10, although its effects may be the same. Secondly, it cannot be interpreted as 'ransom' in the strict sense of that word, for the sacrifice of the righteous which gained deliverance for others was not a price paid, but a representative action accepted as having atoning value.[5] Bearing in mind the force of

[1] It is perhaps noteworthy that the language of the Maccabees passages (2 Macc. 7: 37; 4 Macc. 6: 28 and 17: 21–2) is echoed in Mark 10: 45: προδίδωμι ψυχήν/δοῦναι τὴν ψυχήν: ἀντίψυχον/λύτρον.

[2] E.g. E. P. Gould, *The Gospel of St Mark* (ICC, Edinburgh, 1896) *ad loc.*; H. Rashdall, *The Idea of Atonement in Christian Theology* (London, 1919), pp. 35 ff.　　　[3] Morris, *The Apostolic Preaching of the Cross*, pp. 33–4.

[4] *The Synoptic Gospels* (London, 1927), i, 253.

[5] One of the difficulties with Morris's study of the words for 'redemption' is that in the discussion he subtly shifts from the idea of ransom to that of

the words ἀντὶ πολλῶν, as well as the context and background of thought suggested, we submit that the most adequate interpretation of λύτρον is 'atoning substitute'.[1]

Jesus took upon himself the redemptive mission given by God to his people. He accomplished it and led it to its goal, in his life as well as in his death. For he lived as *the* righteous remnant, as a substitute for the whole nation, revealing in himself what Israel should have been. In bringing this mission to its final and complete accomplishment, he laid down his life, trusting that God would be well-pleased to see his regal claims fulfilled in the one great action of obedient service, which was Jesus' life and death, and would grant to the whole nation deliverance and renewal.

This study clearly exemplifies the importance of giving due consideration to the biblical character of New Testament Greek. This approach to the λύτρον-words suggests that their interpretation should be in terms of 'deliverance' or 'emancipation', except when the context expresses or implies a payment made to gain freedom. By applying the words to the death of Christ, the New Testament writers emphasise the idea of freedom (after the pattern of the great deliverances of Israel) and do not intend to convey, by means of the word-group, a particular theory (the ransom theory) about the method by which this freedom was achieved on behalf of men. The field of meaning to which the words point is that of God's delivering his people. The terminology used to describe such experiences in Israel's history provided the language with which God's new free-men could refer to their deliverance in Christ.

substitution, as if there was no difference. But there is a difference as we have tried to indicate.

[1] J. Downing, 'Jesus and Martyrdom', *JTS*, xiv (1963), 279–93, interprets Mark 10: 45 and other New Testament passages in terms of the Jewish doctrine of atonement through martyrdom. He is of the opinion that this category of Jewish theology was adopted by the early church to expound the meaning of Jesus' death, because Jesus used it himself. Cf. also W. H. C. Frend, *Martyrdom and Persecution in the Early Church*, pp. 32 ff.

81

CHAPTER IV

THE BACKGROUND AND MEANING OF ΔΙΚΑΙΟΣΥΝΗ AND COGNATE WORDS

In the Septuagint the δικαιοσύνη word-group represents words derived from the Hebrew root צדק over four hundred and sixty times. This fact suggests that in the estimation of the translators the extent of semantic overlap between the two word-groups was very great: and this further suggests that the investigation of the use and meaning of the צדק-words would be a useful and valuable preparation for the study of the δικαιοσύνη-words in biblical Greek.

צְדָקָה AND RELATED WORDS IN THE OLD TESTAMENT

The original significance of the root צדק appears to be irretrievably lost, but some instances of its use in languages other than Hebrew provide guidance on its early meaning.

(i) A very ancient example of the use of *ṣdḳ* has been found in the fourteenth-century Ugaritic epic of Keret (line 12), where it refers to right relationship: '*aṭṭ. ṣdḳh* means 'legitimate, rightful or proper wife' and is parallel to *mtrḫt yšrh*, 'legal spouse'.[1] A similar sense is attested in the Tel el-Amarna tablets (no. 287, 32 f.) where Abdi-Hiba (though corresponding in Accadian) uses the Canaanite term *ṣaduḳ* in order to affirm that he has dealt in the right way with the Cushites: *ṣa-du-uḳ a-na ia-a-ši/áš-šum amêlûti ka-ši-wi* ('I am in the right with regard to the Kasi people').[2]

---

[1] C. H. Gordon, *Ugaritic Literature* (Rome, 1949), p. 67, and J. Gray, *The Legacy of Canaan* (Leiden, 1957), Suppl. *VT*, no. 5, pp. 94 ff. At text 32. 5 Gordon reads (*ṣ*)*dḳ kttn*, 'thou shalt admit the right'. On these early examples of *ṣdḳ*, see also J. Swetnam, 'Some Observations on the background of צדיק in Jeremias 23, 5 a', *Biblica*, XLVI (1965), 29–40.

[2] Cf. J. A. Knudtzon, *Die El-Amarna Tafeln* (Leipzig, 1908–15), and S. A. B. Mercer, *Tel el-Amarna Tablets* (Toronto, 1939) *ad loc*. C. J. Mullo Weir (*Documents from Old Testament Times*, ed. D. W. Thomas, London, 1958, p. 39) and W. F. Albright (*Ancient Near Eastern Texts*, Princeton and Oxford, 1950, p. 488) punctuate the passage differently: 'Behold, O King,

(ii) Another early example (*c.* twelfth century) appears, but with a rather different meaning, in the Phoenician epigraphic texts of Byblus. The inscription of Yehimelek contains a plea that his life should be prolonged on the ground that he is 'a righteous and upright king (מלך צדק ומלך ישר)'.[1] The term apparently connotes the quality of his rule, rather than its legitimacy. In this connection, we must take account of the early application of the root to divine beings. When the ancient traditions of Jerusalem speak of Melchizedek (Gen. 14: 18) and of Adonizedek (Josh. 10: 1; cf. Judg. 1: 5–7), it is suggested that the Zedek- part should be construed (analogously with other early names of this type) as a divine name expressing the ideal which the term implies, 'My King, or My Lord is Z(S)edek'. It is possible, however, that the names should be construed like Jehozadak ('Yahu is righteous') to give the meaning, 'My (The) Lord or King is righteous'. Likewise the Ugaritic name *Ṣdk-il* may mean 'Ṣdk is (my) God' or 'Il (El) is righteous'. In either case, its use in personal names suggests the very early association of *ṣdk* with deity, probably with reference to the quality of governing, though the (judicial) interpretation, 'My Lord or King is the right one' is not impossible.

(iii) The root appears in Arabic with a variety of meanings. It may denote what is right, or what is firm and stable and therefore substantial; and when a date is called *ṣdk* it must simply mean that it is 'as it should be', a 'right' date.

On the basis of these illustrations of early usage it is difficult to assert with confidence a single primary meaning of the root צדק. The most we can say is that they suggest that the fundamental idea of צדק available to us is that of conformity to a norm which requires to be defined in each particular case.[2]

my lord, I am *right* (in the right). With reference to the Cushites...'. The meaning of *ṣaduk*, however, is scarcely affected. Weir's and Albright's interpretation makes the word refer to Abdi-Hiba's innocence of charges of disloyalty in the annexation of land; the older view refers it to his treatment of the Cushites.

[1] Cf. M. Dunand, *RB*, xxxix (1930), 321. He finds *ṣdk* in a similar context and with the same connotation in the Yehawmelek inscription (1. 9) which is dated some five centuries later. See also A. Dupont-Sommer, *Semitica*, iii (1950), 35–44.

[2] Cf. E. Kautzsch, *Die Derivate des Stammes tsdq im altt. Sprachgebrauch* (Tübingen, 1881).

Bearing this in mind we turn now to the Old Testament usage. Beginning with occurrences which are not directly religious or theological, we find צֶדֶק used (in the construct state) with 'balances', 'weights', etc. (Lev. 19: 36; Ezek. 45: 10), and adjectivally with 'measure' (Deut. 25: 15), where it clearly connotes conformity to proper standards. The balances, etc., are to be 'as they should be', 'correct' or 'right'.[1] The sacrifices of Deut. 33: 19 and Ps. 4: 6; 51: 21 are the 'correct' sacrifices, those which conform to ritual regulations. The same idea lies behind Gen. 38: 26, where the obligatory standard is accepted customary law. When Judah says of Tamar, 'She is more righteous (צָדְקָה) than I', he is referring, not to ethical uprightness, but to the strength of her case in terms of the levirate marriage law: with reference to a particular act and a particular convention, Judah can say, 'She is "in the right" as against me'. This may be properly called a forensic or judicial meaning, without necessarily implying that a law-suit is actually brought before a judge. But if this action were in fact to take place, the person who is 'righteous' is the person who is 'in the right' and in whose favour the judge would make his decision (cf. Exod. 23: 7).[2] These examples of the meaning of the root are in accord with what we found in the early texts and support our contention that צֶדֶק basically connotes conformity to a norm, but not an absolute ethical norm by which all behaviour is measured, nor an ideal standard of 'rightness' for objects. The norm is furnished by the objective standard of the thing itself:[3] and in cases where

[1] The one instance of the Niph'al of the verb—'the holy place נִצְדַּק (LXX καθαρισθήσεται)' Dan. 8: 14—should probably be interpreted along these lines: 'the holy place shall be put right, restored to what it should be'. Here the LXX translator appears to have interpreted according to the general sense required by the context, since that meaning could not be elicited from δικαιωθήσεται which would have been the normal rendering of the Hebrew.

[2] Cf. W. R. Smith, *The Prophets of Israel* (2nd ed., London, 1897), p. 71, 'Righteousness is to the Hebrew not so much a moral quality as a legal status'.

[3] '*Saddiq* is somebody or something that is as he or it should be; the meaning of the word is "*real*", "pure", "true", that which agrees with the end to which it has been created, that which inwardly, fundamentally corresponds to its external appearance, and therefore actually fulfils the function for which (he) it exists', Th. Vriezen, *Outline of OT Theology* (ET, Oxford, 1958), p. 327.

the term is applied to persons, the rightness or righteousness of conduct depends on the fulfilling of obligations arising from a particular situation or set of circumstances.[1] It might therefore be claimed that צֶדֶק is a formal term, the content of which can only be characterised with reference to the situation within which it is applied. Tamar is the 'righteous' one with reference to the levirate marriage custom. At 1 Sam. 24: 17 David is said to be more righteous (צַדִּיק) than Saul with reference to the duty of preserving the life of the Lord's anointed: and at Ezek. 16: 52, Samaria and Sodom are more 'in the right' at judgment than Jerusalem, because the extent of their sinning is less great.

While custom and duty may thus provide the norm by which the 'rightness' of an action is judged, these were related to a much wider and more basic criterion of behaviour. The Israelite, like the member of other tribal societies, possessed a deep consciousness of the family, tribal and later the national unit, and regarded himself as under obligation to fulfil the demands and laws which made for the well-being and good-ordering of that unit. An action which accords with the claims arising out of the social relation (between two or more persons) may be referred to as צֶדֶק:[2] and the pattern of conduct which adheres to the demands of the community relationship and so preserves society is recognised as צְדָקָה.[3] But in Israelite thinking, one relationship is supremely important, the Covenant relation between Yahweh and his people, and this has great significance for the understanding of personal and community righteousness in Israel and

[1] Cf. W. Eichrodt, *Theology of the Old Testament* (ET by J. A. Baker, London, 1961), pp. 240–1, and G. von Rad, *Theologie des Alten Testaments* (Munich, 1957), Band 1, pp. 368 ff. (ET *Old Testament Theology*, Edinburgh, 1962, pp. 370 ff.).

[2] H. Cremer, *Biblisch-theologisches Wörterbuch der neutest. Gräzität* (7th ed., Gotha, 1893), p. 273: 'Jedes Verhältnis bringt bestimmte Ansprüche an den Verhalten mit sich, und die Befriedigung dieser Ansprüche, welche sich aus dem Verhältnis ergeben und bei welcher allein das Verhältnis bestehen kann, wird mit unserem Begriff (צדק) bezeichnet.' Cf. E. R. Achtemeier, *IDB*, IV, 80: 'צדק is a concept of relationship and he who is righteous has fulfilled the demands laid upon him by the relationship in which he stands.'

[3] In exceptional circumstances, an individual might, out of loyalty to his understanding of the divine purpose, stand over against the community, ceasing to identify himself with its assumed צְדָקָה.

of the righteousness of Yahweh. The Covenant-theme developed as an interpretation of the significance of certain events in Israel's history, and employed already familiar categories and terms.[1] It is therefore not surprising that when צדק was applied to Yahweh and to the covenant-people it should reflect the notions which were associated with the term apart from that particular relationship. This is implied in Eichrodt's statement:

> In the case of Yahweh, his righteousness implies the same kind of right conduct which in Israel upholds the law by means of judicial procedure: the justice appropriate to Israel on her side is determined by her position as the covenant people, in virtue of which she can count on the intervention of the divine assistance in any danger which threatens that position.[2]

We must now examine this two-fold application of the צדק-terms.

1. *The application of* צדק-*words to Yahweh*

The influence on Hebrew usage of *ṣdk* as a title or qualitative description of Canaanite deities is impossible to assess. Some think that צֶדֶק plays an active and personal role in certain Psalms (85, 89 and 97) and that this name refers either to a primitive god who had become Yahweh's servant or to the hypostatisation of the attribute of one great god. Whether this is so or not is difficult to say, but, when we remember the early use of צדק to describe the king (cf. the Yehimelek inscription), it does seem probable that its appearance with reference to a god or gods reflects the early attribution to divine beings of the qualities and functions of the true king. This association of kingly and divine qualities was part of Israel's inheritance and so there is good reason to believe that the characterisation of Yahweh and his rule as צַדִּיק reflects the application of the term to the activity

---

[1] The idea of 'covenant' and the formulation of its terms show parallels with suzerainty treaties between kings and peoples of Western Asia in the second millenium B.C. (cf. G. E. Mendenhall, *Law and Covenant in Israel and the Ancient Near East* [Pittsburgh, 1955], reprinted from *Biblical Archaeologist*, XVII [1954]). The name בְּרִית was in use to describe a relation of mutual obligations and demands: W. F. Albright finds the Accadian forerunner of the word (*biritu*) meaning 'compact' in the Qatna documents of the fourteenth century B.C. ('The Hebrew expression for "making a covenant" in pre-Israelite documents', *BASOR*, CXXI (1951), 21–2).

[2] Eichrodt, *Theology of the Old Testament*, pp. 241–2.

and character of the true king.[1] At this point we may indicate
some aspects of the function of the king in Israel's thought which
are relevant to our understanding of Yahweh's righteousness.
The nation, as a unity, found its focus in the king: on him it
depended for its right-ordering and well being, for it was his
concern to see that the life of the total society and all relations
within it were 'as they should be', that is, were such as to
maintain and promote national unity and prosperity. This state
of affairs constituted the צְדָקָה of the society: in bringing it about,
the king is himself צַדִּיק, both in the manner of his performing his
functions, as well as in his personal character.[2] The king's
concern for the right-ordering of the community's life necessi-
tated his restraining individuals from doing 'what was right in
their own eyes' (cf. Judg. 17: 6) and thus breaking the cohesive-
ness of the nation. To this end, he was the one supremely devoted
to seeing that the sanctions of the group, particularly the nation's
laws, were uniformly observed throughout the various strata of
society. In the event of a dispute, one might go to him, in his
judicial capacity, for a ruling or judgment (מִשְׁפָּט): he 'declared
in the right' (הִצְדִּיק) him who was 'in the right' (צַדִּיק) and
condemned him who was 'in the wrong' (רָשָׁע),[3] the criterion
being whether or not the general well-being of the community
was safeguarded and advanced. This endeavour to create or
promote a state of affairs in which every relationship was 'as it
should be' seems to be the correct point of departure for the
understanding of the peculiar character of justice in Israel and
in the ancient near East generally. For one section of the community things were almost always *not* 'as they should be', that
section variously known as the 'poor', the 'needy' and the 'weak',
and among whom were numbered the widow and orphan. These

---

[1] Cf. A. R. Johnson, *Sacral Kingship in Ancient Israel* (Cardiff, 1955),
pp. 1–7.

[2] Since the activity of the king was to be taken up by the Messiah on a
wider and more perfect plane, it is not surprising to find that the צדק-words
form part of the typical style of all messianic oracles (Isa. 11, and 9;
Zech. 9).

[3] Cf. Deut. 16: 18; 25: 1; Lev. 19: 15. The root ר ע had a development in
many ways parallel to that of צדק. The Hiph'il means 'to decide against
one', 'to condemn'. In view of its associations the root came to have the
general sense of 'wicked'. The meaning of צדק is sometimes best gauged by
the meaning of רשע, which is its opposite.

were the downtrodden who had no means of redress: their only hope lay with the upholder of צְדָקָה, by whose righteous judgments they were not only declared 'in the right', but were *assisted and protected*.[1] An early illustration of this royal duty towards the oppressed is found at 2 Sam. 15: 1–6. Noteworthy among the many occurrences of the theme is Ps. 72: 1–2 and 12–14, a 'royal' Psalm in which the basic thought is that of the king watching over the rights of all his subjects and ensuring that the weaker members of society enjoy his protection, according to their need. This does not mean that there was one law for the rich and another for the poor, or that the weak received preferential treatment (cf. Lev. 19: 15): it simply was that these unfortunates were not receiving equal treatment: they had their right taken away from them: consequently the balance required redress in their favour if the proper ordering of the community's life was to be maintained. This bias in favour of the poor and needy in the meaning of the word צְדָקָה is the beginning of the development by which it came to denote 'mercy', 'benevolence' and 'almsgiving' in post-biblical Hebrew and in Aramaic.[2]

From considering the 'righteousness' of the king, we return to the discussion of the 'righteousness' of Yahweh, King of Israel and of all nations. If the king was responsible for the right ordering of Israel's life by seeing that laws were obeyed and well-being enjoyed, how much more was this the concern of Yahweh, from whom these laws drew their existence and authority, and on whom the nation ultimately depended for its creation and continuance. Accordingly, not only is the norm by which the nation's צְדָקָה is determined provided by the Covenant-relation

---

[1] It is of interest to observe that this special concern for the depressed in judicial righteousness was not new in Israel. The great law-code of Hammurabi (1700 B.C.) affirms this royal responsibility in its prologue (1. 27 ff., v. 15 f.) and epilogue (rev. XXIV. 59 f.): and it is attested as the ideal of Canaanite kingship by the Keret epic, in which the king's son thus chides his ailing father:

Thou canst not try the case of the wretched,
Thou canst not put down them that despoil the children of the poor,
Thou canst not feed the orphan before thy face, and the widow behind thy back...

Cf. G. R. Driver, *Canaanite Myths and Legends* (Edinburgh, 1956), p. 47.

[2] Occasionally the LXX translates צְדָקָה by ἔλεος (Ezek. 18: 19, 21) and ἐλεημοσύνη (Dan. 4: 24; Ps. 24: 5; 33: 5 and 103: 6).

and its responsibilities, but in fact these are regarded, to some extent, in Israel's thought as normative for Yahweh's צְדָקָה.[1] In other words, when both Yahweh and his people are fulfilling their covenant-obligations to one another, things are ideally 'as they should be'; and the state of affairs indicated by צְדָקָה obtains. It is probably by some such line of thought as this that צְדָקָה can come to mean 'victory' or 'triumph'. This meaning appears in the oldest Hebrew text in the Bible, the Song of Deborah (c. twelfth century) where we read of צִדְקֹת יהוה (LXX δικαιοσύνας), Judg. 5: 11, with reference to victory in battle. When Israel's life was threatened from outside by enemies, Yahweh could be expected to intervene on her behalf out of loyalty to the covenant: that the relationship should be maintained was, in this case, his responsibility, and the nation's success in warfare was consequently the proof of his צְדָקָה. The idiom remains in the later period, as at 1 Sam. 12: 7 and Micah 6: 5 where the צִדְקֹת יהוה are the 'righteous acts' which Yahweh performed for his people out of faithfulness to his covenant and which resulted in salvation.

The 'righteousness' of Yahweh reflects more clearly the character of the king's 'righteousness' when it refers to his judicial function.[2] As judge,[3] Yahweh supremely distinguishes between those who are 'in the right' and those 'who are in the wrong': he condemns the latter and 'puts in the right' (Hiph'il

[1] Cf. Achtemeier, *IDB*, IV, 82, 'Yahweh's righteousness is his fulfilment of the demands of the relationship which exists between him and his people Israel, his fulfilment of the covenant which he has made with his chosen nation'.

[2] The 'court-room' scenes in Deutero-Isaiah where Yahweh appears as judge and as spokesman for Israel's case illustrate this. At Isa. 41: 21ff. Yahweh is proclaimed as צַדִּיק ('in the right') where the question is 'Who has the power to control the events of history?' Israel's history is proof of Yahweh's power and he wins the case and is declared 'in the right'. At Exod. 9: 27, after the early plagues, Pharaoh admits, 'I have sinned; Yahweh is in the right (צַדִּיק) and I and my people are in the wrong', i.e. Yahweh has won his case, since he was able both to demonstrate his power and to protect his own people.

[3] In Ps. 50: 6 and 75: 8 Elohim is called שֹׁפֵט: and in Ps. 82 the אֱלֹהִים (the divine beings subservient to Yahweh) seem to possess judicial functions, although they are in fact dispensing false justice. We may claim with certainty that justice was commonly postulated as one of the characteristics of the gods of the Ancient East.

of צדק = declare to be in the right) the former.[1] Just as the righteous judgment of the king took on a special character when it was directed towards the poor and needy, so, in establishing צְדָקָה in the land, Yahweh has a particular concern for the cause of the poor and outcast, the widow and orphan.[2] As early as the thought of the eighth-century prophets the 'righteousness' of Yahweh implies the idea of deliverance. But it is not only the weak and oppressed for whom the righteous judgment of Yahweh means deliverance, the Psalms, for instance, show that it means the same for any humble, trusting man who pleads his cause against the wicked and who is pronounced 'in the right'. His opponent is condemned and punished, while he is declared righteous (הַצַּדִּיק) and *delivered*. This is the character of Yahweh's צְדָקָה.

The conception underlying this use of the term is that a righteous God must distinguish in his dealings between the wicked man, who neither fears God nor deals justly with men, and the righteous man, who though he be not perfect, but is indeed often confessedly a sinner, yet relatively speaking lives uprightly and trusts in God. (Cf. Noah, Gen. 6: 9.) The righteousness of God in this aspect of it, involving the deliverance of the upright, is often spoken of in parallelism with salvation, but without losing sight of the basis of such salvation, in the discriminating righteousness of God.[3]

Thus, within the action of the divine righteousness, there is a place for deliverance and for condemnation, a place for salvation and for punishment. This view of the content of the 'righteousness of Yahweh', as it affected the nation, had its origin—like all Israel's theological statements—in experience and in reflective interpretation of events. National victories in war were regarded as demonstrations of Yahweh's loyalty to the 'right' relationship of the Covenant and were therefore termed צִדְקוֹת יהוה. Time after time this righteous action effected deliverance, but, at other times, it could mean the opposite, condemnation and resulting captivity (cf. Isa. 10: 22). At Lam. 1: 18, the city of Jerusalem, defeated, looted and destroyed, is made to exclaim, not 'The Lord is unjust', but 'The Lord is *in the right* (צַדִּיק): I have rebelled against his word'.

[1] Cf. Gen. 18: 25; Exod. 23: 7; 1 Kings 8: 32; Hos. 14: 8–9; Ps. 7: 7–11; Jer. 11: 20; Zeph. 3: 5 and Ezra 9: 15.
[2] Cf. Amos 2: 6–7; 5: 12–15; Micah. 3: 2 and Isa. 5: 7.
[3] E. D. Burton, *Galatians* (ICC, Edinburgh, 1921), p. 462.

History, to Israel, was God's supreme tribunal...When the decision of history went against the nation, when they were threatened with expulsion from their land and with extinction as a people, that just meant that the Supreme Judge of men was giving His sentence against them, Israel had broken the terms of the covenant. They had lost their right; they were no longer *righteous*.[1]

This should have been the state of affairs in the time of Deutero-Isaiah. But instead of causing condemnation, the operation of God's righteousness in this prophecy almost always brings deliverance and salvation. The great new factor here is that strict justice was not adhered to, so far as the action of Yahweh in Israel's history was concerned: and the prophet's theology was born in interpreting events. Israel was not 'in the right': she had failed on her side of the covenant, and she knew it, *yet* she was being delivered (46: 12–13): the people had no 'right' for which vindication could be expected, *yet* historical happenings could only mean that Yahweh was giving sentence in their favour (54: 17). In Isaiah's theology the explanation is based, not on any just claim won by Israel through her suffering, but *on the character of Yahweh himself.* Yahweh offers to the nation a new beginning because of his steadfast adherence in love and mercy to the purpose he had in his choice of Israel, namely, the perfecting of a fellowship. And that purpose, as the figure and the activity of the Servant show, concerns both Israel and all nations.[2] In order that it may be advanced, Yahweh's righteousness (according to the prophet's interpretation) will give sentence in favour of those whose right it is not.

> Hearken to me, you stubborn of heart,
> You who are far from righteousness:
> I bring near my righteousness;
> It is not far off, and my salvation will not tarry.
>
> (46: 12–13; cf. also 51: 5–8)

The word 'righteousness'—in Deutero-Isaiah's handling of it—has become fundamentally soteriological, close in meaning to 'salvation'. As A. B. Davidson says, 'Salvation is, so to speak,

[1] G. A. Smith, *The Book of Isaiah*, Expositor's Bible (London, 1888–90), II, 218.

[2] Cf. W. Eichrodt, *Theology of the Old Testament*, p. 247, 'The maintenance of the fellowship now becomes the justification of the ungodly'. This theme is clearly represented in the Qumran literature, as we shall see.

the clothing, the manifestation of Jehovah's righteousness'.[1] In his saving activity, Yahweh's righteousness is illustrated and embodied.

This understanding of Yahweh's righteousness was taught by Deutero-Isaiah to the nation. In the book of Psalms it is expressed by the individual believer who can reckon himself among those whom Yahweh will accept and mercifully vindicate (Ps. 35: 24ff.; 37: 6; 71: 2). But the universalism inherent in Isaiah's teaching on Yahweh's righteousness was not everywhere retained: it appears to have been replaced by a narrower view of divine justice as concerned with the distribution of rewards and punishments in accordance with the standards of law.

Throughout our discussion of the 'righteousness' of Yahweh we have claimed that it reflects, to a large extent, ideas associated with the 'righteousness' of the king. However true this claim may be, we must also reckon with the fact that the ideas of kingly and all human righteousness were, in turn, coloured by their having been associated with the Divine. The development of the meaning and content of the צדק-words is not just in one direction, from the human level to the divine: the words come back from their association with the realm of the divine to be used on the human level with added significance.[2] This may be seen in Ps. 72 (a great Psalm of kingship) where we find this plea made to Yahweh, 'Give the king *thy* justice, and *thy* righteousness to the royal son'. The king's righteousness must now be a reflection of the righteousness of Yahweh: therefore the king will defend the poor and needy (*v.* 4) because this is the pattern of Yahweh's judgments. To put the matter more generally, the character of human righteousness in obedience to Yahweh must be in accordance with the character of Yahweh himself.[3] This brings us to the second strand of our discussion.

[1] *Theology of the Old Testament* (Edinburgh, 1904), p. 397.

[2] This kind of threefold development may be quite common. D. Daube has explored it in the case of גֹּאֵל, *Studies in Biblical Law*, pp. 39–62, esp. p. 53.

[3] The righteousness which Yahweh has demonstrated is a righteousness bent on salvation: it is therefore this kind of righteousness, and not strict justice (in the sense of equality of rights before an impartial law) which must be reflected in the judgments of Yahweh's people. We might claim that the common Old Testament ethical pattern or formula operates in this connection also, 'As Yahweh is righteous...so be ye righteous...'.

2. *The application of the* צדק-*words to Israel and to the individual*

Some points relating to this theme have already become clear. In the first place, the righteousness of the judge and of the king has a bias towards 'assistance' or 'deliverance'. Secondly, when the root is used in connection with a plaintiff, it bears the meaning 'in the right' or 'having a just cause'; and the standard or norm is supplied within the situation or from the law with reference to which the claim is made. Thirdly, by virtue of her position as the covenant people, Israel assumed the righteousness of her cause before Yahweh and therefore counted on his intervention on her behalf when danger threatened that position. Yahweh could be expected to honour the 'right' relationship which he had inaugurated and give his people victory in battle.

So long as danger to the claims of Israel within the covenant relationship was reckoned only in terms of a threat from outside enemies, so long could the 'righteousness' of Yahweh be considered in terms of victory and success. With the coming of the prophetic age, however, Israel was made aware not only of the possibility that the rights of the covenant people could be endangered *from within* (by social and political schism breaking up the national unity) but also of the necessity of examining her pretensions. Was Israel 'in the right' simply because she could regard herself as the chosen people? The way was now open for a new approach to the matter of Yahweh's righteousness with reference to the *inward life* of his people. The צדק-words were consequently employed to characterise both the condition of Israel's life which was necessary if the covenant was to be maintained, and the goal of life which the covenant was meant to inspire. If Yahweh was to be faithful to this relationship and declare Israel 'in the right' (with all that that meant to her in terms of success and well-being), then Israel must *be* 'in the right', she must *have* a 'righteous' cause, she must *possess* 'righteousness' that would reflect the character of Yahweh's righteousness. Here again we may see the effect which the association with the divine had upon the content of the term.

It is often urged by historians of Israel's religion that the prophetic emphasis on the necessity of righteousness within Israel amounts to the ethicising of her faith. The amount of

93

truth in this claim can be assessed only when we understand what the 'ethicising' meant and how it came about. The term צַדִּיק, when applied to Israel, retained the idea of status (i.e. 'in the right') but the norm by which the 'rightness' was judged was the covenant relation and its demands: in other words, the content of the term depended upon the situation and the standard. Consequently, when corruption and oppression flourished (as in the time of the eighth-century prophets) and when, as a result, the right-ordering of the community was impossible and the purpose of the covenant contradicted, then that which would put Israel 'in the right' before Yahweh was quite clearly ethical and moral reform of such a kind as would produce the principles of right community order (justice, equality, sincerity, etc.), and so ensure the maintenance of the covenant. Therefore, instead of suggesting that the prophets ethicised Israel's (non-ethical?) religion, it would be of more value to emphasise the fact that (i) the circumstances in which the prophets spoke provided, indeed demanded, specific ethical content for a familiar judicial term, and (ii) that that content was directly concerned with the establishment of social balance which would reflect Yahweh's covenant righteousness. In short, we may regard the prophetic teaching as essentially a recalling of Israel to the covenant and to the standards and way of life which should characterise national and individual existence within the covenant.

The specific content of the צדק-words again depends on the situation with reference to which they are applied when used in the Psalms to denote a class, in opposition to 'evil-doers' or the 'wicked'. The latter have been variously indentified as apostate Jews, foreign enemies, sorcerers and false accusers, but it seems unwise to look for a single explanation according to one formula.[1] Their identity probably varies within the Psalms and *with it* the identity of the 'righteous', whose character is often best gauged by contrast. On many occasions, however, the 'righteous' are those who, in humility and faithfulness, trust in Yahweh, despite persecution and oppression; those who seek to live uprightly and without pride of heart, depending on Yahweh for protection and vindication. 'Righteousness' here is not ethical perfection, but

[1] Cf. A. R. Johnson, 'The Psalms' in *The Old Testament and Modern Study*, ed. H. H. Rowley (Oxford, 1951), pp. 197 ff.

that obedience and uprightness of the faithful who plead with Yahweh for a favourable decision, not always in order to be 'justified' against an adversary, but often, in an absolute manner, to be accepted and saved.

> Who shall ascend the hill of the Lord?
> And who shall stand in his holy place?
> He who has clean hands and a pure heart,
>> Who does not lift up his soul to what is false,
>> And does not swear deceitfully.
> He will receive blessing from the Lord,
>> And vindication (צְדָקָה) from the God of his salvation.
>
> (Ps. 24: 3–5)

In conclusion, we turn to the final chapters of the book of Isaiah. In Deutero-Isaiah we discovered that the 'righteousness' of Yahweh was developing towards meaning 'justification of the ungodly', salvation which is unmerited. There was no affirmation of Israel's righteousness before Yahweh: her only righteousness before the nations was the knowledge and experience of Yahweh's salvation in declaring her to be in the right because of his faithfulness to the covenant promise.[1] The unmerited vindication, the new beginning in grace, brings with it, however, the demand that righteousness in keeping with the covenant should be the character of Israel's subsequent life. That demand finds expression in chapters 56–9 of the book, which begin with the exhortation, 'Keep justice and do righteousness (צְדָקָה)'. And that righteousness means (as in the earlier prophets) social justice, sincere worship and upright conduct (56: 9—58: 9): it means, in short, all that makes for the right-ordering of the nation's life within the covenant. When this righteousness 'is done', there will be national recovery and covenant harmony (58: 8 ff.). In the thrilling vision of restoration presented by the closing chapters of the book, this state of affairs is achieved. 'Righteousness' will be the government of the community

---

[1] Cf. Achtemeier, *IDB*, IV, 85: 'Yahweh will fulfil the demands of the covenant relationship. He will maintain his righteousness. He will do so by justifying Israel, by imputing righteousness to her who has no righteousness, by delivering her who has no right to be delivered (46: 12–13). And this will be Israel's righteousness before all the world, that God helps her (50: 9, cf. 52: 13 — 53: 12)...Despite her failure to do the right, despite her lack of faith, Yahweh...will decide in her favour. Deutero-Isaiah's plea is that Israel but faithfully accept such deliverance.'

(60: 17): the people will be righteous and flourish (60: 21): their righteousness will be known to all nations (61: 10): and all this will be to the glory of Yahweh who chose them, who, with faithfulness and mercy, justified them when they were not righteous, and to whom they now respond with devotion and sincerity.

By way of summary on the 'righteousness' of Israel, we draw attention to Deut. 6: 20 ff., a passage from a book dominated by the theme of the covenant. The question is asked, 'What is the meaning of the testimonies and statutes and ordinances which the Lord commanded?' In the answer given, their meaning is related to the Exodus, the event of election. 'We were slaves in Egypt...and we were brought out...and the Lord commanded us to do all these things, to fear the Lord our God, for our good always, that he might preserve us alive as at this day.' In short, the law has meaning and purpose only within the covenant relationship. 'And', the passage goes on, 'it will be צְדָקָה for us, if we are careful to do all these commandments before the Lord our God, as he has commanded us' (cf. Deut. 24: 13). In other words, the vitality of the community, its right internal ordering, its right attitude to Yahweh, and the personal righteousness of its members, all depend on responsible acceptance of Yahweh's election and on obedience to the law which constitutes divine guidance within the covenant relationship.

Observations on the semantics of the צדק-words

In the course of this study of Old Testament usage—which may be regarded as an exercise in historical semantics—a number of important points have become clear, some of which may also be useful for the interpretation of other biblical terms.

(1) The צדק-words do not appear in biblical Hebrew as *new* words. The root had a previous history and the words derived from it already possessed developed meanings. The use of the root in the Old Testament takes up and builds upon these earlier associations and meanings.

(2) Although the biblical Hebrew use of the צדק-words was founded on the earlier usage which it inherited, the words were given a characteristic content by their particular association with the terminology of the covenant-relation. Yahweh's righteous-

ness is regarded often as faithfulness to the covenant choice and is interpreted in experience as victory for Israel over her enemies: Israel's righteousness also meant loyalty to the covenant and, in particular, obedience to the covenant laws which provided principles for the right-ordering of the nation's life, in its man-ward and Godward aspects: the character of community and personal righteousness depended on the circumstances out of which the demand arose, but it was always regarded as having its ultimate sanction in the obligations of the Covenant: and, finally, because of Yahweh's constancy to the covenant (in the experience of Israel) Deutero-Isaiah found it possible to express by the use of צְדָקָה something almost synonymous with 'salvation'. It would be true to say that it was its incorporation into the terminology of the covenant that secured the special religious character of צְדָקָה in the Old Testament. In more linguistic terms, the covenant idea is the 'emotive force'[1] or the 'predominant thought-trend'[2] which provided the dynamic for the semantic expansion and development of the word.

(3) The suggested threefold development in the history of the צדק-words may be of guidance in the understanding and interpretation of other religious and theological terms. This development takes the word from an association with man and his life (in this case, the 'righteousness' of the king) to an association with Yahweh, and back again to man, with a richer content and colour drawn from its relation to deity.

(4) We must comment on the semantic change in צדק-words within the Old Testament. The idea of conformity to a norm seems to be the basic significance of the root צדק which most satisfactorily accounts for its various developments. This does not mean that that sense was always present or recognisable in the words at every stage of development. The primary meaning may be the key to understanding the *direction* of the semantic development, but usage, which brought the word into association with particular ideas and situations, must be the guide to meaning at any point. Now the Old Testament usage of צְדָקָה does suggest that the word could, when associated with Yahweh, take on the

---

[1] The term belongs to H. Sperber, *Einführung in die Bedeutungslehre* (2nd ed., Leipzig, 1930).

[2] The term is from J. Schwietering, quoted in S. Ullmann, *Principles of Semantics* (2nd ed., Oxford, 1957), pp. 197–8.

meaning of 'that in which Yahweh's righteousness resulted', namely, 'deliverance', 'salvation' and 'victory'. When the word developed thus, it did not necessarily lose the other meanings which it already possessed: the literature of the Old Testament attests the retention of older meanings while changes of emphasis brought about newer meanings. Linguistic study has recognised this. W. Wundt distinguished between partial change of meaning and total change in which a new meaning entirely supersedes the old, which therefore completely falls out of use.[1] We may claim that צְדָקָה underwent the partial semantic change in the Old Testament. When predicated of Yahweh, it changed from meaning the character of his judicial activity to refer to the effects (or expected effects) of that activity: and in ethical contexts, the word could change from meaning 'the status of being in the right' to connote the character of actions and life necessary to achieve that status *within the covenant relation*. Nevertheless, the earlier meanings of the term did not fall out of use as soon as the developments took place.[2]

(5) It is important to remember that the sense or meaning of a formal term like צְדָקָה is frequently fluid or vague and requires delimitation from its context or from the situation-in-life to which it is referred.[3]

δίκαιος AND RELATED WORDS IN GREEK USAGE

Because of its connection with δείκνυμι[4] ('show' or 'indicate') it seems probable that the original connotation of the word δίκη—the basic word of the group—was 'way indicated' or

---

[1] *Völkerpsychologie*, I, Die Sprache (Leipzig, 1900). S. Ullmann, *Principles of Semantics*, p. 174, '...a word may retain its previous sense or senses and at the same time acquire one or several new senses': see also p. 117.

[2] Cf. W. M. Urban, *Language and Reality* (London, 1939), pp. 112f., 'The fact that a sign (i.e. a linguistic sign or word) can intend one thing without ceasing to intend another, that, indeed, the very condition of its being an *expressive* sign for the second is that it is also a sign for the first, is precisely what makes language an instrument of knowing'.

[3] This may be a helpful guide in the interpretation of words like מִשְׁפָּט and תָּמִים which belong both to the judicial terminology of Israel and also to the language of the covenant.

[4] Cf. É. Boisacq, *Dictionnaire Étymologique de la Langue Grecque* (Heidelberg, 1950) and J. B. Hofmann, *Etymologisches Wörterbuch des Griechischen* (München, 1949).

'that which is customary'. The first appearance of the word in Greek literature, referring to a mythical divine being, 'the virgin Δίκη, daughter of Zeus, who is honoured among the gods' (Hesiod, *Works and Days*, 256), suggests that at an early stage of Greek thought the 'established custom' was regarded as the divinely appointed or divinely recognised way of things.[1] It was Solon who 'demythologised' the concept: for him δίκη ('justice') is no longer a divine being, yet is more than a human device: it is *a law*, the law of the universe, which is independent of man and cannot be evaded by him. We may say therefore that δίκη connotes the norm (invested with divine sanction) for human conduct, chiefly for the conduct of men towards one another, and as such was logically regarded as 'right': that which is customary and conforms to the divinely recognised order is 'the right'. After Homer, the implicit juristic reference became increasingly prominent and the word δίκη was frequently used to refer to 'proceedings instituted to determine *legal* rights',[2] a lawsuit, or trial, and even to the objects or consequences of legal action, i.e. 'satisfaction' or 'penalty'. (Cf. Acts 28: 4; 2 Thess. 1: 9 and Jude 7.)

A person whose conduct conforms to the standard δίκη is δίκαιος: he does what is right, according to the traditions of society (Hom. *Od.* 6. 119f.; 9. 174–6): he renders to others their rights and exacts his own. The word may be thus employed with the broad sense 'right'[3] or, in a more specific reference, 'just'.[4] Aristotle defines τὸ δίκαιον as 'that which is legal and fair' (*NE.* 1129*a*, l. 34), thus distinguishing the two parts of justice, legality and equality. It is also defined as 'that which is due from one man to another' (Thuc. 3. 54 and Dem. 572. 14) and this in terms of either one's duty or one's deserts. Although in the older

---

[1] This is confirmed by Hesiod's remark that, 'Unhappy is the city which the divine virgin has fled...', because its affairs will be in chaos: and also by Sophocles, *Ant.* 450–7 which points out that, in the case of a dispute between human and divine right, δίκη will be on the side of the eternal laws of Zeus and against human laws (νόμοι).

[2] In Herodotus, δίκη stands for the 'decision of a judge', conforming to a norm.

[3] Hom. *Od.* 18. 413; Thuc. 3. 40; Plat. *Gorg.* 507*b*; Arist. *NE.* 5. 1129*a*.

[4] Hes. *WD*, 270ff.; Herodas 2. 86—γνώμη δικαίᾳ κρίσιν διαιτᾶτε. 'Just' here connotes the rendering to each of what he has the right to claim according to social rule.

Greek literature the meaning of δίκαιος included reference to the discharge of obligations to the gods as well as to men[1] and τὸ δίκαιον was regarded as having the sanction of divine authority, yet, in the later classical writers, when νόμος had become the source and basis of equality and had taken over the religious significance possessed by δίκη, the predominant reference in δίκαιος was to the mutual relations of men.[2] Thus, in moral philosophy, the term indicates the person who possesses social and political virtue. Though δίκαιος is frequently used in a non-moral sense, the word usually has reference to a standard (either in the nature of the thing itself or outside it) or to a demand requiring to be satisfied, for example, when it means 'exact' (as applied to numbers), 'fitting', 'suitable', 'correct' or 'genuine' (Herod. 2. 149; Xen. Mem. IV. 4. 5 and Aesch. Agam. 1604).

The noun δικαιοσύνη belongs to the third stage in word-formation, following δίκη and δίκαιος, and it is found first at Herod. 1. 96. Through referring to the quality possessed by the person described as δίκαιος (who is the man who conforms to law) the term early bears the sense of the 'prescribed behaviour of the citizen towards society': in other words, it connotes social virtue. With his usual disregard of precise formulation, Plato represents δικαιοσύνη as the *state* of any agent (whether person or association) in which each of the component elements does its own work or performs its proper function. In the city, this means the harmony of the various classes: in the individual, it consists in a certain relation between the different tendencies (the passionate, the rational and the appetitive), a power or principle of order and harmony.[3] For Plato, δικαιοσύνη is not so definite a thing as the virtues of σωφροσύνη, ἀνδρεία and φρόνησις, but is that which makes possible the realisation of these (cf. *Rep.* IV,

[1] Hom. *Od.* 6. 120 and 13. 209f., *Hymn to Demeter*, 386–9.

[2] That justice could not be understood wholly without reference to religion is implied by Plato's association of δίκαιος and ὅσιος (*Gorg.* 507 b; *Rep.* I, 331 a). In *Euthy.* 12 c–e ὅσιον is defined as part of δίκαιον.

[3] In Plato, δικαιοσύνη is not an innate quality, as G. Schrenk (*Righteousness*, Bible Key Words Series, London, 1951, p. 14) suggests. Nor does δίκαιος τὴν φύσιν in Jos. *Ant.* 7. 110 and 9. 216 mean 'naturally righteous', as Schrenk (*loc. cit.*) maintains, but 'just-natured' or 'just by disposition' (cf. English, 'good-natured').

433 b).[1] Aristotle devotes an entire book of his treatise on Ethics to δικαιοσύνη, and describes two kinds: (i) δικαιοσύνη as a particular virtue, the opposite of πλεονεξία, and meaning the 'assigning to a man his due': this may be subdivided into two aspects, a distributive (διανεμητική) and a corrective (διορθωτική), cf. NE. 5. 1130 b; (ii) δικαιοσύνη as co-extensive with the whole of virtue (sic Plato), not as a particular virtue. It is in fact the highest expression of virtue, ἡ τελειά ἀρετή, the realised ἕξις of ἀρετή in man, dealing with his fellow-men. As the performance of all one's social duties, it is essentially πρὸς ἕτερον (NE. 5. 1129 b and 1130 b). For Aristotle, 'justice' (δικαιοσύνη) is less idealistic than it is for Plato: it is realised in concrete relations, and these may subsist in any society. The judicial notion which belongs to δικαιοσύνη when it refers to a particular virtue is found in the definition given by Aristotle in Rhet. 1. 1366 b—'Justice is that virtue by reason of which each has what belongs to him'. The underlying idea here is that of a judge awarding to each his due, and, in fact, δικαιοσύνη occasionally refers to 'justice' as the business of the judge (Plato, Gorg. 464 b–c).

The verb δικαιόω comes from the adjective δίκαιος and, being causative in form, should (by analogy with other verbs) mean 'to make δίκαιος or δίκαιον'. In classical Greek, however, it never has exactly this force.[2] Its uses fall under two main heads: (i) with an impersonal object, it denotes 'to hold or deem a thing to be right or suitable',[3] even 'to decide' or 'claim as a right' that a thing should be done. This use is very common in classical writers and also in Philo and Josephus; (ii) applied to persons, δικαιόω is widely used to mean 'to do one right or justice', 'to treat justly' (i.e. as the opposite of ἀδικεῖν), and this

[1] The works of Philo reveal a lively interest in δικαιοσύνη as one of the cardinal virtues. Linked with the virtues of intelligence, courage and sometimes piety, δικαιοσύνη obviously means 'justice'. Philo takes over from Pythagoreanism the idea that 'equality' (ἰσότης) is the mother of justice (Spec. IV, 231; Plant. 122 and Heres 163) and being so derived δικαιοσύνη is the ordering principle in the human soul and in life.

[2] In a famous fragment of Pindar (169. 3) quoted by Plato (Gorg. 484 b), the verb has the sense of 'to set right', or possibly 'to recognise as right' (νόμος . . . δικαιῶν τὸ βιαιότατον): but this meaning is unusual.

[3] Cf. the verb ἀξιόω: verbs in -οω derived from adjectives expressing a value judgment commonly mean 'to deem or account. . .'.

chiefly *in malam partem*, 'to pass sentence on', 'to condemn and punish'. In the passive, the verb is used in the sense of 'to have right or justice done to one' (cf. Arist. *NE.* 5. 1136 *a*). The use of the word in the Hermetic Tractate 'On Regeneration' (C. Her. 13: 9) calls for special attention: χωρὶς γὰρ κρίσεως ἰδὲ πῶς τὴν ἀδικίαν ἐξήλασεν...ἐδικαιώθημεν, ὦ τέκνον, ἀδικίας ἀπούσης. The writer is describing the way in which the divine nature is implanted in man, who is thus 'reborn' or 'deified'. At each stage of the process, one of the vices natural to humanity is replaced by a god-given virtue (e.g. ignorance by knowledge), and in the passage in question, ἀδικία is replaced by δικαιοσύνη. Instead of expressing the latter by the abstract noun, the writer uses the verb: consequently the meaning is quite simply, 'We have been made righteous, now that unrighteousness is away'. Since the phrase seems to connote ethical change, it is possible that the author here betrays acquaintance with the interpretation which Greek commentators gave of Paul's language.[1]

The noun δικαίωμα means an 'act of right' or 'amendment of wrong', and also a 'plea or claim of right'. It is used frequently in the papyri referring to 'legal deeds or evidence', and appears in Philo, Josephus and the LXX with the meaning 'legal statute', 'demand' or 'ordinance'. The word δικαίωσις is employed with the general sense of 'a putting into action of that which is δίκαιον ("right")': it is judicial 'setting right' or 'doing justice' to someone, especially of condemnation or punishment. It may also be used of a 'plea or demand of right', that is, a 'just claim', and even of 'a judging of what is right'.

At this stage of our study we may observe some points of similarity and of contrast between the Greek δίκαιος-words and the Hebrew צדק-words.

(1) The idea of conformity to a norm and a general forensic reference are common to the meaning and development of the words expressing 'righteousness' in both languages.

(2) The relation of 'custom' to 'right' in early Greek thought recalls the use of root צדק to mean 'in the right', a status which was frequently established with reference to convention or social law.

(3) In both Greek and Hebrew usage the word for 'righteous-

---

[1] Cf. C. H. Dodd, *The Bible and the Greeks*, p. 59.

ness' belongs to the terminology of relationships in community. In Greek, δικαιοσύνη is generally associated with the mutual obligations of men in human society, without reference (except in early writers) to divine sanction: in the Hebrew tradition, on the other hand, the behaviour of man within community is governed by the requirements of the covenant relation, and therefore has reference ultimately to conformity to the divine will.

(4) There is nothing in Greek thought lastingly comparable to the idea of the 'righteousness of God', and consequently no development of the meaning of δικαιοσύνη towards 'victory' or 'salvation'. This significance was added to the word in biblical Greek usage through the LXX translators' use of it to render צִדְקוֹת יהוה.

(5) The particular actions which provide the content for צְדָקָה are often those which the Greek mind would recognise as δίκαια, in the sense of social virtues. Corruption, false dealing, oppression (as condemned by the prophets) would be described in Greek as ἀδικία. But the criterion by which they are adjudged as such in Hebrew thought is primarily the divine demand for equality within the covenant relation, rather than (as in Greek thought) what was socially just or fair.

(6) Throughout most of its development the Greek word δικαιοσύνη tended towards the more precise and narrow meaning 'justice', the giving of what was due to each.[1] Consequently there is nothing parallel to the semantic development of the Hebrew word towards 'deliverance' and 'assistance' and away from the idea of strict justice.

(7) Righteousness, in Hebrew thinking, is distinguished radically from Plato's theoretical and intellectual 'justice' as a state of being in that it is a concrete and experienced thing: צְדָקָה describes a state of affairs which can exist and can be recognised in the life of men. And from Aristotle's notion of 'righteousness' or 'justice' as perfect virtue displayed in society it differs in that its content is determined by something more than social duty: צְדָקָה is determined by the demands of God made known within the covenant relation.

---

[1] Aristotle's division of δικαιοσύνη (as one among the virtues) into a distributive aspect and a corrective aspect is simply a systematisation of current thought on the matter. The Stoic definition is on the same lines— ἐπιστήμη διανεμητικὴ τῆς ἀξίας ἑκάστῳ, Stobaeus, *Ecl.* 2. 102.

THE SEPTUAGINT

The fact that in the LXX the δίκαιος-words translate the צדק-words on 462 out of a possible 476 times implies that, in the estimation of the translators, the amount of semantic overlap between the two word groups was very great: δίκαιος, etc., would appear to have been the most satisfactory words available to render the meaning of צְדָקָה, etc., for the Greek-speaking readers of the Old Testament. Nevertheless, the Hebrew root was occasionally translated differently and sometimes the δίκαιος-words represent other Hebrew words.

In most of the cases where צְדָקָה is not rendered by the words, ἔλεος and ἐλεημοσύνη appear.[1] In our Old Testament discussion we noticed that the word צְדָקָה, when predicated of the judge and of Yahweh, tended towards the meaning 'assistance', 'protection' and 'help'. Now the usual rendering of צְדָקָה by δικαιοσύνη would not convey the idea of 'merciful action', because, as we have pointed out, the Greek term retained the flavour of 'strict justice' throughout its entire usage. Therefore the notion was introduced by the translation ἔλεος and ἐλεημοσύνη.[2] In this connection, it is noteworthy that σωτηρία is *never* used to translate צְדָקָה, although 'salvation' is clearly the area of meaning to which the root צדק frequently approaches in Deutero-Isaiah and in Psalms.

The use of δίκαιος, etc., to render Hebrew words other than those from root צדק is of interest. The adjective δίκαιος is found

---

[1] At Job 4: 17, the Qal of צדק is represented by καθαρὸς εἶναι, and at 22: 3 by ἄμεμπτος εἶναι. N. H. Snaith, *The Distinctive Ideas of the Old Testament* (London, 1944, p. 166) includes in the former category Gen. 24: 8 and Isa. 65: 5, but while καθαρὸς appears in the LXX, the verbs are not צדק in the Hebrew. For the Niph'al of צדק translated by καθαρίζω, see above, p. 84 note 1.

[2] Both human righteousness and divine righteousness are represented by ἔλεος or ἐλεημοσύνη: the former at Ezek. 18: 19, 21; and the latter at Dan. 4: 24 (27); Ps. 24: 5; 33: 5 and 103: 6. This rendering has altered the meaning of the Hebrew in Deut. 6: 25 and 24: 13. The passages state that obedience to the laws of Yahweh will mean צְדָקָה for the people or for the individual. This probably means that obedience is the way to righteousness and the right-ordering of the community (cf. S. R. Driver, *Deuteronomy* [ICC, Edinburgh, 1896, p. 96]) but the rendering ἐλεημοσύνη will refer to the 'merciful action' of Yahweh which Israel will experience if they are obedient to Yahweh's commands.

for יָשָׁר ('straightforward, upright'), in Job. 1: 1; Prov. 3: 32;
11: 3; 14: 9; 21: 2, 18, and δικαιοσύνη once for מֵישָׁרִים ('uprightness') at 1 Chron. 29: 17. The fact that this translation is
almost entirely confined to Job and Proverbs is perhaps significant. Both translators (if indeed there was not only one) of these
books appear to be sensitive to Greek style and usage, and their
work bears traces of familiarity with Hellenistic Alexandrian
culture;[1] in fact they show the early stages of that Hellenisation
of the Old Testament which reached its peak in Philo.[2] In view
of this, their use of δίκαιος for יָשָׁר may betray the Greek understanding of δίκαιος as 'virtuous'.

δίκαιος translates נָקִי ('innocent'), with reference to persons
(Job. 9: 23; 17: 8) and in the phrase αἷμα δίκαιον ('innocent
blood', usually αἷμα ἀθῶον) at Prov. 6: 17 (AS); Joel 4: 19 and
Jonah 1: 14. The noun δικαιοσύνη appears for נִקָּיוֹן at Gen. 20: 5.

The Aramaic זָכוּ ('purity' or 'blamelessness' before God) is
translated by δικαιοσύνη at Dan. 6: 23 (22). The Hebrew root
זכה is twice rendered by δικαιόω:[3] (i) Micah 6: 11—הַאֶזְכֶּה בְּמֹאזְנֵי
רֶשַׁע where the LXX has εἰ δικαιωθήσεται ἐν 3υγῷ ἄνομος.
The RSV renders the Hebrew by 'Shall I acquit with wicked
scales?' Since the Hebrew verb (as it stands) means 'Shall I be
pure?' and makes poor sense, it seems likely that the pointing
should be altered to the Piel or the Hiph'il form. If the Hiph'il was
the reading which the translator had before him, then the
meaning is 'Shall I cause to be, or declare to be pure (righteous)',
and that is adequately represented (when turned into the passive)
by δικαιωθήσεται. The Piel of the verb means 'cleanse', but in
later Hebrew it is often used with the sense 'to acquit' or
'pronounce righteous'.[4] Knowledge of this use may well have

[1] Cf. G. Gerleman, *Studies in the Septuagint:* I. *Job* (Lund, 1946) and
II. *Proverbs* (Lund, 1956).
[2] This does not mean that the translators violently distorted the Old
Testament materials. The content of the books was less characteristically
Israelite from the beginning and therefore a measure of assimilation to Greek
ethical ideas was easier.
[3] G. Schrenk, *Righteousness*, p. 2, includes Ps. 51 (50): 6 among the cases
of זכה being translated by δικαιόω. In fact δικαιωθῇς there renders תִּצְדַּק
and תִּזְכֶּה appears as νικήσῃς ἐν τῷ κρίνεσθαί σε.
[4] Cf. b. Berak. 19a; jer. Sot. 22c, 41; Midr. Ps. 143: 1, 266b, etc. See SB,
III, 134 for examples. Koehler–Baumgartner's Lexicon (under זכה) under
stands the verb here as Hiph'il and as meaning 'für rein erklären'.

influenced the translator in his rendering. (ii) At Ps. 73 (72): 13 רִיק זִכִּיתִי לְבָבִי is rendered by ματαίως ἐδικαίωσα τὴν καρδίαν μου. The Hebrew clearly means 'I have cleansed (i.e. kept clean) my heart in vain', but the Greek will not easily yield that sense. Again the translator may have been influenced by the developing declaratory meaning of the Piel form and may have chosen δικαιόω to convey that sense, rather than some part of the verb καθαρίζω. If this is not the case, we have here the only instance of δικαιόω in the LXX with the meaning 'cleanse', 'make pure or righteous'.

The Hebrew noun חֶסֶד is translated by δικαιοσύνη on nine occasions.[1] Since this term meant 'an act of kindness or loyalty (between persons)' or 'the steadfast loyal love' (of Yahweh for his people), we are confronted with a meaning which lies outside anything that δικαιοσύνη could connote to the Greek mind. Perhaps we may find in this translation evidence that חֶסֶד was not conceived of as entirely a spontaneous feeling, but in terms of what could be expected within a relationship: if so, the idea would be more adequately conveyed by δικαιοσύνη than by the word ἔλεος.[2]

The verb δικαιόω is used twice to render a form of רִיב, at Isa. 1: 17 and Micah 7: 9. The verb רִיב usually means 'to contend', 'to conduct legal proceedings', and may be used in either a favourable or an unfavourable sense. In the two passages where it is translated by δικαιοῦν it bears the sense 'vindicate'.[3]

[1] Gen. 19: 19; 20: 13; 21: 23; 24: 27; 32: 11; Exod, 15: 13; 34: 7; Prov. 20: 28 and Isa. 63: 7.

[2] The translation of חֶסֶד by δικαιοσύνη may be evidence of the growing legalism of the period in which the LXX translation was made: cf. Dodd, *The Bible and the Greeks*, p. 65. Another covenant word which δικαιοσύνη and δίκαιος render is אֱמֶת (usually translated by ἀλήθεια). Some of these occurrences (there are ten in all) refer to the faithfulness or constancy of Yahweh: one means 'security' (Isa. 39: 8); while in two places (Ezek. 18: 8 and Zech. 7: 9) מִשְׁפַּט אֱמֶת ('judgment of truth or faithfulness') becomes δίκαιον κρίμα. In these two passages the forensic reference is dominant in the Greek term, as it is when δικαιοσύνη translates מִשְׁפָּט itself, Isa. 61: 8; Mal. 2: 17.

[3] Snaith (*The Distinctive Ideas of the Old Testament*, p. 166) and Schrenk (*Righteousness*, p. 58) claim that at 1 Sam. 12: 7 δικαιόω renders שָׁפַט. Only LXX MSS. A (generally regarded as unreliable) gives δικαιώσω. All others give δικάσω (fut. of δικάζω = 'judge') which renders שָׁפַט ten times in 1 Samuel, while שָׁפַט is nowhere else in the Old Testament translated by δικαιόω.

Again, δικαιόω appears once (Ezek. 21: 13, MT and LXX, 18) to render בֻּחַן, the Pual of בָּחַן ('to test, try') and the meaning seems to be, 'it has been tested' or 'trial has been made'. Apart from these instances, δικαιόω translates the verb צָדַק.

We must now look at the way in which δικαιόω is used to render the various parts of that Hebrew verb. The Hiph'il (הִצְדִּיק), in which the declaratory and forensic connotation is dominant, is without exception translated by the active of δικαιόω. Snaith claims that 'the forensic sense does not appear to have been as obvious to the LXX translators of Proverbs 17: 15 as it is to the moderns, for there the Greek rendering (of the Hiph'il participle) is δίκαιον κρίνειν, i.e. the actual verb "judge" is inserted in order to make clear the forensic sense'.[1] But surely the reason for this method of translation is the desire for symmetry in style. The translator wanted a verb which could be used in both halves of the sentence and δικαιοῦν could *not* be so used. Occasionally, the active of δικαιόω is used to translate the Piel of צָדַק, with the meaning 'make appear righteous', for example, Jer. 3: 11; Ezek. 16: 51. In these cases an underlying forensic idea seems to be present in the Hebrew and in the translation by δικαιόω.

More interesting is the use of the middle and passive of δικαιόω to translate the Qal of צָדַק, with the meaning 'appear righteous', 'be in the right', even 'to be righteous'.[2] An important example is found in Ps. 143 (142): 2 which the RSV translates, 'Enter not into judgment with thy servant, for no man living is righteous (יִצְדַּק, δικαιωθήσεται) before thee' (cf. Gal. 2: 16; Rom. 3: 20).[3] Does this use of the passive of δικαιόω where the Hebrew means 'appear righteous, be righteous'

---

[1] Snaith, *The Distinctive Ideas of the Old Testament*, p. 166.

[2] In *JBL*, LXXIII (1954), 87, E. J. Goodspeed pointed out that 'Edward Robinson's Greek Lexicon of the NT (current about a century ago) says of the middle of this verb δικαιόω: "to make oneself upright", hence "to be upright, righteous"'. Goodspeed claims that this usage has been ignored by later lexicographers.

[3] Other instances are Gen. 38: 26; Ps. 19 (18): 9 (Heb. and LXX 10); Ps. 51 (50): 4 (Heb., LXX, 6); Isa. 43: 9, 26; 45: 25; also Job 10: 15 Aquil.); Job 22: 3 (Sym.) and Job 15: 14 (Aquil. and Theod.). It is possible that the passive of δικαιόω reflects the Qal of צָדַק in certain passages of the Apocrypha, of which the original Hebrew is no longer extant: see N. M. Watson, 'Some observations on the use of δικαιόω in the Septuagint', *JBL*, LXXIX (1960), 255–66, esp. pp. 262 ff.

imply, as some scholars assert,[1] that the Greek verb has lost its forensic or judicial sense? In answering this question we must recognise the fact that the Qal of צדק (which it renders) generally possesses forensic significance. In the verse quoted from Ps. 143 the Hebrew does not mean 'no one shall be righteous *in himself*', but 'no one shall be righteous *before God*, i.e. in the right at the divine tribunal'. The confirmation of the man's 'in-the-rightness' at some court of appeal (even that offered by the demands of convention, Gen. 38: 26) is an idea present also at Isa. 43: 9, 26 and 45: 25. In Ps. 51: 6, it is Yahweh's being 'in the right' in passing sentence which is expressed rather than his personal righteousness.[2] Now if we may assume that the Greek translators knew the force of the Qal of צדק, we may suggest that they found its particular shade of meaning ('to be in the right') best rendered by the passive form of the Greek verb. Nevertheless, we must admit that the passive of צדק did not always and necessarily bear the specific Hebraic nuance in biblical Greek. Once it had been used to translate 'be righteous' in contexts which were concerned with the confirmation of in-the-rightness, it could easily be used to mean 'be righteous' where that particular emphasis was not present.[3]

From this discussion of LXX usage it will be obvious that the δίκαιος-words underwent considerable expansion and change of meaning through being consistently used to render the Hebrew root צדק. (1) The words were employed to refer to God's character, attitude and actions.[4] In Classical Greek usage,

---

[1] Snaith, *The Distinctive Ideas of the Old Testament*, and M. J. Lagrange, *Épître aux Romains* (Paris, 1931), p. 127.

[2] At Ps. 19: 10 the Heb. says, 'The ordinances of the Lord are righteous (צִדְקוּ)' and the LXX has δεδικαιωμένα. This strange translation, where δίκαια would have been enough, may have been adopted for metrical reasons or for the sake of symmetry, in order to retain a participle in the second part of both halves of the verse.

[3] N. M. Watson (*JBL*, LXXIX [1960], 265) draws attention to some passages in Tobit and Ecclesiasticus (behind which may lie the Qal of צדק) which use the passive of δικαιόω in the sense of 'be righteous', where no idea of 'being in the right' is present. In these cases, δίκαιος + the verb 'to be' might have been a more satisfactory rendering.

[4] Philo applies the adjective δίκαιος to God (e.g. *Somn.* II, 194) and speaks of the δικαιοσύνη of God on two occasions; in *Immut.* 79 he lists it (in Stoic fashion) among the other virtues, and in *Mos.* II, 237 he employs it with reference to God's *justice* in judging.

δίκαιος, etc., were not terms used of the divine, except at a very early date. (2) In the Classical Greek usage of the terms the idea of conformity to a standard was present and the standard was primarily that of social obligation. In the Old Testament use of צְדָקָה the standard implied possesses divine authority and often is the demands of the covenant law. Through being used consistently as the means of translating the Hebrew word, δικαιοσύνη gained this new dimension of reference (i.e. the divine requirement) in biblical Greek. (3) Through being drawn into the covenant terminology the word δικαιοσύνη was supplied, from time to time, with a content which is related to that of 'mercy' (when translating חֶסֶד) and of 'loyalty' and 'trustworthiness' (when translating אֱמֶת). (4) The verb δικαιόω is not found with its secular Greek meanings in the LXX: it has to be interpreted in terms of the Hebrew roots it renders. When it translates the root צדק (and even other roots as well), the forensic sense is almost always present. The only possible exceptions we have found are in Ps. 19 (18): 10 and 73 (72): 13.

THE APOCRYPHA AND PSEUDEPIGRAPHA

In the Apocryphal books δίκαιος is used as in the LXX, except that there are no examples of the meanings 'in the right' and 'innocent'.[1] In the Psalms of Solomon δίκαιος designates the 'upright' man who trusts in God and keeps his law, as distinct from sinners (2:34; 3:4–8; 15:6). When applied to God and his judgments the adjective describes his attitude and action in discriminating between the upright and the sinner.[2] It is applied to the Messiah in a similar sense (17:32). The use of δικαιοσύνη throughout the Psalms of Solomon corresponds to the uses of δίκαιος. In the Apocryphal books δικαιοσύνη appears to have all the usages of the noun in the LXX. It is the 'righteousness' and 'right conduct' on the part of man that makes him acceptable to God, although that 'righteousness' is conceived of in a more

[1] The meaning 'righteous' (applied to man and God, as well as to actions) is found at Tob. 3:2; 14:9; Wis. 2:10; 3:1; Sir. 10:23. The meaning 'just' occurs at Wis. 12:15; 2 Macc. 9:18. The use of the neuter in the sense 'just', that which is right, one's rights or deserts, is common: 1 Macc. 7:12; 11:33; 2 Macc. 11:14; 13:23.

[2] Ps. Sol. 2:10, 18, 32, 34; 5:1; 8:8; 9:2 and 10:5.

external, legalistic way than in the prophets (cf. Tob. 12: 9; 14: 11; Wis. 1: 15). The term also denotes God's 'righteousness' in discriminating between the good and the evil among men, saving the one and punishing the other (cf. Wis. 5: 18; 12: 16). One unusual description of δικαιοσύνη appears at Wis. 15: 3— 'To know thee is righteousness in its entirety (ὁλόκληρος δικαιοσύνη) and to know thy power is the root of immortality'. Here knowledge of God constitutes righteousness, which therefore must connote the status of acceptability before God.[1] In Sirach the verb δικαιόω means (i) 'to do justice to', 'to punish' (42:2), and (ii) 'to recognise or declare to be right or righteous' (7:5; 10:29; 13:22). The verb frequently appears in the passive with the meaning 'to be declared innocent' or 'to acquit' or even possibly to 'accept' (18: 22). The Psalms of Solomon use the verb exclusively with the meaning 'to recognise as just or righteous', that is, man's recognition of the righteousness of God and his judgments.[2]

THE DEAD SEA SCROLLS

Frequent use of the צדק-words is not surprising in the writings of a community whose original leader or founder was called the 'Teacher of righteousness', whose members could refer to themselves as the 'sons of righteousness', whose expectations were fastened to God's vindicating righteousness, and whose mission was 'to practise truth, righteousness and justice in the land' (1QS 1. 5; 5. 4 and 8. 2).

The title מורה צדק or מורה הצדק may mean either (i) 'righteous teacher',[3] or (ii) 'teacher of righteousness'. In the latter case, צדק could refer either to (i) moral uprightness and standards of conduct, or to (ii) deliverance, salvation (as in Deutero-Isaiah). While it is true that the teacher taught his followers and disciples the way of salvation and redemption, as well as inculcating moral uprightness, it may be that the correct understanding of his title lies along a different path. As we have seen, the Hebrew root

---

[1] Cf. Wis. 14: 7 where δικαιοσύνη is used with such special emphasis on the idea that 'righteousness' is the basis of acceptance with God and consequent salvation that it means 'salvation'.

[2] See 2: 15; 3: 3, 5; 4: 9; 8: 7, 23, 26 and 9: 2. The same idea is often expressed in the rabbinic literature by הַצַּדִּיק or צִידֵּק (bab. Ber. 19a, etc.).

[3] The genitive of the noun in the construct state admits of interpretation as a subjective genitive.

appears to have had as its original connotation the idea of
legitimacy or rightfulness, that against which no case can be
made out, and this notion lingered in the various derived forms
throughout much of the Old Testament usage. It seems probable,
therefore, that the name מורה צדק means 'the right teacher',
that is, the legitimate one, in contradistinction to a teacher (or
priest) with falsely assumed rights.[1] This interpretation is consonant with the names given to his opponents, 'the man of
mockery', 'the man of deception'. The designation of the Community as בני צדק (1QS 3. 20; 1QM 1.8; 13. 10) probably means
that they were a company devoted to the ideal of true righteousness, who thus prepare the victory of God's righteousness.[2]

The Qumran writings frequently reiterate the prophetic
emphasis on the righteousness of God. As well as connoting his
activity (1QS 1. 21; 10. 23; 11. 3; 1QM 18. 8), 'righteousness'
also describes God's character. This finds expression particularly
in the Hymns of Thanksgiving. 'There is none righteous beside
thee' (1QH 12. 19, 31 and 16. 9) in the sense that God has the
right on his side to such an extent that none can measure himself
up alongside him:[3] 'none is justified (יצדק)[4] in thy judgment'

---

[1] Among the scholars who take the view suggested are J. L. Teicher, *JJS*,
II (1951), 97; F. M. Cross, *The Ancient Library of Qumran* (London, 1958),
p. 83, and J. T. Milik, *Ten Years of Discovery in the Wilderness of Judaea*
(London, 1959), p. 76. See also A. M. Honeyman, *JJS*, IV (1953), 131:
'The term *sedeq* refers not to the moral content of his instruction but to the
legitimacy of his status and the authenticity of his leadership, to the
"rightness" of his office rather than to the uprightness of his exhortations.'
A parallel is found in משיה הצדק (4Q Patriarchal Blessings 1. 3) which means
the 'right or legitimate Messiah'. J. Weingreen, 'The Title Moreh Sedek',
JSS, VI (1961), 162–74, discusses the use of the words in biblical and rabbinic
Hebrew and concludes that צדק has the effect of an adjective and is to be
interpreted as 'true' in the sense of genuine: 'It expresses the idea of one
publicly recognised in his title to office and in the exercise of his accredited
functions. In this association, the noun צדק has no moral content at all:
it is part of a conventional title and conveys the idea of legitimacy.'

[2] 1QH 2. 13 refers to the members of the sect as 'the chosen of righteousness'. צדק here is not a human ethical ideal: the members were not chosen
in virtue of their own righteousness. The term refers to God's righteous
judgment, dividing between the ungodly and those devoted to the truth,
cf. 1QH 7. 12.

[3] Cf. S. Holm-Nielsen, *Hodayot: Psalms from Qumran* (Aarhus, 1960), p. 207.

[4] The Hiph'il of the verb is used at 1QM 11. 14 in the sense of 'vindicate':
see J. Carmignac, *La Règle de la Guerre* (Paris, 1958), p. 166.

(1QH 9. 15). Now the declaration that righteousness belongs to God alone causes a corresponding emphasis on the frailty and sinfulness of man.[1] The speaker asserts that he has no works of righteousness (7. 17), and declares 'I know that none can be righteous (verb) apart from thee', that is, without God's will and help (16. 11); he goes on to beseech God 'by that spirit which thou hast given me, to fulfil thy mercy towards (thy servant)... and to cleanse me with thy holy spirit'. This note of what we may call 'evangelical piety' is sounded all through the Hymns. The awareness of the weakness of unaided human nature forms the background for the assertion of trust in the mercy of God and in his spirit to guide and direct life and conduct. Two passages give typical expression to this deeply spiritual theme.

I know that righteousness (צדקה) is not unto man
Neither unto the son of man the perfect way.
To the Most High God belong all the deeds of righteousness,
And the way of man cannot be made firm
Except by the spirit which God has formed for him.

But I remembered the strength of thy hand and the multitude of thy mercies,
I was restored and stood upright...
I leaned on thy compassion and thy abundant mercies,
For thou atonest for sin and (purifiest) from guilt through thy righteousness. (1QH 4. 30 ff.)

and at 1QH 7. 28 ff.:

Who is there that is righteous before thee when thou bringest him to judgment?
None is able to withstand thy wrath.
But all the children of thy truth
Thou leadest into forgiveness in thy presence,
To cleanse them from their sins in the abundance of thy goodness[2]
And by the multitude of thy mercies to set them in thy presence for ever.

The acknowledgement of sinfulness and the confidence in God's forgiving mercy which is expressed in these verses comes close to the Pauline doctrine of justification by faith, but, as M. Black

[1] See J. P. Hyatt, 'The View of Man in the Qumran Hodayot', NTS, 1 (1955–6), 276–84.
[2] Cf. 1QH 11. 30 and 13. 17.

112

has pointed out,[1] 'such religious sentiments do not only anticipate the Gospels as *praeparatio evangelica*; they are a continuation
of *Psalmenfrömmigkeit,* the sense of profound trust in God's mercy
in the Psalms, and in the prophets, especially attributed to the
Hasidim'.

The spiritual insights characteristic of the Qumran Psalms
find expression in a significant passage in 1QS 11. 3 ff. and 10 ff.

My justification (משפטי)[2] belongs to God,
The perfection of my way and the uprightness of my heart are in his
    hand;
Through his righteous acts shall my sins be blotted out...
As for me I belong to an evil humanity
And to the company of wicked flesh.

Mine iniquities, my transgressions, my sin...
Belong to...the things that move in darkness.
For a man's way is not his own,
A man cannot direct his steps
But to God belongs justification (משפט)
And from his hand comes perfection of way...
As for me, if I stumble, God's mercies shall come to my help for ever,
If I fall because of the sin of the flesh,[3]
My justification shall be established through God's righteousness
    for ever...
With righteousness and truth he has judged and justified me
And in his great goodness he will atone for all my iniquities,
In his righteousness (צדקתו) he will cleanse me from the impurity of
    man
And from the sin of the children of men.

Of the final lines of this passage Millar Burrows has said, 'In this
verse we seem to have not only justification but sanctification'[4]
and 'The point of prime importance here is that while man has
no righteousness of his own, there is a righteousness which God,
in his own righteousness, freely confers. The meaning of the

---

[1] M. Black, *The Scrolls and Christian Origins* (Edinburgh, 1961), p. 128.

[2] 'Justification' is the usual English rendering of the word here, but
probably it would be more correct to render 'the judgment which, in fact,
justifies': the sentence which is given by God is one which 'justifies' man.

[3] 'Flesh' is probably used, as in Paul, for the seat of wickedness, rather
than for the physical body. The change in man's nature is not in the ontological but in the moral realm.

[4] Cited by W. H. Brownlee, *BASOR*, Suppl. Stud. 10–12, p. 45.

righteousness of God in Rom. iii: 21–6 is thus illustrated and shown to be rooted in pre-Christian Judaism.'[1]

The language of the passage quoted is interesting. The use of the noun משפט (usually translated in the LXX by κρίμα or κρίσις) and the verb שפט implies that the act of justification has a forensic character: it is a justifying judgment.[2] That in which justification is grounded is God's צדקה,[3] and that both describes his character and connotes his action.

According to the passage quoted from 1QS the justification and cleansing of the sinner lies in the grace and mercy of God: it is accepted by man unworthily but joyfully. The whole atmosphere is one of deep trust, even though the writer does not speculate on his own faith and its value. Reliance is placed on God (as in Psalms), but in other parts of the Scrolls there is expressed a faith or confidence in the Law and in the specific revelation brought by the sect. In this connection we must refer to the passage in the Habukkuk commentary (8. 1 ff.) on the great text, Hab. 2: 4.

Its interpretation concerns all those who practice the law in the house of Judah whom God will deliver from the house of judgment because of their suffering and their fidelity to (or faith in) the Teacher of Righteousness.

Whether we translate 'fidelity to' or 'faith in'[4] the Teacher, the passage is significant in that it shows that Paul's famous text had

---

[1] *The Dead Sea Scrolls* (New York, 1955), p. 334.

[2] In Paul's usage, δικαίωμα or δικαίωσις would seem to correspond to משפט here.

[3] The noun צדקה is used, together with משפט, at 1QS 1. 5; 5. 4; 8. 2 for the ideal way of life to which the sect's members must devote themselves. This clearly connotes ethical uprightness and general standards of conduct. Later in this study, we shall see that for Paul also δικαιοσύνη, while referring specifically to God's righteousness and salvation, did describe the ethical righteousness of the believer's life.

[4] 'Fidelity' is the most natural way of rendering the word in Habukkuk and in the pesher. Burrows (*loc. cit.*) thinks that 'fidelity' is meant, but also confidence in the teacher and a belief about him. He claims that the same three elements are included also in what Paul means by 'faith' in Christ, but argues that the belief about Christ which is necessary for salvation goes much further than what was believed about the Teacher of righteousness: and the extra is the belief in the redemptive work of Christ. Recently, however, claims are being made for some kind of redemptive function for

already been used to refer to the relationship of persons to a historic and authoritative teacher.

From this brief study of the terminology of 'righteousness' in the Scrolls, we can see that the issue of justification and the means whereby God accepts the sinner were matters of lively concern within pre-Christian sectarian Judaism.[1]

THE RABBINIC LITERATURE

By way of introduction to the study of the terminology and thought of later Judaism on 'righteousness' we may take notice of the rabbinical treatment of Deut. 33:21 where, with reference to Gad, the Blessing of Moses says:

He chose the best of the land for himself, for there a commander's
  portion was reserved;
And he came to the heads of the people,
With Israel he executed the commands and just decrees of the Lord
(צִדְקַת יהוה).   (RSV translation)

It seems probable that the passage refers to the events narrated in Num. 32 when Reuben and Gad chose fertile land on the east side of Jordan and prepared to settle there, but at the command of Yahweh (made known through Moses) agreed to cross Jordan, win land for their fellow-tribes from the Canaanites and then return to their chosen territory.[2] The phrase צִדְקַת והיה may therefore be interpreted as Yahweh's 'just decision, or command', that is, the obligation placed on Gad to continue fighting before settling down.[3] The rabbinic interpretations of the verse take

the founder of the Sect. These are based on the identification of the speaker in the Hymns with the figure of the Teacher of righteousness. The language used in this connection in the Scrolls may indeed suggest a pre-Christian Jewish martyr-cult: on this see M. Black, *The Scrolls and Christian Origins*, pp. 160–1.

[1] For a study of the relations of the Pauline doctrine to the contents of the Manual, see Sherman E. Johnson, 'Paul and the Manual of Discipline', *HTR*, XLVIII (1955), 157–65.

[2] The suitability of this context to the content of the blessing suggests that *v.* 21 *b* need not be placed after *v.* 4 (referring to Moses) as some scholars think. Mid. Num. XIII, 19 gives Num. 32 as the reference by which to explain Moses' blessing of Gad.

[3] The LXX appears to have overlooked the Hebrew construct state in the phrase and so translates: δικαιοσύνην κύριος ἐποίησεν καὶ κρίσιν αὐτοῦ μετὰ Ἰσραηλ.

Moses as the subject and their rendering of the words צִדְקַת יהוה עָשָׂה is instructive. Sifre Deut. 355 expounds the phrase in terms of the blessings or benefits which Moses (after the manner of Yahweh himself) had shown to the people, especially his concern for the poor (cf. Deut. 15: 7 ff.). This interpretation clearly shows the influence of the common understanding of צדקה as 'act of charity', 'benevolence' or 'almsgiving'. The Fragment Targum (ed. M. Ginsburger, pp. 68, 90) renders the phrase literally, 'He carried out the righteousness (זכותא) of Yahweh'. Both the Pseudo-Jonathan Targum and Targum Onkelos give a somewhat extended version: the former (ed. Ginsburger, p. 364) has מטול דזכון קדם ה' עבד and the latter (ed. A. Berliner, p. 238) has זְכוָן קֳדָם יְיָ עֲבַד: both of these mean 'he wrought righteousness *before* the Lord'. A. Oepke has made use of this interpretation in Jewish commentary to prove that δικαιοσύνη θεοῦ at Rom. 1 : 17 (assuming Paul's knowledge of rabbinic exegesis) means 'the righteousness of man in the eyes of God'.[1] Apart from other criticisms to be mentioned later, this thesis may be questioned on the basis of the frequency with which the rabbis interpreted צִדְקַת יהוה as זכותא 'before God'. To substantiate his claim Oepke would have to show that this was common practice. But in Judges 5: 11 and 1 Sam. 12: 7 צִדְקַת יהוה and צִדְקוֹת יהוה are rendered in T. Jonathan by זכותא דיוי, that is, righteousness of God.[2] In fact the interpretation of Deut. 33: 21 may be unique and may be due to the association of the verse with the figure of Moses whom rabbinic exegesis always wished to exalt.

This, however, does not exhaust the interest of the passage. Its language takes us to the heart of the rabbinic teaching on righteousness. The word צְדָקָה is rendered in the Targums by a part of the root זכה (זכא). This root is found in the Old Testament usually with the meaning 'cleanse',[3] though in later Jewish writers the Piel was used with the sense 'acquit, pronounce righteous', a verdict which God was expected to give either at the Day of Atonement (Pesik. Rab. 40. 169a), or at death (bab.

[1] 'Δικαιοσύνη θεοῦ bei Paulus in neuer Beleuchtung', *TLZ*, LXXVIII (1953), 257–64.
[2] A. Sperber, *The Bible in Aramaic*: vol. 2, *The Targum Jonathan to the Former Prophets* (Leiden, 1959). At these two places he notes no variants in the other Targumim.
[3] Micah 6: 11; Ps. 73: 13—LXX δικαιόω: Ps. 119: 9—LXX κατορθόω: Job 25: 4—LXX ἀποκαθαρίζω.

Erub. 19a) or at the last judgment, on the grounds of a pre-
ponderance of good works (Midr. Ps. 143: 1, 266b; Targ. Ps.
51: 4 (6)). Jastrow lists the various meanings of the verb:[1]
(i) Qal—'to be acquitted', 'be in the right'; occasionally 'to be
worthy or privileged' and 'to benefit another by one's merit';
(ii) Piel—'to acquit', 'to transfer divine favour' and, in a more
theological sense, 'to lead to righteousness', 'to convert', 'to
make purer and better' (cf. Aboth 5: 18). The noun possesses
four main senses: (i) acquittal, favourable judgment; (ii) doing
good, blessing; (iii) the protecting and atoning influence of good
conduct, merit; and (iv) advantage, privilege, benefit. The
pattern of thought suggested by this development of meaning
would seem to be as follows: in order to win the favour of God,
right conduct is essential; one's own righteousness may be supple-
mented by the merit achieved by others, which thus becomes a
source of benefit or advantage to them. Whether or not this
sequence of ideas is chronological,[2] it is at least logical, and it
certainly reflects important aspects of rabbinic thought. Because
of their belief in the justice of God, the rabbis assumed that the
actions of a man are an important factor in the scheme of his
salvation. A man is judged according to the dominant character
of his intentions and deeds (Kid. 40b). If the majority of these are
righteous then he is accounted a 'righteous' man (צַדִּיק), but if
they are otherwise, or if even a few partake of the nature of gross
crimes and immoralities, he is adjudged 'evil' (cf. Sifre 51 b). It
is important to notice the emphasis laid on 'intention' (כַּוָּנָה).
We are guilty of a shallow understanding of Jewish ethics and
religion if we underestimate the seriousness of the demand for
the direction of a man's heart and mind towards God, both in
worship and in action. The intention to do a good act has value,
whether or not the action is carried out, because the desire to
obey is present: it is the intention to do wrong which makes the
wrong act really bad.[3] Now, in intending and carrying out the
good act, it is necessary (according to Jewish teaching) to
repress the evil impulse (יצר הרע) which incites to sin. The chief

[1] *Dictionary of the Targumim, the Talmud Babli and Yerushalmi, and the
Midrashic Literature* (London and New York, 1903).
[2] Rabbinic theology is never systematic, and chronological development
would be extremely hard to assess.
[3] Cf. T. W. Manson, *Ethics and the Gospel* (London, 1960), pp. 39–41.

means of doing this was by the study of the Torah which was the divinely-given remedy for the evil nature of man, the power before which it had to yield. It was partly because they completely repressed the evil inclination (bab. B.B. 16*b*–17*a*) and obeyed the good inclination[1] that the patriarchs were accounted perfectly righteous. Rabbinic theology, therefore, far from encouraging self-righteousness, warns each man to regard himself as partly good and partly evil, and counsels him to seek to determine his own rank by adding (by way of discipline and obedience) to the sum of his own good deeds.

According to Jewish teaching, every good act is a מִצְוָה, a divine command carried out, and every such act of obedience earns merit (זכות) for the doer in the sight of God.[2] The spiritual element is not ignored, for the good deed must be done without ulterior motive, must be performed for its own sake (לשמה) or for God's sake.

Do the words of the Law for the doing's sake and speak of them for their own sake. Make them not a crown with which to exalt thyself, or a hoe with which to weed (Ned. 62*a*).

The calculation of reward and penalty is declared to be contrary to God's intention (Deut. R. 6): these will be the *necessary* consequence of the good or evil deed. But even this causal relation is placed within the circumference of God's grace. When strict justice operates, each is judged according to his own merits acquired by his own righteousness, but the mercy of God permits a man to be judged by the sum total of all the goodness which exists in the world, in an age, in a family (cf. Gen. 18: 22 ff.). This means that merit not only benefits the person who acquired it, but also his contemporaries, and even his ancestors and his posterity, although they have no claim to the advantage.[3] The first exposition or discussion of this topic appears in a conversa-

---

[1] An early reference to יצר הטוב ('good inclination') at Test. Asher 1. 6 says, 'If the soul takes pleasure in the good impulse, all its actions are in righteousness'.

[2] According to some Rabbis, the Torah had been given in order that Israel might have the opportunity of gaining merit by her obedience to it (Makkoth 3. 16).

[3] Cf. S. Schechter, *Some Aspects of Rabbinic Theology* (London, 1909), pp. 170 ff., and A. Marmorstein, *The Doctrine of Merits in the Old Rabbinical Literature* (London, 1920).

tion between two Rabbis of the first century B.C., Shemaiah and Abtalion.[1] The problem which exercised their minds was, 'What merits did the Israelites possess that God divided the sea before them?' Shemaiah says: 'Sufficient is the *faith* with which Abraham their father believed in Me that I should divide the sea unto them, as it is said, "And he believed in God and He counted it unto him (at the sea) for doing charity (with his children)" Gen. 15: 6.' R. Abtalion says: 'Worthy is the faith, they (the Israelites themselves) believed in Me that I shall divide the sea before them, as it is said, "And the people believed" Ex. 4: 31.'[2] Two comments may be made on this discussion. It is of interest to note that in this exposition, which begins a historical review of the doctrine, we find emphasis laid, not on works and external ceremonies, but on the merit of faith in bringing about an event of national importance.[3] Secondly, the issue between the two rabbis—whether merit could be imputed or was only available for one's self—divided the scholars throughout the first century. It is obvious that a doctrine which permitted the merit of one person to benefit another is open to the abuse of fostering moral laxity,[4] and many of the rabbis were acutely aware of this and protested against it, but in time Shemaiah's view prevailed. The reason for this may well have been that the tragic course of Jewish history in the late first and early second centuries A.D. made it natural to appeal to the merits of the faithful in past ages that these might help Israel in her plight. This explanation would do justice to the fact that the twin bases of the doctrine are the assertion of God's mercy and the idea of the solidarity of the race, past, present and future.

Since the attitude of God to men was one of mercy and loving-kindness, mercy must characterise the actions of men. Consequently, the righteousness of men, which wins inestimable

---

[1] Cf. Marmorstein, *op. cit.* pp. 37 ff.

[2] Mek. Beshallah 4. The arbitrary choice of a text to confirm an interpretation and the twofold value of אמן ('to believe' and 'to have faith') resemble Paul's methods.

[3] On the merit of faith, see Marmorstein, *op. cit.* pp. 175 ff., and J. Bonsirven, *Le Judaïsme Palestinien au temps de Jésus-Christ* (Paris, 1934-5), II, 48.

[4] We know from the New Testament and from Jewish sources that many in Israel were tempted to rely on the merit of Father Abraham rather than on their own righteousness (Matt. 3: 9; John 8: 33, 39; Baba Metzia 7. 1).

merit, was almost exclusively interpreted as 'charity', 'alms-giving', 'acts of benevolence'. The real evidence of righteous-ness in a man's inner life is simply *gemilut ḥasadim*, philanthropy (Lev. R. 27). The centrality of charity in Jewish thought, and its religious basis has been well summarised by Mamorstein:

The Torah teaches faith which a Jew has to believe, and leads to works by which this belief can be kept fresh and alive. Faith must inspire man to action and work must express this faith. The climax of both joined together is lovingkindness or charity, צדקה.[1]

For the Jew, the righteousness of life and action which wins merit in the eyes of God is a duty or obligation, and the fruit of disci-pline and obedience. Nevertheless, pride in achievement is not a feature of Jewish religion, as one of the prayers in the Morning Liturgy of the Prayer Book—the depository of Israel's piety—makes clear:

Lord of all the worlds, not because of our righteous deeds do we lay our supplications before thee, but because of thine abundant mercies...[2]

THE δίκαιος-WORDS IN THE USAGE OF THE NEW TESTAMENT

1. *The Synoptic Gospels*

In the study of the word-complex in the Synoptic Gospels, the methods and findings of Form-critical analysis are employed to assist us in discovering the context in terms of which the meaning of the words may most adequately be assessed. Therefore the context treated will sometimes be the sentence or group of sentences which comprised the original kernel or main point of a pericope, as created or remembered by the Church in its mission. The Form-critical approach may also help us to discover whether or not the preaching of the Church caused (by reason of its particular situation or outlook) some alteration in, or addition to the meaning-in-use of the term.[3] We have also

---

[1] Marmorstein, *op. cit.* p. 184.

[2] *The Authorised Daily Prayer Book*, with Commentary, ed. J. H. Hertz (London, 1959), p. 27.

[3] This would appear to be a legitimate application of Form-criticism, since it is essentially a literary method: too often it has departed from its own principles by elevating itself to the level of a definitive historical method.

tried to bear in mind the fact that the particular themes or the apologetic interests which characterise an evangelist's work may be of importance in determining the meaning with which he uses a certain word: in this way, the context of meaning is extended further. One other point: we have attempted to treat separately, as far as possible, the occurrences of the words in the kerygmatic, the hortatory and the eschatological material of the Gospels.[1]

(a) δίκαιος *with the possible meaning 'innocent'*. According to Matt. 27: 4 Judas returns to the chief priests and elders the fee of betrayal with the words, 'I have sinned in betraying innocent blood (αἶμα ἀθῷον)' for which there is attested (Θ it, sa, bo, Orig.) an alternative reading αἶμα δίκαιον.[2] In the LXX αἶμα δίκαιον renders the phrase דָּם־נָקִי (usually translated αἶμα ἀθῷον) at Prov. 6: 17; Joel 4: 19; Jonah 1: 14, while δίκαιος = נָקִי (of persons) at Job 9: 23 and 17: 8. It is therefore legitimate to infer that, within this conventional phrase at least, δίκαιος (in the Old Testament and in Matthew) could bear the unusual[3] meaning 'innocent'.[4] There may, however, be other occasions on which δίκαιος has this connotation. In Matthew's account of the trial of Jesus there are two events recorded which are without parallels in the other Synoptists. The wife of Pilate advises her husband, μηδὲν σοὶ καὶ τῷ δικαίῳ ἐκείνῳ (Matt. 27: 19): and Pilate himself, after washing his hands says, 'I am

---

[1] The study owes much to A. Descamps, *Les Justes et la Justice dans les évangiles et le christianisme primitif* (Louvain, 1950) although I differ from him at several points. The linguistic discussions of ṣdḳ and δικαιόω in C. H. Dodd's *The Bible and the Greeks*, pp. 42 ff., and in *TWNT* (ET, *Righteousness*: Bible Key Words Series) are fundamental to our examination of the New Testament words, and that work is constantly assumed here, even though I may differ from the writers on some points of exegetical interpretation.

[2] There is a second alternative, τοῦ δικαίου (syˢ). It is possible that the use of δίκαιος here with the def. art. (cf. Acts 3: 14) suggests the naming of Jesus as 'the righteous one', or 'the righteous-suffering one' *par excellence*.

[3] Neither LS nor Bauer list it as a possible meaning.

[4] Gen. 20: 5 (LXX) renders בְּנִקְיֹן כַּפַּי by ἐν δικαιοσύνῃ χειρῶν and the idea of innocence rather than of righteousness is dominant. The distinction between 'righteous' and 'innocent' may at times be rather fine. When a man is declared in the right by God and therefore righteous, one would expect his juridical innocence of human charges to be recognised. But this is not necessarily the case.

innocent of the blood of this righteous man (τοῦ δικαίου τού-του) '¹ (Matt. 27: 24). While it would be unwise to claim that all suggestion of Jesus' moral uprightness is absent from the word δίκαιος here, nevertheless it is probable that the idea of innocence is important. Pilate's words occur in the trial context, and it is surely the task of judicial proceedings to declare culpability or innocence, rather than to assess the measure of a prisoner's goodness. We are obviously in touch with the Hebrew-based meaning of δίκαιος, 'in the right', which, with special reference to Jesus, may be extended to connote innocence. Moreover, if the *Sitz im Leben* of these legendary additions to the trial narrative may serve as a pointer to the meaning of δίκαιος, it is plausible to suggest that we are dealing with an apologetic claim of the early Church to the effect that the innocence of Jesus was recognised even by pagans, while the Jews were blind to it.²

A more interesting case is that presented by the words of the centurion at the Cross, in Luke 23: 47—'Surely this man was δίκαιος', where both Matthew and Mark have υἱός θεοῦ. Why is this alteration made? What is the meaning of δίκαιος? Let us assume, with some of the champions of the Proto-Luke hypothesis,³ that the reason for Luke's substituting δίκαιος for υἱός θεοῦ is his use of his non-Markan Passion source. Now examination of Luke's Passion narrative reveals a special interest in the legal guiltlessness of Jesus.⁴ It is declared three times by Pilate (23: 4, 14, 22), once by Herod (23: 15) and by one of the thieves (23: 41). All of these are without parallels in Mark and Matthew and consequently may be claimed to belong to the non-Markan source. If this is what Luke is following, then it would seem legitimate to suggest that δίκαιος in *v.* 47 means 'innocent'.⁵ If, on the other hand, we assume that Luke is deliberately altering the Markan reading, then we must ask why he did so.

¹ Nestle prefers the reading without τοῦ δικαίου, though the words are found in the **א** text.

² Cf. *TWNT*, ΙΙ, 189.

³ E.g. V. Taylor, *Behind the Third Gospel* (Oxford, 1926), pp. 52–9.

⁴ This theme is taken into account by G. D. Kilpatrick, 'A Theme of the Lucan Passion story and Luke 23: 47', *JTS*, XLIII (1942), 34–6. With Kilpatrick's dismissal of the Proto-Luke hypothesis we are not concerned here.

⁵ The RSV so translates: cf. *TWNT*, ΙΙ, 189.

Some suggest, on the basis of Wisdom 2: 18, that the two terms are almost equivalent, υἱὸς θεοῦ meaning 'a faithful man loved by God'. But if that is how Luke understood the Markan υἱὸς θεοῦ, we are obliged to say that he altered it solely for the sake of variety of expression. If it is argued that Luke realised that υἱὸς θεοῦ might be interpreted by Gentiles as akin to the Hellenistic θεῖος ἄνηρ, we must still ask why he changed it to δίκαιος, a word which, if it means 'righteous or upright', does little to clarify the Markan interpretation of υἱὸς θεοῦ. On the whole, it seems preferable to suggest that, if Luke was deliberately altering the Markan source, the use of δίκαιος to mean 'innocent' makes the change more worthwhile and accords with Luke's special theme. For our own part, we incline to the view that Luke was following a non-Markan source at this point, rather than altering Mark: in fact, Mark may have originated the change.[1] But what is of importance for our purpose is that, on either assumption, 'innocent' (*absolutely* 'in the right') is the most satisfactory rendering of δίκαιος.

(*b*) δίκαιος *used of those who wait for or prepare for the Incarnation.* According to Luke 1: 6 the parents of John the Baptist were 'both righteous (δίκαιοι) before God, walking in all the commandments of the Lord, blameless'. There is no difficulty in interpreting δίκαιοι here: these are the faithful and obedient ones (cf. the 'righteous' in the Psalms) who, by reason of their piety and devotion, are worthy to be the parents of the Fore-runner.[2] A similar connotation is evident at *v.* 17 where it is stated that the tasks of the Fore-runner will include, '... to return the rebellious to the wisdom of the righteous', whose righteousness presumably consists in obedience and preparedness for the fulfilment of the promises made to Israel. Whatever be the origin of the Lucan Infancy narratives, a part of the purpose for which the author used them was to demonstrate that the signs of the fulfilment of Israel's hopes were manifested to and recognised by pious Jews, such as Simeon, 'righteous and devout, waiting for the

[1] On the Lucan Passion narrative, see H. Schürmann, *Quellenkritische Untersuchung des lukanischen Abendmahlsberichtes, Luke xxii. 7–38* (Münster, 1953–8) and in *NTS*, vi (1959–60), 193–210.

[2] Cf. G. W. H. Lampe, *New Peake: Luke*, p. 824): 'Here the narrative is moving wholly within the sphere of the piety of the old covenant and the language is correspondingly Septuagintal.'

consolation of Israel' (2: 25) where δίκαιος connotes a man faithful to God and approved to him in spirit and life.[1]

The Gospel of Matthew applies the term δίκαιος to one only of the forebears of Jesus. It says of Joseph, at 1: 19, 'being a just man (δίκαιος ὤν) and unwilling to put her (Mary) to shame, he resolved to divorce her quietly'. Here δίκαιος means 'in the right' before the law in divorcing an unchaste wife-to-be (cf. Deut. 22: 13 ff.). The interpretation of the adjective should not be governed by the clause 'unwilling to put her to shame' so as to make it mean 'discreet' or 'magnanimous'.[2] Joseph's magnanimity is evidenced by his taking advantage of the legal possibility of private divorce before two witnesses (cf. Num. 5: 11–31; M. Sotah 1. 5): but δίκαιος clearly describes Joseph as a man resolved to observe the law conscientiously.

Concerning the death of John the Baptist we read at Mark 6: 20 —'Herod feared John knowing that he was a holy and righteous man' (while Matt. 14: 5 puts it, 'He feared the people, because they held him [John] to be a prophet'). The epithet ἅγιος is never used of men in Hellenistic texts, but in the LXX it is applied to Israelites and especially to priests who were consecrated to the service of God. This association suggests that δίκαιος here bears the meaning 'pious', that is, obedient to the will and law of God, similar to the use of צַדִּיק (δίκαιος) in the Psalms.

In the course of a Matthean passage which deals with the opposition of leading Jews to Jesus we find this statement concerning John the Baptist: 'John came to you in the way of righteousness (ἐν ὁδῷ δικαιοσύνης) and you did not believe him: but the tax-collectors and harlots believed him' (Matt. 21: 32). A. H. McNeile interprets the important phrase as 'with the path of righteousness', that is, with the message of righteousness, and compares for this meaning of ὁδός, Matt. 22: 16; Acts 16: 17 and 18: 25.[3] This view implies that δικαιοσύνη refers to the

---

[1] In the same category we may place the description of Joseph of Arimathea 'a good and righteous man...who was looking for the Kingdom of God' (Luke 23: 50).

[2] So C. Spicq, *RB*, LXI (April 1964), 206–14: see my note in *ET*, LXXVI (January 1965), 133–4.

[3] *The Gospel according to St Matthew* (London, 1915), p. 308. McNeile regards the ἐν as introducing a dative of accompaniment or attendant circumstances, cf. 1 Cor. 4: 21.

'righteousness' which John laid as a standard upon others, and not simply to his own personal righteousness in obedience and saintliness.[1] Consideration of the context suggests that this understanding of the term is basically correct. Verses 28 ff. deal with the refusal of the chief priests to repent and believe in order to enter the Kingdom: these were the obligations of John's baptism, and in fact the connecting link in the passage is the theme of John's baptism, vv. 23–7 dealing with the rejection of its authority and vv. 28–32 with the refusal of its demands.[2] In that case, δικαιο-σύνη must refer to the righteousness which John demanded from those who heard his message:[3] and it is the righteousness of life which comes from obedience to the divine will. We cannot exclude, therefore, its application to John himself, for as P. Benoit rightly says, 'John preached and practised that conformity to the will of God which makes a man righteous'.[4]

The mention of John's baptism leads to consideration of the words of Jesus in accepting that baptism: 'Let it be so now; for thus it is fitting for us to fulfil all righteousness (πληρῶσαι πᾶσαν δικαιοσύνην)', Matt. 3: 15. Matthew alone introduces into the narrative of Jesus' baptism the dialogue with John, and its presence may reflect an attempt to solve the problem (which existed for the Church) of Jesus' accepting water-baptism from his inferior. It is clear from John's words, 'I need to be baptised by you and do you come to me?', that he recognises the personal superiority of Jesus, but, with that recognition given, the evangelist goes on to indicate expressly the motive for Jesus' submission to John's baptism—'thus it is fitting for us to fulfil all righteousness'. Some exegetes interpret these words as meaning

[1] W. Michaelis, *TWNT*, v, 90, claims that John's own righteousness is meant, rather than that required by him of others.

[2] This is probably corroborated by a parallel passage in Luke 7: 29–30— 'When they heard this, all the people and the tax-collectors justified God, having been baptised with the baptism of John; but the Pharisees and the lawyers rejected the purpose of God for themselves, not having been baptised by him.' E. Lohmeyer, *Das Urchristentum*, I, *Johannes der Taufer* (Göttingen, 1932), p. 103 note 1, claims that in the phrase 'in the way of righteousness', δικαιοσύνη is tantamount to 'baptism' as the way to eschatological well-being.

[3] So also SB, I, 866 ff.; G. Schrenk, *TWNT*, II, 201, and G. Bornkamm, *Tradition and Interpretation in Matthew* (London, 1963), p. 28 note 1.

[4] La Sainte Bible, *L'Évangile selon S. Matthieu* (Paris, 1961), p. 132; also G. Strecker, *Der Weg der Gerechtigkeit* (Göttingen, 1962), p. 187.

that Jesus acknowledges that 'every righteous ordinance', including baptism, must be observed.[1] But if δικαιοσύνη means 'righteous ordinance' it is very strange in Matthean usage: why was δικαίωμα not used, a word which, elsewhere in the New Testament, means 'ordinance' or 'righteous act'?[2] Moreover, while the verb πληροῦν can be used in the sense of 'conform to' or 'fulfil (and thus obey) a command', it is always used by Matthew to point to the completion or fulfilment of the Old Covenant in the new realities of the Kingdom.

Recently Oscar Cullmann has suggested[3] that, in submitting to John's baptism, Jesus was identifying himself with the Suffering Servant who takes upon himself the sin of his people. Others came to be baptised for their own sins but Jesus was baptised for the sins of all others in the baptism of his death, of which there is anticipatory notice in this phrase. Therefore, for Cullmann, πληρῶσαι πᾶσαν δικαιοσύνην means 'to effect or acquire righteousness (pardon) for all', echoing Isa. 42: 1 'He will bring forth justice (מִשְׁפָּט, κρίσις) for the nations'. In spite of the possibility that Isa. 42: 1 may lie behind v. 17 ('in whom I am well pleased') is this not a forced interpretation of this peculiarly Matthean expression? It is unusual and non-Matthean for πληροῦν to mean 'procure, acquire', and the use of πᾶσαν δικαιοσύνην to mean 'righteousness for all' is a Pauline form of expression. Cullmann's exegesis seems to be dominated by the Suffering Servant motif and to disregard entirely Matthean usage. Is there another interpretation of the phrase more consonant with Matthew's use of πληρόω and δικαιοσύνη? The contextual reference of the words is to John's baptism; δικαιοσύνη does not simply refer to the righteous character of that baptism as something which conforms to the divine will and which must therefore be accepted: rather it refers to the righteousness of life which was the demand laid on those who accepted that baptism (cf. Matt. 21: 32). By submitting to John's baptism Jesus acknowledges this standard of righteousness as valid for

---

[1] E.g. Loisy, Lagrange, Klostermann, Montefiore, McNeile.

[2] For the reiteration of this criticism and for the suggestion that to understand δικαιοσύνη in this way makes baptism a purely formal act, a ceremony which is fulfilled merely because it is commanded, see *Tradition and Interpretation in Matthew*, p. 138.

[3] *Baptism in the New Testament* (ET, London, 1950), pp. 18–19.

himself and others; but more than that, he affirms the fact that he must realise and establish it (πληρῶσαι) in its entirety (πᾶσαν) as the will of God in the kingdom. δικαιοσύνη therefore bears its Septuagintal meaning of 'righteousness of life' through obedience which is in accordance with the divine will.[1] This interpretation is consonant with Matthew's special use of the term and to that we now turn.

(c) δικαιοσύνη *in Matthew*. The term δικαιοσύνη appears five times in the Sermon on the Mount. Of these the first is in the Beatitude, 'Blessed are those who hunger and thirst for righteousness, for they shall be satisfied' (5: 6). Luke has probably preserved the more original form of the Beatitude, referring to the physical hunger of the poor but devoted saints of God:[2] 'Blessed are ye that hunger, for ye shall be filled.' As in the first Beatitude, Matthew expounds the Lucan form in the interests of clarification and stresses the spiritual character of the hunger. The righteousness which the poor desire intensely is life in accordance with God's will through obedience to God's law. δικαιοσύνη here means more than 'goodness': it is the righteousness of obedience which God desires and approves. The common interpretation of the word here as 'divine eschatological salvation' or 'the vindicating righteousness of God in action' does not seem to be correct.[3] This interpretation is based on the meaning of δικαιοσύνη

[1] G. Strecker, *Der Weg der Gerechtigkeit*, p. 179, considers that the passage comes from a redactor and that δικαιοσύνη means no more than 'right conduct' as it should be carried out by disciples. G. Barth, *Tradition and Interpretation in Matthew*, pp. 140–1, suggests that πᾶσαν δικαιοσύνην refers to the whole will of God which Jesus fulfils himself in that he, as the Messiah-Judge of the world, humbles himself and enters into the ranks of sinners, acts for sinners (cf. G. Bornkamm, *TBlätt.* XVII [1938], pp. 44 ff.). K. Stendahl (Matthew, in *New Peake*, p. 773) speaks of Jesus fulfilling 'the plan of God, which, in Matthew, has righteousness as its ultimate goal'. This view may be incorporated in the total theological significance of the passage, but it stands at some distance from its actual language.

[2] Cf. T. W. Manson, *Sayings of Jesus* (London, 1949), p. 47. Also Ps. Sol. 10: 6.

[3] G. Schrenk (*Righteousness*, p. 35) also suggests that there is no need to think of the judging and saving righteousness of God in a forensic eschatological sense. G. Barth (*Tradition and Interpretation in Matthew*, pp. 123–4) appears, at first, to want to hold together the two meanings: 'they long that God will pronounce upon them in the judgment the verdict "righteous": they long for the rightness of disposition which is acceptable to God.' Yet, in a note, he criticises Schrenk's view that δικαιοσύνη is 'rightness of

in Isaiah and the Psalms (LXX), but it would be unique in Matthean usage: moreover, the gospels do not suggest that the saving action of God comes as a response to human desire, however intense; the attitude of fear and vigilance is more often enjoined upon man as his proper disposition. Those who interpret δικαιοσύνη in terms of the divine activity or God's righteous verdict at 5: 6 do not insist on that meaning at 5: 10: 'Blessed are those who are persecuted (perf.) for righteousness' sake, for theirs is the kingdom of heaven.' The reference is quite obviously to the saints who were down-trodden and despised because of their fidelity to the will and law of God, and probably including the ancient prophets and martyrs who suffered persecution for their obedience (cf. v. 12).[1] The meaning of δικαιοσύνη here is not otherwise than at 5: 6: it is the true righteousness of life through obedience to the word and will of God. The occurrence of δικαιοσύνη at v. 20 in the same chapter ('I tell you, unless your righteousness exceeds that of the scribes and Pharisees, you will never enter the Kingdom of heaven') must, when considered in its context, mean the righteousness of obedience, that faithfulness to the will of God as expressed in the law—that law which Jesus truly establishes (πληρῶσαι, v. 17) but which had been perverted through casuistry by the scribes and Pharisees.[2]

We come now to Matt. 6: 1—'Beware of practising your righteousness before men in order to be seen by them (lit.)'. It is well known that in later Hebrew, both biblical and rabbinical, צְדָקָה could mean 'benevolence' and was translated by ἐλεημο-

disposition' because (he says) it is said that the righteousness is bestowed, and it therefore cannot mean anything else but that God pronounces them righteous in the judgment. But is this necessarily the case? Surely the true righteousness of disposition through obedience leads to divine gift also (cf. Isa. 56: 1; Prov. 21: 21). This is, in fact, what Strecker (*Der Weg der Gerechtigkeit*, p. 157) claims. He reviews both interpretations of the word, but decides for human righteousness. The desire for this righteousness is not passive waiting, but active obedience: and its full realisation is the gift of God, pp. 157–8.

[1] On this possibility, see K. Stendahl, Matthew, in *New Peake*, pp. 775–6. The general reference to persecution in v. 10 is made particular, with reference to the disciples (and the Church), in v. 11, which probably hints at the condition of the Church face to face with Judaism: see W. D. Davies, *The Setting of the Sermon on the Mount* (Cambridge, 1964), pp. 289–90.

[2] At this point the Special-M tradition may have been formed in a Judeo-Christian, anti-Pharisaic milieu.

σύνη (e.g. Dan. 4: 24). Therefore it is sometimes suggested that δικαιοσύνη here is synonymous with ἐλεημοσύνη in *v.* 2, and means 'almsgiving' or 'benevolence'.[1] This would be an unusual use of the noun in the Sermon on the Mount and in Matthew's Gospel as a whole: it would also make 'alms' in *v.* 2 almost redundant. Consequently it is preferable to regard *v.* 1 as an introductory statement to the subsequent teaching on almsgiving, prayer and fasting (note the three occurrences of ὅταν in *vv.* 2, 5, 16).[2] ποιεῖν δικαιοσύνην will then mean something like 'to practise piety' and δικαιοσύνη will be regarded as a general title for acts of devotion and religious duty which conform to the will of God and which are part of a total righteousness of life.

The last occurrence of the noun in Matthew is at 6: 33—'Seek ye first the kingdom and his (its) righteousness and all these things will be added unto you as well'. For Matthew the Kingdom is not a purely eschatological reality,[3] but a present possibility in the lives of those who acknowledge the sovereignty of God. It is present in the person of Jesus and with it also the righteousness of the Kingdom (or God's righteousness). Accordingly, the word δικαιοσύνη must denote 'rightness of life' before God, conduct in agreement with his will, at the heart of which lies the disposition of obedience and devotion.

From the preceding discussion we can see that there is consistency in the Matthean usage of δικαιοσύνη. It refers to uprightness of life, behaviour that is acceptable to God through fidelity to his will and law. The single instance of the noun in Luke (1: 75) is not otherwise. The Benedictus conforms completely to and expresses, in the emotional language of liturgy, the hope of the Old Covenant (both nationalistic and spiritual), '...that we, being delivered from the hand of our enemies, might serve him without fear, in holiness and righteousness before him all our days', where δικαιοσύνη means 'righteousness of life' through obedience. Having thus found a consistent

---

[1] C. H. Dodd, *The Bible and the Greeks*, p. 46 note 1.

[2] So Schrenk, *Righteousness*, p. 36, and G. Barth, *Tradition and Interpretation in Matthew*, p. 139. G. Bornkamm, *Tradition and Interpretation in Matthew*, p. 30, calls it 'the all-embracing notion for the piety of the disciples as a whole'.

[3] Only if βασιλεία was purely eschatological would δικαιοσύνη refer to God's saving activity.

use of the noun in the Gospels, we must now turn to the occurrences of the adjective δίκαιος to see if they corroborate this finding.

(d) δίκαιος *and* δικαιόω *in the Synoptic Gospels.* Some of the occurrences of δίκαιος we have already dealt with, where the meaning seems to be 'innocent'.[1] At Matt. 5: 45, the Father in heaven is described as one who 'makes his sun rise on the evil and on the good, and sends rain on the just (δικαίους) and the unjust'. The context of this affirmation is the exhortation to the disciples to cultivate a benevolent attitude towards their opponents, for thus shall they be the children of their Father who does not discriminate in giving his gifts. The point is not that God is indifferent to moral worth, but that his impartiality is due to his merciful kindness. The traditional Jewish distinction between the righteous or upright in God's sight and the unrighteous is upheld; but the orthodox idea that, by virtue of their superiority, the righteous have privileges over sinners is absent. And the righteous are those who seek to obey God's will.

A more significant case of δίκαιος appears at Mark 2: 17 (Matt. 9: 13; Luke 5: 32): 'I come not to call the righteous, but sinners.' With most commentators we interpret καλέσαι of the call to the Kingdom or to repentance (so Luke) rather than of the invitation of a host.[2] Many exegetes regard this saying as an ironical statement of Jesus and interpret the word δίκαιοι as referring to those who *think* themselves righteous, but who in fact are not.[3] The chief consideration on which this view is based is that of context. The utterance of Jesus comes at the end of a narrative in which the scribes and Pharisees (or the scribes of the Pharisees) have challenged the friendship of Jesus with sinners and publicans. It is assumed therefore that Jesus is hinting at the insincerity of their claims to righteousness. But is this the most

---

[1] We may also note that at Matt. 20: 4, 7 and Luke 12: 57 the neuter adj. (δίκαιον) or noun (τὸ δίκαιον) bears the meaning 'that which is fair and just' in a legal sense; cf. Arist. *NE.* 5. 1129a.

[2] The controversy in the early Church regarding table-fellowship may have led to the preservation of the saying and may have influenced the narrative.

[3] E.g. E. Klostermann, *Das Markusevangelium* (2nd ed., Tübingen, 1926); A. H. McNeile, *The Gospel according to St Matthew*; Hoskyns and Davey, *The Riddle of the New Testament* (London, 1947); and V. Taylor, *The Gospel according to St Mark*, p. 207.

likely interpretation of the saying? We may observe that (i) by giving this meaning to δικαίους, the parallelism with the preceding 'proverbial' utterance is lost: οἱ ἰσχύοντες means 'those who are well', not 'those who think they are well'; (ii) we do not find in the Gospels any other occasion on which δίκαιοι by itself is used in an ironical sense.[1] It seems preferable therefore to regard the utterance as having a straightforward meaning.[2] The δίκαιοι are those who truly live or seek to live in accordance with God's law and will: they are not the object of Jesus' mission. 'The ordinary standards are recognised and the zeal of the "righteous" is acknowledged.'[3] This view preserves the parallelism in the verse and it is strengthened by Luke 15: 7 (which echoes the language of the verse discussed and deals with the same Pharisaic challenge): 'There is joy in heaven over one sinner repenting more than over ninety-nine just persons (δίκαιοι) who do not need repentance.' There is no suggestion of irony here: the 'righteous' are those who remain faithful and obedient to the demands of God. If we interpret δίκαιοι at Mark 2: 17 and parallels to mean the 'zealously righteous', how are we to answer the argument based on context? It should be remembered that Mark 2: 13–17 is an Apothegm or pronouncement story. The emphasis really lies on the utterance of Jesus: the narrative serves as framework, and it may be that the anti-Pharisaic tendency on the part of the evangelist[4] has left its mark on the story, which should therefore not be allowed to influence too strongly the interpretation of the dominical saying.[5] It would seem that if we take the utterance by itself (as an original logion, or at least as being true to the spirit of Jesus), then the word δίκαιοι will bear the usual sense of the faithful and obedient ones of Israel. But if, on the other hand, we integrate

[1] Cf. the expressions in Matt. 23: 28; Luke 18: 9 and 20: 20.

[2] E.g. Loisy, Lagrange and Schlatter. Stendahl, *New Peake*: Matthew, p. 782, does not exclude the possibility that 'Jesus recognises his opponents as in some sense acceptable to God, only pleading for a place also for the despised'.

[3] Schrenk, *Righteousness*, p. 22.

[4] This tendency in the Gospels reflects the later controversy between Church and Synagogue: not all the Pharisees in Jesus' time were unscrupulous and hypocritical, and indeed probably few were.

[5] That is, if we regard 17*b* as original, and not (with Bultmann and Dibelius) as a doctrinal expansion.

the saying closely with the controversy-narrative as it now stands, then it is possible that δίκαιοι may have an ironical connotation.[1] This is one occasion on which a saying of Jesus may have had its meaning altered in the use made of it by an evangelist.

In the course of the Matthean account of the invective against the scribes and Pharisees, Jesus criticises them thus: 'You outwardly appear righteous (δίκαιοι) to men, but within you are full of hypocrisy and iniquity' (23: 28). The second part of the verse implies that sincerity and obedience to the law are the marks of the righteous man: these qualities the Pharisees lack, although they wish to be thought to possess them.[2] Again, the parable of the Pharisee and the publican at prayer is directed to 'some who trusted in themselves (because) that they were righteous and despised others' (Luke 18: 9). The words 'trusted in themselves' should be taken literally: they do not mean 'considered themselves to be righteous', but 'believed in themselves' or 'relied on themselves' (cf. Luke 11: 22; 2 Cor. 1: 9): consequently ὅτι should be rendered as 'because' rather than 'that'.[3] The Pharisees had confidence in themselves because they were able to live up to their standards. Their achievements in piety and morality—which merited their being called 'righteous'—created self-reliance rather than a humble trust in God, and caused them to despise those who did not acknowledge their standard or who failed to live up to it. The publican, the sinner by any standard, 'went down to his house justified (δεδικαιω-μένος) rather than the other (παρ᾽ ἐκεῖνον)'. What is the meaning of 'justified' here? Does it refer to forgiveness, or (as Schrenk suggests)[4] to judicial absolution, as in Paul, but without the reference to the Cross? The latter is closer to the right understanding. The attitude of the publican comprises confession and appealing trust in God's mercy.[5] Despite his sinful record, this

---

[1] Matthew's redactional addition, ἔλεος θέλω καὶ οὐ θυσίαν (Hos. 6: 6) may suggest that this is how he meant the word to be interpreted, if this quotation implies criticism of Israel's religion as insincere.

[2] Cf. Luke 20: 20 for a similar use of the word: 'spies who pretended to be righteous', that is, upright, even scrupulously law-abiding.

[3] Cf. T. W. Manson, *The Sayings of Jesus*, p. 309. He points out that while spiritual pride was a constant danger in Pharisaism not all Pharisees were guilty of it.　　　　[4] Schrenk, *Righteousness*, p. 60.

[5] We may recall the quality of the piety of the Psalms (*Psalmenfrömmigkeit*) and of the Qumran Hodayot—a humble trust in God's forgiveness and

approach means that he is accepted as 'in the right' with God, whereas the self-satisfied Pharisee is not.[1]

In another context concerned with condemnation of the Pharisees Luke puts the following words on the lips of Jesus:

You are those who justify themselves (οἱ δικαιοῦντες ἑαυτούς) before men, but God knows your hearts: for what is exalted among men is an abomination in the sight of God (16: 15).

This saying of Jesus which condemns pride is only very artificially connected with what precedes it by the words 'who were lovers of money', and the Pharisees, in fact, were not specially noted for love of wealth. T. W. Manson makes the attractive suggestion[2] that if the Sadducees were the object of criticism it would fit better with the wider context and would give a word-play within the saying: 'You who justify yourselves' may mean 'you who by taking the name "Sadducee" make public claim to be the party of righteousness': but God looks deeper and sees that the bearers of the name do not possess the reality within. It is the failure to possess the real righteousness which comes from obedience and humility that is the weakness of those criticised. Likewise, at Luke 10: 29, the young lawyer (after receiving Jesus' answer to his question about eternal life) wishes to 'justify himself (δικαιῶσαι ἑαυτόν)' and asks 'Who is my neighbour?'. The Hithpael of צדק is translated at Gen. 44: 16 by the passive of δικαιόω where the meaning is 'to make oneself out to be in the right' or 'to clear oneself of a charge'. It is possible that the active voice (with the reflexive pronoun (as at 16: 15)) bears the same connotation. The lawyer wishes to vindicate himself for failing to do his duty by asking a question which implies that he did not know where precisely that duty lay.

(e) δίκαιος, etc., in eschatological contexts. We come now to

mercy as the only source of acceptance. Together with these expressions of faith, this parable is in some measure an anticipation of the essential spirit of the Pauline doctrine of justification. Cf. T. W. Manson, On Paul and John (London, 1963), p. 55, 'This parable of the Pharisee and the Publican is the connecting link between Jesus and Paul in the matter of justification': also G. W. H. Lampe, New Peake: Luke, para. 731g, p. 838.

[1] παρ' ἐκεῖνον is used in an exclusive sense, like Hebrew מִן.

[2] The Sayings of Jesus, p. 295. The name 'Sadducee' is connected with the root צדק, 'be righteous', and that root is employed to render 'justify yourselves' in the Palestinian Aramaic version of this verse.

those occasions on which the words we are discussing appear in eschatological contexts. The verb is used only once in this type of material.

I tell you, on the day of judgment men will render account for every careless word (ῥῆμα) they utter; for by your words (ἐκ τῶν λόγων) you will be justified (δικαιωθήσῃ) and by your words you will be condemned (Matt. 12: 36–7).

The unexpected change from the 3rd person plural to the 2nd person singular suggests that *v.* 36 is being supported by the quotation of a proverbial saying. However that may be, an eschatological reference is present in the saying, for there is rabbinical evidence for the belief that a man's record, as kept in heaven, included his words, even his harmless utterances, as well as his acts.[1] The verses clearly assert that the words of men are at least part of the basis on which final acceptance with God, final justification, is adjudged.

In the interpretation of the Parable of the Tares we meet this statement: 'Then will the righteous (οἱ δίκαιοι) shine like the sun in the kingdom of their father' (Matt. 13: 43). The verse probably reflects LXX Dan. 12: 3 which promises that in the Resurrection οἱ συνιέντες (LXX and Theod.) ἐκλάμψουσι (Theod.) ὡς φωστῆρες τοῦ οὐρανοῦ (ὡς ἡ λαμπρότης τοῦ στερεώματος Theod.). Here and elsewhere in Daniel (11: 33, 35) οἱ συνιέντες (for which Matthew has οἱ δίκαιοι) represents הַמַּשְׂכִּילִים, a term which is parallel and equivalent to 'those who turn many to righteousness' and which connotes people of understanding who by teaching and example guide others. It is therefore possible that in the use of δίκαιοι Matthew is hinting at the function and fate of true disciples in instructing others towards righteousness. Unlike the causes of offence and the evil-doers, those to whom bliss is promised will have guided others in the right way: theirs will have been a righteousness of life and also of action and service as teachers.[2] At *v.* 49 of the same chapter, the angels are stated to have charge of separating the evil from the righteous (ἐκ μέσου τῶν δικαίων). Again the word refers to those who are acceptable to God at the End because of the

---

[1] SB, i, 639f.

[2] I have developed this argument in greater detail in 'Δίκαιοι as a quasi-technical Term', *NTS*, xi (1964–5), 296–302.

quality of their life and service. If the *Sitz im Leben* of the entire parable in the teaching ministry of Jesus is concern over the problem of who belongs to the kingdom of God, the meaning of 'righteous' is not altered.

In the Matthean parable of the Last Judgment we find that the righteous (δίκαιοι) ask questions about their service and enter into eternal life (Matt. 25: 37, 46). Whether or not πάντα τὰ ἔθνη (*v.* 32) means 'all people' or 'all Gentiles', it is clear that the 'righteous' are those who did good deeds to the brethren of Christ, united with him in the solidarity of the 'Son of man'. Kindness to the poor and suffering finds wide recognition in Jewish writings as a means of meriting salvation:[1] here it is regarded as an evidence of being on the side of the Kingdom of God and as such is a ground of acceptance with God.

(*f*) δίκαιος *in association with 'prophet' and 'martyr'*. In Matthew's gospel the terms προφήτης and δίκαιος are brought into close association on three occasions; twice in the plural form, 13: 17 and 23: 29, and once in the singular, 10: 41. It is noteworthy that on the only other occasion in the gospel when 'prophets' are similarly associated with a class or group, those mentioned are 'wise men and scribes': 'I send to you (the scribes and Pharisees) prophets and wise men and scribes (προφήτας καὶ σοφοὺς καὶ γραμματεῖς), some of whom you will kill and crucify, and some you will scourge...and persecute...' (23: 34). These words have a forward-looking reference: Jesus' own envoys are meant (cf. Luke 11: 49; Matt. 10: 17, 23). It is therefore likely that the terms used of the emissaries reflect conditions in the early Church. On this view, it is plausible to suggest that we have here a reference to the two aspects of Christian missionary work, proclamation (κήρυγμα) and teaching (διδαχή, διδασκαλία), the former being the activity of the προφῆται, and the latter of the σοφοί and γραμματεῖς, that is, the men of understanding and the διδάσκαλοι of the Jewish-Christian community.[2]

---

[1] Cf. Ned. 40*a*. The best rabbinic thought placed 'performance of kindnesses' on a higher level than mere almsgiving, cf. Sukk. 49*b*; Aboth 1. 2—'On three things the world stands: on Torah, the worship, and the performance of kindnesses'.

[2] Cf. G. D. Kilpatrick, *The Origins of the Gospel according to St Matthew* (Oxford, 1946), pp. 110ff., 126; also G. Strecker, *Der Weg der Gerechtigkeit*,

In the same Woe-saying as that in which the text just discussed appears we find the declaration that the Scribes and Pharisees hypocritically 'build up the tombs of the prophets and adorn the monuments of the righteous (τὰ μνημεῖα τῶν δικαίων)' (Matt. 23: 29). It seems certain that οἱ δίκαιοι here means more than the saintly and obedient servants of God in old time: the 'righteous' are those who, because of their piety and obedience, were persecuted, even to death: they are the martyrs of the Old Testament who sealed their testimony to righteousness with their blood. Now, in the biblical understanding of 'martyrs' and 'martyrdom' the emphasis firmly lies on the idea of witness and witnessing: the martyrs are pre-eminently those who have faithfully witnessed to God's truth, and the unfavourable reception accorded to their prophetic message resulted in their being put to death. Accordingly, when we interpret δίκαιοι in Matt. 23: 29 to mean 'righteous martyrs' we should acknowledge that the idea of witness, of teaching or declaring the will and judgments of God, adheres to the term as well: the 'righteous' are those who faithfully testified and they can be reckoned among the teachers whom Israel rejected.

We turn now to Matt. 13: 17 where Jesus speaks of the privilege which the disciples have in experiencing the present reality of the Kingdom. What was for the best men of the past only an object of faith and hope has become for them a matter of present experience. 'Many prophets and righteous men (πολλοὶ προφῆται καὶ δίκαιοι) longed to see what you see and did not see it, and to hear what you hear and did not hear it.' It is probable that Luke 10: 24 has preserved the more original form of this logion: Matthew has taken it and made it refer to the general use of parables and at the same time has changed the collocation to 'prophets and righteous men'. Who are these δίκαιοι? The Matthean form and context of the saying suggest that they are more than simply upright and saintly men who desired the fulfilment of the Kingdom: they are men who, like the prophets, had eyes open to search for the purpose of God, and who, again like the prophets, sought to disclose their understanding of God's will to an unheeding audience. The term may refer obliquely to

pp. 37–8. Matt. 13: 52 confirms the view that the Christian 'scribe' had a teaching function. Acts 13: 1 and Didache 15. 1 link 'teachers' (διδάσκαλοι) with 'prophets'.

those who followed the prophets in the post-exilic period, namely, the scribes or teachers of the law who, when they were faithful, may be rightly described as having desired to see the Kingdom. The disciples have the advantage over these in that they now experience that for which the seers and teachers of old earnestly hoped.

Does the suggestion that δίκαιος, when found in conjunction with προφήτης, contains an allusion to a witnessing or teaching function help us in interpreting Matt. 10: 41? At the conclusion of the Mission-charge to the disciples, Jesus declares:

40. He that receiveth you receiveth me, and he that receiveth me receiveth him that sent me (Q, or possibly M). 41. He that receiveth a prophet in the name of a prophet shall receive a prophet's reward: and he that receiveth a righteous man (δίκαιον) in the name of a righteous man shall receive a righteous man's reward (M).

Some commentators[1] admit that *v.* 41 (peculiar to Matthew) belongs to the time of Jewish Christianity, when Christian prophets were a recognised class distinct from the apostles. This seems a correct observation, but no commentator allows it to affect the interpretation of δίκαιος. This word is understood as referring to followers of Christ who practise the righteousness which exceeds that of the scribes and Pharisees: they are people who exemplify faithful, upright living. However, in view of the context of the verse and because it belongs to Matthew's special material, it seems plausible to suggest that δίκαιος, like προφή-της, may refer to a semi-distinct class in the early Church. As at 23: 34, Matthew may be alluding to the preaching and teaching functions. If δίκαιος is understood as an archaic way of referring to 'teacher', the passage yields a greater sense. The person who receives a prophet in the name of a prophet (i.e. for his own sake as a prophet, or in his capacity as a prophet) will receive the reward which the prophet gives: he will hear the *proclamation* of God's message. He that receives a righteous man (teacher?) in the name of a righteous man will receive the reward offered by the righteous man:[2] he will be *instructed* in the understanding of

---

[1] E.g. A. H. McNeile, *The Gospel according to St Matthew*, p. 149; P. A. Micklem, *St Matthew* (Westminster Commentary, London), p. 108.

[2] Thus προφήτου and δικαίου are interpreted as genitives *originis*, not as objective genitives: cf. the construction with μισθός in LXX Isa. 40: 10, 62: 11 and Rev. 22: 12.

the message. οἱ δίκαιοι may then be used occasionally in Matthew's gospel to refer to those in the community who witness, instruct and teach.[1]

(g) *An unusual use of the verb* δικαιόω. We conclude this discussion by making reference to the unusual use of the verb δικαιόω in Luke 7: 29.

When they heard this all the people and the tax-collectors justified God (ἐδικαίωσαν τὸν θεόν) having been baptised with the baptism of John, but the Pharisees and the lawyers rejected the purpose of God for themselves, not having been baptised by him.

It is clear from the antithetic form of the saying that ἐδικαίωσαν τὸν θεόν must be approximately opposite to 'rejected the purpose of God'. Is there any usage in biblical Greek which would make this possible? Earlier we pointed out that in the Psalms of Solomon δικαιόω always means 'to recognise the justice of God' (Ps. Sol. 2: 15; 3: 5; 4: 9; 8: 7, 23). This is also a common meaning of הִצְדִּיק and צִדֵּק in rabbinic works.[2] Thus δικαιόω here may most suitably mean 'to recognise and acknowledge the righteousness of God'.[3] In submitting to the conditions of baptism the people acknowledged that God's judgment on them, expressed in John's preaching, was a just judgment. A similar sense may be applied to the verb in the enigmatic saying at Matt. 11: 19: 'and wisdom is justified (ἐδικαιώθη) by her (its) works', which Luke renders as 'by its children' (7: 35). Whether 'wisdom' refers to Jesus or to the wise plan of God of which he is the manifestation, the context requires the saying to mean that this wisdom is recognised as righteous (i.e. proved to be in the right and accepted by God) by reason of its results accomplished. Luke changes the wording to suggest, probably, on the basis of *v*. 29, that the action of 'wisdom' is acknowledged as right by her *true* children who have been changed; for example, the publicans and sinners who justified God by accepting John's baptism.[4]

---

[1] I have discussed this quasi-technical use of the δίκαιος/צדק words (illustrating it from the usage of Qumran and the Inter-testamental literature) in *NTS*, xi (1964–5), 296–302.

[2] Cf. bab. Ber. 19a, Sif. Deut. 307 on 32: 4 and Sif. Lev. on 10: 3.

[3] So also G. W. H. Lampe, *New Peake:* Luke, p. 831.

[4] A. Schlatter, *Der Evangelist Matthäus* (Stuttgart, 1957), pp. 374–5, interprets the verb in Matt. 11: 19 as 'condemn'. This is a Hellenistic use and is not found in the New Testament.

From the preceding discussion it is clear that the meaning of δίκαιος and related words in the Synoptic Gospels must be interpreted within the framework of thought of the Old Testament, the witness to Israel's religious faith. 'Righteous' and 'righteousness' stand squarely within the faith of Judaism, as a religion of obedience and devotion to the will of God. The content of the terms owes much to the use and meaning of the δίκαιος-words in the Septuagint.

2. *Paul*

After this survey of the words for 'righteousness' we turn to the writings of Paul, bringing with us the fruits of our background study, in an effort to find out where the roots of his use of δικαιοσύνη lie. How far does the Old Testament idea of צְדָקָה as channelled through LXX usage explain his usage of the term? To what extent are the expressions of 'evangelical piety' in the Scrolls the clue to his understanding of 'righteousness'? How far, if at all, has he introduced new elements from secular Greek thought and usage or through his own Christian conceptions?

Our survey of the rabbinic teaching on righteousness and related themes will have demonstrated to the reader the intensity of the desire, on the part of the individual Israelite, to win, both in life and especially at the final judgment, the approbation of God. The path to this end was obedience to the precepts of the Torah, the inclusive expression of the whole Jewish religion. Within Judaism, the Law defined the demands of the Covenant and obedience was therefore the test of Israel's faithfulness to the Covenant. By faithfully observing the precepts of the Law, each Israelite renewed, as it were, the Covenant and accomplished in himself Israel's mission to and for mankind. Now the relevance of the Covenant and of Torah was not confined to certain moments of life: it covered its whole extent. Legal prescriptions were multiplied so as to enclose the whole life of the individual, the family and the nation in a network of observances, thus making almost every action of life a fulfilment of the law. These prescriptions, operative in the spheres of worship and morality,[1] had been drawn from the written Torah, from the oral Torah (i.e. the

---

[1] Between these two spheres there is no clearly drawn frontier. In each it is a matter of carrying out the will of God. To a people dedicated to the service of God, worship concerns morals and morals relate to worship.

living and authentic tradition of God's people) and, thirdly, from the halachic tradition which found in the Torah and in other sources of tradition practical interpretations and authoritative rules of conduct believed to go back to Moses and Sinai. Although obedience to Torah was considered to be the ground on which the Jew won 'merit' both for himself and others, the Rabbinic literature does bear witness to the quest for a pure and disinterested fidelity. The doctrine of כַּוָּנָה or religious intention played an important part in Jewish spirituality, and tradition always set before the Israelite the highest motives for his actions and observances: that the Law should be fulfilled for its own sake because it is God's will, and that present obedience is the necessary proof of faithfulness to the engagement entered into by God and his people at the inauguration of the Covenant.

We may fairly claim that the directions of thought outlined here formed part of Paul's inheritance as a Jew, within the mainstream of Pharisaic Judaism. Yet in his epistle to the Galatians[1] there is set forth a doctrinal position which amounts to a fundamental rethinking and restatement of the conception of 'righteousness'. Paul firmly rejects the Judaizers' attempts to make obedience to the law the necessary extension or completion of faith in Christ: the break with 'works of the law' must be complete.

We ourselves, who are Jews by birth and not Gentile sinners, yet who know that a man is not justified (οὐ δικαιοῦται) by works of the law, but through faith in Jesus Christ, even we have believed in Christ Jesus in order to be justified (ἵνα δικαιωθῶμεν) by faith in Christ and not by works of the law, because by works of the law shall no one be justified (δικαιωθήσεται) (Gal. 2: 15ff.).

In these verses we have the middle/passive of δικαιόω used three times (a fourth appears in the next verse), the third of them being in a quotation from LXX Ps. 143 (2): 2. In our study of LXX usage we had occasion to comment on the use of the middle and passive of the verb to render the Qal of צדק with the meaning 'appear righteous, be in the right, even, to be righteous', and one of the examples cited was Ps. 143: 2. Some interpreters of

---

[1] For arguments which make Galatians the earliest letter, see G. S. Duncan, *Galatians* (MNTC, London, 1934), pp. xxii ff. Most scholars date it closer to the Corinthian and Roman letters.

Paul lay stress on this oft-neglected meaning of δικαιοῦσθαι, and either state or imply that it necessitates a radical revision of the understanding of 'justification', since 'to be righteous' is a *qualitative* term, not judicial. But the Qal of צדק rendered by the middle and passive of δικαιόω and translated by 'to be righteous' is *not* qualitative, but retains its forensic significance. The 'righteousness' is a matter of being '*in the right before God*', that is, a reckoning at the divine tribunal, not of being righteous in oneself. Consequently, whether we render the word δικαιοῦσθαι as 'be in the right, be righteous' or, more conventionally, as 'to be justified', the word has forensic meaning. 'Righteousness' connotes status rather than the character or content of life.[1] In opposition to Jewish teaching, Paul asserts that 'to be righteous (in the right) before God' depends not on a man's achievement through obedience to the Law, but solely on his trust in Christ.

Now if there is implicit in the verb the idea of judicial pronouncement, we must ask, When, in the Pauline scheme, does the pronouncement take place? According to Jewish teaching, the judicial act was postponed to the Last Judgment: and the future tense at Gal. 2: 16 (cf. Rom. 3: 20) would probably be taken by the Jews as pointing to this future judgment. Did Paul understand it in this way? The use of the future tense here cannot be decisive, since it falls within a quotation, and in any case other strands of the Apostle's teaching imply that the judicial act belongs to the time of this life. What is a matter of hope for the Jew becomes for Paul a present possibility and reality. When a man is united by faith to Christ in his death and new life, when he is found *in Him* who is adjudged supremely 'The Righteous One' in God's sight, then he too is declared 'in the right' and set within the sphere of God's righteousness. The declaration of the believer's 'in-the-rightness' or 'righteousness' is the consequence of his being *in Christ*.[2]

Among the passages which witness to Paul's association of 'justification' with the idea of 'being in Christ' we may cite

---

[1] That δικαιοσύνη and cognate words are used also of the character of the Christian life will be demonstrated later.

[2] Paul, of course, continued to associate justification with the Last Judgment in the sense that at the End the believer's 'righteousness' is consummated, not just pronounced.

(i) Gal. 2: 17—'if, while seeking to be justified (δικαιωθῆναι) in Christ...' where 'in Christ' connotes the sphere within which, as it were, the declaration of righteousness takes place. (ii) 2 Cor. 5: 21—'Him who knew no sin he made to be sin for us in order that we might become the righteousness of God (δικαιοσύνη θεοῦ) in Him'. Paul will not say that God made Christ to be sinful or a sinner, but uses the noun ἁμαρτία = 'sin' (probably with the LXX meaning, 'sin-offering'): for the sake of parallelism in construction he uses the noun δικαιοσύνη to describe believers, but what he means is that through identification with Christ (in his death and resurrection) we are given the status of 'being in the right before God'. Once more, 'in Christ' is the sphere of justification. (iii) Rom. 6: 6–7—'We know that our old self was crucified with Him so that the sinful body might be destroyed and we might no longer be enslaved to sin. For he who has died is freed from sin (δεδικαίωται ἀπὸ τῆς ἁμαρτίας)'.[1] The believer who is crucified and dies with Christ appropriates for himself the atonement won by the death of the Righteous One (or the Righteous martyr)[2] and is justified (in the right) against sin's charges. 'The real point of his argument', says Schrenk,[3] 'is conformity, through faith, with Christ's death, which holds the secret of justification' (cf. Gal. 2: 21). (iv) The idea is again set forth in Phil. 3: 8–9—'All things I count as refuse in order that I may gain Christ and *be found in Him*, not having a righteousness of my own, based on law, but that which is through faith in Christ, the righteousness from God (ἐκ θεοῦ) that depends on faith, that I may know him and the power of his resurrection...'. Here, in Schrenk's words, 'the juridical is combined with the mystical'[4] as Paul expresses his desire to be found in Christ, not possessing the relative righteousness of life which is derived from obedience to the law, but that which proceeds from God and is accorded to faith. Although the first

---

[1] The last sentence is a rabbinic cliché (e.g. Sifre Num. 112 on 15: 31) associated with the doctrine of Atonement through martyrdom: see K. G. Kuhn, *ZNW*, xxx (1931), 305 ff. This parallel may reveal how justification and atonement are brought together.

[2] R. Scroggs, *NTS*, x (1963), 104 ff., has stressed the idea of the atoning value of the righteous martyr's death in explanation of this verse.

[3] Schrenk, *Righteousness*, p. 65. Cf. C. K. Barrett, *The Epistle to the Romans* (London, 1957), p. 125.

[4] Schrenk, *op. cit.* p. 51.

δικαιοσύνη has ethical connotation, the second must be interpreted as 'the status of being in the right', of being acceptable to God, because it comes 'from God and in response to faith'.[1] Now this 'righteousness' or 'justified status' is related to, if not actually dependent on, Paul's being found *in Christ*. And this is not a purely eschatological hope. The reference is to the aspirations of Paul for the entire course of his life. By reason of his faith, Paul is 'in Christ': he desires to *maintain* that relationship and the status of 'righteousness' which he receives in it.

The association of 'righteousness' and 'union with Christ' seems to be confirmed by the connection which Paul makes between Christ's death and the believer's identification with it and freedom from condemnation under the law. At Gal. 2: 19 he declares, 'I through the law died to the law, that I might live to God', and then goes on, as if to explain this, by referring to 'crucifixion with Christ' and entering new life through this death. This is elucidated by Gal. 3: 10 ff. Inability to fulfil the demands of the law brings man under a curse, for Scripture has said 'Cursed (ἐπικατάρατος) be everyone who does not abide by all the things written in the book of the law to do them' (Deut. 27: 26; Gal. 3: 10). Freedom from the oppression of this curse can be attained only through death: 'the law is binding on a person only during his life' (Rom. 7: 1) is a principle well known in Jewish teaching (bab. Shab. 30a, 151b). By his death, Jesus not only broke the tyranny of the law but also identified himself with man's plight by becoming himself 'cursed', through the method of his execution (Deut. 21: 23; Gal. 3: 13). It follows then that those who are united with him in this death are also freed from the tyranny of the law 'You have died to the law through the body of Christ...Now we are discharged from the law, dead to that which held us captive' (Rom. 7: 4, 6). And to be discharged from the law as the way to righteousness, through identification with Christ, means to be free to receive, in Christ, the righteousness which comes from God.

[1] Of this righteousness which proceeds from God and is accorded to faith, F. W. Beare writes, 'It is not a higher kind of moral attainment, but is basically a *right relationship* with God, which God himself creates through Christ and opens freely to all who believe in Christ. It is always and only the gift of God and not in any degree the achievement of man' (*Epistle to the Philippians* [London, 1959], p. 120).

It may be objected at this point that Paul does not clearly state that 'righteousness' or 'justification' depends on 'being in Christ' but rather that the status was obtained through *faith* (Phil. 3: 9; Rom. 3: 28; 4: 5, etc.). There is no contradiction here. 'Faith' means for Paul, not an intellectual assent to dogmatic statements, but 'a joyful self-committal of the whole personality of God',[1] which is the origin of an intensely personal relation with Christ. 'Faith' always implies for Paul its object, Christ, and involves a relationship with him. Our understanding of Paul's message is seriously weakened, if not distorted, unless we give to 'faith' its full significance in the expression 'justification by faith'. When 'faith' is understood as involving union with Christ in his death and new life (Rom. 6: 11), with all that that means in terms of surrender and sacrifice, then it is indeed the basis of our acceptance with God, the means of justification and righteousness. Any lesser appreciation of the meaning of 'faith' is in danger of making 'justification by faith' a semi-magical process without theological depth. It may be that to make the doctrine a part of the wider Pauline theme of 'union with Christ' is to give it secondary importance within Paul's doctrinal scheme. But may that not be, in fact, its proper place? It is not the essential pivot of his theology. The centre of his thought lies in the twin conceptions of 'dying and rising with Christ' and of undergoing a New Exodus in him and of being thus incorporated in a new Israel, the community of the Spirit. This is not to deny the importance of the doctrine of 'justification by faith' nor its significance in Christian theology, but is simply to see it in truer perspective in its relation to Pauline teaching as a whole.[2]

Paul's use of the phrase 'righteousness by faith' was probably derived from the Old Testament passages which he cites in support of his teaching. In a controversy with those who insisted on the centrality of the Torah—legalistically interpreted—and the necessity for universal obedience to it the only kind of support which would carry conviction to his opponents was scriptural, and so Paul appealed to two passages, Gen. 15: 6 and Hab. 2: 4, and argued from them that faith, rather than works of obedience

---

[1] C. Anderson Scott, *Christianity according to St Paul* (Cambridge, 1927), p. 133.

[2] Cf. W. D. Davies, *Paul and Rabbinic Judaism*, pp. 222–3.

to the law, was, according to Scripture itself, the means of salvation. Both these verses are used in Galatians and require some discussion. Gal. 3: 6—'Abraham believed God and it was reckoned to him for righteousness'. From this it follows that it is men of faith (πίστις) who are the sons of Abraham and inherit the blessing.[1] Probably Paul has in mind here an argument available to or used by his opponents to the effect that it was clear from Gen. 12 and 17: 10–14 that no one could participate in the blessings of God's covenant with Abraham and so in the Messianic salvation (which is inseparably associated with it) unless he was circumcised, thus fulfilling the obligations of the law. Paul's quotation, however, is meant to show that before there was any mention of circumcision Abraham's faith was the means of his pleasing God and inheriting the blessing. What is meant here by δικαιοσύνη? In the Hebrew version (of which Paul quotes the LXX translation) צְדָקָה clearly means an act which is right or 'as it should be', and therefore approved by God. The Targumic rendering of the verse (Onkelos and Ps. Jonathan) reveals that the act of fidelity was understood as a source of merit.[2] Now Paul cannot mean by δικαιοσύνη 'merit', but there is nothing in the word itself, nor in λογίζεται εἰς, which can be claimed as deciding between (i) 'it was attributed to him as *right conduct*', that is, he was regarded as having acted righteously, in the right way, and (ii) 'it was reckoned to him as a *ground of acceptance* with God'. If a strong recollection of the Hebrew צְדָקָה is uppermost, we should probably decide for the former, but that would not altogether exclude the second, since the 'right action' was the type of conduct or attitude of mind which God desires and which is pleasing to him. It would appear that Paul draws the word (which he found in Gen. 15) into his own vocabulary of

[1] From the Jewish point of view the faith of Abraham was not faith in Paul's sense, but an act of fidelity and therefore a good work which acquired merit, cf. 1 Macc. 2: 51. But Judaism has really no place for the rigid distinction between faith and works: faith can only fully exist when it is embodied in works.

[2] Rabbinic sources also magnify the *faith* of Abraham. R. Shemaiah (first century B.C.) claimed that 'Abraham received possession of this world and the world to come by the merit of faith', quoting Gen. 15: 6 (Mekh. Ex. 14: 31). There were other views, too, but in Palestinian and Diaspora Judaism Abraham remained the great pattern and symbol of faith or fidelity to God.

'justification', thereby giving to it a precision of meaning which it probably did not possess in Genesis. The same applies to his use of the words πιστεύω and πίστις.

The second of the Old Testament passages used by Paul is Hab. 2: 4, introduced at Gal. 3: 11—'No one is in the right or righteous before God on the basis of law, for it is written, "He who is righteous by faith shall live" (ὁ δίκαιος ἐκ πίστεως ʒήσεται)'. There seems to be no doubt that this is how the Habakkuk verse must be rendered here: the sequence of thought and argument demand it, for Paul is concerned to establish the basis on which a man may be righteous, not how the righteous shall live. In using the text Paul alters both syntax and meaning. The Hebrew text has, 'The righteous man will live by his faithfulness',[1] and the LXX, 'The righteous man will live by my faithfulness'. Paul understands πίστις as 'faith' and not 'faithfulness' and links it with ὁ δίκαιος to give the meaning he requires.[2] The 'righteous man' is the one who is in the right before God and therefore acceptable to him: he possesses the status on the basis of faith, and will live (eternally): those who depend on works of the law stand under the curse (Gal. 3: 10).

Before turning to the Epistle to the Romans we may comment on some passages from the Corinthian correspondence. 1 Cor. 1: 30—'He is the source of your life in Christ Jesus, whom God made our wisdom, our righteousness (δικαιοσύνη) and sanctification and redemption'. Once again, δικαιοσύνη is brought into association with the death of Christ and life in him, for the context

---

[1] The interpretation of the verse in the Habakkuk pesher from Qumran (8: 1) has already been mentioned.

[2] Cf. A. Schweitzer, *The Mysticism of Paul the Apostle* (ET, London, 1931), p. 208. G. S. Duncan, *The Epistle of Paul to the Galatians*, pp. 94–5, interprets thus and adds, 'It must be remembered that for him (Paul) the true meaning of any passage was to be found, not within the narrow limits of its historical context, but in its relation to the eternal truths of divine revelation'. The use made by Paul of δικαιοσύνη and πίστις in a different sense from that originally meant in the quotations raises an interesting semantic problem. It may be said, however, that collections of Old Testament quotations probably had been formed for the purpose of facilitating discussion with the Jews and demonstrating the truth of Christianity. Paul may have used some of these, and this would explain his method of quoting and interpreting Scripture to prove a point.

makes it clear that it is supremely in the Cross that God has revealed the true wisdom which is composed of righteousness, sanctification and redemption.[1] It seems probable that these terms refer to three aspects of 'deliverance in Christ' and therefore δικαιοσύνη is best interpreted (as in Galatians) as 'justification', the status of being in the right before God, achieved for man by Christ in his death and possessed by those who are in Christ.[2] The forensic connotation of δικαιοσύνη is undoubtedly present in 2 Cor. 3: 9 where the dispensation of justification (i.e. which pronounces righteous) is contrasted with the Mosaic dispensation of condemnation. It seems likely that the three verbs in 1 Cor. 6: 11 'you were washed, you were sanctified, you were justified (ἐδικαιώθητε)' refer to three aspects of the signficance of baptism 'in the name of Christ'. By undergoing that union with Christ in his death and resurrection which was symbolised and sealed in baptism, the Corinthian believers were sanctified, that is, separated to a life of holiness, and declared 'righteous' before God.[3]

When we turn to Romans the first appearance of the verb occurs, somewhat surprisingly, perhaps, in the statement—'For it is not the hearers of the law who are righteous before God, but the doers of the law who will be justified (δικαιωθήσονται)' (2: 13). The context makes it clear that Paul, respecting the obligations of the law for Jews, is claiming that Jews will be judged by that law, and that the test will be, not knowledge of its provisions, but obedience. Complete conformity to God's will as expressed in the Torah may, in theory at any rate, put a man in a right relation with God. But no Jew has achieved that status, for not one of them renders this total obedience. Their failure to keep the commands, however, does not release God from the obligation to keep his promises: he remains faithful to his

---

[1] To treat the three terms as explanatory of 'wisdom' seems the most satisfactory procedure, see W. D. Davies, *Paul and Rabbinic Judaism*, p. 154.

[2] So Schrenk, *Righteousness*, p. 43, and C. S. C. Williams, *New Peake*: 1 Corinthians, p. 955. Even if the terms are interpreted of the stages of progress in Christian living, our view of the meaning of δικαιοσύνη need not be altered.

[3] Some commentators interpret that passive of δικαιόω here as 'were made righteous' in character. This is doubtful. Paul does not seem to use the verb at any time with this meaning.

covenant, even when men default, and Ps. 51:6 proves it—'God is in the right in his judgment'. This, however, does not mean that man's wickedness demonstrates more clearly the righteousness of God (i.e. God's fidelity and rightness in judging), for then the wrath of God against the sinner would be unjust. All men, Jews and Greeks alike, are under the power of sin and lacking in righteousness, but, since law brings the knowledge of sin, obviously 'no one will be justified before him', quoting Ps. 143: 2, 'on the basis of works of law'. As in Gal. 2: 16 this quotation has a forensic reference and means 'no one is in the right before God'. The law which demands righteousness cannot create it. There is only one remedy, the Gospel.

The great passage which follows, 3: 21 ff., will be taken up at a later stage in our discussion. The theme of the superiority of faith to works is resumed in 3: 27 and continues through chapter 4. There is no room for boasting, for the self-confidence which claims its duty done: faith is the sole means of becoming accepted, of being in the right before God (3: 28) and Scripture itself illustrates this in the case of Abraham. If he had been judged righteous on the basis of works, then he would have had grounds for boasting: but, in fact, he had no such grounds, for it was faith which was counted to Abraham as righteousness (4: 3). The content of the terms 'faith' and 'righteousness' here, as in Galatians, comes from Paul's own theological standpoint, rather than from the Hebrew words translated by them in the LXX. Now the argument from Gen. 15 means that 'to one who does not work, but trusts him who justifies the ungodly (τὸν δικαιοῦντα τὸν ἀσεβῆ) his faith is reckoned as righteousness' (4: 5). The words δικαιοῦντα τὸν ἀσεβῆ are a striking allusion to the Old Testament and describe God as doing precisely what the Old Testament forbids (Exod. 23: 7; Prov. 17: 15; Isa. 5: 23). These passages indicate that in the remarkable phrase under discussion Paul is using δικαιόω in its forensic meaning 'to justify', 'to give the status of being in the right', and by so doing he declares a great paradox in the divine action. The NEB rendering 'him who acquits the guilty' seems to overstate the paradox, and F. W. Beare is right in questioning the accuracy of this translation.[1] 'To acquit the guilty' seems to go further

---

[1] In a review of the NEB in *NTS*, VIII (1961–2), 91.

than the literal sense 'justify the impious' permits,[1] especially since the quotation in *v.* 7 from Ps. 32: 1 (introduced because it contains the verb λογίζομαι) makes it clear that δικαιοῦν here is tantamount to 'to forgive'.[2] The 'counting of righteousness' becomes equivalent to the 'not-counting of sin'. And is 'to forgive' the same action as 'to acquit', even though the result be the same? Verses 11 ff. declare that Abraham's circumcision did not confer righteousness on him, and was not a token that he was under obligation henceforth to keep the law in order to be justified: it confirmed by a visible sign the fact that he *had been justified* by faith. Likewise the promise of Gen. 22: 17 ff., though made after Abraham had been circumcised, was not therefore dependent on his observing the law, but rather 'through (or "in the context of", so Barrett) the righteousness (or justification) which comes by faith' (διὰ δικαιοσύνης πίστεως). By this affirmation Paul shatters the synthesis between law and promise which was a fundamental principle of Judaism. Throughout these passages Paul uses δικαιοσύνη with a sense and precision which it did not really possess in Gen. 15: 6.[3] In this he would appear to be applying rabbinical exegetical methods which tolerated the practice of interpreting words without much reference to their contextual meaning.[4]

In the fifth chapter of Romans 'justification' is again associated with faith and with the death of Christ.

Since we are justified by faith (δικαιωθέντες ἐκ πίστεως) we have peace with God... Since we are now justified in his blood (δικαιω-θέντες νῦν ἐν τῷ αἵματι αὐτοῦ), much more shall we be saved by him from the wrath of God (5: 1, 9).

[1] 'For Paul, in all cases where man is concerned, the meaning "acquit" is excluded. For "acquit" means to pronounce guiltless or innocent: and it is of the very essence of Paul's argument that no man is guiltless before God' (T. W. Manson, *On Paul and John*, p. 54).

[2] W. A. Stevens made much of this for his understanding of 'justification', *AJT*, I (1897), 443–50. Cf. also C. K. Barrett, *The Epistle to the Romans*, p. 89, and F. J. Leenhardt, *The Epistle to the Romans* (ET, London, 1961), p. 116.

[3] Cf. J. H. Ropes, *JBL*, xxII (1903), 225, 'The term in these passages goes in...as moral excellence; it comes out, after Paul has used it, with his peculiar stamp upon it'.

[4] We have seen this in Mek. Beshallah 4, see p. 119. Cf. Paul's use of the principle *gᵉzerah shawaʾ* in Rom. 4, on which see Barrett, *op. cit.* p. 89. The principle states that when the same word occurs in two biblical passages, each may be used to illuminate the other.

'Justification', the setting of us right with God, takes place on the basis of faith and has been effected (lit.) 'in his blood'. Whether the ἐν is instrumental ('by means of') or reflects the Hebrew *beth pretii* and means 'at the cost of',[1] the sacrificial and atoning death of Christ is declared to be the means of the present justification, which itself guarantees deliverance at the final judgment. Where the Epistle to the Galatians developed the doctrine of 'righteousness' before God without directly mentioning forgiveness and the atoning death of Christ, Romans clearly associates justification with atonement. In both epistles, however, the idea of identification with Christ is implicit. Whoever, by faith, dies with Christ, thus applying the atoning sacrifice of Christ to himself (as having taken place for him along with others), is included among those for whom it was offered: consequently, he has part in the forgiveness which has been thus obtained and which is the 'favourable verdict' involved in justification.[2] The Adam–Christ typology affirms the character of this verdict. 'The judgment, following one trespass, brought condemnation, but the free gift following many trespasses brings justification (δικαίωμα)' (5: 16). The word δικαίωμα requires different translations elsewhere (1: 32; 2: 26; 5: 18; 8: 4) but in using it here Paul may be governed by rhetorical considerations:[3] it chimes with κατάκριμα. There is no doubt, however, that he means 'justification' (possibly even, 'acquittal'), the opposite of 'condemnation'. The use of the same word in v. 18, with the meaning 'a righteous act', is probably again dictated by the stylistic necessity of finding a word to chime with παράπτωμα ('act of transgression'). Having employed δικαίωμα to mean 'righteous act', Paul chooses δικαίωσις to express 'justification' (which he uses elsewhere only at 4: 25).[4] The words εἰς δικαίωσιν ζωῆς (lit. 'unto justification of life') are explained by reference to v. 17, 'those who receive the abundance of grace and the free

---

[1] So Barrett, *The Epistle to the Romans*, p. 107, stressing the sacrificial reference in 'blood'.

[2] Cf. Schweitzer, *The Mysticism of Paul the Apostle*, p. 218.

[3] Leenhardt, *The Epistle to the Romans*, p. 147, speaks of 'a studied effect of alliteration'.

[4] 'Christ was delivered up for our trespasses and was raised διὰ τὴν δικαίωσιν ἡμῶν.' It seems best to translate διά prospectively, 'with a view to...'. According to v. 17 Abraham's justification is the result of faith in God who quickens the dead. We need not make fine distinctions as to what

gift of righteousness reign in life. . .'. This 'gift of righteousness' may mean the conferment of righteousness upon man, or the gift which proceeds from God's righteousness, but in either case it is the ground on which man can share in the blessing of victorious living. Justification leads to life. In a more cautious fashion, v. 21 asserts the same view. 'Because grace reigns, righteousness (δικαιοσύνη) becomes possible and righteousness leads to eternal life', where the meaning of 'righteousness' includes both initial acceptance with God and the righteousness of life (following justification) which progresses towards eternal life. This verse confirms the impression that 3ωῆς (in εἰς δικαίωσιν 3ωῆς, v. 17) should be understood eschatologically, as well as of the Christian life. 'For Paul, justification looks forward to the perfecting through which alone it receives its ideal and its final manifestation'[1] (cf. also 5: 19b). In Rom. 8: 33 the present participle of the verb (δικαιῶν) refers to God's declaring a person righteous. The future consummation of 'justification' is implied in Gal. 5: 5, 'For through the Spirit, by faith, we wait for the hope of righteousness': as G. S. Duncan has said, 'Though the believer is "accepted as righteous" here and now, he relies on Christ to complete the good work that has been begun in him and to make him righteous so that he can be accepted on the day of judgment'.[2]

There has been some discussion among exegetes about the correct interpretation of δικαιοσύνη in Rom. 8: 10—'If Christ is in you, the body is dead because of sin, but the Spirit is life because of righteousness (τὸ δὲ πνεῦμα 3ωὴ διὰ δικαιοσύνην)'. The setting in antithesis with 'the body (of man) dead because of sin' may suggest that πνεῦμα here refers to the spirit of man quickened by the presence of Christ for the attainment of ethical righteousness.[3] That interpretation, however, would require εἰς δικαιοσύνην rather than διὰ δικαιοσύνην. As is the case throughout the section πνεῦμα means the Spirit of God and the use of 3ωή itself would suggest this. The Spirit is at work giving life to a man

is achieved by Christ's death and what by his Resurrection. The two events are inseparable in the New Testament. The Crucified is what he is only because he was raised, and Paul can say that we are justified by his death and that he was raised for our justification.   [1] Schrenk, *Righteousness*, p. 73.
[2] *The Epistle of Paul to the Galatians*, p. 156.
[3] So H. Lietzmann, *An die Römer* (4th ed., Tübingen, 1933), *ad loc.*, and M.-J. Lagrange, *Épître aux Romains* (Paris, 1931), p. 199.

because of justification, because he has been rightly related to God, in whose gift the Spirit lies. The NEB renders the verse, 'The Spirit is life itself, because you have been justified', and T. W. Manson speaks of 'life which comes from God because we are now right with him'.[1]

In the course of our discussion of the words for 'righteousness' we have often used the phrase 'being in the right before God' and have based this interpretation on the meaning of the Hebrew צְדָקָה. But what does it mean to be 'in the right'? In what does this righteousness consist? We have rejected Goodspeed's argument that it is a righteousness of character, a qualitative righteousness,[2] since this is at variance with the Hebrew background of the term. Others have explained 'justification' as a kind of fictitious righteousness, the declaring righteous a person who, in fact, is not righteous. Bultmann claims that the justified man is actually made righteous in terms of a forensic righteousness: he has righteousness in the verdict of the law-court.[3] C. H. Dodd puts the emphasis on vindication by God,[4] and J. H. Ropes on the vindication of the sinner against the sin which wrongly accuses him.[5] While all these interpretations are valid, it is Bultmann who sets forth the meaning with greatest clarity. By affirming that the act of justification creates a *status* rather than a character, Bultmann rightly insists that the believer has an actual but *forensic* righteousness, not a quality of life, but a relationship based on the forgiveness of sins and the experience of dying and rising with Christ by faith. This divine verdict, however, must have consequences for ethical conduct (as Dodd, Bultmann and others fully realise) in that the justified man seeks, through obedience to the will of God and the 'law of Christ', to become a righteous man.[6]

---

[1] Romans (in *New Peake*, p. 946). Cf. K. Barth, *The Epistle to the Romans* (ET, London, 1933), p. 286, '... because of the righteousness which has been established in him'.

[2] *JBL*, LXXIII (1954), 87f.

[3] *Theology of the New Testament*, I (London, 1952), 272. The section pp. 270–85 is extremely valuable throughout.

[4] *Epistle to the Romans* (MNTC, London, 1932), pp. 12ff. and 51–3.

[5] *JBL*, XXII (1903), 211–27.

[6] Cf. T. W. Manson, *On Paul and John*, p. 64, 'There is no such thing in Hebrew or Christian thought as a salvation which does not take immediate effect in the creation of a new moral achievement here and now'.

We turn now to this use of δικαιοσύνη to characterise the life of the Christian man between the time of his acceptance on the basis of faith and his final acquittal at the last Judgment. The use of δικαιοσύνη in this connection agrees with the classical Greek use of the term to describe man's moral life. It will be remembered, however, that in our earlier discussion we pointed out that, while the idea of conformity to a norm is the meaning of 'righteousness' in both biblical and Classical Greek, the norm itself is very different. In Greek thought the norm was regarded as being the citizen's duty to the state or community: in Hebrew thinking it was conceived of as the will of God within the covenant community. In Pauline thought there is a great awareness of the social side of a Christian's life and his responsibilities as a citizen, but these are brought within the framework of God's will for his whole life within the new community.[1] Obedience to ethical standards which have their source in the will of God and the 'law of Christ' must be the character of Christian living, and this obedience is never opposed to faith, but follows from it. By emphasising 'justification by faith' in isolation from its context, it is possible to make too much of the contrast between Pauline Christianity as a religion of liberty and Judaism as a religion of works of obedience. According to Paul, to die with Christ is to be free from subservience to the Law as a means of acceptance with God. Faith alone makes possible or creates this relationship of identification within which a man is accepted. The life to follow must be a 'new life' in Christ, lived in the power and freedom of the Spirit; but it is also a life of discipline, obedience and of righteousness well-pleasing to God. The Roman Christians must offer their members to God as 'instruments of righteousness' (6: 13), and be slaves of obedience which leads to righteousness and sanctification (16, 18). The translation of εἰς δικαιοσύνην as 'justification' here would be entirely out of place: what is meant is 'righteousness of life'. Those who, by faith, are accepted by God must, through the power of the Spirit, enter the service of righteousness (cf. 2 Cor. 6: 7). This life of

---

[1] Within the Pauline doctrine of 'justification' the covenant relationship (i.e. the new covenant in Christ) is assumed, though δικαιοσύνη is not directly associated with the word διαθήκη. P. J. Achtemeier (*IDB*, IV, 91 ff.) makes the concept of the Covenant (broken, restored and accepted) basic to his entire explanation of δικαιοσύνη in the New Testament.

faith, though a life of freedom from observances, is a life under the rule of God. 'For the kingdom of God is not eating and drinking, but righteousness (δικαιοσύνη), peace and joy in the Holy Spirit' (Rom. 14: 17). Both 'righteousness' and 'peace' usually describe the objective relation with God, but 'joy' here is certainly subjective and probably determines the sense of the other two words. 'Righteousness' therefore is 'righteous living' (which springs from the objective relation of 'righteousness') and 'peace' means a 'peaceful state of mind and affairs' which also arises from a peaceful relation with God. At 2 Cor. 6: 14 this 'righteousness' of life is contrasted with the iniquity and lawlessness of pagan living.

In Phil. 1: 11 Paul expresses the hope that, in view of the day of Christ, the Philippian Christians may be 'pure and blameless, filled with the fruit of righteousness (καρπὸν δικαιοσύνης) which comes through Jesus Christ, to the glory and praise of God'. Most commentators interpret δικαιοσύνης as a genitive of definition: the Philippians are to bring forth 'righteouness'. But F. W. Beare argues that the phrase means 'the fruit which springs from justification':

The thought is not that righteousness itself is the harvest, but that it is the right relationship with God which produces the harvest. The Christian character developed in all its clearness and purity is the end product of the grace by which we were 'justified'.[1]

This point of view is certainly true to Pauline theory, but it is doubtful if it finds explicit expression here.[2]

According to Eph. 4: 22-4, the 'new' (Christian) man is formed after the image of God in righteousness and holiness. Both terms refer to the quality of life. The same is true of the meaning of δικαιοσύνη in Eph. 5: 9 and 6: 14. It has been suggested that 'almsgiving' or 'benevolence' is the meaning of δικαιοσύνη in the quotations from Ps. 112: 9 and Hos. 10: 12 found at 2 Cor. 9: 9f. because the context is concerned with the 'collection'. On the other hand, v. 8 speaks of 'every good work' and δικαιοσύνη is probably used to connote righteousness of life of which charity is an expression.

Because of the assumed divergence in doctrine between Paul

[1] F. W. Beare, *The Epistle to the Philippians*, p. 55.
[2] The understanding that 'righteousness' as fruit comes, not naturally, but only through Christ and from a relation to him, is always implicit in Paul.

and James, it will be valuable to refer to the use of δικαιοσύνη in the latter. At 1: 20 'righteousness of God' means righteous actions such as God may approve, and at 3: 18 'the fruit of righteousness' probably refers to the harvest of righteous life produced by those who cultivate the seed of peace. At 2: 23 James uses Gen. 15: 6 to prove that Abraham was righteous in God's sight on the basis of his action in offering up Isaac and to declare that a man is justified by works and not by faith alone. The difference between this declaration and Pauline teaching may be relatively small when it is remembered that (i) for James, 'faith' tends to connote mere credal orthodoxy rather than that personal trust which unites a man to Christ, and (ii) that 'works' means, not the detailed observance of law in the rabbinic sense, but actions of practical love and service which (according to Paul as well) are the characteristics of Christian living. Nevertheless, it must be granted that Paul could not have agreed with James' contention that Abraham was justified on the ground of an action of sacrificial obedience which accompanied and authenticated his faith. Both, however, would have been at one in desiring the faith which produces the right kind of obedience.[1]

We come now to the phrase δικαιοσύνη θεοῦ and especially to Rom. 1: 17 and 3: 21 ff. Very familiar is the 'text' of the letter to the Romans:

I am not ashamed of the gospel of Christ for it is the power of God unto salvation for everyone who has faith, to the Jew first and also to the Gentile. For in it the righteousness of God (δικαιοσύνη θεοῦ) is revealed from faith to faith (lit.), as it is written, 'He who through faith is righteous shall live'.

Exegetes and theologians have long argued whether δικαιοσύνη θεοῦ here connotes a divine attribute or the gift which God grants to the believer and as a result of which God can proclaim the believer righteous. This debate has been complicated by confessional differences and loyalties. The Roman tradition has been inclined to insist on righteousness as a gift which transforms the nature of the believer: the Reformed tradition to

---

[1] The polemic of James is directed against a doctrine of 'faith without works' which is different from what Paul meant by 'faith apart from works of the law'. Was the former a development from the latter, comparable to Corinthian libertinism? See A. Schlatter, *Der Brief des Jakobus* (2 Auf., Stuttgart, 1956), pp. 51 ff.

emphasise righteousness as an attribute of God by virtue of which he makes a declaration in favour of the believer, who remains in himself what he was before. The basic error holding these views apart lies in the fact that static modes of thought were followed in medieval theology and insufficiently discarded by Reformed teachers. With the increasing study of the LXX and the Hebraic background of Paul's vocabulary it has become clear to both Protestant and Roman Catholic exegetes that the 'righteousness of God' is essentially a term involving action. For example, the Jesuit scholar S. Lyonnet, writing on the meaning of *iustitia Dei* in Rom. 1 : 17, quotes Old Testament passages from Isaiah and Psalms where 'righteousness of God' is parallel to 'salvation' and asks, 'Can we doubt that Paul is indebted for the meaning of this expression to these texts, so clear and having similar contexts?'[1] Are we then to equate 'righteousness of God' with 'salvation' in Romans? If one stresses the importance of Isaiah and the Psalms for the understanding of Rom. 1 : 17 and assumes Paul's acquaintance with the meaning of God's righteousness in the Old Testament, then one must also credit the Apostle with awareness of the distinction between 'righteousness' and 'salvation' which pertains to the passages in Isaiah. The two ideas are admittedly very close, but the words are not synonymous. 'Salvation' is the situation or state of affairs ushered in (even the action taken) as a result of Yahweh's righteous decision for Israel or his righteous verdict on Israel:[2] in short, the righteous action (God's righteousness) brings about salvation, but is not equated with it. The Old Testament distinction remains in the Romans passage under discussion, for 'righteousness of God' is parallel, not to 'salvation', but to the phrase 'the power of God unto salvation'.

Although this approach to the interpretation of ' the righteousness of God' runs counter to the attempts to explain it as 'the righteousness (of life)' which God gives to man,[3] its validity can

---

[1] *Verbum Domini*, xxv (1947), p. 29.

[2] C. H. Dodd, *Epistle to the Romans* (MNTC), p. 12, interprets 'the righteousness of God' as 'an activity whereby the right is asserted' through God's merciful vindication of his people even when they have broken the covenant relation.

[3] Cf. Lagrange, *Épître aux Romains*, on 1 : 17. We have already mentioned the attempt by A. Oepke (*TLZ*, LXXVIII [1953], 257–64) to revive this interpretation on the basis of the claim that the Rabbinic explanation of צִדְקַת יהוה at Deut. 33 : 21 (with which Paul is assumed to have been

be demonstrated by consideration of the context and its Old Testament background. The righteousness of God, says Paul, is revealed in the Gospel which itself leads to salvation. Now, in Judaism, salvation belongs to the realm of eschatology, but, according to Christian teaching, it has been anticipated in the present through the death and resurrection of the Messiah. Consequently the Gospel is not merely an announcement that salvation will take place in the future, but a divine activity and power leading to salvation now. Paul knows from the Old Testament, however, that salvation presupposes righteousness and that the initiative in establishing both lies with God. Salvation results from God's action in doing right and in seeing right done, even to the extent of vindicating those who do not deserve such treatment, but to whom he has bound himself in covenant mercy and love. By reason of this action on his behalf, man is 'put in the right' before God: in judgment he will secure a favourable verdict. In the Gospel this 'righteousness' is revealed, for the Gospel means essentially 'God in action in Jesus Christ' doing right with his people and establishing them 'in the right' before him. This is the power of God that works towards salvation, and this righteous action is being revealed on the basis of faith (ἐκ πίστεως) for all who have faith (εἰς πίστιν),[1] as it is written, ὁ δε δίκαιος ἐκ πίστεως ζήσεται. As in Gal. 3, the context demands that this be interpreted 'he who is righteous on the basis of faith shall live'. This agrees with the intention of the Apostle, which, as A. Feuillet puts it, 'is not to establish how the righteous shall live, but rather with what kind of righteousness he must be clothed in order to be able to live: that from faith or that which comes by works?'[2]

acquainted) is 'righteousness of man in the eyes of God'. The strength of the argument is seriously undermined by our discovery that this rabbinic rendering of צְדָקַת יהוה was not common and may, in the discussion of Deut. 33: 21, have been dictated by special circumstances. Oepke seeks confirmation of his claim in Test. Dan 6: 10, ἀποστῆτε οὖν ἀπὸ πάσης ἀδικίας καὶ κολλήθητε τῇ δικαιοσύνῃ τοῦ θεοῦ (i.e. 'righteousness before God'), but he must take account of the likelihood of post-Christian influence at this point, as well as of the possibility that τοῦ νόμου between τοῦ and θεοῦ (attested by α A β S¹) may be original.

[1] This interpretation of the phrases seems best and accords with what seems to be the parallel thought of 3: 21.

[2] 'La citation d'Hab. 2: 4 et les huit premiers chapitres de l'épître aux Romains', NTS, VI (1959–60), 52.

With the observation that δικαιοσύνη θεοῦ at 3: 5 certainly means exclusively the 'righteous action of God in judgment', we come to the great passage, 3: 21 ff., in the study of which the strands of our discussion may be brought together. This passage is one of the turning-points of the epistle. The law has been proved ineffectual in bestowing righteousness on man: all, without distinction, stand under condemnation, guilty before God:

But now, the righteousness of God (δικαιοσύνη θεοῦ) has been manifested apart from law, although the law and the prophets bear witness to it, the righteousness of God through faith in Jesus Christ for all who believe.[1]

As the passage proceeds, it becomes clear that God's righteousness is manifested in his action and the action shows that 'he is righteous in himself' and that 'he justifies'; that is, it shows that he is in the right, or righteous,[2] and that he does right, putting others who did not deserve it *in the right*, solely on the basis of faith in Jesus Christ. These are 'justified by his grace as a gift....', which does not mean that they were made ethically virtuous or righteous, nor that they were treated as righteous although they were not in fact so: it means that 'they were put in the clear' (in God's court), given the status of being in the right. This verdict is made possible because Christ died and his atoning death dealt decisively with sin that had been formerly passed over. Here again, justification and atonement are brought together: the possibility of justification rests on the propitiatory sacrifice which reconciles (ἱλαστήριον). The wrath of God against sin required righteous judgment upon it so that God's own righteousness might be maintained and that he might put in the right those who have faith in Christ (*v.* 26). And that faith, as chapters 5 and 6 make abundantly clear, means the union of the believer with Christ in his atoning death and resurrection life which is the sphere of 'justification'.

[1] The parallel in thought and expression with 1: 17 is close: πεφανέρωται corresponds to ἀποκαλύπτεται; διὰ πίστεως to ἐκ πίστεως; and εἰς πάντας τοὺς πιστεύοντας to εἰς πίστιν.

[2] We ought to remember that God's righteousness includes not only the idea of his righteousness in personal character and action, but also that of his loyalty to the covenant-people. His action proves his 'in-the-rightness' (with reference to covenant faithfulness) over against man's 'unrighteousness'.

Finally, at Rom. 10: 3, Paul speaks of his fellow-Jews thus:

ignorant of the righteousness of God (τὴν τοῦ θεοῦ δικαιοσύνην) and seeking to establish their own (righteousness), they did not submit to God's righteousness (τῇ δικαιοσύνῃ τοῦ θεοῦ): for Christ is the end of the law for righteousness to everyone who has faith.

If the first 'righteousness of God' is interpreted as the ethical or qualitative righteousness which is granted to the believer by God, the passage will mean: the Jews sought the righteousness which they thought was achieved by obedience to the law, because they did not understand the righteousness which comes from God as a gift, and therefore they failed to submit themselves to God's righteousness. But if the second occurrence of 'righteousness of God' means the same thing, then the force of the last clause is weakened. Unless the second 'righteousness of God' means 'Christ, as the embodiment of the divine righteousness' (as Leenhardt suggests),[1] we must surely see it as a reference to the operation of God's righteous activity. In the light of this, it is likely that the first δικαιοσύνη connotes, not a quality, but God's justifying action. This the Jews did not understand, and so continued to try to establish their own righteousness through the law. This way, says Paul, is not valid, because (i) Christ is the end (τέλος) of the law as a way to achieving the status of being righteous or acceptable,[2] and (ii) the law itself proclaimed that 'faith' is the way to righteousness (Gen. 15: 6).

Apart from Paul's writings the phrase 'righteousness of God' occurs at James 1: 20 and 2 Pet. 1: 1. In the former passage it probably means 'what is right in God's eyes, right conduct of which he may approve'. In the second passage, the phrase appears in the formula, 'to those who have obtained a faith of equal standing with ours in the righteousness of our God and Saviour Jesus Christ', and probably refers to God's just (rather than justifying) activity in relation to his people which gives equal privilege to all.[3]

This discussion of Pauline usage makes clear the following points:

[1] *The Epistle to the Romans*, p. 265.
[2] If τέλος is interpreted as 'purpose', 'intention', 'fulfilment', then εἰς δικαιοσύνην must mean 'by bringing about righteousness' (i.e. justification) for the believer.
[3] Cf. Schrenk, *Righteousness*, p. 35.

(1) The verb δικαιόω does not seem to be used in the Epistles (nor, in fact, in any of the New Testament documents) in either of the senses normally attaching to it in non-biblical Greek: it does not mean 'to deem right', nor 'to treat (someone) justly or rightly'.

(a) Its use in the active form is the same as that of δικαιόω in the LXX where it translates the Hebrew הִצְדִּיק, with the meaning 'to cause to be in the right', 'to put someone in the right' by giving judgment in his favour.

(b) In the middle and passive forms, it reflects the LXX rendering of the Qal of צדק, 'to be in the right', and therefore 'righteous' before the bar of judgment.

Consequently, we may say that the verb is primarily and predominantly a forensic term,[1] a word of the law-court, describing a relation to, or a status before God, the judge of all men. It is not a case of God 'making righteous' a person who is not so: he 'puts in the right' the person who is in the relationship of faith (i.e. trust, surrender and identification) with Christ, in whose life and death the righteousness of God in covenant-faithfulness to man has been manifested.

(2) The words 'righteous' and 'righteousness' also possess a wide area of meaning which is strange to Greek usage, but closely related to the Hebrew צְדָקָה and the LXX δικαιοσύνη. When the noun is used with reference to man's salvation it means 'the *status* of being in the right' graciously given by God. In the words of Bultmann:

It does not mean the ethical quality of a person. It does not mean any quality at all, but a relationship. That is, δικαιοσύνη is not something a person has as his own; rather it is something he has in the verdict of the 'forum'...to which he is accountable. He has it in the opinion adjudicated to him by another.[2]

When predicated of God, 'righteousness' refers to his being 'in the right' by reason of his loyalty to the covenant, and to his action in setting men right.

(3) In a manner akin to Greek usage, both δίκαιος and δικαιοσύνη are used in an ethical or qualitative sense. This is the

---

[1] Cf. H. St J. Thackeray, *The Relation of St Paul to Contemporary Jewish Thought* (London, 1900), p. 87.
[2] R. Bultmann, *Theology of the New Testament*, I, p. 272.

case when they refer to that 'righteousness' which must characterise Christian living in obedience to the will of God and the
law of Christ. While Christian 'righteousness' may thus be
regarded as a virtue, there is an important difference between it
and Greek 'justice'. The latter was thought of predominantly in
terms of what was dutiful and good within the community or
state: Christian righteousness (and social justice) was placed
within the context of the supreme will of God. This is the insight
of Old Testament teaching and religion, and Paul retains it,
adding his own Christian interpretation. The will of God for
the new community of the Covenant has been made known in
the life and teaching of Jesus Christ. Obedience to this is the
'righteousness' of life which God expects and which will lead to
the consummation of the 'justifying' verdict at the last Day.

We may claim then with confidence that Paul's use of the
group of words is firmly rooted in biblical Greek usage, rather
than in that of Classical Greek writers. Awareness of this fact has
provided us with an essential clue to the interpretation of Paul's
language of 'justification'. Now we may legitimately ask whether
the *faith* expressed in the language to which Paul was indebted
also provided him with the doctrine he set forth in those
(borrowed) terms: in other words, does the Old Testament
provide the substructure of Paul's doctrine of 'justification by
faith'? In some measure it does. Not only do we find in the Old
Testament the affirmation of God's 'righteousness' in his
faithfulness and 'in-the-rightness' with reference to the covenant-
relationship, but we also discover in the prophets and especially
in the Psalms that 'the righteous' (those who are 'in the right')
are those who have a profound trust in the divine mercy and seek
to do his will. Is not this a foretaste of the essential spirit of Paul's
doctrine? That this kind of piety continued as one strand of
Jewish religion is proved by the contents of the Qumran Manual
of Discipline (1QS) and Hodayot (1QH). In our discussion of
these we referred to their declaration of human weakness and of
the justification (i.e. the judging as righteous, מִשְׁפָּט) of the sinner
through faith in God's forgiving mercy, a justification which was
grounded in God's righteousness (צְדָקָה). The new materials
therefore show that the question of the means whereby God
accepts the sinner remained an issue of importance at least in
sectarian circles.

In the teachings of the Old Testament and pre-Christian sectarian Judaism we see the framework of Paul's doctrine and the background of his thought as he faced a degenerating and legalistic religion, but the special *content* of his doctrine was his own. Two factors are responsible for it. First, he was writing at a particular moment in the life of the Church: the doctrine of 'justification by faith' was crystallised in opposition to the thesis of contemporary Judaism that acceptance with God was based on merit achieved by works of the law. As a result of the controversy, the doctrine gained precision of statement and a pronounced negative reference, 'not by works'. The second factor contributing to the uniqueness of the Pauline doctrine is vastly more important. Paul writes from the standpoint of belief in Jesus as the Messiah. He begins with the Cross and Resurrection, and, from this centre, rethinks the entire realm of theology and religion, including the doctrine of the means of justification. The *sola fide* of Jewish evangelical piety becomes *sola fide Christi*. Faith gains its characteristic Christian connotation—trust in and identification with Christ in his saving act—and justification its reference both to God's supremely righteous act and to man's acceptance as 'in-the-right' in Christ alone. Greatly indebted though Paul is to the best in Jewish thought, it is his understanding of the Christ-event and the influence of that understanding on his entire theology that makes his doctrine of justification something different from, and an advance upon the deep spiritual insights of the Old Testament and of Qumran piety.[1] We cannot claim to have understood the Pauline doctrine when we have located anticipations of it in the religious faith of Judaism.

[1] See on this, S. Schulz, 'Zur Rechtfertigung aus Gnaden in Qumran und bei Paulus', *ZTK*, LVI (1959), 155–85, and especially, W. Grundmann, 'Der Lehrer der Gerechtigkeit von Qumran und die Frage nach der Glaubensgerechtigkeit in der Theologie des Apostels Paulus', *Revue de Qumran*, II (1959–60), 237–59. The latter ends his study with these words, 'The uniqueness of Paul lies not in special concepts and ideas, not even in their new arrangement in a new theological system, but in their being brought into relation to Christ Jesus, who encountered Paul and who thenceforth determines his life in time and in eternity. Paul recognises in the crucified and risen Jesus the promised Messiah, who in Qumran was awaited but remained unknown' (p. 259).

CHAPTER V

THE BACKGROUND AND BIBLICAL USAGE OF ΖΩΗ AND ΖΩΗ ΑΙΩΝΙΟΣ

THE OLD TESTAMENT

In the Old Testament there are two words which, in English versions, are frequently rendered by 'life': these are חַיִּים and נֶפֶשׁ. The latter is regularly translated in the Septuagint by ψυχή but never by ζωή, whereas חַיִּים and related words are almost always rendered by ζωή and its cognates.[1] Since the aim of this study is to investigate the Greek word ζωή, our attention will be directed towards the understanding of the use and meaning of חַיִּים. Nevertheless, it would be unwise to ignore completely the word נֶפֶשׁ, since knowledge of its meaning may help us towards a more precise understanding of חַיִּים.[2]

While being aware of the danger of imposing a false uniformity on Hebrew thought by offering a general meaning for this much-discussed term, we may with some assurance say that the word נֶפֶשׁ connotes the power of vitality which animates the body. This power is associated with the activity of breathing[3] (Gen. 2: 7; 35: 18; 1 Kings 17: 22) and with the presence of blood (Gen. 9: 4; Deut. 12: 23; Lev. 17: 11, 14), and נֶפֶשׁ can frequently mean 'a life' as a physical entity (e.g. Gen. 12: 13; 19: 19, 20): 'to spare or save a נֶפֶשׁ' means 'to spare or save a life'.[4] When the physical entity is particularised, נֶפֶשׁ means 'individual person', 'someone' (pl., 'persons' or 'people')[5] or denotes 'self', or even the

---

[1] On a few occasions ψυχή appears in the LXX where חָיָה or חַיִּים stands in the MT. These will be dealt with later.

[2] The two words belong to one semantic field, and therefore illumine one another: see Barr, *Semantics*, p. 235.

[3] 'There is no reason to doubt that the primary meaning of *nephesh* was "breath", like that of the Arabic *nafsun* = soul (*nafasun* = breath), though there is but one instance in the OT in which "breath" is the most natural rendering (Job 41: 19, 20)', H. W. Robinson, 'Hebrew Psychology', in *The People and the Book*, ed. A. S. Peake (Oxford, 1925), p. 356.

[4] Also Gen. 19: 17; 37: 21; 44: 30; 2 Kings 1: 13; Ps. 6: 5, etc.

[5] Gen. 12: 5; Exod. 1: 5; 12: 4, 15, 16, 19; Lev. 4: 2, 27; 5: 1, 2, 4, 15, 17.

personal pronoun.[1] In a third main group of usages the word נֶפֶשׁ denotes the subject of the vital manifestations of life, both psychical and physiological:[2] it is the seat of appetites such as hunger (Lam. 1: 11) and thirst (Isa. 29: 8), of emotions and passions, such as love (Gen. 44: 30), disgust (Num. 21: 5), hatred (2 Sam. 5: 8), anger, wrath and sorrow. Desires and emotions are characteristics of life that is genuine and meaningful, and it is a man's נֶפֶשׁ which expresses his life, as well as being the subject of living, and of its opposite, dying.

The word to which we give greater attention is חַיִּים. We may begin by noting the application of the term to ordinary physical existence (a) in relation to its antithesis, death (Jer. 21: 8; Jos. 2: 13), (b) in relation to time only, where the emphasis is on the continuance of a person's existence, for example, 'the days of one's life' (Deut. 4: 9; 1 Sam. 7: 15), 'the years of one's life' (Gen. 23: 1; Exod. 6: 16), and (c) in relation to actions and events which occur during a lifetime, e.g. valorous deeds (Judg. 16: 30), marriage (Lev. 18: 18), praising God (Ps. 104: 33).

Although the term חַיִּים itself signifies only physical, organic life, and that with reference mostly to the extent of existence in time, there are sufficient indications in the associations of the word to justify the claim that, in Israelite faith, 'life' is something more than the mere continuance of physical existence.[3] There is a clear recognition of the distinct character and dignity of man's life. It is true that the animals were created by God and that each, like man, was נֶפֶשׁ חַיָּה (Gen. 1: 21, 24; 2: 7), but into man alone did 'God breathe the breath of life' (נִשְׁמַת חַיִּים)': man's life is, in a direct way, the gift of God. The high place given to man by God in his world-order is reflected in the character and content of the life man may and should enjoy. To be worthy of the name, 'life' must be something exuberant and joyous, to which the possession of goods, wealth and family contribute. When the Israelites say, 'Let the king live (יְחִי הַמֶּלֶךְ)', 1 Kings 1: 25 and 2 Sam. 16: 16, their desire is not exhausted by his being granted

---

[1] Gen. 27: 4 (= 'I'); 27: 19 (= 'thou'); Isa. 44: 20; 47: 14; 51: 23; Ps. 3: 3.

[2] Cf. Th. Vriezen, *Outline of OT Theology*, p. 202, '*Nefesh* is the motor impulse in a man's life, physically as well as psychically'.

[3] Cf. *From Death to Life*, R. Martin-Achard (ET, Edinburgh, 1960), ch. 1, esp. pp. 5 ff.

continuance of earthly life: they desire that he should be rich and great, strong in himself and for his people (cf. Ps. 72: 15). 'May the king live for ever', they also say (1 Kings 1: 31; Dan. 2: 4) for life shows its strength by not perishing, and the possession of life is, in itself, an unqualified good (cf. Job. 2: 4).[1]

Man's life, however, is more than simply length of days and abundance of possessions: it consists rather in what he is by virtue of his goals and ideals. In this connection the Wisdom literature is important. The pessimistic outlook which characterises Ecclesiastes focuses attention on enjoyment, but in Proverbs the ideal is the good life, the life of righteousness. 'In the paths of righteousness is life' (Prov. 12: 28; cf. 11: 19; 10: 16); wisdom is the source and means of life (3: 2; 8: 35), and the fear of the Lord leads to life (19: 23). The spirit of these passages, and indeed their vocabulary, is Deuteronomic. We recall the utterance of Deut. 8: 3, 'Man lives (יִחְיֶה) by everything which proceeds from the mouth of the Lord': in the promulgation of the law, Moses sets before Israel life (חַיִּים) and good, death and evil (Deut. 30: 15 ff.); and Deut. 30: 20 '...loving the Lord your God, obeying his voice and cleaving to him, that is your life (חַיֶּיךָ) and the length of your days'. The Holiness code expresses the same point of view: Lev. 18: 5 (quoted at Neh. 9: 29, and developed at Ezek. 18: 21) 'You shall keep my statutes and ordinances, by doing which a man shall live'. The choice between life and death confronts man: by hearkening to the word and will of God he will live.[2] Length of days and fullness of life depend on obedience and righteousness.[3] Amos presents the same challenge to Israel: 'Seek the Lord and live' (5: 4, 6), where 'seeking the Lord' means seeking and loving good, establishing justice and fairness where injustice and dishonesty existed (vv. 14, 15). Only by faithfulness, that is, by loyalty to Yahweh and his covenant, will the righteous man live (Hab. 2: 4). In these instances the verb חָיָה connotes not only physical survival in a time of disaster, but also living in right relation to God.

The sense of security which comes to the godly man from his

---

[1] See J. Pedersen, *Israel: its Life and Culture*, I–II (London, 1926), 152 ff.

[2] BDB remark (p. 311, *sub* חיה) that the verb often has 'the pregnant sense of fullness of life in the divine favour'.

[3] See R. Bultmann *et al.*, *Life and Death* (Bible Key Words Series, London, 1965), p. 19.

consciousness of fellowship with God requires comment. The Psalms have many expressions of this theme. For instance, Ps. 16: 10–11—'Thou dost not give me up to Sheol or let thy godly one see the Pit. Thou dost show me the path of life (אֹרַח חַיִּים): in thy presence there is fulness of joy and in thy right hand are pleasures for evermore.' Against the view that the Psalmist here expresses belief in a full life with Yahweh after death, it is pointed out that 'death' and similar terms frequently connote diminished vitality or deep affliction, and that to 'be restored to life' or 'delivered from Sheol' may mean 're-established in vigour and well-being'. If this is the case, then the Psalmist's total meaning will be that Yahweh delivers him from present affliction (which brought him near to death) and will enable him to live to a ripe old age. But, even if this interpretation is accepted, the Psalm clearly declares that communion with God is the supreme good, and that assurance is a central element in the final biblical view of life after death.[1] It finds expression again in Ps. 73, which probably originated in Wisdom circles:

> I am continually with thee:
> Thou dost hold my right hand,
> Thou dost guide me with thy counsel
> And afterward thou wilt receive me to (in) glory.
> Whom have I in heaven but thee?
> And there is nothing on earth I desire beside thee:
> My heart and my flesh may fail,
> But Yahweh is the strength of my heart
> And my portion for ever. (vv. 23 ff.)

The Hebrew does not suggest life beyond death as strongly as the English versions, and some think that only blessing and deliverance in this life are referred to, but (i) 'afterward' seems to be parallel to 'their end' (v. 17), the *ultimate* fate of the wicked; (ii) the root לָקַח ('receive') may be used in the special sense of God taking a man hence;[2] and (iii) the context of the passage describes an experience of communion with Yahweh which is fullness of life in spite of present affliction and injustice, and which

[1] On this Psalm and on Ps. 73, see G. W. Anderson's commentary in *New Peake*, pp. 416, 428.

[2] The idea of 'rapture' was current in Israel and in ancient Babylon. It is illustrated in the taking away of Elijah (2 Kings 2: 1) and of Enoch (Gen. 5: 24): see also Ps. 49: 16.

the Psalmist considers to be unbreakable.[1] G. von Rad has rightly warned against seeing in expressions of this kind any dramatic religious breakthrough:[2] in Israel's thought security and joy depend solely on a sense of Yahweh's presence, and what we have in these statements of personal faith is a special emphasis on the *unlimited extension* of this life-fellowship (*Lebensgemeinschaft*), even beyond death.[3] This assurance, however, does not indicate a general belief in a resurrection after death: the possibility of life beyond death envisaged here depends on a personal relationship of special, almost exceptional, intimacy with Yahweh.[4] This personal casting of oneself upon Yahweh in life, which brings the faithful over the threshold of death, underwent a profound change in apocalyptic thought which expressed the hope of a collective resurrection of the faithful (Isa. 26: 19, 'thy dead shall live')[5] caused by the vivifying 'dews' of God, and later of a more general resurrection, of some to eternal damnation, and some to eternal life, לְחַיֵּי עוֹלָם, Dan. 12: 2[6]—the first and only time in the Old Testament canon when these words appear. By the time of the book of Daniel the old reserve towards ideas of a life after death, caused by reaction against the mythology of dying and rising gods, had been overcome in Israel, and it was possible to state in a new form the victory of life over death for the faithful.[7] No picture is drawn of the conditions of this

[1] J. Pedersen, 'Wisdom and Immortality', *VT*, Suppl. III (1955), 245, 'The approaches to a belief in an individual resurrection found in the Old Testament are due to a demand for the accomplishment of justice'.

[2] *Old Testament Theology*, I (ET, Edinburgh, 1962), 406.

[3] Cf. W. Eichrodt, *Theologie des Alten Testaments*, Band III (Leipzig, 1939), 165.

[4] The significance of this is increased if we regard the 'I' of the Lament-Psalms as the king, high-priest or prophet. For the view that there is no belief in immortality or resurrection in these Psalms, see C. Barth, *Die Errettung vom Tode in den individuellen Klage- und Dankliedern des AT* (Basel, 1947).

[5] This passage is contained in the so-called Apocalypse of Isaiah which almost all scholars consider to be post-exilic. Some have dated it in the Maccabean period, others in the fourth century B.C.

[6] It is now almost universally agreed among scholars that the book of Daniel, as we now have it, was written in the time of Antiochus Epiphanes, about 165 B.C.

[7] For a study of the development of the doctrine of resurrection, see H. Birkeland, 'The Belief in the Resurrection of the Dead in the Old Testament', *ST*, III (1950), 60–78. He makes a distinction between (i) the

coming time: the form of the expression עוֹלָם חַיֵּי simply connotes 'life of the remotest time (forwards) ',[1] the life of perpetuity, that is, continuing life as contrasted with continuing corruption.

In conclusion we may reiterate what is perhaps the most significant aspect of the Hebrew understanding of 'life', namely, its dependence on God. Wherever there is life, it is God's gift. 'He breathed into man the breath of life' (Gen. 2: 7): obedience in righteousness to his will is the means of entering into the enjoyment of his gift in its reality and fullness. The life after death is also a gift from God, given within his indestructible fellowship or by his resurrecting power. That life in all its aspects should be so dependent on God need not surprise us, for the God of the Old Testament is himself the Living God, active and creative. Oaths are sworn 'as truly as Yahweh lives': praise is offered to the living God (Ps. 18: 47; 42: 3; 84: 3). He is *the* 'Living One'.[2] Alive himself, this God is the fountain of life (Ps. 36: 10), its inexhaustible source. Life here and now, life after death, are given and sustained by him.

Note on the form חַיִּים

Some scholars regard חַיִּים as an example of the plural of mystery or majesty, denoting what escapes man's grasping. GK-Cowley lists it among the plurals which intensively focus the characteristics in-

possibility of a life beyond death, dependent on a miracle by God (as in Psalms and in the Suffering Servant Songs), (ii) the belief in the restoration of the people, and (iii) the actual belief in an eschatological resurrection. The last development (he thinks) was due not to association with agricultural and fertility religions, but to Iranian influence on Israelite belief. 'There is no plain evidence of any belief in a (relatively) *general* resurrection of the dead in the OT before the Persian-Hellenistic time. Before that time only the belief in some exceptional wonders is testified. Still more: before the Persian-Hellenistic time, we find no special attention paid to the resurrection of the *body*, even in the few exceptional cases mentioned' (p. 75). See also, R. Martin-Achard, *From Death to Life*, pp. 74–181, 186–205.

[1] The phrase is from E. Jenni, 'Das Wort *'ōlām* im AT', *ZAW*, LXIV (1952), 244 ff. Cf. J. Barr, *Biblical Words for Time*, pp. 69 ff. and 117 ff. We cannot translate the words as 'life of the age', for the sense of 'age' or 'period' for עוֹלָם is of very late origin in Hebrew, and probably does not occur in the Old Testament, except possibly, though doubtfully, at Eccles. 3: 11.

[2] The emphasis on God's being everlastingly alive probably developed as an antithesis to Canaanite belief in dying and rising deities, cf. Vriezen, *An Outline of Old Testament Theology*, p. 171.

herent in the idea of the stem,[1] so that חַיִּים will mean 'the abstract idea of the qualities of the living being'. Brockelmann's comparative grammar suggests that חַיִּים is an abstract noun expressed by the plural of the related concrete or adjectival form, and goes on to explain it in terms of the primitive tendency to attribute vitality to various parts of the body and not to one single source.[2] F. C. Burkitt suggested that the plural form must be interpreted as having temporal significance, not as expressing an abstract idea.[3] The word is plural 'because the Hebrews regarded life as consisting of successive instants or moments or days or years. A man's חַיִּים is the period during which he is alive.' While not denying the fact that the Hebrews were concerned about length of life, it seems unlikely to us that we can read off so much about their understanding of life from this plural form. Still others see the word as an intensive plural, denoting diversity in unity: חַיִּים expresses life in its many modes and manifestations.

It is impossible to explain with certainty the form of the word as we have it (and it is plural in other Semitic languages), but it seems to be most helpful to interpret it along the lines suggested by Brockelmann. The adjective חַי means 'living', 'a living being', and its plural is חַיִּים, 'living beings'. That which all these living beings share, the one characteristic common to each and to all of them, is 'life' or 'existence', and this comes to be expressed by the same word חַיִּים.

Whether this is the case or not—and it is not our task to explain the form, but to discuss use and meaning—it soon becomes clear that the word חַיִּים represents the state of being alive, with emphasis on the character and quality of the process, whereas נֶפֶשׁ emphasises the *personal* vitality of the being who lives.

THE CLASSICAL GREEK USAGE OF ζωή

The noun ζωή appears only three times in the Homeric poems and on each occasion bears the sense 'property' or 'a man's substance'.[4] After Homer, it usually and frequently means 'the physical life or existence' of living organisms (animals, men, plants) and, as such, is the opposite of 'death'. 'Life' is not regarded as a thing, but as the quality of being alive by which all living beings are characterised: consequently ζωή is scarcely

---

[1] Para. 124 a–d.
[2] *Grundriss der vergleichenden Grammatik der semitischen Sprachen* (Berlin, 1908–13), II, 59–60.
[3] *ZNW*, XII (1911), 228–30.
[4] *Od.* 14. 96, 208; 16. 429. Cf. also Herod. 8. 105 and Arist. *HA.* 608 b 21.

ever used in the plural. Very occasionally the word connotes 'way of life'.[1]

From the earliest literature onwards the verb ʒῆν is used of animal life, 'to live' (Hom. *Il.* 24. 559; Arist. *NE.* 1097*b*33, etc.). Aristotle's language seems to suggest some kind of difference between 'existence' (τὸ εἶναι) and 'life' (τὸ ʒῆν), *NE.* 1170*b*, and this may be explicable in terms of his definition of 'life'— 'Life is defined in the case of animals by the capacity for sensation, in the case of man, by the capacity for sensation and thought' (1170*a*). The second main use of ʒῆν (as equivalent to βιοῦν) means 'to pass one's life', e.g. *Od.* 15. 491 and Soph. *El.* 599.

Liddell and Scott draw attention to an uncommon use of the verb with the pregnant sense, 'to live fully, or in the fullest sense'. For instance, Xen. *Memor.* 3. 3. 11 speaks of 'excellent principles by which we understand how to live', where there is undoubtedly the suggestion of true or right living: this idea may also be present in Isoc. *Paneg.* 27 which mentions the foundation of a city 'in which we may be able to (really) live'. Again, Dio Cassius relates how Similis was promoted by Trajan to the command of the guards, but, on finding the post wearisome, resigned and spent the last seven years of his life privately: his epitaph is 'Here lies Similis, having lived so many years (βιούς), but having really lived (ʒήσας) seven years' (69: 19). Menander also appears to have made use of the word in a similar sense (if a fragment from the Πλοκίον has been rightly completed by Seneca), 'It is but a small part of life (βίος) wherein we really live (ʒῶμεν)'. The verb βιόω does not seem to have developed any comparable 'high' sense.

It is frequently assumed, particularly in discussions of New Testament usage,[2] that the ethical and qualitative idea commonly associated with βίος in Classical Greek was transferred in the sacred literature to ʒωή, but was not present in the classical use of ʒωή. This assumption is not strictly accurate. As well as meaning 'manner of living', βίος often indicates 'period, or term of life',[3]

---

[1] Herod. 4. 112, 114. This sense generally belongs to βίος. 'Βίος indicates the way of life, the character, and is closely related to ἦθος', Bultmann, *Life and Death*, p. 23.

[2] E.g. Moulton and Milligan, *VGT*, p. 274.

[3] Hom. *Od.* 18. 254; Aristoph. *Pax* 439; Isoc. 6. 45; Plato, *Leg.* 870*e*; Soph. *Ant.* 1114; Arist. *Pol.* 1272*a*37.

and indeed this may be the basic meaning of the word. Its ethical connotation depends on the context and particularly on adjectives qualifying it, e.g. τελεῖος (Arist. *NE*. 1098 *a* 18), ἡδύς (*ibid.* 1169 *b* 26) and ἀγαθός (*Od.* 15.491), etc.[1] But the same may be said of ζωή. Arist. *NE*. 1170 *a* 23 mentions μοχθηρὰ ζωὴ καὶ διεφθαρμένη, i.e. 'vicious and corrupt life': and in a notable passage Plato (*Rep.* 521 *a*) speaks of rulers who are 'rich in that wealth which makes happiness, namely a wise and virtuous life (ζωῆς ἀγαθῆς τε καὶ ἔμφρονος)'. Again a qualitative suggestion is present in μακαρία ζωή, a phrase by which Plato (*Leg.* 713 *c*) recalls the Life of the Golden Age. This use of ζωή may be infrequent in classical literature, but it nevertheless shows that the ethical and qualitative connotation was not associated solely with the word βίος.

THE USAGE OF THE SEPTUAGINT AND INTERTESTAMENTAL LITERATURE

Of the 149 appearances of the noun חַיִּים in the Old Testament, 130 are translated by ζωή and ten by the verb ζῆν. In three of the remaining nine all reference to 'life' is missing in the LXX, and the other six use various terms. For instance, at Prov. 31: 12 יְמֵי חַיִּים is rendered by βίος, although at that point A S Θ have the literal form ἡμέραι τῆς ζωῆς. At Prov. 4: 10 'years of life' becomes ὁδοὶ βίου, either through a misreading of the Hebrew or because ὁδούς was found in the following verse. In Proverbs the 'duration of life' is expressed by βίος, the common word in classical literature for 'lifetime': in fact the use of the noun βίος (translating the Hebrew יוֹם) and the verb βιοῦν belongs almost exclusively to Job and Proverbs in the Canon[2]— books whose Greek translators were sensitive to Greek style and usage.[3] On two occasions (Ps. 64: 2; Job 33: 30; cf. Job 38: 39) the noun חַיִּים, and on two occasions (Ps. 74: 19; Job 33: 28) the verb חָיָה are translated by ψυχή, the usual word for נֶפֶשׁ, a living being.

[1] It would seem that βίος never refers to the character of life without a qualifying adjective.
[2] The words are found also in Sirach, Wisdom and 2, 3, 4 Maccabees. Cf. Bultmann, *Life and Death*, p. 33 (G. Bertram).
[3] Cf. G. Gerleman, *Studies in the Septuagint: Job* (Lund, 1946), and *Proverbs* (Lund, 1956).

When we inquire what other words are translated by ζωή in the LXX there is nothing of importance to record. Once (Job 7: 1) it renders יָמִים: twice (Prov. 23: 3; 27: 27) it represents לֶחֶם, a translation which recalls the ancient classical use of ζωή to mean 'substance, means of sustaining life'. At Prov. 18: 4 ζωή appears in the LXX for חָכְמָה ('wisdom') and at Hos. 10: 12 for חֶסֶד ('steadfast love'). It would be difficult to explain satisfactorily these varied Septuagintal readings, assuming they are not due to simple error, but we may spare ourselves the attempt by reason of the infrequency of their occurrence and the consequent un-likelihood of their having affected the background of the New Testament term ζωή: the word generally corresponds to the Hebrew חַיִּים, even when the latter possesses the pregnant sense of 'real life' achieved through obedience to and fellowship with God.

At Isa. 26: 19 the phrase 'thy dead shall live' is translated in the LXX by οἱ νεκροὶ ἀναστήσονται, the verb ἀνίστημι being specially associated with *resurrection* into life. The later translators, Aquila, Symmachus and Theodotion, all use ζήσονται. In the important 'resurrection' passage (Dan. 12: 2) the first mention of the 'eternal life' of the pious is rendered in the LXX by εἰς ζωὴν αἰώνιον, this being the only place in the canonical Old Testament scriptures where this conjunction of noun and adjective occurs. The adjective αἰώνιος first appears in Plato, and from that period onwards it is used to mean 'enduring for an indefinitely long time, perpetual, eternal': bearing this meaning, it is a satisfactory rendering of the Hebrew עוֹלָם.[1]

When we pass to the Apocryphal and Pseudepigraphical writings (both Hellenistic and Palestinian) we find most of the uses of ζωή which we have noticed still present. The word is very frequently used to connote the duration of life, and the continuance of life is considered as good (Tob. 8: 17).[2] The ideas associated with the word are those of the Old Testament. The commands of God are the commands of life (Bar. 3: 9), and length of days and life are associated with the learning of wisdom (Bar. 3: 14). Life (with stress on the physical aspect) is regarded as a recompense for righteous living: 'They that do alms and

---

[1] See p. 168 for remarks on the meaning of עוֹלָם.

[2] ζωή, like βίος, may be used to mean 'a man's living' (Sir. 4: 1; 31: 25?). Both words can bear this meaning in Classical Greek.

righteousness shall be filled with life' (Tob. 12: 9, cf. Sib. Or. 4. 45).

In this literature, however, there comes into greater prominence what we may call the conception of eschatological life. In the pre-Christian Psalms of Solomon we read (3: 12), 'They that fear the Lord shall rise to life eternal (ἀναστήσονται εἰς ζωὴν αἰώνιον) and their life (ἡ ζωὴ αὐτῶν) shall be in the light of the Lord and shall come to an end no more': at 13: 11, 'the life (ζωή) of the righteous shall be for ever (εἰς τὸν αἰῶνα)': and at 14: 10 'the saints of the Lord shall inherit life (κληρονομήσουσι ζωήν) in gladness'.[1] The same expectation is affirmed in Slav. En. 50: 2; Sib. Or. proem 84–5; Apoc. Baruch 42: 7, and throughout the seventh chapter of Fourth Esra *vita* and *vivere* are the usual words employed to express participation in salvation.

Considerable interest attaches to the eschatological outlook of the Book of Enoch. At 37: 4 Enoch claims that 'the lot of eternal life'[2] has been given to him by the Lord of Spirits, and in his Third Similitude he declares that 'the righteous will be in the light of the sun and the elect in the light of eternal life: there will be no end to the days of their life' (58. 3; cf. 91. 10; 103. 4). The blessed righteous and elect dwell in a garden (60. 8), called the 'garden of life' (61. 12), located (according to 70. 3–4) between the north and west, and (according to 77. 3) at the furthest extremity of the quarter of the earth called north.[3] Most of these passages are found in the Similitudes section of Enoch, and the fact that no fragments of these chapters have been found at Qumran creates a strong presumption that they are substantially of late (even post-Christian) origin. But Aramaic fragments of ch. 77 (which locates the garden of righteousness in the north) have been discovered, one of which contains the words לפרד[ס קושטא ('the paradise of righteousness');[4] and a strong case can

---

[1] The passages 3: 12 and 13: 11 suggest contact with Dan. 12: 2 and point to the idea expressed there. Some other verses in the Psalms (e.g. 9: 5) may refer to eschatological life, but their interpretation is uncertain.

[2] At Enoch 10. 10 ζωὴ αἰώνιος is used of long life, where an ultimate termination is expected (after 500 years).

[3] A full study of these geographical details is made by P. Grelot, 'La Géographie Mythique d'Hénoch et ses Sources Orientales', and J. T. Milik, 'Hénoch au pays des aromates', *RB*, LXV (1958), 33 ff. and 70 ff.

[4] See Milik, *op. cit.* p. 76.

be made out for the antiquity of chapter 70.[1] Probably, therefore, we have two pre-Christian Jewish passages in 1 Enoch testifying to the belief that the righteous and elect live eternally in a paradise 'in the north'.[2]

The Hellenistic–Jewish books of Maccabees frequently express the certainty of a life beyond death. As he dies, the second of the seven martyred brothers says, 'The King of the Universe will raise us up to everlasting life (εἰς αἰώνιον ἀναβίωσιν ζωῆς) because we have died for his laws' (2 Macc. 7: 9), and the fourth brother exclaims to the tyrant, 'There will be no resurrection into life (ἀνάστασις εἰς ζωὴν) for you' (7: 14): while the youngest of the martyrs claims that 'our brothers are under the covenant of God for everlasting life (ἀενάου ζωῆς ὑπὸ διαθήκην θεοῦ)' (7: 36). The mother of the martyrs is described in 4 Macc. 15: 3 as follows, 'She loved religion which preserves to eternal life (εἰς αἰώνιον ζωὴν) according to God's premise'. The idea of the restoration of life and breath (or spirit) to the dead is expressed at 2 Macc. 7: 23 and 14: 46. The formulation of such ideas may be regarded as the response to the tragic loss of Hebrew manhood in the Maccabean persecutions. It is a response which (whatever foreign influences contributed to it) is true to essential Old Testament religious insights in its emphasis on the lasting worth of righteous living. This is a theme basic to the future hope: 'the life of the righteous shall endure for ever' (Ps. Sol. 13: 11); the hope of the righteous, in death, is full of immortality (ἀθανασία) (Wisd. 3: 2–4); 'The righteous live for ever' (Wisd. 5: 15), and in summary, 'Righteousness is immortal (ἀθάνατος)' (Wisd. 1: 15).

When we ask if the Intertestamental writings offer any explanation of the enduring life, we find hints in such passages as Slav.

[1] M. Black, *JTS* (n.s.), III (1952), 4–10 claims that chs. 70–1 represent an older Son of Man/Enoch tradition (integral to 1 Enoch) 'out of which the Similitudes have grown, by a rewriting of the Enoch legend in support of a doctrine of a supernatural Messiah, foreign to the original conception of 1 Enoch'.

[2] Milik, *op. cit.* p. 77 note 1, offers as a reason for the popularity of the Enoch writings in Qumran the fact that in them the question 'Where is Paradise?' receives an answer. He suggests that the north–south orientation of the Qumran graves (the head at the south-end) was governed by the wish that at the general resurrection the Covenanters would rise to face north and then proceed towards the Paradise.

En. 30: 8 and Wisd. 2: 23–4 ('God created man for incorruption, ἐπ' ἀφθαρσίᾳ, and made him an image of his own proper essence') which imply an original indestructible element in man which, in the case of the righteous, is the pledge of immortality.[1] Where the ideas of Palestinian Judaism are dominant, the life after death is considered as created by God through the resurrection of the dead.

PHILO JUDAEUS AND THE HERMETIC WRITINGS

In the writings of Philo the term ζωή is frequently used in the general sense of the 'life' of animals and men,[2] of which life God is author and source.[3] The term is used also in the more particular sense of 'mortal life' as opposed to θάνατος (*Heres* 209), and, whereas death is an evil, life is a good (*Fug.* 58). But 'life' may vary in quality and worth:

some people are dead while living (ζῶντες) and some alive (ζῶσι) while dead;...bad people, prolonging their days to extreme old age are dead men, deprived of the life in association with virtue (τὸν μετ' ἀρετῆς βίον), while good people, even if cut off from their partnership with the body, live for ever (ζῆν εἰσαεί) and are granted immortality (ἀθανάτου μοίρας ἐπιλαχόντας) (*Fug.* 55).

The importance of the quality and character of 'life' is underlined as this passage continues with an interpretation of Deut. 4: 4 ('Ye that did cleave unto the Lord your God are alive, all of you, at this day')—'only those who have taken refuge in God and become his suppliants does Moses recognise as living (ζῶντας), accounting the rest to be dead men'. This *real* life (ἡ ἀληθινὴ ζωή) was obtainable from the 'tree of life' (i.e. wisdom) but was not accepted by man, who chose instead misery (*Leg. All.* III, 52). What was this ἀληθινὴ ζωή?

We must here take account of the distinction made by Philo between the life of the body and the life of the soul or of reason. There are two kinds of men: those who live by reason, the divine

---

[1] The 'death which entered the world by the envy of the devil' (*v.* 24) refers to spiritual death, not physical. Both the righteous and the evil experience the latter: but the evil must endure the former, while the righteous enter life.

[2] *Spec.* III, 198, 201; *Virt.* 143; *Mut.* 223; *Congr.* 33; *Som.* I, 20.

[3] *Opif.* 30; *Aet.* 106; *Fug.* 198.

in-breathing, and those who live by blood and the pleasure of the flesh (*Heres* 56). The blood-life or life of sensation is opposed to the life of mind and reason: the former finds its material, so to speak, in the physical organisation, and is irrational: only its subordination to the divine element, reason, can produce life that is true life. An attempted blend of Platonic, Stoic and Aristotelian conceptions enables Philo to claim that life in accordance with reason (the divinely in-breathed gift) is the real life of man, ὄντως ʒῆν (*Deter.* 84). Since reason, however, enables us to be indifferent to the so-called bodily and external interests and to be superior to the allurements of passion, it is the fountain of all virtue: hence to live 'rationally' is to live 'virtuously'. For Philo the most generic virtue is called 'goodness' (ἀγαθότης);[1] but occasionally (and in accordance with the genius of the Hebrew mind) piety (εὐσεβεία), which includes justice and philanthropy, assumes the leading place among the virtues. It requires us to love God as benefactor,[2] to fear him as Lord, to serve him and keep his commandments. To do this is to achieve real life (*Congr.* 87 on Lev. 18: 1–5).

We may fairly claim, then, that for Philo life according to reason, the life of virtue and the life of piety and holiness are essentially the same in character and manifestation. As their source and support is one, namely the Logos,[3] so also do they share in one fulfilment, namely ἀθανασία.[4] The rational soul or

[1] This is represented by the river which watered Paradise and flows out of the Wisdom of God. It is therefore, in a sense, identical with the sacred Logos, in conformity with which it was made. As the river is said to have parted into four great streams or dominions, so goodness divides into the four great virtues. Cf. J. Drummond, *Philo Judaeus* (London, 1888), II, 315.

[2] The element of love in man's approach to God is strongly emphasised by Philo. 'This is the most noble definition of endless life (ἀθάνατος βίος) to be possessed by a love of God with which flesh and body have no concern' (*Fug.* 58).

[3] The Logos, as God's Thought or Reason, is 'imaged' in human reason, and 'each rule of conduct which we can treat as an injunction of reason is itself a Logos, one of those innumerable thoughts or laws into which the universal thought may, through self-reflection, be resolved' (Drummond, *op. cit.* p. 273). The universal Logos finds partial expression in various Logoi, identified with divine ethical ideas, by which the soul ought to be governed.

[4] Throughout his writings Philo speaks of immortality rather than of resurrection of the body. References to the latter doctrine in the traditional literature were understood as figurative means of referring to immortality. Cf. H. A. Wolfson, *Philo* (Harvard University Press, 1947), I, 404.

mind is incorruptible and immortal (*Prob.* 46 and *Congr.* 97): created man, inspired by the divine spirit or breath, which is the essence of the power of this rational principle, does not differ, when placed in the paradise of virtues (Eden), from the tree that brings forth deathless life (*Plant.* 44), since both are imperishable. The life of the body is, as we have pointed out, in opposition to the life of the mind, but the eternal possibilities in the latter are illustrated by *Gig.* 14 which speaks of those philosophers who study to die to the life in the body in order that a higher existence, immortal and incorporeal, may be their portion. In short, reason leads to virtue, which is the path to immortal life. The plants of life, immortality and knowledge, will not grow in the barren soul, but in the reasonable soul (λογική ψυχή), whose path towards virtue has, as its end, life and immortality (*Plant.* 37). The life of virtue is, for the Jew, essentially the life of piety and holiness: it is not therefore surprising that Philo suggests that righteous conduct here and now has within it the seeds of immortal life.[1] Commenting on the promise of the fifth commandment ('...that thy days may be long upon the land') he says (*Spec.* II, 262), 'It offers deathlessness given by a prolonged vitality and age-long life (ἀθανασίαν διὰ πολυχρονίου ζωῆς καὶ βίου μακραίωνος) which thou wilt keep nourishing (θρέψεις), even while in the body, if thou live with a soul purged clean of all impurity.'

Having already drawn attention to the fact that the life of reason, the life of virtue and the life of piety are united in their source, the Divine Logos, we may note that the same Logos is the ultimate source of the eternal life which is promised as their reward. In expounding the meaning of 'the cities of refuge' in which suppliants might save their lives, Philo declares (*Fug.* 75), 'Is not life eternal (ζωὴ αἰώνιος)[2] to take refuge with him who is?' and proceeds to explain that the six cities correspond to six divine powers, but the chief of them is the divine Logos.

[1] Cf. F. von Hugel, *Eternal Life* (Edinburgh, 1913), p. 52, writing of Philo, points out that, since God is the fount of reason, a reasonable life is a life of God, and adds, 'Indeed this divine life, even as a man can begin to live it here by a holy life, and still more as, after such a life, he will live it in the Beyond, is sometimes characterised as strictly eternal'.

[2] This the only occurrence of the word-combination in Philo's writings.

The swiftest runner, fleeing from involuntary faults, must urge his breathless course to the highest divine Logos, the fountain of wisdom, that he may draw thence, instead of death, eternal life (ἀΐδιος ζωή) (*Fug.* 94).

The various aspects of the Philonic teaching on immortality, like most of his characteristic teachings, find their synthesis in his comprehensive doctrine of the Logos.

In the Hermetic writings[1]—which illustrate a type of religious thought akin to some aspects of Johannine thought —we find 'life' defined as the union of mind and soul (XI. 14) or of mind and Logos, the offspring or image of Nous (God) (I. 6). The significance of this is explained as follows by C. H. Dodd:

The creative Word is the offspring of the eternal Mind, just as articulate thought and speech in us are the offspring of the human mind; not that these are to be thought of, in either case, as separate entities; life, as a concrete activity, depends on their unity. For a mind not expressing itself is not really alive, and speech which is not the expressed thought of a permanent rational personality is *vox et praeterea nihil*. Similarly, this living universe is such only as it is the expression of the Eternal Mind.[2]

At Tractate I. 9 (Poimandres) the Primal God (Nous) is himself described as being ζωὴ καὶ φῶς (cf. XIII. 18–19) and Dodd suggests the influence of Old Testament symbolism from Ps. 36:9, 'With thee is the fountain of life; in thy light we shall see light'.[3] Philo also draws attention to the presence of these two ideas at the beginning of the Creation story (*Opif.* 30) and so witnesses to the fact that the view that the union of 'light' and 'life' gives the most satisfactory account of God in his creative aspect was well established in the Christian era, where Jewish and Hellenistic thought met in the Egyptian environment. The archetypal man (οὐσιώδης ἄνθρωπος) shares the same attributes: he was originally of the substance of the Father (i.e. life and light) and became 'from life and light, soul and mind; from life, soul and

---

[1] The writings were produced in Egypt, for the most part, in the second and third centuries A.D.
[2] *The Bible and the Greeks*, p. 119; cf. *Corpus Hermeticum*, ed. Nock and Festugière (Paris, 1945), I, 18.
[3] *The Interpretation of the Fourth Gospel* (Cambridge, 1953), p. 19.

from light, mind' (I. 17).[1] In Tractate XII we find the remarkable statement, 'As heaven, water, earth and air are parts of the world, so life and immortality (ζωὴ καὶ ἀθανασία)...are parts of God' (XII. 21), which Dodd interprets as meaning that 'as God is manifestly the cause of physical life in the world, so we can look to Him for life everlasting'.[2] To describe the life after death the usual word in the Hermetic literature is ἀθανασία, but ζωή is used for the divine life into which man may enter either here and now or after death. Chapter 21 of Tractate I suggests that the way for an individual to regain the immortality which belongs to Essential Man is to know his origin.

The God and Father of whom man came is life and light. If therefore you hear that you are of light and life, and believe (πιστεύῃς) that you are of these, you will enter into life again (εἰς ζωὴν πάλιν χωρήσεις).

In other words, to know God and one's origin in the eternal God is to be immortal.[3] The passage into life is described as an ascent, corresponding to man's primal fall. On this journey man is purified from his passions and at last experiences communion with God. Thus we read in Poimandres 32, 'I believe and testify: I enter into light and life. Blessed art Thou, O Father'. The spiritual and mystical awareness of the truth is at the same time an entrance into life and light, a union with God, and it apparently takes place in this life, when the bodily life has been put to death by asceticism.

Ζωή is used of ordinary physical life where the name of Adam's wife is called Ζωή, life.[4] 'Life' allured man to love her and so brought him low, by affording indulgence for his love of material nature. In this connection, ζωή is clearly not transcendental life, but physical existence.

The writings of Philo represent what may be called an early

---

[1] Probably there is here an echo of Gen. 2: 7. The doctrine of both writers is that the life which is in God is manifested in man as the 'soul'. Cf. Philo, *Leg. All.* I. 32. The Hermetic author adds that the light—which is the other aspect of the divine nature—appears in man as 'mind'.

[2] Dodd, *op. cit.* p. 18.

[3] Cf. *Corp. Herm.* IV. 5, also Philo, *Spec.* I. 345.

[4] The name 'Eve' in Hebrew (חַוָּה) resembles the word for 'life', and the LXX renders the name by Ζωή. Speculation on the name is witnessed to in the *Apocryphon of John*, and in Philo, *Heres* 53.

Jewish gnosticising type of thought which uses pagan religious thought to elucidate the Jewish scriptures. The Hermetic writings, on the other hand, represent a fuller and more developed Gnosticism where the Jewish scriptures become the handmaid of philosophy. It becomes clear from our brief discussions of these works that they represent life as possible on two levels, that of ordinary animal existence, the merely physical plane, and that of mind (cf. *C. Her.* XII. 1–3), of awareness of one's true nature and origin, which is knowledge. All men possess the divine element of the potential life, but only some achieve salvation and ἀθανασία. This is attained, not by the redemption and transformation of the whole man, but by the release of the divine nature which is fettered within the lower levels of existence, a release which is made possible by the imparting of γνῶσις in mystical experiences. Dr F. Müssner sums up the matter well when he says that 'Gnostic redemption does not bring life as a divine gift, but is the drawing back again of the separated sparks of life into transcendent heavenly unity in which they are freed from cosmic forces'.[1] The question whether 'the transcendental form of the Gnostic myth comes to the fore in the concept of "life" in the Fourth Gospel must be answered in the negative, although there are many formal and terminological points of contact between John and Gnosis'.[2]

THE RABBINIC LITERATURE

The phrase 'eternal life' (חַיֵּי עוֹלָם) first appears at Dan. 12:2 to describe the reward of the righteous. The same idea finds expression in various works of Palestinian Judaism. When we turn to the writings of rabbinic Judaism we find the phrase חַיֵּי עָלְמָא appearing in the Targums where the Old Testament speaks simply of 'life', e.g. Lev. 18:5; Deut. 33:6 (Ps. Jon. and Onk.). Here and at Ezek. 20:11, 13, 21, where a similar method of translation is adopted, it seems clear that the meaning intended is 'eternal life'. Judaism has found reference to the idea of a

---

[1] Müssner, ZωH — *Die Anschauung vom 'Leben' im vierten Evangelium* (Munich, 1952), p. 186. See Dodd, *op. cit.* part 1, ch. 5, pp. 97 ff.

[2] Müssner, *loc. cit.* A. Feuillet, *Études Johanniques* (Bruges, 1962), pp. 176 ff. also criticises those who interpret the Johannine teaching in terms of Hellenistic mysticism.

future life where the Old Testament confined its hope to the blessings of longevity through obedience to God.

In the Talmud חַיֵּי עָלְמָא is used occasionally in antithesis to חַיֵּי שָׁעָה, 'temporary, or ephemeral life'. The earliest example of this seems to be the criticism by Eliezer (c. A.D. 90–100) of those who put aside the eternal life and occupy themselves with the transitory life, b. Bez. 15b. The same contrast is imputed to Simeon ben Jochai (c. A.D. 150) at b. Shab. 33b and to Simeon ben Gamaliel (c. A.D. 140) in jer. Moed qat. 82b. Here the emphasis lies on the duration of the life (and perhaps also on the quality) and we might even translate as 'everlasting life'.

Along with the use of חַיֵּי עוֹלָם as the correlative of חַיֵּי שָׁעָה, there arose a different usage which distinguished two עוֹלָמִים, 'this age' and 'the age to come'. The doctrine of the Two Ages is found in developed form in Fourth Ezra (c. A.D. 100), but there appear to be references to it in Enoch 48 and 71, and it is implied in the language of Paul, the Synoptic gospels and Hebrews. The general distinction between the two ages has often been described and here we need only refer to the treatment of the subject in Strack-Billerbeck,[1] Bonsirven[2] and G. F. Moore,[3] while drawing attention to three significant points. First, the doctrine evidently arose in apocalyptic circles. Secondly, while it was undoubtedly well known to the rabbis, references to it are scarce and uncertain in rabbinic sayings before the end of the first Christian century. If the addition to a saying of Hillel, given in P. Aboth. 2. 7, is genuine ('He who acquires for himself the words of the law acquires for himself the life of the Age to come (חַיֵּי הָעוֹלָם הַבָּא)' then this would be the earliest witness to the use of the expression. A second and securer witness is Johanan ben Zaccai (c. A.D. 80) who declares that God revealed to Abraham this age, but not the age to come (Gen. R. 44, cf. also Tos. Peah 4. 18, p. 24). The currency of the expressions is thus well-established from the end of the first century A.D.[4] Thirdly, in the rather confused discussions of Jewish theology concerning the Age to come two lines of thought are present: (i) the Age to come is conceived of as eternally existent: it always *is* in the heavens and

---

[1] SB, IV, 799 ff.
[2] *Le Judaisme Palestinien au temps de Jésus-Christ* (Paris, 1934–5), I, 307 ff.
[3] *Judaism* (Oxford, 1927–30), vol. II.
[4] Cf. G. Dalman, *Words of Jesus* (Edinburgh, 1902), p. 151.

we awake to it at death[1] (1 Enoch 71: 15; P. Aboth 4. 16) and then experience judgment (b. Ber. 28 b): (ii) the Age to come is said to come into being *after* the Messianic age and the general resurrection. The examples of this usage are legion and need not be given at this point.[2] It seems that SB impose too neat a system on the rabbinic doctrine when they interpret these two views as referring to a first and second phase of the world-to-come.[3] In the teaching of Judaism on the עוֹלָם הַבָּא there is neither uniformity nor careful system. We must reckon not only with differences of emphasis in the earlier and later Rabbis, but also with the continuance of apocalyptic ideas (Enoch 71) as distinct from rabbinic conceptions. Moreover, the presence of the two views of the Age to come is not inconsistent with the Old Testament idea of immediate entry into everlasting life after death (Psalms) as well as of its delay till after the Resurrection (Isaiah and Daniel). In fact these two strands of thought probably form the basis of all the strange variety of statement by which apocalyptic and rabbinic Judaism expressed their confident hope in the reality of life in the Age to come.

As one would expect within the teaching of Judaism, the condition of entry into the life of the Age to come is associated with the Torah and obedience. In addition to P. Aboth 2. 7, a late gloss to Aboth 6. 7 affirms that 'Great is the Torah, for to those who practice it it gives life in this world and in the world to come'. Likewise Sifra Lev. 5. 85 d (on 18: 5): '"Keep it", that means to keep and to do it (the Law) and "a man shall live" in the Age which is coming' (cf. Sifre Deut. par. 47–8, p. 110; Mech. Ex. 13. 3 and Pesik. 102 b). According to R. Eliezer (c. A.D. 90) consideration for others, concern for the welfare of children, knowledge of and reverence for God mark the pathway by which men may come to share in the life of the Age to come (b. Berak. 28 b).

While the phrase 'the life of the Age to come' is common in the later Jewish literature, the simple term 'life' is occasionally

---

[1] Cf. W. D. Davies, *Paul and Rabbinic Judaism*, p. 316. Cf. also the works of Moore and Bonsirven, and also J. B. Frey, 'La Vie de l'au-delà dans les conceptions juives au temps de Jésus-Christ', *Biblica*, XIII (1932), 135 ff.

[2] Cf. *A Rabbinic Anthology*, ed. C. Montefiore and H. Loewe (London, 1938), ch. 31. Reference is made on pp. xlvii and 581 to the variety of rabbinic opinion on the theme.　　　　　[3] SB, IV, 819 ff.

used with the same meaning, but only when the antithesis 'life-death' is implied or expressed.[1] We may therefore distinguish within Judaism three main forms of expression: (i) 'life' as contrasted with 'death'; (ii) 'eternal life' as contrasted with the transitory life of time; and (iii) 'the life of the Age to come' contrasted with the 'life of this Age'. In all three there is reference to life beyond the grave.

THE DEAD SEA SCROLLS

From an investigation of the Qumran Scrolls it becomes clear that some of the uses of חַיִּים found in the Old Testament reappear. The use of the word for a man's life or lifetime is common,[2] and its use in association with 'light' and 'wisdom'[3] recalls passages from the sapiential literature, and describes that light and wisdom by which men truly live. It is remarkable that, unlike the rabbinic writings, there appears to be no direct association of the Torah and 'life', although the Torah played a very significant part in the life of the sect. Nevertheless, obedience to God and the entry to the Covenant, which will result from that obedience, constitute the path to real life[4] and ensure incorporation in the Book of life.[5] Those who have entered this path, the elect of God, will be rewarded by '...all everlasting blessings, ever-lasting joy in eternal life (חיי נצח) and perfect glory with fulness of splendour in eternal light' (1QS 4. 7):[6] and CD 3. 18–20 says of the faithful, 'God...forgave them their trespass and pardoned their sin. He built them a sure house in Israel...They who hold fast to it shall possess eternal life (חיי נצח) and all the glory of Adam'.

---

[1] Cf. Dalman, *Words of Jesus*, pp. 159–60 and the examples cited there. Note the use of 'life' to denote life beyond the grave in Ps. Sol. 14. 10 and 2 Macc. 7: 9, 14.

[2] E.g. CD 4. 21; 1QH 5. 6; 9. 6, 11; 2. 17(?); 8. 29(?) and 1QS 1. 1.

[3] 1QS 2. 3 and 3. 6–7.

[4] 1QS 3. 1; 1QH 7. 15. At 1QH 8. 6 'trees of life' is probably an allegorical reference to the members of the sect who acknowledge (or put faith in) the 'fountain of life', which is possibly an allusion to the Teacher of Righteousness (so A. Dupont-Sommer, 'Le Livre des Hymnes', *Semitica*, VII [1957], 62).

[5] 1QM 12. 3.

[6] Over against this 'joy in eternal life' is set 'destruction in the fire of dark regions' (*v.* 13) which is presumably an eschatological reality.

These passages bring us to the debated question of the sect's expectation of immortality. A passage of importance in this connection is 1QH 3. 19–23:

I give thanks unto thee, O Lord,
For thou hast delivered my soul from the pit;
And from Sheol Abaddon thou hast brought me up to the summit of
    the world (to an everlasting height).
I walked on a plain without bounds:
And I knew that there is hope for him whom thou hast fashioned from
    dust for the communion of eternity.
The perverse spirit thou hast cleansed from a great transgression,
To take its place with the host of holy ones (the angels?)
And to enter into fellowship with the company of the sons of heaven.
For thou hast appointed to man eternal lot (destiny) with the spirits
    that have knowledge,
To praise thy name together with them
And to recount thy wonders before all thy works.

With this passage in mind, M. Black claims that 'there is no doubt that, as contrasted with Sadducaean doctrine, the Zadokites did believe in a doctrine of immortal or eternal life'.[1] R. B. Laurin has taken issue with this interpretation and asserts that the passage refers to a deliverance from present distress and suffering into security.[2] He compares the passage with (i) 1QS 6. 7–35, which refers to the restored Israel and to those who are associated with 'angels of the presence', but *on the earthly sphere*, and with (ii) 1QSb 4. 24b–28 where 'the holy dwelling place' in which the priests will share the lot with the 'angels of the presence' is located (by Laurin) in the restored Kingdom. But this latter passage may be interpreted as referring to the dwelling-place of God in heaven,[3] rather than to the sanctuary of a restored

---

[1] *The Scrolls and Christian Origins* (Edinburgh, 1961), pp. 138–9. Black thinks that the immortality included both body and soul, thus differing from Dupont-Sommer (*The Dead Sea Scrolls*, Oxford, 1952, p. 72) who claims that the passage teaches the immortality of the soul only, in harmony with Josephus' account (*BJ*, II, 8. 11) of the Essenes' hope of the immortality of the soul. Cf. J. van der Ploeg, 'L'Immortalité de l'homme d'après les Textes de la Mer Morte', *VT*, II (1952), 171–5.

[2] 'The Question of Immortality in the Qumran "Hodayot"', *JSS*, III (1958), 344 ff.

[3] Earlier in this study we drew attention to the likelihood that the Qumran covenanters located this paradise of God in the North, following the Enoch

Jerusalem. If this is so, the sect's doctrine of immortality would be the same as that of Luke 20: 35 ff. where, in the resurrection of the dead, men and women become ἰσάγγελοι in heaven. Laurin, however, concludes that the Thanksgiving Hymns do not express the hope of immortality for the righteous.

As we would expect, they used the timeless expressions of the biblical Psalms but 'this is implicit in any real fellowship with God' (H. W. Robinson, *Inspiration and Revelation in the Old Testament*, 1946, p. 118). They caught the spirit of the Psalmist when they looked for fellowship with God to last 'forever', yet they remained bound to the belief that one day they would die and that would be the end of it.[1]

If we look beyond the Thanksgiving Hymns and especially to the two passages in which the words חיי נצח appear (CD 3. 20 and 1QS 4. 7) it seems difficult to deny that the sectarians did possess the hope of eternal life. F. Nötscher claims that the words for 'eternal' should not be understood eschatologically in this connection, but merely of long duration:[2] but, while it is true that this is a common meaning of עוֹלָם, the word may also connote infinite prolongation when associated with that which God establishes or gives.[3] Moreover, the probability that we should take the phrase חיי נצח to mean life without cessation by death is increased by the fact that in the two passages where it appears, the context is clearly eschatological. 'All the glory of Adam' (and that probably included original deathlessness) will be restored, the splendour and joy of the Beginning will be renewed; in fact, the state of things before the Fall will be restored and the new obedient mankind will be given life for a thousand generations (CD 7. 5–6), an expression which, as Black says, 'practically means eternal life'.[4]

tradition which was popular among them. The north–south orientation of the graves at Qumran may be explained on this hypothesis. If it is correct, then we would have irrefutable evidence for the sect's belief in life after death.

[1] Laurin, *op. cit.* p. 355.
[2] *Zur theologischen Terminologie der Qumran-Texte* (Bonn, 1956), p. 157.
[3] Cf. J. Barr, *Biblical Words for Time*, p. 70.
[4] Black, *op. cit.* p. 139.

THE MEANING AND USE OF αἰώνιος

Before entering upon the detailed discussion of ζωή and ζωή αἰώνιος in the New Testament, we must investigate the meaning of the adjective αἰώνιος. The word first appears in Plato with the meaning 'perpetual', 'enduring for an indefinitely long time' (*Rep.* 363 *d*), 'everlasting' (*Tim.* 37, 38 *c*; *Leg.* x. 904 *a*). Throughout classical and later Greek usage it retains this sense, cf. Diod. Sic. I. I. 5. The LXX uses it to translate only עוֹלָם and cognates, modifying such words as διαθήκη (Gen. 17: 1) and νόμιμος (Exod. 27: 21): here the adjective retains its classical meaning. The phrase ζωή αἰώνιος, so frequent in the New Testament, occurs only at Dan. 12: 2 and (as suggested earlier) there is no deviation here from previous usage: indefinite duration is increased to infinite, as a suitable description of that which is divine in origin. When ζωή αἰώνιος is used at 4 Macc. 15: 3 and Ps. Sol. 3: 12, and similar phrases at 2 Macc. 7: 9 and 1 Enoch 15: 4, 6, the adjective bears the durative connotation. 'In general the word depicts that of which the horizon is not in view, whether the horizon be at an infinite distance, or whether it lies no farther than the span of a Caesar's life.'[1]

Now it is well known that in discussions of the New Testament use of ζωή αἰώνιος it is generally assumed that the adjective refers to the 'Age to come' and that the phrase means 'the life of the Age to come', explicable in terms of the Jewish doctrine of the Two Ages. Many years ago E. D. Burton disputed this[2] and maintained (i) that the force of the adjective is always purely temporal and quantitative, and (ii) that 'it has no association with ὁ αἰὼν οὗτος or ὁ μέλλων αἰών: it came into existence before these terms were in use and its kinship of meaning is not with them, but with the αἰών of Plato, meaning "for ever"'. The mainstream of the usage of αἰώνιος certainly does connote duration. Should we then interpret ζωή αἰώνιος in the New Testament in a temporal manner (i.e. 'eternal' = enduring for an indefinitely long time), or are the many commentators correct who, while not denying temporal value to the term, claim that it also bears a distinctly qualitative reference associated with 'the

---

[1] Moulton and Milligan, *Vocabulary of the Greek Testament, ad loc.*

[2] *Galatians* (ICC, Edinburgh, 1921), pp. 344 and 432. The quotation given is from p. 432.

Age to come'? If so, what is the new factor supporting this interpretation?

In answering these questions we must try, first of all, to assess the approximate date at which the idea of the Two Ages entered Jewish thought in order to discover whether or not it could have influenced the New Testament documents. The doctrine of the Two Ages is clearly developed in Fourth Ezra (c. A.D. 100) and the variation of view in this book as to the time of the beginning of the New Age (cf. 6: 7–10 and 7: 29) suggests that speculation about the two ages had been for some time a feature of Jewish thought. C. H. Dodd draws attention to apparent references to the two ages in Enoch 48: 7 and 71: 15,[1] but, since both these passages are in the Similitudes section whose early date is uncertain and indeed unlikely, it would be unwise to build upon them any argument for the early appearance of the two-ages doctrine. At a number of points in the Apocalypse of Baruch a contrast is made between 'this age' and a coming age (14. 13; 15. 7f.; 44. 15; 48. 50), but all these passages come from parts of the book which are usually dated after A.D. 70. Somewhat earlier than this, but still in the first Christian century, the Slavonic Enoch mentions 'the future age' or 'the endless age' (61. 2 and 65. 7). In discussing rabbinic usage we drew attention to words ascribed to R. Hillel (a contemporary of Herod the Great) in P. Aboth 2. 7 which, if genuine, would form the first rabbinic reference to the doctrine: but the authenticity of the ascription is doubted by some. The earliest certain rabbinic witness to the use of the phrases 'this age' and 'the age to come' is Johanan ben Zaccai (c. A.D. 80) in Gen. R. 44. From the extra-biblical material therefore we may conclude that definite statements concerning the doctrine of the Two Ages are late: the expressions are current by the end of the first century A.D., but rare and questionable before that date. Nevertheless, we must bear in mind the possibility that the *idea* was current before it found clear expression.

On this matter, however, we must admit New Testament evidence and it seems clear that the theme of the Two Ages was known to Paul. The expression 'this age, ὁ αἰὼν οὗτος' occurs seven times in the genuine letters.[2] In Gal. 1: 4 there occurs the

[1] *The Interpretation of the Fourth Gospel*, p. 145.
[2] Rom. 12: 2; 1 Cor. 1: 20; 2: 6 (*bis*), 8; 3: 18 and 2 Cor. 4: 4.

phrase 'this present evil age', but only in Ephesians, among the letters ascribed to Paul, do the two expressions 'this age' and 'the coming age' occur together (1: 21). The distinction is also suggested at Matt. 12: 32; Mark 10: 30; Luke 16: 8 and 18: 30.

Since the idea of the Two Ages appears to have been known to the New Testament writers, we must go on to ask whether it is likely that they would use the word αἰώνιος to describe aspects, and in particular the 'life' of the coming age. It is plausible to suggest that, since עוֹלָם in the Old Testament was regularly rendered by αἰώνιος when both the Hebrew and the Greek terms connoted 'indefinite, or infinite duration', when עוֹלָם came to bear the meaning of αἰών (= 'age, definite period of time'),[1] the adjective αἰώνιος would be retained with the corresponding change of meaning, that is, 'of the age'. We may go one step further. On analysing certain statements in the Gospels concerning ζωή αἰώνιος, we are confronted with a very close parallelism between them and passages in Jewish writings which include the words חַיֵּי הָעוֹלָם הַבָּא. For instance, Mark 10: 17 and par. pose the question as to the means of having or inheriting ζωή αἰώνιος. This recalls the request made to R. Eliezer by his disciples, 'Teach us the paths of life that by them we may acquire the life of the Age to come' (b. Ber. 28b): and with the answer of Jesus we may compare Sifra Lev. 5. 85d (on 18: 5) which declares that the keeping of the law assures a man of life in the age which is coming. The dating of these rabbinic statements is notoriously difficult and creates great uncertainty as to their usefulness for the elucidation of New Testament sayings, but the likeness of the ideas expressed suggests a strong possibility that ζωή αἰώνιος means 'the life of the Age to come'. Similarly, some passages in John's Gospel (if we may anticipate our later discussions) seem to contain reminiscences of the Jewish doctrine, e.g. John 5: 39 and 4: 36.[2]

It would appear therefore to be legitimate and right to interpret ζωή αἰώνιος to mean 'life of the Age to come'. To do so, however, does not mean that the idea of duration is absent. The future Age is brought in and established by God's action, and in

---

[1] On this semantic development, see Dalman, *The Words of Jesus*, pp. 152–3.

[2] C. D. Dodd, *op. cit.* p. 146 mentions other passages.

so far as it is his age it is enduring and eternal: those who experience it share in 'life' which is infinitely prolonged. In other words, ζωὴ αἰώνιος in the New Testament contains a temporal reference but stresses the qualitative reference.

THE USE OF ζωὴ αἰώνιος IN THE NEW TESTAMENT

1. *Paul*

In many passages Paul uses ζωή in the straightforward sense of 'physical life' whose antithesis is death.[1] At 1 Cor. 15: 19 he uses it to mean 'lifetime' (cf. James 4: 14; 1 Tim. 4: 8). The verb is used to mean 'be alive',[2] 'to live a lifetime'[3] and 'to get a living' (1 Cor. 9: 14). God is the living God,[4] alive himself and able to make alive (Rom. 4: 17). At Rom. 12: 1 Christians are exhorted to present their bodies to God as 'living sacrifices (θυσία ζῶσα)': here the adjective connotes what is alive, active and effectual: Christians should have all their powers and faculties alive to the will of God.[5] The noun ζωή is also frequently used in the eschatological sense, referring to a future reward or blessing which God will bestow; with this meaning it is generally qualified by αἰώνιος. Thus at Rom. 2: 7 'eternal life' is the reward of perseverance in well-doing and of the quest for glory and immortality: in Rom. 5: 21 it is the goal or aim of the reign of grace through Christ, and at Rom. 6: 22 it is the ultimate result of freedom from sin and servitude to God, being described as the gift of God. According to Gal. 6: 8 'eternal life' is the harvest reaped by life that is dominated by the Spirit. These passages suggest that 'eternal life' is not just something added on at death or at judgment, but is organically related to the actual life lived. 'One man's act of righteousness led to acquittal and life (εἰς δικαίωσιν ζωῆς) for all men' (Rom. 5: 18) and that 'life' is 'both the immediate and ultimate result of that state of things into which the Christian enters when he is declared righteous or

---

[1] Rom. 8: 38; Phil. 1: 20; 1 Cor. 3: 22.
[2] Rom. 14: 8; 2 Cor. 1: 8; 1 Thess. 4: 15.
[3] Rom. 7: 1, 2, 3; 1 Cor. 7: 39.
[4] Rom. 9: 26; 2 Cor. 3: 3 and 6: 16; 1 Thess. 1: 9.
[5] On the participle of ζάω used as an adjective, and for its meaning, see E. G. Selwyn, *The First Epistle of Peter*, p. 159.

receives the sentence of absolution'.[1] Through being justified man has life and will have life.

Although Paul regards ζωὴ αἰώνιος as predominantly eschatological, he also sees 'life', even 'eternal life', as a present possession of the believer. It is the result of the indwelling of the Spirit and may even be regarded in terms of the actual and active presence of the Spirit in the human personality. 'The law of the Spirit of life in Christ Jesus (i.e. the life-giving Spirit) has made me free from the law of sin and of death' (Rom. 8: 2). To have one's attitude determined by the Spirit will issue in life and also has in itself already the germs of life (Rom. 8: 6, 10). The new life of the believer is also associated with participation in the death and resurrection of Jesus through baptism.

We were buried therefore with him by baptism unto death, so that as Christ was raised from the dead by the glory of the Father, we too might walk in newness of life (ἐν καινότητι ζωῆς). For if we have been united with him in a death like his, we shall certainly be united with him in a resurrection like his... If we have died with Christ, we believe that we shall also live with him (Rom. 6: 4f., 8).

It is clear that *v.* 4 represents the new life as a present possibility, but is the union with Christ's resurrection (*v.* 5) present or future? C. K. Barrett interprets it as futuristic, as in *v.* 8;[2] but F. J. Leenhardt argues convincingly for the present:

Is the future verb chronological, or logical? Is it an allusion to the general resurrection, or to the present participation of the believer in the life of the Risen Lord which should flow logically from his participation in the death of the Crucified? The second meaning is preferable both because of the indissoluble unity constituted by the Cross and Resurrection and also because of the parallel thought in Col. 2: 12, where ideas of death and resurrection are associated with baptism.[3]

[1] Sanday and Headlam, *Romans* (ICC, 5th ed., Edinburgh, 1902), p. 142. 1 Tim. 6: 12 refers to the 'eternal life' into which Timothy was called at baptism: cf. also Rom. 5: 17.

[2] *The Epistle to the Romans*, p. 123.

[3] Leenhardt, *Epistle to the Romans* (ET, London, 1961), *ad loc.* Barrett admits that the future in *v.* 5 might be a purely 'logical' future, but thinks this would not agree with the undoubtedly temporal reference in the future at *v.* 8. He adds that Paul is always cautious of expressions which might suggest that the Christian has already reached his goal. H. Koester, *NTS*, VIII (1962), 329 note 2, claims that in the genuine Pauline letters 'the resur-

Furthermore, at *v.* 11 Paul alludes to the new life of the believer in such a way as to make it clear that it is a present sharing in the life of the Risen Lord: the Christian must consider himself alive to God in Christ Jesus.[1] Not only so, but his life should manifest the life of Christ, through re-enactment (2 Cor. 4: 10–11). Col. 3: 1–4 ('You have been raised with Christ... You have died and your life is hid with Christ in God. When Christ who is our life, ἡ ζωὴ ἡμῶν, shall appear, you also will appear with him in glory')[2] affirms that the continuing source of the believer's present resurrection (or raised) life is Christ himself: and Rom. 5: 10 ('Having been reconciled, we shall be saved in his life') suggests the same thought—as T. W. Manson says, 'the reconciled share the life of Christ and to share this divine life is to be saved indeed'.[3] In claiming that entry into real life is possible for man on earth Paul is consistent with his expressed view of the original divine purpose for man. God's original design was to give man life. The commandment of God was intended to bring life (ἡ ἐντολὴ ἡ εἰς ζωήν, Rom. 7: 10) though its purpose was unfulfilled: 'if law had been able to make alive (ζωοποιῆσαι), then righteousness would indeed have sprung from the law' (Gal. 3: 21). In other words, the possession of life is the ideal for humanity, but law could not give it. The power of the Spirit, however, enables the believer to receive newness of life (Rom. 6: 4). By participating in the death and resurrection of Christ the man of faith receives the transformation of life now, in humility and hope, and also the entry into the life which is eternal.

2. *The Synoptic Gospels*

In discussing the significance of the adjective αἰώνιος we suggested that in Synoptic usage the phrase 'eternal life' represents the Jewish חַיֵּי עוֹלָם הַבָּא, the life of the Age to come. For

rection of the believer remains a future expectation': but Rom. 6: 1 ff. suggests clearly that we are *now* risen with Christ and have entered into the new life.

[1] Verse 8 of the chapter suggests a future hope pointing to the final resurrection (συζήσομεν αὐτῷ): but we should not make a too sharp distinction between the verse and the neighbouring verses, since the formula 'with Christ' may be interpreted sacramentally (Col. 2) as well as eschatologically.

[2] Here and at Eph. 2: 6 the past tense is used of the resurrection of Christians, but Koester (see above) doubts the authenticity of both letters.

[3] *New Peake*: Romans, p. 944, para. 820 *b*.

example, Jesus promises (Mark 10: 30) that the faithful disciple will receive 'in the world to come, life everlasting'. This is a future good belonging to a future age, and having the enduring quality of divine life. The use of ζωή by itself is infrequent, but significant. In Mark 9: 43–7 ζωή (*vv.* 43, 45) is synonymous with 'the kingdom of God' (*v.* 47).[1] According to the teaching of Jesus, entrance into the Kingdom is the great end to be sought and it is made possible by discipleship. That this 'chief end' is also described in his teaching as 'life' suggests that when John chooses this term to refer to the supreme good he is not inventing something new, but is interpreting something which lies in the primitive tradition: the roots of the Johannine theme are in the teaching of Jesus.[2] And (to anticipate a little) John's characteristic emphasis on the *present* possibility of 'eternal life' is also explicable in terms of the equation with the 'kingdom', for, however much the 'kingdom' bore a future reference, it was in a real sense inaugurated in the coming of Christ and membership of it was a present possibility for his disciples.

At Matt. 19: 17 ζωή is synonymous with ζωή αἰώνιος in *v.* 16, while Matt. 7: 14 ('the gate is narrow and the way hard that leads to life') suggests that acceptance of the demands of discipleship is the only path to the enjoyment of real life, both present and future.

3. *The Fourth Gospel*

Without proceeding to discuss in detail the background of Johannine thought, we may legitimately claim that our survey reveals that the background of the phrase ζωή αἰώνιος is predominantly Jewish-Hellenistic rather than Graeco-Hellenistic.[3]

---

[1] That Mark 9: 41 ff. is an original word of Christ is strongly suggested by the fact that the section has a clear poetic character when rendered into Aramaic: see M. Black, *Aramaic Approach*, pp. 127–8.

[2] On this see T. W. Manson, *On Paul and John*, pp. 110 ff. He shows that the different New Testament terms for the content of salvation—kingdom, justification, life—connote essentially the same thing, and that the means of reaching it is also constant, although the terminology may differ. 'Whatever the form of words that is used, two factors remain constant from the Synoptics to John: that the thing that is to be attained is something that belongs to God—He gives it or it is found in his presence—and the attainment of it always depends on some relation of the individual to Christ' (p. 111).

[3] By means of these terms we try to designate emphases within Hellenistic thought, which itself cannot be simply contrasted with Jewish.

At the level of terminology, the Fourth Gospel's preference for ζωή αἰώνιος (rather than ζωή ἀθάνατος) betrays the Jewish affiliation of its language, for the Greek phrase is found only in LXX Dan. 12:2; Ps. Sol. 3:12; Philo *Fug.* 75 and 4 Macc. 15:3: and, at the level of meaning, the term is associated with the Jewish doctrine of the Age to come. To the detailed consideration of this we now turn.

In the fourth verse of the Prologue we find the affirmation: 'In Him (the Logos) was life (ζωή) and the life was the light of men.' While it is true that the ideas represented by 'life' and 'light' are characteristic of Hellenistic religion and philosophical thought, the closest parallels to this statement are found in the Old Testament and Jewish thought. The words of Ps. 36 (35):10 spring to mind immediately and probably influenced John, 'With thee is the fountain of life, and in thy light shall we see light.' The sapiential literature declares that Wisdom is ἀπαύγασμα... φωτὸς ἀϊδίου (Wisd. 7:26), that 'he who finds wisdom finds life' (Prov. 8:35) and that through Wisdom one may possess ἀθανασία (Wisd. 8:13, 17). Now the identification of Wisdom with Torah in Jewish thought is certainly pre-Christian (cf. Sir. 24) and therefore we may infer that the application of the descriptions of Wisdom (namely, 'life' and 'light') to Torah need not be a late development, though many expressions of it are relatively late.[1] The application is implied in the Johannine prologue and its legitimacy denied. One of the dominant themes of the Fourth Gospel is the contrast between the Torah and the Incarnate Word. The evangelist is concerned to show that the revelation in Christ offered *in reality* what Judaism was meant to offer, but failed to provide, namely a genuine knowledge of God bringing life to men.

The Law as such is not for John a way to the knowledge of God's will... It claims to be, but is not, the divine Wisdom, the light of the world, the life of men.[2]

But the Logos *was* the light, revealing knowledge of God: and the Logos *was* the life, giving life to men. Christ possessed and manifested life, true life in dependence upon the Father and therefore eternal, and that life is available to men through him.

---

[1] Sifre Deut. 11:22, par. 48; Deut. R. 7:3 on Canticles 1:3.
[2] C. H. Dodd, *Interpretation of the Fourth Gospel*, p. 86.

'Thou has given to the Son power over all flesh that he might give eternal life to all whom thou hast given him' (17:2; 1 John 2:25). That the purpose of the mission of Jesus is to give to men life or eternal life is stated unequivocally at 10: 10, 28, and elsewhere under symbolic language. The gift is received by faith. But it is necessary for the Son of Man to be lifted up (in crucifixion and in glory)[1] in order that everyone who has faith in him may have eternal life (3: 15). The following verse (16) again connects the possession of 'life' with πίστις, as does 3: 36 as well. The theme recurs in 5: 24. 'Verily I say unto you, He that heareth my words and believeth on him that sent me has (ἔχει) eternal life: he does not come into judgment, but has passed from death to life' (cf. 20: 21; 6: 40, 47; 7: 38 and 11: 25). Concerning these verses a number of important points should be noted.

(i) The phrase ζωὴ αἰώνιος first appears at John 3: 15 after the only reference in the Gospel to the kingdom of God (3: 3, 5). The idea of 'life' or 'eternal life' replaces that of the Kingdom in the Fourth Gospel, but the equivalence of the two themes is witnessed to in Mark 9: 43–7.

(ii) What is characteristic of the Fourth Gospel is its declaration of the possibility of the *present* possession of life eternal. He who believes in Christ *has* eternal life.[2] This emphasis accords with the eschatology of the whole Gospel which is essentially a realised eschatology. Judgment has come in Christ: those who are related to him by faith now *possess* eternal life. This profound reinterpretation of the primitive Christian eschatology may have had its roots in the Synoptic tradition which was aware that somehow the Kingdom had come in the coming of Christ: it is also consistent with the Pauline doctrine that 'life', the sharing in the risen life of Christ, is possible now for the justified man.

(iii) John 5: 24 is very similar to the Pauline doctrine of justification. The believer does not come into judgment, but leaves the courtroom acquitted. Although John connects faith

---

[1] The verb ὑψοῦν in John refers to ascending the Cross and to exaltation. The verbal play is stronger in Syriac and Palestinian Aramaic since in these languages אזדקף means 'to be lifted up' and 'to be crucified'.

[2] Since πιστεύω is only once in John followed by ἐν (3: 15), Barrett, (*The Gospel according to St John* [London, 1955], p. 179), thinks it probable that the ἐν αὐτῷ should be construed with ἔχῃ ζωὴν αἰώνιον. If this were so (and it seems doubtful: א reads εἰς) it would be unique, for the passages listed above amply demonstrate that 'eternal life' *is* the result of belief in Christ.

and the possession of life directly, without 'righteousness' as a middle term, his doctrine affirms what the Pauline soteriology expressed by the forensic metaphor of 'justification by faith', an experience which involves the believer's dying with Christ and rising with him into newness of life.[1]

(iv) But what does ζωὴ αἰώνιος mean for John? Is it 'everlasting life', with the idea of duration paramount? We have already pointed out that ζωὴ αἰώνιος in the usage of the Synoptics almost always refers to the 'life of the Age to come', and this appears to be the case in John's gospel also. The Jewish doctrine is very probably referred to in 5: 39: 'You search the Scriptures (ἐρευνᾶν = שׁרַד, the technical term for biblical study and exposition), for you think that in them you have eternal life, and it is they which bear witness to me. Yet you refuse to come to me that you may have life (ἵνα ζωὴν ἔχητε).' The view that study of Torah was the way to the life of the Age to come is a common-place of rabbinic teaching; e.g. Aboth 2: 7 (R. Hillel): 'If a man has gained for himself the words of the Law he has gained for himself the life of the Age to come', and Aboth 6: 7 'Torah gives to them that practice it life in this Age and in the Age to Come'.[2] The allusion in the verse, and also in 4: 36 and 12: 25,[3] to the Jewish doctrine creates a strong possibility that John means by ζωὴ αἰώνιος 'the life of the Age to come'.

(v) Assuming this to be the case, how can John claim that this 'life of the Age to come' is a *present possibility* for those who have faith in Christ, that in Christ eternal life is present? In the first place, the replacing of the Synoptic 'kingdom of God' by 'eternal life' may have enabled John to posit presentness of 'life', since the Synoptics were aware of the Kingdom's presence in the coming of Christ. Secondly, the fact that John writes 'within and for and from the standpoint of the post-resurrection church'[4] may have influenced him in his declaration that what was commonly regarded as a future possibility has become a present fact. Christ's risen, exalted, present life was the life of the promised Age to come, and all who came in faith to Christ might share in it. A third and fruitful line of approach to this question may be developed from a consideration of the type of

---

[1] See above, pp. 141–4.   [2] Cf. jer. Berak. 6a; Mechil. Ex. 13: 3.
[3] Dodd, *The Interpretation of the Fourth Gospel*, p. 146.
[4] Barrett, *The Gospel according to St John*, p. 179.

dualism with which John works. That there is a dualism in John's thought between two worlds—that of God, light and salvation and that of Satan, darkness and corruption—is undeniably clear and has been illumined by the writings of the Qumran sect. But in John the two worlds are not distinguished according to a horizontal line (as in Judaism), i.e. the present world and the world to come, but rather in a vertical line, the world above and the world below (8: 23), a celestial and a terrestrial (3: 12, 31). The temporal, successive idea of the two ages was, in John, in process of dissolution. It was no longer necessary, or even possible, to safeguard the otherness of God, as Judaism had done, by declaring that *at some future time* the Kingdom would descend from heaven with power. *Already* it was possible for a new existence (still 'from above') to possess a man so that he might see and enter the Kingdom of God. The two worlds co-exist and overlap. Humiliation and glory, hiddenness and revealed-ness, this Age and the Age to come, are no longer conceived of as in temporal succession, but co-existent aspects of the one act of revelation in Christ.[1] It is in the perspective of this kind of dualism that we must place the Johannine idea of 'life', if we are really to understand it. 'Life' is the characteristic of the world above: it belongs to God, while to the earth belongs corruption and death. God has sent his Son, the Logos, the bearer of Life, to save men and give them Life: the Incarnation is the appearing of the divine life. The eschatological life is thus a present reality in the 'now' of the Christ-event. Paradoxically, however, it is the death of Christ which is the necessary preliminary to the reception of the gift: by that death man is delivered from the dominion of this world and can then receive the gift of life through faith and the Sacraments.

Thus far we have dealt only with the present possibility of 'eternal life'. There are also in John's gospel statements concerning 'life' which reflect the usual late Jewish and Christian eschatology. Bultmann and other commentators ascribe these to Church redaction, but it is not necessary to resort to 'textual surgery' to solve this Johannine problem. Let us examine the statements in context.

[1] Cf. C. K. Barrett, 'The Place of Eschatology in the Fourth Gospel', *ET*, LIX (1947–8), 302–5: also F. Müssner, ΖΩΗ — *Die Anschauung von 'Leben' im vierten Evangelium*, p. 56, and *L'Évangile de Jean* (Recherches Bibliques, III, ed. F. M. Braun, Louvain, 1958), p. 184.

He who hears my words and believes on him that sent me has eternal life: he does not come into judgment, but has passed from death to life (5: 24).

This is the statement of realised eschatology. With *v.* 25 the imagery takes on an apocalyptic ring, and *v.* 28 asserts:

The hour is coming when all who are in the tombs will hear his voice and come forth, those who have done good to the resurrection of life (εἰς ἀνάστασιν ζωῆς) and those who have done evil to the resurrection of judgment (28–9: cf. Dan. 12: 2).[1]

This view is not antithetical to the other: both are in an organic relation. The evangelist agrees with, and here affirms, the popular Christian eschatology that the believer will enter into eternal life at the Resurrection. But this truth is of less importance to him than the fact that the believer may now possess eternal life. The point of unity between the two strands of teaching is formed by the Johannine Christology. Christ is the life-giving one: the present and continuing 'life' is his gift: the life after the death of the body and the end of the world is also his gift: it is the consummation of true life begun, the final fulfilment of the saving work of Christ.[2]

In Johannine thought 'eternal life' is mediated by faith and through Sacraments. Several of the statements relating 'faith' to the possession of eternal life have been recorded above, and to these may be added 6: 40, 47; 7: 38 and 11: 25. The characteristic construction of πιστεύω in this connection is with εἰς αὐτόν (cf. 'ב האמין) and this denotes not simply 'to give credence to a message', but 'to have a firm reliance upon Christ', recognising as valid the claims made for his person, and being identified with him. 'This is eternal life, that they know thee, the only true God, and Jesus Christ whom thou hast sent' (17: 3). This 'knowledge' is both objective and a personal relation. The new life which is given by it is born out of the death of the old.

Verily, I say unto you, unless a grain of wheat falls into the earth and dies, it remains alone; but if it dies, it bears much fruit. He who loves his life loses it, but he who hates his life in this world will keep it for eternal life (the life of the Age to come) (12: 24–5).

[1] This saying is dramatised in 11: 25.
[2] The 'inaugurated' and 'to be consummated' aspects of the Kingdom of God and of entry into it in the Synoptic Gospels are united in the doctrine of the person and work of Christ.

The death and resurrection of Christ is the source of new life: in death and resurrection with Christ (i.e. the identification which is 'faith', for both Paul and John) the new life is acquired by man.[1]

'Eternal life' is mediated also through the Sacraments. The connection with baptism seems to be implicit in 3: 3–5, 'Unless a man is born ἄνωθεν... unless a man is born of water and Spirit, he cannot see the Kingdom of God'. Since John elsewhere always uses 'eternal life' instead of 'kingdom of God', we may justifiably claim that the entry into 'life', like the entry to the kingdom, is conditional upon rebirth from above, or regeneration through baptism and endowment with the Spirit. The possibility of re-birth, like the possiblity of life, lies in the descent in love of the Son of Man and his 'elevation' of the Cross (3: 13–15);[2] the possibility becomes an actuality for those who have faith and are baptised.

The association of 'life' with the Eucharist is found at 6: 52 ff. The argument of the chapter (from *v.* 22) develops the theme of the 'bread of life' in three stages.

(i) Man must labour, not for the bread which perishes, but for the bread which abides unto eternal life (εἰς ζωὴν αἰώνιον) which the Son of Man will give. This bread which gives life to the world Jesus identifies with himself, who, as Son of Man, came down from heaven (6: 33). In this section a contrast appears to be drawn between the Torah and the true bread of God. In rabbinic teaching bread is a common symbol for Torah, and this tradition can be traced back to the time of Eliezer ben Hyrcanus and Joshua ben Chananiah (*c.* A.D. 90).[3] It was therefore natural to regard Torah as the bread of Moses and a simple step to identify it with manna.[4] But the Torah was not able to give eternal life, although it promised to do so: the true

---

[1] Paul affirms the same truth in terms of δικαιοσύνη.

[2] 1 John 5: 6ff. brings together the baptism and death of Jesus and the two Sacraments of Baptism and Eucharist.

[3] See Gen. R. 70. 5 and R. Berechiah on Prov. 25: 21 in Pesik. 80 *b*.

[4] Dodd, *Interpretation of the Fourth Gospel*, p. 336, 'The equation of manna with σοφία in Philo almost necessarily implies that in some circles it was taken to be a symbol of Torah'. In late rabbinic tradition the second giving of manna is a fixed feature of Jewish eschatological expectation. Thus another level of meaning in the narrative is that the Jews are asking Jesus to establish his messianic claims by the sign of renewing the gift of manna.

bread of God (Jesus) gives eternal life to those who receive it in faith.

(ii) The second section (41–51) makes the significant addition that the bread which Jesus will supply is his flesh, given for the life of the world.

I am the living bread which came down from heaven: if anyone eats of this bread he will live for ever. And the bread which I shall give is my flesh (given) for the life of the world (51).

This is a clear reference to the sacrificial death and it points forward to the allusion to the Eucharist in the final section, *vv.* 52–9.

(iii) The main verses are 53 and 57. 'Unless you eat the flesh of the Son of man and drink his blood, you have no life in you. He that eateth my flesh and drinketh my blood has eternal life and I will raise him up at the last day' (53), and 'He who eats me will live through me'. The flesh and blood of Christ are life-giving food and drink to those who receive them, because, by means of them, a reciprocal indwelling of Christ and the believer is established, and through this union with Christ, by mutual indwelling, man experiences and enjoys eternal life.

The whole discourse is illumined by the reference to the Spirit in the verses which follow. The flesh of which Jesus has spoken gives life because it becomes the vehicle of the life-giving Spirit to those who believe (63); likewise, the words which he has spoken are spirit and therefore generate life. The words of Moses were unable to do this, although they promised it—'The words of the law which I have given you are life for you' (Mechil. Ex. 15: 26; cf. Gal. 3: 21). Jesus alone has the words of eternal life (6: 68), for they are alive and convey life to those who hear and believe (5: 24 and 12: 50). There is no opposition between the life-giving flesh and the life-giving words: each has its life-giving quality, not in itself, but in its witness to the life of Jesus, and in its being the vehicle of the Spirit to bring men into communion with the living Christ.[1]

At 7: 38 the Spirit is mentioned under the image of 'living water' (ὕδωρ ζῶν). In order to retain the parallelism within the saying and in view of the context, it seems preferable to interpret the verse in the following way: 'If anyone thirst, let him come to

---

[1] Cf. C. H. Dodd, *op. cit.* p. 342 note 3.

me; and let him drink who believes on me: as the Scripture says, "Out of the midst of him (i.e. of the Christ) shall flow rivers of living water"".[1] If we interpret the verse in this way, the saying is clearly connected with the subsequent assertion that it is from Christ (for John, the glorified Christ) that the Spirit proceeds. The image of 'living water' occurs again in the conversation with the Samaritan woman (4: 14)—'The water which I shall give to him (who drinks) will be in him a spring of water welling up to eternal life'. Now 'living water' as a metaphor for the quickening energies of God appears in the Old Testament (Ezek. 47: 9; Zech. 14: 8; Jer. 2: 13); and in the rabbinic literature the image of 'water' is used both for the Torah[2] and for the Holy Spirit. While it would be unwise to deny that John is here again suggesting the contrast between the power of Christ to give life and the failure of Torah to provide it, yet he seems to want the metaphor to refer to the Spirit. Strack–Billerbeck (II, 434 ff.) draw attention to the use of 'water' and 'living water' as a symbol of the Spirit and it is of interest that Gen. R. 70. 8 interprets the water-drawing of Tabernacles as a drawing of the Spirit, in view of the fact that the setting of the Johannine saying (7: 38) is the Feast of Tabernacles. The 'living water' is the gift of Holy Spirit which brings men into life-giving contact with Christ.

We have already discussed the present reality of 'eternal life' in response to faith. Now, in conclusion, we turn our attention briefly to the Johannine understanding of the content and character of this life. Two categories predominate: that of joy (15: 11; 16: 20–4; 17: 13 and 1 John 1: 4) and especially that of love (ἀγάπη). The availability to men of eternal life is grounded in God's self-giving love (3: 16), and, just as the life of Jesus illustrates this comprehending and sacrificial love, so also will

---

[1] The punctuation of this verse remains in dispute, and scholars are almost evenly divided in opinion. Dodd, Bultmann and Jeremias prefer the interpretation given here, but Barrett and Lightfoot retain the traditional view that believers themselves give life. In a useful discussion Hoskyns and Davey (*The Fourth Gospel* [London, 1943], pp. 365 f.) suggest that both meanings are Johannine: Jesus is the donor of life and those who believe are the creative source of new life to others. This passage was the subject of a series of articles in *RB*, LXV–LXVII (1958–60).

[2] See A. Schlatter, *Der Evangelist Johannes* (Stuttgart, 1948), *ad loc.*; and C. H. Dodd, *Interpretation of the Fourth Gospel*, p. 83.

the lives of his disciples (15: 12ff.). The words of T. W. Manson on this theme may stand as the conclusion to our study:

The vitality of God overflows into the world: it is creative life, and what it creates is a fellowship of love. 'We know that we have passed out of death into life, because we love the brethren' (1 John 3: 14)...

The new life shows its divine quality by the way it becomes creative in the love of the brethren. Salvation for John is life—life that is eternal, continually creative, continually spending itself in love yet never diminished, the kind of life that age does not weary nor the years condemn. It is a life of fellowship—with God who gives it, with Christ who mediates it, with the brethren who share it.[1]

On the basis of our examination of the Johannine use of ζωή αἰώνιος and of the various symbols by which it is explained, we may claim that, while the terminology and thought of the evangelist resemble those of Greek philosophy, the roots of the theme are to be found in Jewish teaching. In his treatment of 'eternal life' as the content of salvation John is essentially true to the Jewish–Synoptic–Pauline tradition, though he emphasises, in a unique way, the present reality of 'the life of the Age to come' in the experience of the believer. This special emphasis is explicable in terms of the revised dualism (vertical rather than horizontal) with which John works, and by means of which he can declare that the life of the realm above, real life, inter-penetrates and overlaps this world. This is the life of the incarnate, crucified and glorified Christ. It is shared by those who, through faith and obedience, come to him and are renewed in their being through identification with him. It is mediated and maintained by the Sacraments which, like the words of Christ, are the vehicles of the Spirit to create life-giving communion between the living Christ and his people, a communion which is to be consummated at the general resurrection.

[1] *On Paul and John*, pp. 113 and 115.

CHAPTER VI

THE BACKGROUND AND BIBLICAL USAGE OF THE TERM ΠΝΕΥΜΑ

THE CLASSICAL USAGE

The word πνεῦμα (derived from πνεῖν 'to blow', 'to breathe') is not found in Homer, Hesiod or Pindar, but first appears in Aeschylus.[1] The meanings attached to it in Greek literature may be classified as follows.

(1) *Wind*, whether gentle breeze or violent blast. This is the most frequent meaning of the word and is found in all the main writers of the classical period.[2] (Cf. Aesch. *Pers.* 110; Herod. 7. 16. 1; Pl. *Phaedr.* 229 b; Arist. *Prob.* 940 b 7; Polyb. *Hist.* 1. 44. 4.) The word is also used metaphorically to refer to a force affecting the mind, what LS call 'genial breeze or influence'.[3] The examples of this usage show that, while πνεῦμα could be employed in figurative expressions referring to relationship, destiny and attitude, the word itself had not yet acquired the secondary meaning of 'disposition'.

(2) *Air breathed* (in or out), breath of a living being, man or animal. This usage is frequent in all the major writers from Aeschylus onwards.[4] (Cf. Aesch. *Eum.* 568; Eur. *Phoen.* 787 and *Bacch.* 128; Pl. *Tim.* 78 a–b.) Scarcely distinguishable from the idea of 'breath' is that of 'air', as available for breathing (Eur. *Hel.* 867; Polyb. *Hist.* 24. 8 d). The word denotes 'air' as necessary to life (not precisely 'the breath of life') in Plato, *Tim.* 77 a, 'life depends on fire and air'. At 84 d–e of the same dialogue πνεῦμα

---

[1] The occurrence of the word in Xenophanes and Anaximenes (both sixth century B.C.) is known from the testimony of later writers and will be examined later.

[2] The word πνο(ι)ή is more common in the poets, and is used by Homer for 'wind'.

[3] Cf. Aesch. *Theb.* 708 and *Prom.* 884; Soph. *O.C.* 612; Aesch. *Supp.* 30 reads 'Receive this suppliant female train with air (or spirit) of respect on the part of the country' (so LS).

[4] Whether 'breath' or 'wind' is the first sense cannot be decided on the basis of occurrence: both are present as early as Aeschylus.

seems to refer to the air in the various parts of the body which is furnished to these parts by the lungs, themselves called ὁ τῶν πνευμάτων τῷ σώματι ταμίας.

(3) In some passages (scattered over a considerable period of time) πνεῦμα has the meaning 'breath of life', 'life' and even more generally 'the basic principle of life': cf. Aesch. *Theb.* 981; Eur. *Orest.* 864 and *Hec.* 571; Polyb. *Hist.* 13. 1 *a.* 2.

Of interest are two fragments from Epicharmus, a contemporary of Sophocles.

No. 126: joined it was, is now severed and is gone again whence it came; earth to earth, and spirit (πνεῦμα) above.

No. 146: if with pious mind thou shouldest live, thou wouldest suffer no ill at death: above, the spirit (το πνεῦμα) will continue to exist in heaven.
(Quoted from Diels, *Die Fragmente der Vorsokratiker*, 3 Auf. 1, p. 122.)

It is difficult to know exactly the meaning of πνεῦμα in these two passages. Possibly, the reference is to the 'breath of life' (rather than the 'spirit') being re-absorbed in the universal πνεῦμα, that is, the air or soul-substance. A statement similar to that of Epicharmus appears at Eur. *Suppl.* 532–4, but editors agree in not ascribing the lines to Euripides, and Stobaeus (*Florileg.* 123. 3) attributes them to Moschion (second century A.D.). Their meaning, however, is clear: everything returns to its origin, the body to the earth and the 'spirit' to the air, the 'spirit' being the breath of life, the air by which men live.

Xenophanes (sixth century B.C.) is said by Diogenes Laertius (IX. Xen. 3) to have been the first to declare that the soul (ψυχή) is πνεῦμα. The context leads one to suspect that by this statement Xenophanes did not mean that the soul is 'spirit', but rather that (as against the views of his predecessors who maintained the the soul lives after death as a shade) everything which comes into being is also subject to extinction, and that, under this general law, the soul also is merely 'air' or 'breath'. Plutarch (*Plac. Phil.* 1. 3) ascribes to Anaximenes, a contemporary of Xenophanes, the statement: 'as our soul, being air, controls (or holds together) us, so wind (πνεῦμα) and air encompass the whole world'. While πνεῦμα is not here predicated of 'soul', it is evident that πνεῦμα and ἀήρ are almost synonymous terms. Aristotle uses the expression σύμφυτον πνεῦμα to denote air that belongs in, or is born in the body, as distinct from that which is inhaled (*de Part. Anim.* 659*b*, 17–19).[1]

It appears then that from the sixth century B.C. πνεῦμα was predicated of the soul, meaning a substance identical with or akin to 'air', and that, from the time of Sophocles at least, the idea of life was associated with the term. In Epicharmus, it denotes 'soul substance', and by the time of Pseudo-Aristotle πνεῦμα comes to signify the basis of all life. In none of the passages cited, however, is the term *individualised*, so as to denote the 'soul' of a person, or the 'human spirit' conceived of as the seat or organ of psychic life.[2] πνεῦμα remains a term of substance, meaning 'spirit' in a non-individualised sense, a substance constituting (according to some writers) the soul, and (according to others) a sort of reservoir of soul-stuff or life-principle.

In the late Greek authors the word πνεῦμα retains the meanings 'wind', 'breath of life', 'life' and 'air'. Dionysius of Halicarnassus witnesses to its use, by metonymy, to mean 'energy or forcefulness' in speech (*Demos.* 20) and he also uses the term to mean 'a spirit' (*Antiq.* 1. 31). This latter usage is attested by the LXX (1 Sam. 16: 23; 1 Kings 22: 21) for a period earlier than Dionysius, but his appears to be the first example of its use in this sense in non-Jewish Greek literature.

The Stoics made much use of the term πνεῦμα. The early representatives of that school still employed the word to mean 'wind'. Stobaeus (*Ecl.* 1. 17) says that Chrysippus defined the ultimate reality as πνεῦμα, or air endowed with the power of self-motion, not just air in motion, as in the earlier writers. As predicated of the soul πνεῦμα means, not the 'perishable breath' (as in Xenophanes), nor 'inert matter', but 'soul-stuff' which while being material is also, by virtue of its permeation by *logos*, active: its activity within (as πνεῦμα σύμφυτον ἡμῖν—so Chrysippus) is the extension of itself from the governing soul to the organs of sense-perception (πνεύματα νοερά), as a vital nervous fluid.

So far as we know Posidonius was the first among the Greeks to

[1] Pseud. Arist. *Mund.* 394*b* uses πνεῦμα to denote a substance in both plants and animals which permeates all living things, that is, as a universal principle of life or existence. The passage is probably very much later than Aristotle's genuine work.

[2] This is roughly the connotation of ψυχή.

say that God was πνεῦμα (Stob. *Ecl.* 1. 1), to which characterisation he added 'intelligent and fiery', the latter adjective suggesting that the notion of material still adhered to the term. Two hundred years before Posidonius, Menander (frag. 482) used the phrase πνεῦμα θεῖον of Τύχη in such a way as to suggest that some of his contemporaries employed the term to designate the power controlling human affairs, but how far it was individualised or personalised (with reference to deity) is far from clear. In the pseudo-Platonic *Axiochus* 370c we read that there is in the soul some divine breath (θεῖον πνεῦμα) through which it possesses intelligence and knowledge. The context makes it obvious that the notion is of 'divine inspiration' residing in the soul. Again, there is no evidence of the personalising of πνεῦμα, and in fact it would seem that πνεῦμα remains, till the end of the first Christian century, a name of the substance, refined, ethereal, penetrating the whole cosmos (*anima mundi*) but not yet immaterial, the substance of which God and the human soul[1] are composed: it denotes neither the human spirit nor personal divine spirit.

THE OLD TESTAMENT USE OF רוּחַ

The Hebrew word which most nearly corresponds to the Greek word πνεῦμα and which is usually translated by that word, is רוּח. This term, ordinarily translated 'spirit' has as its primary sense (like πνεῦμα) 'air in motion', and therefore means 'wind' or 'breath'. While there may be divergence of opinion as to which of these two meanings came first, it is not correct to claim that the meaning 'breath' did not appear until after the Exile.[2] According to C. Virolleaud, רוּחַ signifies 'vital breath' (of animals) in the Ras Shamra texts,[3] and the same meaning is implied in several Old Testament passages which predate the Exile. In Exod. 15: 8 and 2 Sam. 22: 16 (= Ps. 18: 16) 'the רוּחַ of the nostrils of Yahweh' signifies the 'wind' and רוּחַ must be under-

---

[1] Plutarch, *de prim. frig.* 2. 5.

[2] E. D. Burton, *Spirit, Soul and Flesh* (Chicago, 1918), p. 61; J. Hempel, *Gott und Mensch im AT* (2nd ed., Stuttgart, 1936), p. 105; H. W. Robinson, 'Hebrew Psychology' (in *The People and the Book*, ed. A. S. Peake, p. 360) and *Inspiration and Revelation in the Old Testament* (Oxford, 1946), p. 75.

[3] *Syria*, XVIII (1937), 86. Cf. A. R. Johnson, *The Vitality of the Individual in the Thought of Ancient Israel* (Cardiff, 1949), p. 27.

stood as 'breath'.[1] On the basis of these poetical passages, which express the primitive belief that the wind is the breath of God, one is tempted to claim that the original meaning of רוּחַ is 'breath' (emerging from nose or mouth) and that this has been extended to 'wind', regarded as the 'breath' of a superhuman being.

Speculation on primitive ideas and original meanings is not significantly fruitful for our study: we are concerned with the range of meaning of רוּחַ found within the literature of the Old Testament. Of the 378 occurrences of רוּחַ, about one-third,[2] spread throughout the whole period of the Testament, denote 'wind' or are closely associated with that idea. Among the latter are those passages (mostly poetical) mentioned above in which 'the רוּחַ ("breath") of Yahweh' signifies the 'wind'. The contexts of a few of the many occasions on which רוּחַ must itself be translated 'wind' will demonstrate the Israelite conviction that the wind is under Yahweh's control and is one medium through which he exerts his power. Yahweh brings forth the winds from his treasure (Ps. 135: 7; Jer. 10: 13): he makes them his messengers (Ps. 104: 4): he creates the wind and regulates its force (Amos 4: 13; Job 28: 25): he sends a wind to assuage the Flood (Gen. 8: 1): in the story of the Exodus, the wind is the agent in bringing the plague of locusts (Exod. 10: 13b, 19) and in causing the sea to recede before Israel (14: 21). When רוּחַ means 'wind', the notion of strength or violence is generally present (e.g. Prov. 27: 16; Ps. 55: 9; Isa. 7: 2), only occasionally is there no sense of power and force expressed (e.g. Ps. 78: 39; Zech. 5: 9; Gen. 3: 8).[3] The wind is also invisible, mysterious and impalpable; it knows no limits, yet no one knows its origin. To this extent, any mysterious, unpredictable power is akin to the wind. It is not surprising, therefore, to find that exceptional displays of power in men are ascribed to the action of the רוּחַ of

---

[1] Cf. Hos. 13: 15; Isa. 11: 4 and 30: 28, where the 'breath' of God signifies the 'wind'.

[2] H. W. Robinson, *Inspiration and Revelation*, p. 74, reckons the number at 131.

[3] Cf. N. H. Snaith, *The Distinctive Ideas of the Old Testament*, p. 152. There is a derived used of רוּחַ meaning 'a point of the compass', e.g. 'Come from the four winds...'. This is found ten times in Ezekiel, four in Jeremiah, three in Zechariah and once in 1 Chronicles. We may be confident in assuming that this is a post-exilic use of the word.

Yahweh: the same characteristics—strength and mystery—belonged to those prodigious exploits as to the energies of the wind.

This brings us to the second main use of רוּחַ, to denote supernatural influences acting upon men, and very occasionally on inanimate objects;[1] we may call this the 'inspirational' or 'charismatic' רוּחַ יהוה (or Elohim) and רוּחַ is translated 'spirit'. In the historically earliest sources, the רוּחַ (in this sense) acted or was experienced in an intermittent fashion: it fell unexpectedly on certain individuals, particularly the early prophets and the warriors who saved Israel.[2] When the רוּחַ was upon Othniel (Judg. 3: 10) and upon Jephthah (11: 29), when it 'put on' Gideon (6: 34) and 'rushed upon' Saul (1 Sam. 11: 6), these men, obscure in themselves, became heroic and won unexpected victories over the enemies of Israel. When the רוּחַ 'pushed' Samson (Judg. 13: 25) or 'rushed on' him (14: 6), he slew a lion with his hands, killed thirty men (14: 19), broke his bonds like flax and slew a thousand Philistines (15: 14ff.). Two observations may be made here: first, the coming of the רוּחַ יהוה on a man was the occasion of his experiencing an access of divine power, violent and overwhelming, but the endowment was temporary, not permanent, given to him to deal with a specific crisis: secondly, these crises were moments of supreme importance both for the safety and for the faith of the nation; the evidence of divine power in victorious leaders restored confidence in the Covenant and in eventual liberation.[3]

The ecstasies and oracles of the early prophets were also attributed to the action of the 'spirit of Yahweh'. Indeed the 'spirit' was so characteristic of the prophet that he could be called 'man of the spirit' (Hos. 9: 7). In the days of Samuel, the strange actions and outbursts of the נְבִיאִים were ascribed to the effects

[1] H. W. Robinson, op. cit. p. 74, reckons that this use accounts for 134 of the total occurrences of the word.

[2] The רוּחַ does not seem to have been ascribed to the kings in their ruling function: their decisions were based on oracles (2 Sam. 14: 17, 20; 1 Kings 3: 11, 12). But 1 Sam. 16: 13–14 and 2 Sam. 23: 2 attribute the 'spirit' to David. The second passage comes from a poem which has similarities to the Wisdom writings and may be a late composition: but 1 Sam. 16: 13f. suggests a connection between the anointing of the king and the bestowal of the spirit: this supports the view that the gift was virtually limited to leaders of the people.

[3] Cf. J. Guillet, Thèmes Bibliques (Paris, 1950), p. 233.

of spirit-possession (1 Sam. 10: 6ff.; 19: 20ff.). On meeting a company of such men, the spirit 'rushed on' Saul and he was transformed into another man and began to prophesy (1 Sam. 10: 9f.). The connection between the accession of 'spirit' and prophesying is clear from Num. 11: 29 where Moses says, 'Would that all the Lord's people were prophets, that the Lord would put his spirit upon them'. Examples of specific oracles attributed to action of the spirit are later and less numerous (cf. Num. 24: 2). the But the coming of the רוּחַ יהוה to the early prophets, as to warriors of Israel, was a strange, violent and temporary endowment, not an abiding gift.

In the case of the later and great prophets, the claim to spirit-possession is very infrequent, although the power of the 'spirit' is present in their activities. The pre-exilic prophets never (with the possible exception of Micah 3: 8, if the words 'the רוּח of Yahweh' are not a later interpolation) speak of being possessed by the spirit in order to justify or authenticate their inspiration. It may be that opposition to the irrational and extravagant frenzies provoked by the 'spirit' in the early prophets accounts for the suppression of the idea.[1] Possession of the word of God, the knowledge that 'Thus saith the Lord...' qualifies the later prophet for his ministry.[2]

After the Exile, the 'spirit' reappears as an essential element in the inspiration of the prophets. Ezekiel speaks and acts under the control of the 'spirit' (2: 2; 3: 24; 11: 5, etc.) and it is to the 'spirit' that he attributes his reception of the divine message and his power to proclaim it. Some post-exilic texts view the history of Israel as the result of the nation's attitude to the 'spirit of God' manifesting itself through the prophets.

Thou didst warn them by the spirit through the prophets, yet they would not give ear: therefore thou didst give them into the hands of the people of the lands (Neh. 9: 30).

They made their hearts like adamant lest they should hear the law and the words which the Lord of hosts had sent by his spirit through the former prophets (Zech. 7: 12).

[1] See S. Mowinckel, 'The Spirit and the Word in the pre-exilic reforming Prophets', *JBL*, LIII (1934), 199–227.

[2] We ought not, however, to differentiate too radically between 'spirit of Yahweh' and 'word of Yahweh'. Ps. 33: 6 (and possibly Gen. 1) brings together the creative breath and the creative word. See P. van Imschoot, 'L'esprit de Yahvé, source de vie dans l'AT', *RB*, XLIV (1935), 481–501.

The continuing inspiration of prophets presupposes that the action of the 'spirit' was not solely an explosive and spasmodic phenomenon, and many texts (mostly of late origin) describe it as a *permanent* endowment to enable a man to fulfil a certain function. The 'spirit' was *on* Moses (Num. 11:17, 25) and was transmitted to his successor, Joshua (Num. 27:18; Deut. 34:9). A part of the 'spirit' of Moses rested on the seventy elders chosen to assist him in the judging of the people: the 'spirit' rested or settled on Elisha (2 Kings 2:15): it filled the artisans who were commissioned to fashion the furniture of the cult (Exod. 28:3; 31:3; 35:31): and it was *in* Joseph, as the source of wisdom for his good government of Egypt (Gen. 41:38–40). In these cases, just as in the instances of temporary inspiration, the רוּחַ of Yahweh may be considered as the source (or explanation) of capacities and powers beyond normal human experience: the natural gift was of knowledge, strength or insight; its exceptional heightening was attributed to the accession of divine power, the 'spirit of Yahweh'.[1]

The past history of Israel was not regarded as the only scene of the spirit's action. The future was expected to witness outpourings even more wonderful. The future age was to be characterised by abundant fruitfulness, judgment and righteousness in the social order—all of which would be the results of the 'spirit' from on high (Isa. 32:15 ff.). The 'shoot from the stem of Jesse', the messianic king, would be endowed with the 'spirit' to direct all his activities (Isa. 11:1 ff.). Likewise, the 'spirit' was expected to rest upon the Servant of Yahweh: 'I have put my spirit upon him, and he shall bring forth justice to the nations' (Isa. 42:1): and the prophet-messenger of Isa. 61 declared, 'The Spirit of the Lord God is upon me, because the Lord has anointed me to bring good tidings to the afflicted...' (61:1 f.). But the endowment with 'spirit' was not to be the prerogative of special individuals only: in the future age, all might receive the gift.

---

[1] A. R. Johnson, *The One and the Many in the Israelite Conception of God* (2nd ed., Cardiff, 1961), pp. 15 ff., interprets the Spirit acting upon man as an 'extension of Yahweh's personality'. 'God', he says, 'is thought of in terms similar to those of man as possessing an indefinable extension of the Personality, which enables him to exercise a mysterious influence upon mankind.' In its creative aspect this appears as 'blessing'; in its destructive aspect it makes itself felt as a 'curse' (p. 16). Other extensions of Yahweh's personality include his Name, the Word, Angels, and the Ark.

'I will pour out my spirit upon all flesh...' (Joel 3: 1; cf. Isa. 44: 3). When this 'spirit' was spread abroad in the hearts of the people, it would bring forth obedience, deliverance and renewal (Ezek. 36: 26ff.): when the divine presence and power is acknowledged and experienced, the whole life of the community is regenerated. Only once is moral renewal by the spirit desired by an individual for himself: in Ps. 51: 12–14 (MT) we read:

Create in me a clean heart, O God, and put a new and right spirit (רוּחַ נָכוֹן) within me.
Cast me not away from thy presence and take not thy holy spirit (רוּחַ קָדְשְׁךָ) from me:
Restore me to the joy of thy salvation and uphold me with a willing spirit (רוּחַ נְדִיבָה).

In this prayer, v. 12 pleads for stability or steadfastness of disposition, and v. 14 for a spirit that is ready and willing to respond obediently to God's demands.[1] In the context of such a prayer for self-renewal the meaning of 'thy holy spirit' will have some ethical content, and it must also be parallel to the preceding petition, 'Cast me not away from thy presence'. We would submit that the phrase refers to that inward sense of the presence and power of God which both purifies and inspires to obedient and righteous living: in short, it is the inward power which makes for holiness.[2] Elsewhere רוּחַ occasionally refers to the

[1] Cf. Exod. 35: 21. The adj. נָדִיב means also 'noble or princely' and the LXX has ἡγεμονικόν: but that nuance of meaning is unlikely here.

[2] Cf. H. J. Kraus, *Biblischer Kommentar, Psalmen I* (Neukirchen, 1960) *ad loc.* This is the usual interpretation of the phrase: cf. A. Weiser, *The Psalms* (ET, London, 1962), *ad loc.*; and M. Buttenwieser, *The Psalms* (Chicago, 1938), p. 191, calls the 'holy spirit' the power of good within man. T. W. Manson, *On Paul and John*, p. 34, speaks of the holy spirit here as being 'the moral and religious consciousness that tells a man when he sins', or even 'the better self'. But this is to neglect the positive and active role of the Spirit's presence which Manson himself suggests when he later uses the phrase 'a power that inspires man to holy and righteous life'.

In a book devoted to the study of the Psalm (*Psalm Fifty-One*, Leiden, 1962), E. R. Dalglish puts forward a new interpretation (pp. 157ff.). Because the gift of the Spirit was reserved for special individuals in Israel, the Psalmist must be a select personage: he had the holy spirit resident within him, and the only official who had this permanent possession of the רוּחַ יהוה was the king, since the anointing with oil was the sacrament of the bestowal of the spirit. Therefore, the 'spirit of holiness' will mean 'royal inviolability' rather than moral power: the notion of holiness must be understood as sacredness rather than as having ethical import. To interpret

spirit which guides and instructs towards righteousness: Ps. 143:
10, 'Teach me to do thy will...Let thy good spirit lead me on a
level path'; and Neh. 9: 20 (referring to Israel's past), 'Thou
didst give thy good spirit to instruct them'. This aspect of the
Spirit's activity is parallel to the work of 'wisdom' in the sapiential books (cf. Job 32: 8).[1]

Apart from Ps. 51, the only occurrence of the phrase 'the holy
spirit' (lit. 'spirit of holiness') is in Isa. 63: 10–11.

But they rebelled and grieved his holy spirit (רוּחַ קָדְשׁוֹ); therefore he
was turned to be their enemy and himself fought against them.
Then he remembered the days of old, Moses and his people, 'Where
is he that brought up from the sea the shepherds of his people?
Where is he who put in the midst of them his holy spirit?'

The 'holy spirit' here is the active, directing presence of God
in Israel's life, embodied in the spirit-inspired ministry of the
prophets (cf. Neh. 9: 30; Zech. 7: 12). The 'grieving of his holy
spirit' means the rejection of the prophetic instruction by which
God sought to guide his people towards holiness and righteousness,[2] and in *v.* 11 the 'holy spirit' refers to the endowment of
Moses, the prophetic agent of God's warning and instruction
(cf. Num. 11: 17).[3] The phrase 'holy spirit', both in Ps. 51 and

'holy spirit' thus (of status rather than of character) seems to do less than
justice to the context, despite Dalglish's attempts to prove otherwise. Moreover, the gift of the spirit to the king (even if linked with anointing) was not
given simply by virtue of his position: it was essentially related to his
character. The few references we have to the gift of the spirit to David and
to Saul prove that the endowment of power for leadership came to them
because they were of upright and obedient character, because they possessed
the qualities necessary for kingship over the people of God.

[1] In the sapiential literature (apart from the book of Wisdom) the 'spirit'
plays an insignificant role. In Wisdom, however, many passages suggest that
'wisdom' like 'spirit' is a divine power active in Creation (9: 2, 9); that it
assists the righteous man to do God's will (9: 11 and 10: 5): again, it appears
to be (again like 'spirit') a principle of moral life, communicated to the
righteous. On the close relation between 'wisdom' and 'spirit', see P. van
Imschoot, 'Sagesse et Esprit dans l'AT', *RB*, XLVII (1938), 23–49.

[2] The Hebrew verb 'vex' or 'grieve' almost always has a personal object:
this suggests a degree of personification in the term 'holy spirit' which is
preserved in the interpretation we have adopted.

[3] 'This spirit is a national endowment, residing in the community: it is
the spirit of prophecy, resting on Moses, but manifesting its presence also
through other organs of revelation', J. Skinner, *Isaiah* (Cambridge Bible,
1898), vol. 2, chs. 40–66, p. 201.

Isa. 63, has as its essential background God's holy will, the divine demand for righteousness. Within Israel's national life, this standard was revealed and proclaimed in the instruction and theology of the prophets: in the life of the individual (Ps. 51), the inner awareness of the divine demand—evidence of the directing presence of God—is itself the inspiration and power for holy living.

Broadly speaking, then, the רוּחַ יהוה is the divine presence experienced in terms of power for action, whether it be prophetic utterance, heroic exploit or righteous living. The רוּחַ is not an agent with its own existence and actions.[1] A. R. Johnson speaks of it as an 'extension of Yahweh's personality', by which he exercises influence on mankind,[2] and Manson calls it 'the power through which God works and manifests himself in the world'.[3] The רוּחַ יהוה is the means of expressing God's presence to, and action within the world: it is the divine, creative, energising and renewing power in the lives of men and communities.

The Spirit of God is hardly considered another distinct from Him; it is God exercising power, communicating himself, or operating. This power may be simply vital power, physical life; or it may be intellectual, moral and religious life. These are all communicated by the Spirit or רוּחַ of God.[4]

We turn now to the use of רוּחַ to denote the principle of life in both human beings and animals,[5] and found usually in association with נְשָׁמָה (Isa. 42: 5; 57: 16; Job 4: 9; 33: 4 and 34: 14) or נֶפֶשׁ (Isa. 26: 9; Job 7: 11; 12: 10). רוּחַ חַיִּים is used at

---

[1] That the Hebrews did sometimes represent the רוּחַ as a concrete entity, separable in some way from Yahweh (e.g. Ps. 104: 30, 'When thou sendest forth thy spirit...') does not conflict with this judgment. The thought of the Hebrew was imaginative: he expressed himself in the language of pictures drawn from sense impressions, and that language remained poor in abstract terms, being dominated by concrete images. Now 'spirit' (like the 'word') is rather more exterior to a person and more separable than hands, arms and mouth: breath, like speech, acts when it has gone forth from a living being. Consequently, the רוּחַ could, in a sense, be represented as an entity acting apart from Yahweh, though never really distinct from him. Cf. E. Jacob, *Theology of the Old Testament* (ET, London, 1958), p. 121.

[2] *The One and the Many in the Israelite Conception of God*, p. 36.

[3] *On Paul and John*, p. 33.

[4] A. B. Davidson, *Theology of the Old Testament*, p. 193.

[5] H. W. Robinson, *Inspiration and Revelation*, p. 74, reckons that there are thirty-nine such occurrences.

Gen. 6: 17; 7: 15 (as is נִשְׁמַת חַיִּים in Gen. 2: 7) to denote the breath of life in men and in animals.[1] In lifeless idols there is no רוּחַ (Ps. 135: 17; Jer. 10: 14). The Anointed of the Lord, under whose shadow Israel lives, is called the 'breath (רוּחַ) of our nostrils', the very means of existence (Lam. 4: 20). Life only lasts as long as the breath (רוּחַ or נְשָׁמָה) remains in the living being: when it is withdrawn, death ensues (cf. Ps. 104: 29). Yahweh both gives and takes away 'breath' and is the source of life to all creatures, just as in Egyptian, Babylonian, Canaanite and Phoenician thought the god gives life by communicating the vital breath or his own breath.[2] Yahweh is God of the 'spirits' (or 'vital breath') of all flesh (Num. 16: 22; 27: 16) and to him, at death, the רוּחַ returns (Eccles. 12: 7; cf. Ps. 31: 6). The vital character of רוּחַ is further witnessed to in Ezek. 37, which proclaims the restoration or resurrection of the nation by the coming of the breath of God (רוּחַ) from the four winds or compass-points. We find intermingled here the ideas of רוּחַ as 'wind', as the 'principle of life' and as the agent of moral renewal (cf. 36: 22 ff.), but it would be unwise to press out of the mixed symbolism support for the Greek (Orphic) notion that vivifying spirit was borne through the universe by the wind.

There is some similarity between the ideas of Ezek. 37 and those expressed in Gen. 1: 2 (P), which may be the only Old Testament passage in which רוּחַ is brought into association with cosmological activity: וְרוּחַ אֱלֹהִים מְרַחֶפֶת עַל־פְּנֵי הַמָּיִם. Great diversity of opinion exists among interpreters of this verse, and it is impossible to deal with it in detail here. That there is present some reminiscence of the Babylonian cosmogony and the triumph of Marduk over Tiamat seems certain, but that admission does not necessarily mean that the P writer did not have his own content for the words used. For that reason, we think that the translation 'a mighty wind (i.e. wind of godlike

[1] Gen. 7: 22 (J) combines רוּחַ and נְשָׁמָה, but LXX omits רוּחַ and translates πνοὴ ζωῆς. Most scholars claim that רוּחַ is not original, being interpolated from 7: 15; but cf. A. R. Johnson, *The Vitality of the Individual*, p. 31. The expression נִשְׁמַת רוּחַ is found in the ancient poetical passage of 2 Sam. 22: 16 (= Ps. 18: 16) and it is not impossible that the MT has preserved the authentic J reading in Gen. 7: 22.

[2] Cf. J. Hehn, 'Zum Problem des Geistes im Alten Orient und im AT', *ZAW*, XLIII (1925), 210–25.

proportions) swept over the face of the deep'[1]—an interpretation which leans heavily on the fact that Marduk clothed himself in the winds to conquer Tiamat—is rather improbable. Would an author, who used אֱלֹהִים for the creating God, have employed the same word to describe violence, when other unambiguous terms were available?[2] Moreover, the verb מְרַחֶפֶת suggests a slow, fluttering movement, like 'hovering' (cf. Deut. 32: 11), rather than a violent pressure.[3] What then is meant here by רוּחַ אֱלֹהִים?[4] It seems probable that more than one idea is present. In רוּחַ אֱלֹהִים there is an allusion to the 'spirit of God', the purposeful power of the divine; but, at the same time, the רוּחַ is the 'breath of God' which, like the wind, is creative and vivifying. 'By the word of the Lord the heavens were made, and all their host by the breath (רוּחַ) of his mouth' (Ps. 33: 6). The divine word and the divine breath are not rigidly distinguished: both are active, efficacious entities, involved in the Creation process. Consequently, although there is no further mention of רוּחַ in the narrative of Gen. 1, it is fair to claim that the action of the life-giving breath is given order and direction by the divine word.[5] The creative 'breath', which is also the mighty power of the spirit, hovers, waiting, and at the command of God, enters into action constructively.

Returning to the use of רוּחַ in connection with the life of

---

[1] So von Rad, Eissfeldt, Goodspeed and others. The question here raised is this: 'Is that cosmological idea what the author *wished* to communicate?'

[2] E. Jacob, *Theology of the Old Testament*, p. 144.

[3] The meaning 'cover' does not seem adequate in view of the image at Deut. 32: 11. The Syriac use of the root suggests 'brood over' and recalls the idea of the fertilised egg in the Phoenician primordial myth. The verb רחף appears in the Ras Shamra texts (Aqhat 3. i. 20, 21, 31 and 32) with the meaning 'hover' or 'soar'.

[4] H. M. Orlinsky, 'The New Jewish Version of the Torah', *JBL*, LXXXII (1963), 254ff., defends the translation 'a wind from God, or of God', mainly on the basis of traditional Jewish understanding of the verse and the Mesopotamian creation stories. He claims that it was because of the influence of Philo's tendency to allegorise רוּחַ as 'spirit' that the interpretation 'wind' was lost. While doubting the truth of this claim, we would admit that the translation advocated may be correct, but we are prepared to suggest that further overtones may be present in the meaning of the term in the usage of the P writer.

[5] J. Hehn, *ZAW*, XLIII (1925), 218f., cites a number of texts which prove that among ancient near Eastern peoples the breath and the word from the mouth of a god were identical entities, both producing life.

human beings, we must point out that, whereas in the event of the רוּחַ as temporary endowment being withdrawn the individual returned to normality, remaining entirely alive, when the רוּחַ as vital breath or the principle of existence is withdrawn, the result is a loss of strength and consciousness (cf. Judg. 15: 19; 1 Kings 10: 5) and ultimately death. The absence of רוּחַ causes some kind of diminished vitality: its presence or return increases strength and well-being. Consequently, we may say that רוּחַ means not only the principle of existence (that which makes the difference between death and life) but denotes also the principle of *full* vitality, that which makes the difference between half-life (caused by hunger, grief or fainting) and real 'spirited' living. In both cases, the action of breathing (observed as present or not present, as strong or weak) may provide the key to the understanding of the Hebrew usage.

We now pass to the fourth main group of the uses of רוּחַ, where the word is used psychically and denotes (like נֶפֶשׁ and לֵב) the seat of the affections, emotions and passions, of the will, and of the intellectual and moral life.[1] This usage develops naturally from the close association observed between breathing and various feelings and emotions: in anger the breath (רוּחַ) is hot (Ezek. 3: 14); in impatience it becomes short (Micah 2: 7; Exod. 6: 9; Job 21: 4); in terror it is excited or troubled (Gen. 41: 8; Dan, 2: 1, 3). Given this usage, it is not surprising that the step was taken to the use of רוּחַ to describe the dominant impulse or disposition of an individual (cf. Gen. 26: 35; Ps. 32: 2). Confusion, impatience, obstinacy and sadness are termed the רוּחַ of trouble (Gen. 41: 8), of shortness (Exod. 6: 9), of hardness (Deut. 2: 30) and of grief (1 Sam. 1: 15). The 'humble' person is the man 'of contrite spirit (רוּחַ)' (Isa. 66: 2) and 'sorrow of heart' is equivalent to the 'breaking of the רוּחַ' (Isa. 65: 14).

The word רוּחַ may also refer to the seat of thought (Ezek. 20: 32; 11: 5) and even to the controlling power of the moral and religious life. 'Take heed', says Malachi (2: 15), 'to your spirit, that ye deal not treacherously with the wives of your youth.' Restoration of character involves the renewal and regeneration of the spirit and the heart (Ezek. 11: 19; 18: 31, etc.), that is, a complete change of inner life and attitudes. In this use, the

---

[1] Cf. H. W. Robinson, 'Hebrew Psychology', *The People and the Book*, pp. 360f.

meaning of רוּחַ overlaps with the meaning of לֵב: but, as N. H. Snaith has pointed out,[1] this does not mean that 'heart' and 'spirit' were equivalent in Hebrew thinking: both words (and נֶפֶשׁ as well) had smaller and larger circles of meaning, and in the case of all three, these circles overlap in the common area where each connotes the controlling power in man, the seat of desire, will and emotion.

This leads to our final point. The usage (mostly late) which we have just discussed suggests that 'spirit' is part of man himself, the controlling element within him. How is this inner רוּחַ related to the נֶפֶשׁ? Is there a dichotomy between soul and spirit in the Hebrew understanding of man? When it refers to 'inner controlling element' רוּחַ denotes, as we have said, the same thing as נֶפֶשׁ when it means the directing element in man's energies, attitudes and emotions. In any case, the נֶפֶשׁ is not opposed to the רוּחַ in scriptural statements, but is parallel to it (Isa. 26: 9; Job 7: 11; 12: 10). It has been suggested by H. W. Robinson[2] that even when רוּחַ became 'naturalised' in human nature (as a synonym of לֵב or נֶפֶשׁ) it still suggested a reference to the common and continued use of the word to denote a supernatural influence acting on man from outside, and thus supplied a point of contact between man and God. While not wishing to be dogmatic, we are inclined to doubt this. There is no passage to suggest that the רוּחַ יהוה acted only on the רוּחַ of man, or that there is any substantial likeness between them. The two uses of the word in question seem to stem from two different strands of meaning which had attached themselves to the word in the course of its historical development, one relating to human psychology, the other to divine power endowed. The Hebrews never failed to distinguish between God and man: the use of a word, which bore several senses, in ways which *suggest* the minimising of that distinction is an insufficient basis for Robinson's statement.

This sketch of the use and meaning of רוּחַ in the Old Testament may be concluded by restating the four main senses in which it is found: (i) as the description of the 'wind', especially as created and controlled by God; (ii) in the charismatic sense, the רוּחַ יהוה

[1] Snaith, *The Distinctive Ideas of the Old Testament*, pp. 148–9.
[2] *Inspiration and Revelation*, p. 76.

being the source of special powers in men, either as a temporary phenomenon or as a permanent gift to fulfil certain functions. Within this usage, the presence of the 'spirit' becomes a sign of God's renewing and regenerating activity in the messianic age. The special usage 'holy spirit' refers to the directing presence of God, the awareness of the demand of God's holy will, both in the community (through the prophetic ministry) and in the individual, in whose experience this awareness inspires to righteousness of life. (iii) It is used to refer to the principle of existence and vitality, the vivifying breath communicated to men and animals; and, as the powerful divine breath, it is occasionally related to the action of Creation. (iv) רוּחַ is used to denote aspects of, or impulses within the psychical life of man.

Appended Note. The Old Testament speaks also of 'evil spirits', I Sam. 16: 14; Judg. 9: 23 and I Kings 22: 21. In accordance with the exclusiveness of the Old Testament faith in God, these spirits were regarded as having been created by God: they were employed in the service of his anger, and therefore related to the fulfilling of his will. Later these spirits were personalised in 'Satan', but behind this idea lies a strong ethicising and 'transcendentalising' of the being of God which refused to believe that God could be in any way responsible for evil, even when it was demonstrably under his control. A. R. Johnson thinks of these evil spirits in terms of his thesis of Yahweh's extended personality (*The One and the Many*, p. 16). He claims that we must be prepared to think of Yahweh acting not only through the instrumentality of his own רוּחַ, but also through the agency of some subordinate רוּחַ who, as a member of his immediate entourage, may be thought of as an individualisation within the corporate רוּחַ of Yahweh's extended personality. In this way, the 'evil spirits' would be related to the idea of the Heavenly Court, as were the אֱלֹהִים (Ps. 82: 1 and 89: 8–9).

THE USAGE OF THE SEPTUAGINT

The Septuagint translators reveal a strong tendency to render the Hebrew word רוּחַ by πνεῦμα,[1] and this in spite of the fact that the Hebrew had a wider range of meanings than the Greek. The survey of Greek usage showed that πνεῦμα covered the

---

[1] Baumgärtel (*TWNT*, vol. VI, πνεῦμα in LXX) reckons that of the 378 occurrences of רוּחַ, 277 are rendered in the LXX by πνεῦμα.

meanings 'wind', 'breath of life' and 'air', but did not denote 'spirit', either human or divine: in biblical Greek πνεῦμα is employed to render רוּחַ when it bears this meaning.

In about fifty of the passages where רוּחַ denotes 'wind' the translators chose to render it by ἄνεμος rather than by πνεῦμα.[1] There does not seem to be any real distinction in the meaning of the two words, when applied to 'wind', and if they are not identical, they are at least closely synonymous. On a few occasions when רוּחַ denotes 'wind' the LXX has either paraphrased the original or misunderstood it (Jer. 10: 13; 51: 16; LXX 28: 16), with result that neither ἄνεμος nor πνεῦμα appears in the text. At Ezek. 13: 13 רוּחַ ('wind') is translated by πνοή.

When רוּחַ denotes 'breath' it is almost always rendered by πνεῦμα, cf. Gen. 6: 17; 7: 15; Exod. 15: 8; 2 Sam. 22: 16; Ps. 18: 16 and Ps. 104 (LXX 103): 29–30. Occasionally, even נְשָׁמָה ('breath') is rendered by πνεῦμα,[2] and this is a sign of the extent to which the meaning 'breath' was identified with the Greek word.

The Greeks possessed nothing that corresponded to the Hebrew conception of the Spirit of God, and it is not strange therefore that they lacked a means of expressing it. The LXX translators simply extended the use of πνεῦμα to cover this meaning of רוּחַ as well, and they did so quite consistently. The charismatic רוּחַ יהוה, as the temporary gift to warrior and prophet, as the permanent endowment of the prophets and the messianic king, and as the regenerating, re-creating power in the future community, is consistently rendered by τὸ πνεῦμα τοῦ θεοῦ.[3] When discussing the Old Testament idea of the Spirit of God, we pointed out that the 'spirit' is not a separate agent with its own existence and action, but rather the divine power entering into action. Now it is impossible to discover on the basis of usage alone whether the Greek rendering preserved this Hebrew idea or whether it suggests some kind of power or personality separable from God. Ordinary Greek usage, as we have seen, consistently understood πνεῦμα in terms of substance. Did something of this conception pass over into the term 'spirit

---

[1] Exod. 10: 13, 19 and 14: 21; 2 Kings 22: 11, etc.

[2] 3 Kings 17: 17; Job 34: 14; Dan. 5: 23 and 10: 17, where Theodotion has πνοή.

[3] Gen. 1: 2 reads πνεῦμα θεοῦ not τὸ πνεῦμα τοῦ θεοῦ.

of God' as it was interpreted from the Greek Bible by Greek speakers? In other words, did the possibility of regarding the Spirit as independent of God enter because of the connotation πνεῦμα possessed for the Greek mind? Some passages suggest that this may be so. The important verse in Ps. 51, 'Take not from me thy holy spirit (lit. the spirit of thy holiness)' becomes τὸ πνεῦμα τὸ ἅγιον σου, a rendering which may imply a degree of distinction between 'spirit' and the source of the gift which the Hebrew would not support. At Isa. 63: 10f. the same change is at work. In 1 Sam. 16: 14 and 1 Kings 22: 21 f., what is implicit in the Hebrew concerning 'spirits' under Yahweh's control becomes explicit in the Greek version. Further evidence for the idea of 'spirits' with separate existence is found in the translation of Num. 16: 22 and 27: 16. The Hebrew reads, 'God of the spirits (i.e. the vital breath) of all flesh': the Greek has θεὸς τῶν πνευμάτων καὶ πάσης σαρκός where the πνεύματα are probably understood as 'spirits' acting as God's messengers. On discovering renderings of this kind, one is caused to wonder if we have here (in the Greek translation) the beginnings of the idea of possession by spirits and the source of the later use of πνεύματα to describe beings surrounding God, akin to the אֱלֹהִים and angels in the Old Testament.

When רוּחַ is used in the psychical sense, as the seat of the affections, passions and will, there is considerable variation in the method of translation. Only about half of the passages in which this sense belongs to the Hebrew are rendered by πνεῦμα. This is not surprising in view of the fact that in Greek a psychological use of that word does not occur. To obviate this difficulty, the translators resorted to other renderings. They sometimes used ψυχή ('soul'), as in Gen. 41: 8; Exod. 35: 21, or some form of that word, ὀλιγοψυχία (Exod. 6: 9), ὀλιγόψυχος (Isa. 54: 6; 57: 15; Prov. 14: 29; 18: 14). More often they used θύμος (Job 15: 13; Zech. 6: 8, etc.) or some derived form of the word. Such terms as ἡσυχίος, ταπεινόφρων, κακοφροσύνη, φρόνησις and νοῦς (Isa. 40: 13) occur once in rendering רוּחַ: and occasionally a different expression was substituted (Ps. 32: 2; Prov. 15: 13) thus avoiding a direct translation of the word. So consistently did the translator of Proverbs use these expedients that only once, in ch. 15: 4, does πνεῦμα appear where רוּחַ stands in the Hebrew —and there the meaning of the passage is misunderstood! Since the translator of Proverbs (and of Job) was more alive to Greek usage and ideas,[1] it is not surprising to find variety and precision in the psychological terms he employs.

THE APOCRYPHA AND PSEUDEPIGRAPHA

The usage of πνεῦμα in these writings is, in general, the same as that found in the Greek translations of the canonical books, but, in addition there are some developments to be considered. The use of πνεῦμα for 'wind' is frequent in both the translated and the Greek books,[2] and the meaning 'breath' or 'breath of life' is found throughout the literature.[3]

The phrase 'spirit of God' is not frequent in the Intertestamental books. Apart from Judith 16: 14, where the divine πνεῦμα is equated with the Word of God in the action of Creation, the Spirit of God is always associated with 'wisdom' in these writings:

Who ever gained knowledge of thy counsel, except thou gavest wisdom (σοφία) and sentest thy holy spirit (τὸ ἅγιόν σου πνεῦμα) from on high (Wisd. 9: 17, cf. 7: 7).

Wisdom is itself equated with 'a holy spirit of discipline or instruction (ἅγιον πνεῦμα παιδείας) which flees deceit' (1 : 5): it is a spirit that loveth man (1 : 6) and a spirit of understanding (Sir. 39: 6).[4] In so far as there was a hypostatisation of 'wisdom' in the sapiential literature, the same process tended to draw the concept 'spirit of God' towards the idea of substance in the Alexandrian theology.

The spirit of the Lord has filled the inhabited world, that which holdeth all things together (τὸ συνέχον τὰ πάντα) hath knowledge of every voice (Wisd. 1: 7).

Thine incorruptible spirit is in all things (Wisd. 12: 1).

[1] Cf. G. Gerleman, *Studies in the Septuagint: II. Proverbs* (Lund, 1956).

[2] Sir. 39: 28; 43: 17; Song of Three 27, 43 (Dan. 3: 50, 65); Wisd. 5: 11, 23; 7: 20 (?); 11: 20 (?); 13: 2; 17: 18 and Ep. Jer. 61.

[3] Sir. 38: 23; Tob. 3: 6; Judith 10: 13; 14: 6; Bar. 2: 17; Wisd. 2: 3; 15: 11, 16; 16: 14; Ep. Jer. 24; 2 Macc. 7: 22, 23; 3 Macc. 6: 24 and 4 Macc. 11: 11; 12: 19. At Dan. 3: 86 (Song of Three 64) the phrase 'spirits and souls of the righteous' denotes the living righteous, not departed spirits.

[4] According to Wisd. 7: 22 ff., '*in* wisdom there is a spirit, quick of understanding, holy...penetrating all things': this assertion shows the extent to which 'wisdom' was viewed under the form of human personality.

These passages suggest that πνεῦμα is some formless, all pene-trating being or material substance pervading the entire universe (cf. the Stoic *anima mundi*). But on the other hand, 'spirit' (like 'wisdom') may denote divine power, active in the sphere of the intellect, and enabling the righteous to know and to accomplish the will of God: in other words, the function of the Spirit is to build up morality and increase knowledge of God. The good man experiences this power or shares in it (Test. xii. Sim. 4: 4; Benj. 8: 2): and the Messiah was expected to possess the spirit in fullness:[1]

God will cause him to be mighty in holy spirit (ἐν πνεύματι ἁγίῳ) and wise in the counsel of understanding, with strength and righteousness (Ps. Sol. 17: 37, cf. 18: 7).

There is no reference here to a personal being. The Psalms of Solomon (standing in the main stream of Jewish thinking) reaffirm the old idea of endowment with divine power for a special task (cf. Sir. 48: 12, 24).

The use of πνεῦμα for 'a personal spirit' is almost entirely confined to the books of Enoch, Jubilees and the Testaments of the Twelve Patriarchs.

(*a*) The angelic beings who had their home in heaven and left it to consort with mortal women are called 'spirits' (πνεύματα) (Enoch 15: 4–8). In the Ethiopic portion of Enoch the phrase 'Lord of Spirits' (found 104 times, of which 28 are in interpolated passages) seems to take the place of the older 'Lord of Hosts', and the two titles may reflect a kinship of ideas concerning God's control of the powers.[2]

(*b*) The giants, who were born of the union of angels with human kind, are 'evil spirits', and from them, at their death, go forth evil spirits (Enoch 15: 8–12; 16: 1). These spirits are demons, living on earth without restraint, and tormenting living persons until the day of consummation, the great Judg-ment. This demonology is found in the book of Jubilees and in

---

[1] Cf. Test. xii. Levi 18: 7, and Enoch 49: 2–3, 'In him (the Elect One) dwells the spirit of wisdom'.

[2] The title יְהוָה צְבָאוֹת was frequently translated in the LXX by κύριος τῶν δυνάμεων, which may suggest the idea of lordship over divine agencies: see Dodd, *The Bible and the Greeks*, pp. 16–17. In 2 Macc. 3: 24 God is called ὁ τῶν πνευμάτων καὶ πάσης ἐξουσίας δυνάστης.

the Testaments. Acting under the rule of Beliar or the Devil, the 'spirits of deceit' (the most common designation) concern themselves primarily with the temptation of men. According to Test. Reub. 2: 1–2 and 3: 3–6 the 'seven spirits of deceit' (fornication, insatiableness, fighting, etc.) appear to be the inclinations to various sins, located in the various organs of the body.[1] Test. Jud. 20: 1 claims that two spirits wait on man, the spirit of truth and the spirit of deceit, and the works of both are written upon the hearts of men and each one of them is known by the Lord. Instead of 'spirits' Test. Asher 1: 3 ff. speaks of 'inclinations':

If the soul takes pleasure in the good (inclination) all its actions are in righteousness; if it inclines to the evil, all its actions are in wickedness and...it is ruled by Beliar. (Cf. also Test. Benj. 6: 1.)

Once in Tobit (6: 8,) a demon inhabiting a human being is called πνεῦμα πονηρόν.

(c) A new meaning for πνεῦμα—'a human being after death' —is found in Enoch 9: 3, 10 and 20: 3. When used thus, the term seems to be a synonym of ψυχή, and in ch. 22 the two words are used interchangeably. In using the word πνεῦμα in this way the author may have been influenced by his own application of it to the 'spirits' which proceeded from the dead giants, but the innovation of usage was not followed by any other writer of the period.

The use of πνεῦμα in the 'psychical' sense (denoting the seat of affections and emotions) is almost non-existent in the Intertestamental books composed in Greek. This is additional evidence that among Greek-speaking people there was no such meaning in use. There are, however, several instances in the books which translate a Hebrew original. The 'spirit' (i.e. courage) of the people revived when they selected Simeon as their leader, 1 Macc. 13: 7. God changed the spirit of Ahasuerus into mildness towards Esther (Greek addition to Esther 15: 10; cf. also 1 Esdras 2: 2, 8). The 'spirit' (πνεῦμα) is the seat of excitement and impulse (Sir. 9: 9), of anxiety (Bar. 3: 1), of humility

---

[1] Test. Reub. 2: 3 — 3: 2 uses πνεύματα to denote the sense organs or appetites. This use of πνεῦμα is found in Stoic philosophy in which the five senses, together with the powers of reproduction and speech, discharge themselves into the body in the form of immaterial currents (πνεύματα) (Plut. *Plac. Phil.* 4: 21; Philo, *Opif.* 40). The passage in Test. Reub. is a late Greek interpolation.

(Song of Three 16) and of fear (Judith 7: 19). These examples of the use of πνεῦμα are interpretable only in the light of the 'psychical' use of רוּחַ in the Old Testament.

PHILO JUDAEUS

In the writings of Philo, the word πνεῦμα is not so frequent as one would expect. It appears about 110 times, whereas ψυχή occurs about seventeen times as often. Although πνεῦμα is not a leading term with Philo, his usage throws valuable light on the use of the word in the Alexandrian philosophy at a time coincident with the period of the writing of some of the New Testament documents.

Philo employs the word πνεῦμα (sing. and pl.) to denote 'wind' over forty times. The old Jewish idea of the wind as under the direct control of God seems to be entirely abandoned, presumably because Philo had adopted the Greek conceptions of physical nature. This suggestion is borne out by his use of πνεῦμα to denote one of the *elemental* substances. Associated with 'heaven', 'earth' and 'water' (*Ebr.* 106; *Sacr.* 97) πνεῦμα means 'air', the air we breathe which is life-giving (*Opif.* 29–30) and is equivalent to ἀήρ (*Gig.* 10; *Cher.* 111). To denote 'breath' (both human and animal) Philo employs πνεῦμα eleven times. 'Breath' (being part of the air outside) is inhaled through the nostrils and mouth (*Legat.* 18; cf. *Mos.* 1. 93) and travels through the wind-pipe (*Immut.* 84).

In harmony with Stoic thought and expression, Philo occasionally uses πνεῦμα when referring to the permeating and building force within physical bodies: *Immut.* 35, 'Cohesion in stones and wood is a breath or current (πνεῦμα) ever returning to itself'; *Opif.* 131 says that the earth is bound together by the power of (or by virtue of) the life-breath (?) that makes it one (πνεύματος ἐνωτικοῦ δυνάμει) and by moisture; and *Fug.* 182 declares that the dominant faculty in the soul 'waters the face, which is the dominant part of the body, extending to the eyes the spirit (or current, πνεῦμα) of vision, that of hearing to the ears' and so on with the various senses which are faculties of the irrational soul.[1]

---

[1] We noted earlier, in connection with Test. Reub. 2: 3 — 3: 2, the Stoic use of the word πνεύματα to describe the senses and the powers of reproduction and speech.

It is impossible to find any satisfactory English equivalent for the Stoic πνεῦμα, denoting an immaterial force, akin to the element of air and associated with the principle of cohesion in the body and with the power of sense-perception.

Sometimes Philo uses πνεῦμα with reference to Reason or Mind (νοῦς).[1]

To that faculty which we share with irrational things blood was assigned as its *substance*, but that flowing from the fountain of reason has for its substance breath (πνεῦμα), not air set in motion (i.e. not just 'air' or 'wind') but a sort of stamp and impress of the divine power...the εἰκών, showing that God is the archetype of rational nature and man its copy... (*Deter.* 83).

In other words, 'the Spirit which forms the essence of man's rational soul is the impress of the Logos',[2] and for this the proof-text is Gen. 2: 7, 'And the Lord God breathed into his face the breath of life'.[3] We have already mentioned Philo's application of πνεῦμα ('breath') to the irrational soul,[4] but here we have the term applied to the rational soul, the image or impress of the Divine reason.[5] In *Plant.* 18 Philo speaks, in notable terms, of the rational soul of man as 'the genuine coinage of that divine and

---

[1] This use of πνεῦμα links it to one aspect of ψυχή. On the one hand, ψυχή (when applied to man) possesses the vital energy, the principle of life in matter, irrational and common to men and animals: the essence of this vital principle is blood (Lev. 17: 11) and life lived in accordance with it is opposed to the life of reason. On the other hand, ψυχή possesses a rational capacity, the impress of the divine reason, and, being described as 'breathed into man by God', it is called πνεῦμα: it may also be named νοῦς or λόγος since it is an undivided part of the divine Reason.

[2] J. Drummond, *Philo Judaeus*, II, 215.

[3] The LXX uses πνοή here, and in quoting the verse Philo uses πνοή five times and πνεῦμα once, as if the words were interchangeable. Yet in *Leg. All.* 1 : 42 he distinguishes between them: πνεῦμα, he says, applies to the rational mind when conceived as something created 'after the image and idea', i.e. after the idea of mind, without reference to its connection with the irrational soul. The term πνοή refers to the rational mind, when conceived as connected with the irrational soul created of matter.

[4] *Opif.* 67, and cf. Frag. on Gen. 9: 4, 'the breath (πνεῦμα) rather than the blood is the essence of the soul', i.e. the irrational soul. See H. A. Wolfson, *Philo*, I, 385 ff.

[5] Wolfson, *op. cit.* p. 394: 'In its application to the irrational soul, the term "breath" is of Stoic origin and it means something corporeal: in its application to mind, it is of scriptural origin and it means something incorporeal.'

invisible spirit (πνεῦμα) marked and stamped by the seal of God, whose impress is the eternal Logos': and in *Heres* 55-7 he refers to reason as 'the divine inbreathing' (θεῖον πνεῦμα). In these quotations we observe that the term πνεῦμα θεῖον (as well as πνεῦμα) can be used to describe the essence of the *incorporeal and rational soul* breathed into man. The same use is found in *Opif.* 135 and *Spec.* IV. 123.

There is another use of πνεῦμα θεῖον in Philo. In order to understand its place in his scheme we must recall that man's rational soul (the substance of which is πνεῦμα or πνεῦμα θεῖον) is not regarded by Philo as having any knowledge of its own: it has only a capacity for knowledge, and that capacity may be fulfilled in one of two ways: the soul may take data of the external world supplied to it by the senses and transform them, by its native power, into rational concepts; or, by freeing itself from the bodily influence and from its own rational concepts based on sense-perception, the incorporeal soul may become filled with 'divine spirit' (or prophetic spirit) and through this receive a new kind of knowledge of things incorporeal, that is, a supernatural order of rational knowledge (cf. *Plant.* 24; *Gig.* 22 f.). In this use of πνεῦμα θεῖον to refer to inspiration there are echoes of both Stoic and Platonic ideas and terminology, but Philo is also sensitive to the Old Testament idea of the 'spirit' as a divine endowment, or equipment.[1] In fact, Philo illustrates this aspect of the 'divine spirit' by the special equipment of wisdom and understanding bestowed on Bezaleel for the construction of the Tabernacle, and by the imparting to the seventy elders of the spirit of Moses. This 'spirit' leads the mind to truth (*Mos.* II. 265): it is the author of inspiration (*Somn.* II. 252; *Mos.* I. 175, 297) and takes over from reason the control of man (*Spec.* IV. 49; *Heres* 265). It is not, however, a permanent gift. The biblical statement, 'My spirit shall not always dwell with men, because they are flesh (σάρξ)' (Gen. 6: 3), is interpreted of the divine inspiring power which remains only temporarily with

---

[1] Cf. E. Hatch, *Essays in Biblical Greek* (Oxford, 1889), p. 127: 'The conception of this special form of πνεῦμα seems to be required on the one hand by philosophy, in order to account for the fact that some men have a knowledge and intellectual power which others have not, and, on the other hand, by theology, since the Pentateuch speaks of men being filled, in some special sense, by a divine Spirit.'

men, because men, as flesh, do not always desire or receive a notion (ἔννοια) of the Highest (cf. *Immut.* 2). Nevertheless the divine spirit may be encouraged to remain if we refrain from doing wrong (*Gig.* 47). Only with one type of man does the divine spirit *dwell*, namely he who has stripped off all that belongs to the world of becoming, 'and with unrestricted and open mind reaches God' (*Gig.* 53).[1]

What is the relation between 'divine spirit' as the essence of the rational (incorporeal) soul and 'divine spirit' in the sense of prophetic spirit? No clear solution of this problem emerges from Philo's writings, but it seems that the connection must be sought in the relation of both to the Logos.[2] The πνεῦμα θεῖον which forms the essence of the rational soul is the impress of the Logos: it is the communicated divine idea, the sharing of the universal Reason, the Logos immanent in man. As the inspiring endowment of man, πνεῦμα θεῖον is identified with Wisdom in its highest sense (*Gig.* 22) and is therefore indistinguishable from the Logos, which, by reason of this endowment of itself, is manifested in varying degrees in individual men. Through uniting philosophical thought with Jewish teaching Philo presents the idea that the source of the possibility of the life according to reason is essentially the same as the divine endowment which inspires and equips for noble living.

By way of summary, we may say that in the works of Philo the word πνεῦμα is used of 'wind', the element 'air' and 'human breath'; of the cohesive force in physical bodies and of the power of sense-perception (both Stoic ideas); as the inbreathing of God in creation, it is the essence of the rational soul of man, the stamp of the Logos: this soul is also called πνεῦμα θεῖον, a term which may also denote the source of inspired, prophetic knowledge, identifiable with Wisdom and Logos.

THE RABBINIC LITERATURE

We have already noticed that the attribution of cosmic functions to the רוּחַ is very infrequent in the Old Testament (Gen. 1: 2; Ps. 33: 6 and 104: 30) and in the Intertestamental books: like-

---

[1] See H. A. A. Kennedy, *Philo's Contribution to Religion* (London, 1919), pp. 186 ff.

[2] See H. A. Wolfson, *Philo*, II, 30; J. Drummond, *Philo Judaeus*, II, 214–16, and H. A. A. Kennedy, *op. cit.* p. 188.

wise, among the Rabbis, the 'spirit' is not conceived as the life-giving creative power of God. 'In early Rabbinic literature', says E. Schweizer, 'the "cosmic" function of the Spirit does not appear to be mentioned at all.'[1] There are, however, passages in which the Spirit is spoken of as the *re*-creating, *re*-vivifying power of the Messianic Age. Ex. R. 48 (102*d*) distinguishes the functions of the Spirit in this Age and in the Age to come:

God said to Israel, 'In this world my spirit has put wisdom in you, but in the future my Spirit will make you to live again, as it is said (Ezek. 37: 14) "I will put my Spirit in you that you may live".' (Cf. also Gen. R. 96 (60*d*).)

The Spirit of God was to be the creative power of life in the Age to come, active, mainly, in the raising up of those who were to share in the messianic blessings.

The use of רוּחַ for 'wind' is retained in the Targumim to those passages in which this is the Old Testament meaning. The same is true of the use of the word to denote 'breath' and in the various psychological expressions of 'spirit'. The dependence of mankind upon God for vital breath expressed in Num. 27: 16 ('God of the spirits of all flesh') is explained as 'The Memra of God who rules over the breath of man and from whom is given the spirit of breath to all flesh' (Ps. Jonathan). In this connection we may draw attention to the strange interpretation of Gen. 2: 7, 'God breathed into man's nostrils the breath of life and man became a living being'; Targ. Onk. says, 'the breath of life became in Adam a discoursing spirit (רוּחַ מְמַלְלָא)'. This interpretation bears witness to the close connection that was thought to exist between 'breath' and 'word, or speech'.

When we turn to the frequent use of רוּחַ and רוּחַ יהוה to denote charismatic endowment, we discover that, in rabbinic interpretation, the character of the gift is predominantly the spirit of *prophecy*. The gift of the Spirit to the Seventy elders probably means divine inspiration to govern well, but according to Targ. Ps. Jon. it refers to the spirit of prophecy. The spirit upon Samuel (1 Sam. 10: 6, etc.) is again the 'spirit of prophecy',

---

[1] E. Schweizer, *The Spirit of God* (Bible Key Words Series, London, 1960), p. 14. In Gen. 1: 2 the רוּחַ אֱלֹהִים is understood by T. Onkelos as 'a wind from before God...': Ps. Jon. 1 and 2 speak of 'the spirit of mercy from before God' and so discern in the passage the thought that God created the world with *mercy*: see SB, 1, 48–9 and G. F. Moore, *Judaism*, 1, 389.

as is the endowment of Balaam (Num. 24: 2). In the description of the comprehensive spiritual enrichment of the messianic ruler (Isa. 11: 2), in which the 'spirit' assumes varied forms to meet varied duties, Targ. Onk. placed first and equivalent to 'spirit of the Lord' the phrase 'the spirit of prophecy from God'.[1] A further example of the association between the divine spirit and prophecy is to be found at Isa. 63: 10f. where 'spirit of holiness' is rendered by 'the words of His holy prophets'—an interpretation which accords with the rabbinic inclusion of the patriarchs in the category of God's prophets and which makes explicit what we suggested was implicit in the Old Testament passage. This rabbinic emphasis on the spirit of prophecy means that the term 'prophecy' is not restricted to reference to the special inspiration to foretell the future and proclaim the divine judgments: it comprises the possession of deeper insight into the will of God, the infusion into man of a more than ordinary power, knowledge and discernment, enabling him to perform what is right and good more effectually than the person who lacks the gift. Thus the 'spirit of prophecy' may be attributed to warrior and craftsman, king and messianic ruler—men whose activities would not all be included within the narrow definition of prophecy.

In addition to being essentially 'prophetic spirit' the Holy Spirit, according to the Rabbis, was the inspirer, even the composer, of the books of the Old Testament. Indeed, in such measure is the Old Testament Holy Writ one of the great visible results of the Holy Spirit's activity that the two are regarded as equivalent: a saying from the Old Testament can be quoted either as a saying of Torah or as a saying of the Spirit. Within this general framework of scriptural inspiration, the Holy Spirit may have a special function in the dramatisation of biblical verses and passages. Israel or a biblical character recites part of a verse and Holy Spirit responds by quoting the remainder of the same verse or a neighbouring verse (cf. Cant. 8: 5–6; Tosef. Sotah 9. 9).[2] What is arresting in this usage is the extent to which Holy Spirit

[1] Targ. Onk. to Isa. 42: 1 does not reinterpret the gift of the Spirit there in terms of prophetic endowment.

[2] Cf. H. Parzen, 'The Ruaḥ Hakodesh in Tannaitic Literature', *JQR*, xx (1929–30), 56–60; and J. Abelson, *The Immanence of God in Rabbinical Literature* (London, 1912), pp. 225 ff.

is personified: the Spirit speaks, cries, laments, weeps, rejoices, comforts, but always effects these actions by introducing scriptural quotations. Probably this is a graphic attempt to express the presence and involvement of God in the affairs of his people. The 'Holy Spirit' is the representative of God, and may even be used as a synonym for God speaking in Scripture (Mid. Ex. 15: 3; Sifre Deut. 335 on 33: 26). The reason for this metynomy, as for many other rabbinic substitutes for the actual name of God, is the desire to avoid desecrating the Tetragrammaton, regarded reverently as the proper name of God.

The sanctity of the divine name gave rise to the frequent use of the term 'Shekinah', referring to the divine presence, and this is often employed interchangeably with 'Holy Spirit'. Similar phraseology clusters round both terms: the sins that drive away the Spirit also drive away the Shekinah: the virtues which qualify one to possess the Holy Spirit also qualify for the Shekinah. Although the two terms were often used indiscriminately, 'Holy Spirit' is employed far more sparingly in the rabbinic literature, and where the two are parallel it is found mostly in the later, rather than in the early writings.[1] The exact relation between 'Spirit' and 'Shekinah' is difficult to determine, but it does not seem correct to regard them as identical. While the idea of the abiding presence of God is common to both, there is not attributed to Shekinah the function of revelation or inspiration which is so central to the activity of the Spirit in Jewish thought.[2]

In contrast to the teaching of the Old Testament writers, the Rabbis universalised the gift of the Spirit. In the former it is the endowment only of recognised prophets, of specially prominent individuals and of the Hebrew nation at certain points of its career, but in the thought of the Rabbis and in succeeding Jewish theology the Holy Spirit may be acquired by any individual who orders his life in accordance with the fear of God.[3] It is not given by Heaven miraculously, that is, without any sufficiently evident reason; its existence in a man is the effect of a clear cause, and that cause is persevering obedience to the Torah (Lev. R. 35. 7 on 26: 3 and Num. R. 15. 20 on 11: 6). Once the Spirit is given,

[1] Abelson, *op. cit.* Appendix, p. 379.
[2] G. F. Moore, *Judaism*, I, 437, and *HTR*, xv (1922), 58.
[3] The idea of the possession of the 'spirit of holiness' in Ps. 51 may be moving in this direction.

it inspires men to even greater holiness of life.[1] The perfectibility of man towards the possession of the Spirit as an ideal state is well brought out in the celebrated dictum of R. Phinehas ben Jair (second century A.D.):

Torah leads to carefulness, carefulness to diligence, diligence to cleanliness (ritual purity), cleanliness to self-control, self-control to purity, purity to piety, piety to humility, humility to fear of sin, fear of sin to holiness, holiness to the Holy Spirit, and Holy Spirit to the resurrection of the dead. (Mish. Sotah 9. 15; b. Abodah Zarah, 20 b.)

The possession of the Holy Spirit is the culmination of what the religious life should mean in the case of each man who lives it.

Just as holiness is a condition for the gift of the Spirit, so also is wholeness of the body. Every physical imperfection or emotional disturbance of the organism of the body acted as a barrier to the accession of the Spirit (cf. Gen. R. 91. 6). The same applied to unclean material surroundings. When a devout man sins the Holy Spirit departs (Gen. R. 60. 3 on 32: 14), but the same happens when he approaches a place which is under the power of sin. When Esther approached the idolatrous palace of Ahasuerus the Holy Spirit departed from her (Yalk. Est. 5. 2). As a development of this idea, the diminution of prophecy—or the cessation of the Spirit—was traced to the sinfulness of Israel, Sif. Deut. 173 on 18: 12. A sinful nation is no longer a suitable environment for the Holy Spirit, and even outstanding Rabbis who were personally worthy of the Spirit were debarred from its enjoyment because of the sinful age. 'When the sages entered the house of Guryo at Jericho, they heard the Bath-Qōl[2] announce, "One man is present here who is worthy of the רוח הקדש, but his generation is not worthy of it"' (Tos. Sotah 13. 3). In short, a favourable religious milieu must exist as well as saintly men before the Spirit will appear. This view enables us to understand the passages in

[1] In connection with the idea of the Spirit as the power for righteous living, it is of interest to note that Jer. Targ. on Gen. 6: 3 ('My Spirit shall not always strive with man') interprets the verse as referring to man's failure to perform good works.

[2] 'Bath-Qōl' (lit. 'daughter of the voice') was, in a sense, an agent of revelation. It often recited Scripture for the guidance of men and gave advice on matters of Halakah (see A. Marmorstein, *Studies in Jewish Theology* [Oxford, 1950], pp. 135 ff.). Its authority was not equivalent to that of the Spirit because, on occasion, its guidance could be set aside, b. Bab. Metz. 59 b.

which the geographical location of the Spirit's activities is discussed. According to some Rabbis, Palestine alone was sanctified and the only place, outside the Holy Land, on which the Spirit could be experienced was on the seas which were considered pure. Other teachers suggested that, while God reveals himself everywhere, it was only in Palestine, and in Jerusalem in particular, that the Spirit remained constantly active. 'In order to understand the issue involved in this difference of opinion,' says Parzen, 'we must bear in mind that Palestine is the Holy Land. Therefore it is the proper place for Revelation. Foreign lands are, from the rabbinic viewpoint, "impure", consequently, not suitable for Divine Revelation.'[1]

From discussion of the persons and places in which the Spirit is operative we turn to the times or epochs of its functioning.[2] With their broad view of the nature of prophecy, the Rabbis claimed that the Spirit rested on all the devout and righteous of earlier generations. Moses, David, Solomon, priests, patriarchs and their wives were all equipped and inspired by the power of the Spirit. The *past*, the remote past, was indeed the great era of the Spirit. What of the present? In the Apocryphal books it is assumed that, although the great period of prophetic activity has passed, the Spirit may still be granted to men (Wisd. 7: 7; 9: 17; Sir. 39: 6). The Rabbis, on the other hand, clearly state that after the last prophets the Spirit departed from Israel.

When the last prophets, Haggai, Zechariah and Malachi, died, the Holy Spirit ceased out of Israel: but nevertheless it was granted them to hear (the communications from God) by means of a Bath-Qol. (b. Yoma 9*b*; b. Sotah 48; b. Sanh. 11*a*; Mis. Sotah 9. 12; Tos. Sotah 13. 2.)

Some Rabbis even denied that the Spirit had ever been present in the Second Temple (b. Yoma 21 *b*; Num. R. 15. 10). Despite this testimony to the cessation of the action of the Spirit, some scholars (e.g. I. Abrahams[3] and A. Marmorstein[4]) have suggested that it

---

[1] H. Parzen, *JQR*, xx (1929–30), 53: see also Abelson, *The Immanence of God in Rabbinical Literature*, pp. 275–7.

[2] For this and other aspects of the Jewish doctrine, see W. Foerster, 'Der Heilige Geist im Spätjudentum', *NTS*, viii (1961–2), 117 ff.

[3] *Studies in Pharisaism and the Gospels* (Cambridge, 1917–24), 2nd ser., pp. 120 ff.

[4] *Studies in Jewish Theology*, 'The Holy Spirit in Rabbinic Legend', pp. 122–44.

was still often experienced in life. It is not our purpose to review these arguments here: instead, the reader is referred to the careful statement and consideration of them by W. D. Davies in *Paul and Rabbinic Judaism* (2nd ed.), pp. 209–15. His conclusion seems essentially correct, especially in drawing the distinction between the general drift of rabbinic teaching and the experience of devout individuals.[1]

The evidence, both direct and indirect, of belief in the frequent activity of the Holy Spirit in Rabbinic Judaism is unconvincing. The weight of the evidence suggests that the activity was regarded as a past phenomenon in Israel's history, a phenomenon which had indeed given to Israel its Torah, its prophets and the whole of its Scriptures, but which had ceased when the prophetic office ended. This, however, does not mean that we are to regard Rabbinic Judaism as an arid desert scorched to barrenness by its belief in a transcendent God, who no longer revealed himself to his people. On the contrary, the phenomena...are eloquent of the awareness of the near presence of God, and we need not deny that there may have been individuals who were conscious of the Holy Spirit as active in their lives (p. 215).

But if Judaism tended to relegate the activity of the Spirit to the past, it nevertheless sustained a strong hope for the outpouring of the Spirit *in the future*. The Messiah would possess the Spirit of God. Rooted in such passages as Isa. 11: 2, this belief was firmly held throughout Jewish history and finds expression in Ps. Sol. 17: 37; 18: 7; Test. Levi 18: 7; T. Jud. 24: 2. The Targum to Isa. 11: 2 reiterates the hope and Targ. Isa. 42: 1 ff. makes God say concerning the Servant Messiah, 'I will make my Spirit rest upon him'. In the Last Age, the righteous also would receive the Spirit as the agent of regeneration, and for this expectation of national revival Ezek. 36: 26–7 and 37: 14 were the foundation texts. The evil impulse would be taken out of Israel's heart in the Age to come, and the Spirit, as a power for moral renewal,

---

[1] It may be to suggest such a distinction that Abelson (*op. cit.* p. 260) differentiates between three senses in which the 'Holy Spirit' is employed in rabbinic writings, viz. the Spirit as inspirer of classical prophecy and of the Old Testament books, as the giver of a secondary prophetic endowment to various lesser Old Testament characters, and thirdly, as an enrichment to the life of any man of achievement in morality and devotion: this last is not a thing of the past.

would rest upon her (Pesik. 165 a). But the prophetic-inspirational aspect of the Spirit remains important, and for this Joel 2: 28 ff. is the decisive passage.

The Holy One, blessed be He, said: In this world individuals were given prophetic power, but in the world to come, all Israel will be made prophets, as it is said (Joel 2: 28), 'I will pour out my Spirit on all flesh'. (Num. R. 15. 25.)

In concluding the discussion of the rabbinic material, we may draw attention to two points. First, it is a striking fact in the rabbinic writings that the Spirit is often conceived in material terms, such as light, fire, sound, water or a dove.[1] Conceptions like these, Abelson suggests, are understandable as the attempts to give expression to mystical, visionary experiences, and should therefore be treated as metaphorical descriptions: the rabbis did not think of the Spirit as an actual material object.[2] Secondly, in rabbinic literature, the Spirit is frequently spoken of in personal categories: the Spirit speaks, weeps, laments, and addresses God. Does this mean that in Judaism the Spirit is regarded as a hypostasis, or as a personal angelic being? No: the use of personal categories to describe the activity of the Holy Spirit is meant to represent it as 'an objective divine reality which encounters a man and lays claim to him...a reality which to some extent represents the presence of God and yet is not identical with him'.[3] Abelson also denies that the personification of the Spirit suggests any metaphysical divisions in the godhead: as well as being a circumlocution for the divine Name, it is primarily a means of expressing the action of God in the life of man.

The Holy Spirit is God's Holy Spirit. It is not itself God; it is a property of God, it is an emanation of God, a visible, or rather perceptible, trace of His workings in the world and in the heart of man. It is the Rabbinic portrayal of God in action, it is the emphatic declaration of the *nearness* of God, His direct concern in the affairs of men, the ever possible accessibility of man to his grace.[4]

[1] Targ. Can. 2: 12, 'the voice of the turtle-dove' is paraphrased as 'the voice of the Holy Spirit concerning redemption'.

[2] Abelson, *The Immanence of God in Rabbinical Literature*, pp. 212 ff.

[3] E. Schweizer, *The Spirit of God*, p. 15.

[4] Abelson, *op. cit.* pp. 205–6.

THE DEAD SEA SCROLLS

In the Scrolls discovered at Qumran the word רוח (and its
plural) occurs frequently and in a variety of senses.[1] Once it
refers to the breath of animals (1QM 6: 12); and on a few
occasions both singular and plural forms connote 'wind(s)'.[2]
The plural form is used at 1QM 9: 13 (as occasionally in Ezekiel) to
mean 'compass points' or 'directions'. At 1QH 7: 29 רוח appears
to mean 'emptiness, vacuity, vanity, vapour'—a sense associated
with 'wind' and 'air' and found in the book of Ecclesiastes.

The use of רוח in the psychological sense to denote 'disposition, mood or attitude' is very common and a few examples
must here suffice. An upright and humble spirit (רוח יושר וענוה)
is required if a man's sin is to be atoned (1QS 3: 8). The three
priests in the Council of the community are to be men 'who
maintain faithfulness on earth with unshakeable purpose and
with a contrite spirit (רוח נשברה)' (1QS 8: 3 and 11: 2). Those who
are contrite in spirit (נכאי רוח) (1QM 11: 10), and those who are
humble in spirit (עניי רוח)[3] (1QM 14: 7) will be strengthened to
fight and conquer in the great battle. All those who volunteer for
the great battle (1QM 7: 5) must be 'perfect or blameless in
spirit and body (flesh)'.[4] The 'spirit' is the seat of fear (1QS

[1] See A. A. Anderson, 'The Use of "Ruaḥ" in 1QS, 1QH and 1QM',
JSS, VII (1962), 293–303.

[2] CD 8: 13 and 19: 25; 1QM 10: 12; 1QH 1: 10; 1QH 7: 23, and
possibly 1QH 6: 23 and 7: 5, although there the word may be used metaphorically.

[3] The interpretation of this phrase is a matter of some importance. The
explanation 'poor or impaired in courage' (see E. Best, *NTS*, VII [1960–1],
255–8) has been rightly criticised by S. Légasse ('Les Pauvres en Esprit et
les "Volontaires" de Qumran', *NTS*, VIII [1961–2], 336–45) on the
grounds that it is based on a misunderstanding of what is the correct context
of interpretation: the contrast affirmed at this point is not between force
and weakness, but between moral qualities and impious cruelty. J. Carmignac, *La Règle de la Guerre* (Paris, 1958), p. 204, translates the phrase as 'les
humbles d'esprit' and B. Jongeling, *Le Rouleau de la Guerre* (Assen, 1962),
p. 321, as 'les pauvres en esprit'. The latter explains (pp. 312–13) that the
'poor in spirit' are in fact poor in material goods, but the reason for their
poverty is that they walk in the fear of Yahweh and are therefore oppressed
in this world. For this view see also, J. Dupont's study of the phrase in
Neutestamentliche Aufsätze: Festschrift für J. Schmid (Regensburg, 1963).

[4] Although 1QM emphasises the sinfulness of the flesh, there is no contrast
between 'flesh' (as evil) and 'spirit' (as good). The phrase here expresses

7: 18); and behaviour which contravenes the rules of the Community is called 'a spirit of rebellion' (1QS 8: 12). On a few occasions, a man's 'spirit' connotes his willingness or ability to endure affliction, and is almost equivalent to 'courage' (1QH 1: 32; 4: 36; 5: 36).

Within the Manual of Discipline, the term רוח several times bears a wider connotation. On entering the Covenant, a man's 'spirit' was examined regarding his understanding and works in the law (5: 21): the yearly investigation of the 'spirits' and deeds of entering members determined promotion (5: 24, cf. 6: 17). Among the duties of the enlightened Instructor (משכיל) of the sect was the task of weighing or discerning members according to their 'spirits', that is, judging each man according to the cleanness of his hands (his deeds) and his understanding (9: 14–16). In these instances 'spirit' (רוח) appears to denote 'a man's disposition', and in particular his attitude and devotion to the ways of the sect, as revealed in his behaviour. While the emphasis here on the religious aspect of a man's life may permit us to interpret 'spirit' as 'spirituality', we cannot agree with D. Flusser in associating it with the degree to which a member of the Sect possessed the gifts of the Holy Spirit.[1] Probably we have here an extension of the Old Testament use of רוח to describe the controlling impulse or attitude.

The use of πνεῦμα to denote 'a spirit' or supernatural power was found in Jubilees, Enoch and the Testaments, and רוח is similarly used in the Qumran material. According to their function or nature, the spirits are either good or bad, but all are inferior to God who created them and who is Lord of every spirit (1QH 10: 8). The chief of the wicked spirits is Belial, and the spirits of his party (1QM 13: 2, 4, 11) are 'spirits of perdition' (14: 10) able to influence men. But God has his spirits also, and these 'spirits of truth' (under the leadership of the Prince of Light, 1QM 13: 10) assist his people.

A special section of the Manual of Discipline (1QS 3: 13 — 4: 26) deals with the origin and function of the spirits. The God of all knowledge, the Source of all things, 'created man to rule

the totality of a man. It is just possible that the words may refer to adult vitality, something like 'sound in wind and limb'.

[1] *Aspects of the Dead Sea Scrolls* (Scripta Hierosolymitana, vol. IV, Jerusalem, 1958), pp. 246–8.

the world, and assigned him two spirits in which to walk' till the time of the final visitation. These are the 'spirit of truth' and the 'spirit of wickedness'. The former originated in the abode of light and is identical with the Prince or Spirit of light and the Angel of truth: the spirit of perversion had its source in darkness and is equivalent to the Angel of darkness. God created both spirits and on them founded all conduct. The ways or 'counsels' of the spirit of truth include wisdom, humility, patience, compassion, goodness, knowledge, integrity, mercy, purity and prudence:[1] the ways of the spirit of error include greed, slackness, wrong-doing, pride, deceit and cruelty.

Under these two spirits are the generations of all the sons of men, and all their hosts...have an inheritance in their divisions: and in their ways do they walk, and in either of them (lies) all their action and conduct, according to the inheritance of each, whether great or little (in the two spirits) in equal parts until the last period (3: 15–16).

At the last time, the season of God's visitation, wickedness will be destroyed: the 'truth of the world' (probably a synonym for the 'spirit of truth') will emerge, and men will be cleansed and refined (4: 20–1). The section ends with a restatement of man's present situation: 'Until now the spirits of truth and wickedness strive within the heart of man: men walk in wisdom and in folly.'

Because of the sharp opposition between the two spirits described in this section, many scholars have interpreted it in terms of the cosmic dualism and determinism of Zoroastrianism or of a pre-Christian Jewish Gnosticism. This explanation seems to overemphasise the uniqueness of the unit in the Manual and to forget that (by virtue of its preservation and incorporation in the document) it was accepted Qumran teaching, and therefore is best interpreted in terms of the general drift of Qumran thought which is rooted in the Old Testament. Neither the ultimate origins of the 'two spirits' theme, nor parallels to it, need determine the meaning of the doctrine for the Sect.[2] The 'two spirits' *may* have cosmic functions, but the emphasis in the passage under

[1] Both Flusser, *op. cit.* p. 262 note 157, and M. Black, *The Scrolls and Christian Origins*, p. 132 note 1, have drawn attention to the similarities between the 'ways' of the good spirit and 'the fruits of the spirit' in Gal. 5: 18 ff.

[2] For a careful treatment (with bibliographical details) of the various interpretations of 1QS 3: 13 ff. see P. Wernberg-Møller, 'The Two Spirits

discussion is not on their transcendent character, but on their persistent involvement with the life and behaviour of men.[1] We may compare Test. Jud. 20: 1 ff., 'Know therefore, my children, that two spirits wait upon man, the spirit of truth and the spirit of error (τὸ τῆς πλάνης [πνεῦμα]) '[2] where the function of the spirit

in 1QS 3: 13 — 4: 26', *Revue de Qumran*, III (1961), 413–41. The writer correctly distinguishes between the idea of a doctrine, *ultimately* Persian in origin, being transformed and reinterpreted in Jewish and Christian circles, and that of a doctrine being adopted by Qumran in basically the same form as it was taken over from the Gathas, except that the Jewish monotheistic faith was preserved by regarding the two cosmic spirits as created by, and subservient to, God. As a result of the influence of the latter view, many argue that the Qumran sect held strictly dualistic and deterministic doctrines: but when taken in its context, the two-spirits passage is capable of a different interpretation.

[1] H. G. May, 'Cosmological Reference in the Qumran doctrine of the Two Spirits and in OT Imagery', *JBL*, LXXXII (1963), 1–14, holds together the cosmological setting and expression of the doctrine and its present psychological reality: also E. Schweizer, in *The Background of the New Testament and its Eschatology* (Dodd Festschrift, Cambridge, 1956), pp. 482–508, esp. 488–93.

[2] The question of the dating of the Testaments is disputed. The earlier opinions of M. de Jonge (*The Testaments of the Twelve Patriarchs*, Assen, 1953) that the document was written by a Christian author using Jewish material have been modified, to some extent, by the study of the DSS (see 'Christian Influence in the Testaments of the Twelve Patriarchs', *NT*, IV [1960], 182–235) but he still posits extensive Christian influence. A. S. van der Woude, *Die messianischen Vorstellungen der Gemeinde von Qumran* (Assen, 1957) discusses parallels between the Testaments and the Scrolls and suggests that the former was originally a Jewish document, but that the *Grundschrift* is impossible to reconstruct because the book has been rewritten and abbreviated and subjected to some interpolation. M. Philonenko, *Les Interpolations chrétiennes des Testaments des Douze Patriarches et les Manuscrits de Qumran* (Paris, 1960) suggests a very close link between the two writings and reduces Christian influence on the Testaments to an almost negligible minimum: the passages which have been called Christian are the work of an Essene interpolator: the similarity between the Testaments and the Qumran literature is such as to suggest a common origin. The debate will be continued, but it seems fair to declare that (i) it seems certain that a Jewish *Vorlage* underlies the present form of the Testaments—as Qumran would suggest, and that (ii) the difficulty in deciding the extent and form of this pre-Christian material is so great that we ought to be very cautious in using the Testaments for the elucidation of New Testament themes. In the matter of the 'two spirits' theme, the similarity of the Qumran view and that expressed in the Test. Jud. suggests that the teaching had a single origin in *Jewish* thought: it was certainly well established there.

of truth is 'to witness to all things and to condemn all things'.[1] The words τὸ πνεῦμα τῆς πλάνης would correspond to רוח תועה, and, although this exact phrase has not been found in the Qumran text, we do read (1QS 3: 21) that the spirit of wickedness leads astray all the sons of righteousness, and also of the people whose spirits have been led astray (תועי, 11: 1). Now if the Qumran doctrine of the 'two spirits' can be paralleled in the teaching of the Jewish apocalyptic books, then it is probably also akin to the rabbinic doctrine of the good and evil inclinations.[2] The passage in the Manual is not concerned with a metaphysical theory of dualism, but with psychological insights and the realities of life. The 'spirits' are the forces, inwardly experienced, which drive a man to act in a certain way, the influences which condition or bring about behaviour: they create, and to some extent become equivalent to, attitudes and dominant dispositions. If these forces are born of error and wickedness, the resulting conduct is evil and perverse: if they have their source in light and truth, conduct is righteous and good.

There are three other points of interest in connection with this important passage. First: in the literature of a sect which was deeply concerned with the nearness of the End, this is the only place where a strictly eschatological significance is ascribed to the Spirit (4: 20).[3] Secondly, the function of the spirit in the End-time is both purificatory and illuminative: the spirit of truth is sprinkled upon the faithful to give knowledge and to cleanse. Thirdly, the spirit of truth and 'holy spirit' seem to be identical. If our understanding of the 'two spirits' is correct, this identity means that God's holiness or truth, when known and acknowledged, is itself a powerful impetus towards the fulfilment of righteousness in conduct: as that 'spirit' operates on man, it

---

[1] Cf. John 14: 17; 15: 26; 16: 8, 13.

[2] Cf. A. A. Anderson, *JSS*, VII (1962), 299, 'We are not told of the way in which these influences of the spirits, etc., are exercised upon man, but it is possible that the author of 1QS 3–4 may have thought of something *approximating* to the Rabbinic doctrine of the good and evil inclinations.' W. D. Davies, 'Paul and the DSS: Flesh and Spirit', in *The Scrolls and the New Testament*, ed. K. Stendahl (London, 1958), p. 173, considers that the spirits are 'two constant currents of good and evil forces in conflict'. But the emphasis in the passage seems to be on describing how these currents are experienced by man.

[3] On the Spirit and Eschatology in Qumran, see W. Foerster, 'Der Heilige Geist im Spätjudentum', *NTS*, VIII (1961–2), 117–34, esp. pp. 122 ff.

exerts a cleansing influence and leads to knowledge and righteousness. This is closely related to what we found it possible to say in explanation of 'the spirit of holiness' in Psalm 51.

It would be difficult to classify the many uses of רוח in the Thanksgiving Hymns, and the very presence of such variety may lend weight to the suggestion made by Davies that the Hymns reflect a later stage in the community's history than that of the other writings, a time when greater Hellenistic influence had taken place.[1] The author of 1QH 1: 22 refers to himself as 'a structure of sin... a spirit of error (רוח התועה) perverted without insight', and in 3: 21 the writer alludes to himself, or to the community in general, as 'a perverted spirit (רוח נעוה)' who is cleansed from transgression and made fit to share in the fellowship of eternal spirits. Since the phrase רוח נעוה appears to be parallel to איש in 3: 22, both phrases probably refer to a man in the entirety of his being. At 1QH 13: 13 and 17: 25 we find the expression 'a spirit of flesh' which, because it is parallel to 'one born of woman' (13: 14), means 'a human being', 'a man'. There is no rigid contrast between 'flesh' and 'spirit', the one being evil and the other good: it is the whole of man which is sinful, the whole personality which is perverted. The doctrine of the 'two spirits' seems to underlie 1QH, although it may not be so explicitly expressed as in 1QS 3–4. We find reference to the 'spirits of badness' (1QH 3: 18), the 'spirits of wickedness' and of 'perversion' in Frag. 5. 'A perverted spirit (רוח נעוה)' rules in man, according to 13: 15, and the phrase seems to refer to a man's corrupted spirit or disposition (cf. 1: 22). On the other hand, there are 'holy spirits' or 'spirits of holiness' and 'spirits of knowledge' who appear to belong to the same class as the 'sons of heaven' and the 'host of holy ones' (3: 22). The use of the phrase 'holy spirit' or 'spirit of holiness' is important in the Hymns. It is described as the agent of cleansing (16: 11–12); it brings knowledge (12: 11, 12; 13: 19 and 14: 25) and gladness (9: 32). By this spirit a man is strengthened in the way of righteousness (7: 6–7). What we said concerning the meaning of 'holy spirit' in 1QS is true also here:[2] the influence on a man of

[1] *Op. cit.* p. 165.
[2] Foerster, *op. cit.* pp. 129 ff., has compared what is said about the 'spirit of truth' in 1QS and what is said by the writers of the Hymns 'through the holy spirit', and he posits the essential similarity of the two expressions.

the acknowledged holiness and will of God has a cleansing and stabilising power.

In the Damascus Document the phrase 'holy spirit' occurs three times. Twice (5: 11 and 7: 4) the reference is to the 'holy spirit' within people which may be polluted or defiled by denying the truth of the principles of the community of God: the disposition towards holiness may be overwhelmed by disobedience. At CD 2: 12 we read, 'God made known his holy spirit unto them (the Remnant) through his anointed one', that is, either prophet(s) or priest(s).[1] In other words, God revealed, through the custodian of his truth, his power and presence as a holy God who requires his people to be holy (cf. Isa. 63: 10–11).

The Manual of Discipline has three references to 'holy spirit'. 'United through the holy spirit of God's truth, man shall be cleansed of all his iniquities: because of an upright and humble spirit his sin shall be atoned' (1QS 3: 6f.). Here we are in touch once more with the thought expressed in Ps. 51 that the powerful influence on man's life of God's truth and righteousness creates the desire for and will to achieve holiness through obedience and righteous conduct. At 8: 16 the 'holy spirit' denotes the source and inspiration of the prophetic proclamation. Finally, we read at 9: 3—

When these things shall come to pass in Israel [i.e. the institution of the community], according to these rules, for a foundation of holy spirit, for eternal truth, to make atonement for the guilt of the offence and for the sin, and for divine favour to the land, without [i.e. rather than] the flesh of burnt offerings...At that time the men of the community shall be set apart, a house of holiness for Aaron.

---

[1] For the problems and various interpretations of this passage, see Davies, *op. cit.* p. 175 and p. 280 note 60. It is doubtful if 'anointed one' should be understood as a reference to the Messiah(s). The idea that the Messiah imparts holy Spirit is possibly suggested by the messianic interpretation of Isa. 52: 14f. in the Qumran Isaiah scroll, but not here (see W. H. Brownlee, *The Scrolls and the New Testament*, ed. Stendahl, pp. 43–4). Test. Jud. 24: 2–3 tells us that the Messiah pours down the spirit of grace: but M. de Jonge (*The Testaments*) and M. A. Chevallier (*L'Esprit et le Messie dans le bas-Judaïsme et le Nouveau Testament* [Paris, 1958]) think that the passage is Christian, with material from the Qumran sect or a related group incorporated. The reconstruction of the pre-Christian text of the passage would be extremely difficult, and so it is probably wise to lay little emphasis on it for the affirmation of the Messiah's role in giving the Spirit. Within Judaism it is always God who bestows the Spirit.

It has been suggested that this passage means that the possession of holy spirit is the necessary preparation for the End, or that the discipline of the sect is the foundation on which the spirit will be given in the Age to come.[1] However, since the section deals with the creation of the covenant-community it seems that the phrase in question may well mean 'an institution of spiritual holiness', that is, a community whose life is ordered by the search for righteousness and truth, through acknowledgement of the holiness of God and obedience to his will. 'Holy spirit' is then essentially a description of the character and direction of the sectarians' total life and piety.

THE NEW TESTAMENT USAGE

1. *The Synoptic Gospels: Mark, Q, Special M and L*

We commence this survey of the use of πνεῦμα in the Synoptic Gospels with a brief mention of the application of the term to the 'spirits' or demons of evil and illness. We find that the word bears this connotation fourteen times in Mark, usually with the adjective ἀκάθαρτον.[2] Matthew 8: 16 has τὰ πνεύματα, without any qualifying adjective, where Mark (1: 34) has δαιμόνια. Both Matthew (12: 43) and Luke (11: 24) use ἀκάθαρτον πνεῦμα in a passage for which there is no Markan parallel, namely, the sequel to the Beelzebub controversy.[3] This use of πνεῦμα is already familiar to us from our discussion of the demonologies of 1 Enoch, Jubilees and the Testaments of the XII Patriarchs: and the later rabbinical literature (especially the Babylonian Talmud) contains many allusions to 'spirits' and their harmful activities among men: the same is true of the literary and non-literary texts of Hellenism.

The 'psychological' use of πνεῦμα is attested three times in Mark. At Mark 2: 8 Jesus knows 'in his spirit' the thoughts of others, where 'spirit' connotes the seat of knowledge and sensi-

[1] Davies, *op. cit.* p. 176, discusses the views and mentions as 'possible' the interpretation here suggested as likely.

[2] Mark 1: 23, 26, 27; 3: 11, 30; 5: 2, 8, 13; 6: 7; 7: 25; 9: 25; 9: 17 and 25 (πνεῦμα ἄλαλον, κωφόν) and 9: 20 (πνεῦμα). Where the Matthean and Lucan parallels do not use the same expression, the words δαίμων, δαιμόνιον or some part of the verb δαιμονίζω generally appear.

[3] These passages and Mark 3: 30 will be discussed later when the contexts of the sayings are investigated.

241

tivity (cf. Ezek. 11 : 5; 20: 32). There is no reference to the Holy Spirit, nor is the knowledge necessarily supernatural in character (cf. 5: 30, 'Jesus knew in himself'), although, if the events took place as recorded, the impression given might easily have been of supra-normal insight. The statement that 'Jesus groaned in his spirit' (8: 12) accords with the Old Testament use of 'spirit' (רוּחַ) to denote the seat of deep emotion. At Mark 14: 38 (cf. Matt. 26: 41) the contrast is drawn between 'willing spirit' and 'weak flesh'. This contrast ('spirit-flesh') immediately directs the mind to Paul, but the Apostle's meaning is not that of the Gospel.[1] In Mark, 'flesh' does not refer to 'life in opposition to God and the Spirit', but to the frailty of the body, which may hinder the noble desires of the will ('willing spirit') from being fulfilled. E. Schweizer claims[2] that πνεῦμα is not 'some better part of man's nature', but is 'the Spirit of God which is temporarily imparted to a man and fights against human weakness'. In support of this exegesis Schweizer states that the phrase 'willing spirit' is derived from the Hebrew text of Ps. 51: 14 (Eng. verse 12)[3] where it is identical with the 'Spirit of God'. But the nature and sequence of the parallelism in Ps. 51: 12–14 (MT) suggests that 'willing spirit' is *not* identical with 'holy Spirit' but is closer in meaning to the experience of joy in God's salvation, and connotes a human spirit responsive to God and capable of meeting the demands of the new situation. The logic of the narrative in Mark requires that the distinction between πνεῦμα and σάρξ be understood, not in terms of the difference between God and man, but between the will of man and his physical weakness. At Matt. 27: 50 πνεῦμα is used to denote 'life-breath': 'Jesus gave up the spirit', where Mark and Luke use the verb ἐξέπνευσεν, 'expired'.

All the evangelists declare that at the Baptism of Jesus the Spirit descended upon him, like a dove.[4] The narrative of the

[1] Lagrange, *Saint Marc* (6th ed., Paris, 1942, p. 390) suggests that there may be some foundation for the Pauline doctrine in this saying of Jesus. This may be true, if we accept the saying as a genuine utterance.

[2] *The Spirit of God*, pp. 24–5.

[3] R. G. Bratcher, *Interpretation*, xvi (1962), 409 ff., criticises the view of Schweizer as if it were based on v. 12 of the MT, instead of on v. 14 of MT (i.e. 12 in Eng. verse). See also Schweizer's reply in the same journal, xvii (Jan. 1963).

[4] In late Judaism the dove was a symbol for the Holy Spirit (cf. Targum to Cant. 2: 12) as well as for the community of Israel.

Baptism marks off the event as something different from the call of a prophet and his endowment with the Spirit by emphasising its messianic character. The utterance of the voice (the Bath-Qōl, the substitute, in Jewish thinking, for the lost guidance of the Spirit) echoes Ps. 2: 7 and Isa. 42: 1 and indicates that Jesus is both 'Son of God' and 'Elect Servant'. Now the declaration that Jesus is the Servant makes necessary his endowment with the Spirit, since Isa. 42: 1 goes on to declare, 'I have put my spirit upon him' (cf. Isa. 61: 1). Likewise, since the use of Ps. 2: 7 suggests that, at his baptism, Jesus becomes or is revealed as Son of God (because he is then installed as King Messiah),[1] the Spirit becomes an indispensable gift: in Jewish thinking, an endowment of Spirit was to be part of the equipment of the Anointed One. Ps. Sol. 17: 37 (first century B.C.) declares 'God will make him (the Messiah) mighty by means of holy spirit, and wise by means of understanding with strength and righteousness' (cf. 1 Enoch 49: 3). And the messianic hymn in Test. Levi 18: 6 ff. asserts:

The heavens shall be opened and from the temple of glory shall come upon him sanctification,
With the Father's voice, as from Abraham to Isaac:
And the glory of the Most High shall be uttered over him,
And the spirit of understanding and sanctification shall rest upon him (in the water).[2]

---

[1] Cf. C. K. Barrett, *The Holy Spirit and the Gospel Tradition* (London, 1947), p. 41.

[2] The words 'in the water' are generally considered to be a post-Christian interpolation. But in view of the fact that there is no unanimity on the dating of the Testaments, caution must be exercised in the use of this (or any passage) for the interpretation of New Testament teaching. Sometimes C. K. Barrett (in the work cited) is too ready to accept its evidence uncritically. In the matter before us, however, the Ps. Solomon provide reliable evidence for the tradition of the Messiah's being endowed with Spirit. It must be admitted that, if Test. Levi 18: 6 ff. was post-Christian and reflected the narratives of Jesus' baptism, the words 'with the Father's voice...' would be difficult to understand. In *From Babylon to Bethlehem* (ed. L. E. Browne [2nd ed., Cambridge, 1951], pp. 95 ff.) M. Black has interpreted these words on the basis of Abraham's only recorded utterance to Isaac, 'God will provide himself a lamb' (Gen. 22: 8). On this view, the theme of sacrifice is inherent in the Messiah's election and ordination. The words υἱός ἀγαπητός recall the description of Isaac at Gen. 22: 2, 12 (LXX) τὸν υἱόν σου τὸν ἀγαπητόν. For the view that Test. Levi 18 is dependent on the New Testament, see M. A. Chevallier, *L'Esprit et le Messie dans le bas-Judaïsme et le Nouveau Testament*, pp. 125–30.

16-2

The descent of the Spirit at Jesus' baptism may be understood then as his being endowed with power, wisdom and holiness for the fulfilment of the messianic ministry. The meaning of 'spirit' here is rooted firmly in the use of the term with a charismatic sense in the Old Testament and Jewish writings. There may then be no new interpretation, but when we remember that Judaism denied the activity of the Spirit in the present time and expected it to be renewed only in the Last Time, we may see a deep significance in the narrative. The fact that the Spirit is regarded as having been poured out suggests that the moment of Baptism is being pin-pointed as the beginning of the New Age, the Age of the Messiah. This event is as far as Mark takes back the question of messianic origins, whereas Matthew and Luke press the matter right back to the birth of the Messiah as a human being.

At this point we may investigate the saying of John the Baptist concerning the baptism with which the 'Stronger One' will baptise his people. The logion has been preserved in two forms: the shorter Markan form at 1: 8, 'He will baptise you [ἐν] πνεύματι ἁγίῳ'; and the Q version (Matt. 3: 11 and Luke 3: 16) which reads, 'He will baptise you ἐν πνεύματι ἁγίῳ καὶ πυρί', and which continues, 'whose fan is in his hand, throughly to cleanse his threshing-floor, and to gather the wheat into his garner: but the chaff he will burn with unquenchable fire'. Many commentators have decided that, in the Q version, the words ἐν πνεύματι ἁγίῳ are a Christian insertion and that the original form of the saying was 'He will baptise you with fire'. Not least among the reasons for this view is the unsuitability to the context of a reference to the Spirit: the prophecy is concerned with the purifying judgment of Israel and a reference to the gracious gift of the Spirit (or Holy Spirit) is therefore scarcely consistent with that theme. The same assumption may underlie the suggestion that the original form did include the word πνεύματι, but with the meaning 'wind'; the baptism was to be by 'wind and fire'. Although this interpretation implies that the meaning of the prophecy was recast under the influence of the Pentecost event,[1] it has the merit of providing an understanding of πνεῦμα which is in harmony with the verses following: the *wind* winnows the grain and the fire *burns* the chaff. We may summarise the position on the Q version in this way: the theme

---

[1] Cf. E. Best, 'Spirit-Baptism', *NT*, IV (1960), 236–43.

of the prophecy is purification and judgment; the agents or instruments of this cleansing are πνεῦμα (ἅγιον) and πῦρ; the judgment theme has created difficulty for the interpretation of πνεῦμα as 'the Spirit'. Most commentators are of the opinion that the Markan version of the saying must have been understood by its readers, and probably by Mark himself, as a reference to the outpouring of the Spirit on the Church (cf. Acts 1: 5 and 11: 16) and that the form of the saying was influenced by Christian baptismal practice as illustrated by Acts 2: 38 and 19: 1 ff., in which 'water-baptism' conveyed the gift of the Spirit. Recently, J. E. Yates has challenged this view.[1] He claims (i) that Acts 1: 5 is an editorial comment which shows that it was *Luke* who intended the Baptist's words to be understood as fulfilled in the Pentecostal outpouring; (ii) that the Markan and Q versions of the saying preserve an earlier and correct understanding, according to which the promise was fulfilled in the ministry of Jesus, from his baptism to his death; that is, the Baptism with the Spirit is the 'visitation' and 'overwhelming' of *all Israel* (not just of believers within the New Israel) by the presence and power of God active in the proclamation of the Kingdom by Christ. According to this view, the Spirit in Mark (as in Q) is the agent or instrument of cleansing and judgment, not a gift of something static and impersonal; and the claim that the theme of judgment is important throughout Mark (even if the promise of the Spirit is not specifically related to it) lends support to this view; (iii) Yates argues that if, as is possible, Mark's form has been influenced by the Christian practice of Baptism, the influence was not according to the pattern in Acts 2: 38 and 19: 1 ff., but according to the earlier pattern in Acts 10–11, in which the Spirit is the agent of the divine action.

This interpretation of Mark 1: 8 certainly brings the verse into harmony with the Q version by taking the dative case (with or without ἐν) as instrumental,[2] and by suggesting that in both places the 'holy Spirit' is the agent of purification. It is difficult, however, to accept the explanation of 'baptise' as meaning (metaphorically) 'overwhelm': this sense of the word appears in Mark 10: 38 and Luke 12: 50, but it does not refer, in Jewish

---

[1] Originally in 'The Form of Mark 1: 8b', *NTS*, IV (1957–8), 334–8, and in extended form in *The Spirit and the Kingdom* (London, 1963).
[2] With Lohmeyer, *Das Evangelium des Markus* (Göttingen, 1937), p. 19.

writings, to a visitation of the Spirit of God in judgment and cleansing. Furthermore, Yates appears to find it impossible to hold together the conceptions of the Spirit as *agent* of spiritual purification and as gifted *endowment*. Now these two conceptions are hard to hold together if we imagine that Mark must have been referring to the Pentecost outpouring, but, when we remember that the saying is a prophecy of the Baptist (whose message was essentially one of eschatological judgment), is it not possible that the agent of cleansing and judgment is also an endowment of the people who experience the action?

Without entering into the question of the relation of John to the Qumran sect,[1] it is pertinent to mention here a language-parallel to the Baptist's promise in 1QS 4: 20f. The section describes the visitation of God when a portion of mankind will be refined and purged.

Then God will cleanse by his truth all the deeds of a man (or men)[2]
And will refine him some of the children of men,
In order to abolish every wicked spirit out of the midst of their flesh;
And to cleanse them by a holy spirit from all evil deeds;
And he will sprinkle[3] upon him a spirit of truth like purifying water...
Thus he will give the upright insight into the knowledge of the Most High and the wisdom of the sons of heaven...

Here in an eschatological context, with references to 'refining' and to 'fire', the Spirit is both agent of cleansing and an endowment. What does 'holy spirit' or 'spirit of truth' mean here? We suggest that it is close to what we discovered to be the meaning of 'holy spirit' in Ps. 51: it is that inward sense of God's holiness and knowledge of his presence (cf. *v.* 22) which both purifies man and directs him in the way of holiness.[4] As pointed out earlier, we

[1] See J. A. T. Robinson, 'The Baptism of John and the Qumran Community', *HTR*, L (1957), 175–91, esp. 183 ff., where the importance of the passage to which we refer is stressed.

[2] The 'man' may be a special individual (a prophet-Messiah) or each member of the community: see W. H. Brownlee, *BASOR*, CXXXV (1954), 36–8.

[3] It is possible that the Spirit was expected to come in connection with the sect's lustral rites, for the gift of the spirit is associated with a sprinkling of clean water in Ezek. 36: 25.

[4] Cf. pp. 236–9 for this interpretation, and its relation to the context in the 'two-spirits' passage.

have been too ready to think of the baptism with holy Spirit in Mark and Q solely in terms of the gift of *the Holy Spirit* at Pentecost: we would submit that the expression originally referred to a *sprinkling* of God's people in the time of His visitation: *in the presence and action of the Stronger One (Jesus)*[1] this people will receive a powerful experience of cleansing and renewal of life.

One of the features common to the Synoptic accounts of the Temptation of Jesus is the declaration that, at the time, Jesus was under the influence of the Spirit: Mark 1: 12 has, 'the spirit drives him...' and the verb ἐκβάλλω indicates strong propulsion and recalls the violent seizures of men in the Old Testament. The Matthean modification (4: 1) retains the suggestion that the Spirit exercised a controlling influence upon Jesus, but according to Schweizer, this is changed in the Lucan version (4: 1)—

Luke avoids giving the impression that the Spirit is an agent set over Jesus. He is not satisfied with the OT idea of the power of God falling on a man. Instead, Jesus becomes the agent—'in the Holy Spirit'. He is no longer a Man of the Spirit (Pneumatiker), but is now Lord of the Spirit.[2]

However true this last statement may be for Luke's general view of the relation to Jesus and the Spirit, it is very doubtful if it can be drawn from the verse in question. The inward possession of the Spirit may be implied by the Lucan addition 'full of holy Spirit' (though the phrase could also mean 'filled by the Holy Spirit'), but the subjection of the Spirit to Jesus is by no means evident in the words ἤγετο ἐν τῷ πνεύματι. The verb is passive and ἐν τῷ πνεύματι can be interpreted only as (i) denoting agency, 'by the Spirit', or (ii) as descriptive of Jesus, and equivalent to 'in the power of the Spirit': but even this second view does not support the idea of Jesus' control over the Spirit.[3] In fact all three Evangelists regard the Spirit, at this point, as a power leading Jesus to and (as Luke emphasises) equipping him to meet the messianic temptations. We are still in touch with essentially Old Testament ideas of the Spirit's function.

[1] The Scrolls have provided no exact parallel for the idea that it is through the 'coming One' that God would baptise his people with Holy Spirit. It is very unlikely that CD 2: 10 ff. bears this meaning.

[2] Schweizer, *The Spirit of God*, p. 37.

[3] In *Interpretation*, XVII (1963), 123, Schweizer comes near to accepting the explanation of ἐν τῷ πνεύματι in terms of status.

The conception of the Spirit as the divine power which makes possible certain actions is again evident at Mark 3: 29, the logion on blasphemy which occurs in the context of the Beelzebub controversy: 'whoever blasphemes against the Holy Spirit has never forgiveness'. The following verse and the general context make it clear that the blasphemy means the assertion that Jesus cast out demons by being in league with the prince of evil powers. The 'holy Spirit' is the divine presence and power which inspires the works of Jesus: to say that Jesus has an 'unclean spirit' (v. 30) is to attribute his actions to diabolical inspiration. The form of the saying in Matthew and Luke is less easy to interpret. At Matt. 12: 31 ἡ τοῦ πνεύματος βλασφημία corresponds to the Markan logion and causes no difficulty. In the following verses, however, Matthew has a Q form of the saying, which Luke also gives (though in a different context which it does not easily fit) as 12: 10. In this version the contrast is not between blasphemy and all other sins, but between 'blasphemy' (Luke) or 'speaking against the Holy Spirit' (Matthew) which is not forgiven, and 'speaking against the Son of Man', which can be forgiven. If a genuine dominical utterance is preserved here, then the saying will mean that 'speaking against the *person* of the Son of Man (Jesus)' is forgivable, but 'speaking against the *power* by which he works' (i.e. the divine endowment), is not, and 'the holy Spirit' will mean (as in Mark) the gift of God for the healing works of the messianic ministry. The difficulty with this view is that it implies a distinction between the person and the power of the Son of Man: but to speak against the one surely involves speaking against the other! Consequently many scholars think that the saying has emerged from the Church's consciousness of itself as the spirit-filled community. The Holy Spirit is the constitutive factor in the Church's life, and to speak against it would be tantamount to apostasy, being a denial of the very root of the community's existence. Blasphemy of, or speaking against the Son of Man would then denote the attitude of a person outside the Church who fails to recognise who Jesus is: his sin could be forgiven, because he might later be brought to repentance and faith. In other words, blasphemy against the Holy Spirit is a sin committed within the Church, blasphemy against the Son of Man is a sin committed outside the Christian fellowship. Both interpretations of the verse understand the 'spirit' in terms of power:

if the logion is authentic the 'Holy Spirit' is the divine inspiring power by which Jesus acts; if it is a church tradition (perhaps reinterpreting the Markan saying), the 'Holy Spirit' refers to the endowment of power experienced within the Church.

The Matthean account of the Beelzebub controversy provides the context for another occurrence of the word πνεῦμα. 'If I, by the Spirit of God, cast out devils, then the Kingdom of God has come upon you' (12: 28). Luke 11: 20 reads, 'by the finger of God', and the arguments in favour of the priority of this form seem better.[1] Both phrases, however, connote the mighty power of God which inspires Jesus in his exorcisms. These, like the healing miracles, are messianic actions and signs of the Kingdom's imminence or presence (ἔφθασεν).

At Mark 12: 36 Jesus introduces the quotation of Ps. 110: 1 (LXX) with the words, 'David spake in the Holy Spirit'. Matthew reproduces the thought and recasts the sentence, omitting the word 'holy' (22: 43), while Luke has, 'David says in the book of Psalms' (20: 42). The allusion to 'holy spirit' shows that David (the assumed author of the Psalm) is regarded as having been inspired, like a prophet, in this saying. The rabbinic view that the Old Testament scriptures were inspired, even written, by the prophetic Holy Spirit was mentioned earlier, but this is the only occasion (with Matt. 22: 43) on which it is referred to in the Gospels, and it is introduced because the argument required the citation of an acknowledged authority.[2] We might have expected the Synoptists to speak more often of the Holy Spirit (of prophecy) in reference to the Old Testament, but presumably its authority was sufficiently recognised without adducing any reference to the source of its inspiration.

In the course of his teaching ministry Jesus promised divine

---

[1] Would Luke, with his interest in the Holy Spirit, have changed the reference to δακτύλῳ? The Matthean version may well be an explanation of the sense of the other reading, giving Matthew a convenient introduction to the saying about blasphemy against the Holy Spirit. J. E. Yates (*The Spirit and the Kingdom*, pp. 90 ff.) thinks that Luke made the substitution because he did not wish to connect 'the Spirit' with action: his predilections associated it with inspiration. Here, as elsewhere in his book, Yates distinguishes too rigidly between the Spirit as agent and as a possessed endowment.

[2] The fact that Jesus' words accord well with a conventional Jewish usage may be taken as evidence of the historicity of the saying in the Markan/Matthean form.

help to his followers when they were put on trial before human authorities. The tradition to this effect is strongly attested and is probably authentic. At Mark 13: 11 (in the Apocalyptic discourse) we read

And when they bring you to trial and deliver you up, do not be anxious beforehand what you are to say, but say whatever is given you in that hour, for it is not you who speak, but the holy Spirit.

Matthew 10: 20 (in the Mission charge) says, 'It is not you who speak but the Spirit of your Father (τὸ πνεῦμα τοῦ πατρὸς ὑμῶν) which speaketh in you'. The Lucan passages are 21: 14f. (appearing in a context similar to that of the Markan saying) which affirms that, not the Holy Spirit, but 'I (Jesus) will give you mouth and wisdom', and 12: 12 (referring to arraignment before authorities) 'The Holy Spirit will teach you in that hour what you must say'. When we attempt to discover which form of the saying is original, Luke 21: 15 appears to invite confidence. It comes from a primitive source, and, in view of Luke's special interest in the doctrine of the Spirit, it is unlikely that he would have altered a reference to the Spirit's action. Nevertheless, there is good reason for doubting the originality of this form. As V. Taylor says, 'It has a distinctly Johannine ring and appears to reflect the doctrine of the Exalted Christ'.[1] It represents Jesus as speaking in a manner reminiscent of God's address to the prophets. The combined testimony of Mark and Q (reflected in Matthew and probably in Luke 12: 12) is hard to set aside: and these versions of the saying speak of the 'Holy Spirit' (or 'the spirit of your Father'). The promised action of the Spirit results in inspired speech and this concurs with the Old Testament understanding of the charismatic 'spirit of God'. It ought to be observed, however, that this is not a promise of a universal outpouring of the Spirit, but an endowment of power or inspiration for a specific kind of situation. When persecution, betrayal and accusation happen as a result of faithful witness to the Gospel, the divine aid and inspiration will be given.

We have now completed the references to πνεῦμα in Mark and in the Q tradition. Of those which are theologically significant, only Mark 13: 11 and par., and possibly Mark 3: 29, can be attributed with any degree of certainty to Jesus, and in these two

[1] *The Gospel according to St Mark*, p. 509.

places the understanding of 'spirit' is in harmony with the Old Testament idea of a charismatic endowment of power. According to the latter case, the 'spirit', signifying God's power and presence, marks the action of Jesus, and according to the former, is available to assist faithful disciples in times of extreme need. Most of the references in the early tradition are associated with the messianic interpretation of the ministry of Jesus, and in this context, the 'spirit' refers (again following the Old Testament and Judaism) to the special equipment in wisdom and strength which enables him to fulfil the tasks of Messiahship.

Special M. Of the passages peculiar to Matthew in which the word πνεῦμα appears we take first Matt. 5: 3: 'Blessed are the poor in spirit (οἱ πτωχοὶ τῷ πνεύματι), for theirs is the Kingdom of heaven.' This cannot mean 'poor in the holy Spirit': the reference is to human spirit, and the dative (πνεύματι) is one of reference or respect (cf. 5: 8). It seems probable that the Matthean version of the Beatitude is drawing out the essential meaning of the Lucan and more original form (6: 20). There 'the poor' does not mean merely those who possess no material wealth, but those who, in addition to, and even because of their poverty, have a firm trust in the faithfulness of God. Now the Matthean addition reflects a Semitic period of transmission of the text, rather than a Hellenistic, for πνεῦμα was not used in common Greek for 'human spirit'. Consequently, it seems certain that behind the Matthean saying lies an original Hebrew or Aramaic form, עניי רוח (cf. Ps. 37: 11 ff.). Now this phrase actually appears in 1QM 14: 7 and, earlier in this study, we accepted the interpretation 'the humble poor who trust in God's help'. If this is correct, then the meaning of the single discoverable example of עניי רוח (= πτωχοὶ τῷ πνεύματι) confirms our understanding of the Lucan version and also demonstrates the accuracy with which Matthew expanded and explained it. The 'poor' and 'the poor in spirit' are the oppressed poor who maintain a humble trust in the mercy and power of God, and such indeed are blessed.[1]

At 12: 18 ff. Matthew quotes Isa. 42: 1 ff. to provide a testimonium for secrecy, and suggests that the endowment of Jesus as the Servant with the Spirit is the explanation of his power to work miracles of healing.

[1] See P. Bonnard, *L'Évangile selon St. Matthieu* (Paris, 1963), p. 56.

The apostolic commission at Matt. 28: 18ff. contains the command to 'baptise them (the nations) in the name of the Father, the Son and the Holy Spirit'. It is possible, though not likely, that the triple formulation is an ancient insertion.[1] But, in assuming that the words belong to the correct text of the Gospel, we are not assuming their historicity. Luke, John and Paul, and even Mark 16: 15ff., have no knowledge of it: the primitive Church seems to have baptised in the name of the Lord Jesus only (Acts 2: 38; 8: 16) and to have engaged in long controversy before undertaking any mission to the Gentiles. The saying reflects the situation and thinking of the Church at least a generation after the death of Jesus. Triadic formulae appear occasionally in Paul and in other New Testament writers[2] in passages which are doxological or liturgical in character, and some scholars would include the Matthean text in the latter category, since it does not advance any particular Trinitarian doctrine.[3] On the other hand, because of the precision of the formulation, some writers regard it as the product of theological fixation, and suggest that it reflects a settled and familiar credal statement.[4] This view, however, requires a much later date for the formula. Whatever be the date of its origin, this passage uses πνεῦμα in a sense unique in Matthew: 'Holy Spirit' does not here refer to an endowment with divine power, but is personalised and elevated into relationship with the Father and the Son.

The Matthean account of the birth of Jesus refers twice to his conception by the Holy Spirit: 1: 18 says of Mary, εὑρέθη ἐν γαστρὶ ἔχουσα ἐκ πνεύματος ἁγίου, and 1: 20 gives the words of the angel to Joseph, τὸ γὰρ ἐν αὐτῇ γεννηθὲν ἐκ πνεύματός ἐστι ἁγίου. Many lines of interpretation have been advanced, many parallels adduced, to elucidate the meaning of conception by the Holy Spirit. These are reviewed and evaluated by Professor Barrett in his book *The Holy Spirit and the Gospel Tradition* and followed by his own explanation. He draws attention to Old Testament passages which present the Spirit as active creatively in relation to the primal birth of the world and of man[5] and in the

---

[1] Cf. Barrett, *The Holy Spirit and the Gospel Tradition*, pp. 102–3.

[2] 2 Cor. 1: 21; 13: 13; 1 Pet. 1: 2; Jude 20ff. and Rev. 1: 4–6.

[3] Cf. Schweizer, *The Spirit of God*, p. 31.

[4] Cf. O. Cullmann, *The Earliest Christian Confessions* (ET, London, 1949), p. 36 note 1, for the distinction between liturgical formulae and creeds.

[5] Gen. 1: 2; 2: 7; Ps. 33: 6; 104: 30; Job 27: 3; 32: 8; 33: 4; Prov. 8: 22.

redemption or re-creation of the people of God (Isa. 44: 3f. and Ezek. 37: 1–14). While this creative aspect of the Spirit's activity is mentioned in some of the Intertestamental books (Wisd. 7: 22; 15: 11; Judith 16: 14; 2 Bar. 21: 4), it was not retained in Palestinian (rabbinic) Judaism, although it finds expression (in a philosophically reinterpreted fashion) in Philo and in Judaism as it came under the influence of Hellenistic thought (*Opif.* 29 ff.). In rabbinic Judaism there lingered, however, the notion of the Spirit's activity as the *re*-creating, *re*-vivifying power of the messianic era (Ex. R. 48. 102 *d*, and Gen. R. 96. 60 *d*). With this background of thought, the Christians appear to have believed that 'just as the Spirit of God was active at the foundation of the world, so that Spirit was to be expected also at its renewal'.[1] Since the renewal of the world was intimately bound up with the messianic hope and eschatology, the entry of the Messiah upon the stage of history could be regarded as the work of the Spirit, and therefore the activity of the Spirit in creating the life of the messianic child was introduced into the birth narratives on the basis of Hellenistic rather than Palestinian interpretation of the Old Testament.[2] In short, the 'holy Spirit' here connotes the creating power and activity of God inaugurating the New Creation by the conception of the messianic redeemer. To Barrett's interpretation we would add the observation that, on this view of the Birth narratives, Jesus' birth becomes the *type* of what Paul calls the New Creation and John the New Birth (cf. John 1: 13; 3: 5ff.).

Special Luke. We turn now to the special Lukan tradition and we find that, in its birth narratives, the conception of Jesus is again attributed to the action of the Holy Spirit: 'the Holy Spirit shall come upon you (Mary) and the power of the Highest shall overshadow thee' (1: 35). The 'Spirit' is equated with the power of God, while the verb 'overshadow' (ἐπισκιάζειν) recalls, in thought and sound, the 'Shekinah', the name for the visible presence of God.[3] The Spirit, as the power and presence of God, is the life-giving agent in the birth of the New Man who inaugu-

[1] Barrett, *The Holy Spirit and the Gospel Tradition*, p. 23.

[2] Barrett, *loc. cit.* In Hellenistic thought there was a prepared ground for ideas of miraculous conception which encouraged theories of virgin-birth.

[3] Cf. D. Daube, *The New Testament and Rabbinic Judaism*, p. 33.

rates the New Age. The belief that the New Age has indeed come is strikingly demonstrated by Luke's emphasis on the presence of the Spirit of prophecy throughout the birth-narratives. John is to be filled with 'holy spirit' even from his mother's womb (1: 15): he is to walk 'in the spirit' and power of Elijah (1: 17). Elizabeth, his mother, becomes a prophetess, filled with the Spirit, and her husband Zacharias is also filled with the Holy Spirit, and prophesies (1: 67). The Spirit rests on Simeon (2: 25): he receives a divine oracle 'in the Spirit' (26), and enters the Temple under the inspiration of the Spirit (27). In our survey of Jewish thinking about the Spirit (predominantly the spirit of prophecy) we pointed out that, while the action of the Spirit in the present was not affirmed, there was a lively expectation of its coming in the future age, the messianic era. In the events of the Birth narratives, we see this hope fulfilled: we find the Spirit in the full vigour of its operation at the beginning of the Gospel story. The new dawn has broken; the new age has arrived: the signs of its presence are experienced.

The persistence of the connection between the gift of the Spirit and the coming of the messianic age is evidenced by the Marcionite reading of the Lord's prayer (Luke 11: 2): 'let thy holy Spirit come (upon us) and cleanse us'. This text may represent a variant used at Baptism,[1] or Luke's own interpretation of the clause 'Thy Kingdom come' found in his source,[2] but it is completely in harmony with Luke's view that the supreme object of prayer is the gift of the Spirit.[3] At 11: 13 we read, 'How much more shall the Heavenly Father give the Holy Spirit to them that ask him'. The text of Luke is somewhat uncertain at this point and the Matthean version good things' is probably original. Luke appears to be reading into the saying his own thought and affirming the gift of the Spirit in a time before that in which he generally states that it will be given, namely, after the death and resurrection of Jesus (Luke 24: 49; Acts 2: 33).

One of the distinctive features of Luke's work is the emphasis he

---

[1] The reading expresses the meaning inferred from Acts 11, where the Spirit 'comes upon' the audience while Peter is speaking and water-baptism follows.

[2] On the Lucan text of the Lord's Prayer, see A. R. C. Leaney, *NT*, 1 (1956), 103–11.

[3] Throughout his writings Luke emphasises the Spirit as *gift*, something inwardly possessed.

lays on the Spirit in relation to the life of Jesus.[1] He alone emphasises the completeness of Jesus' possession of the Spirit at the time of Temptation (4: 1). Jesus returns to Galilee 'in the power of the Spirit' (4: 14), that is, filled and inspired by the Spirit (as a prophet) rather than 'one who possesses the power of the Spirit'.[2] In the synagogue at Nazareth Jesus proclaims himself to be the Spirit-anointed prophet of Isa. 61: 1 whose mission is to bring in the age of salvation. This important passage stands like a prologue to Luke's work: it is the charter of the ministry, the messianic programme: 'The Spirit of the Lord (πνεῦμα Κυρίου) is upon me for he has anointed me to preach the gospel to the poor...' (4: 18).[3] At 10: 21 Luke declares that Jesus rejoiced in the Holy Spirit (ἠγαλλιάσατο τῷ πνεύματι τῷ ἁγίῳ) where Matt. 11: 25 has simply 'Jesus answered and said'. Some manuscripts omit τῷ ἁγίῳ but the words are probably original and draw attention to the important saying which follows and which Luke may have thought to be an inspired or even ecstatic prophecy.[4] It is, at any rate, another instance of Luke's tendency to heighten the spirit-filled character of Jesus.

It is possible that a suggestion concerning the presence of the Spirit in Jesus underlies Luke 2: 40. His growth and advance is wisdom (τὸ δὲ παιδίον ηὔξανεν καὶ ἐκραταιοῦτο πληρούμενον σοφίας) are described in terms parallel to those concerning John's development (τὸ δὲ παιδίον ηὔξανεν καὶ ἐκραταιοῦτο πνεύματι, 1: 80), but the absence of πνεύματι with reference to

[1] On this theme, cf. G. W. H. Lampe, 'The Holy Spirit in the Writings of St Luke', *Studies in the Gospels,* ed. D. E. Nineham (Oxford, 1955), pp. 159–200.

[2] Schweizer, *The Spirit of God,* p. 37.

[3] The quotation (which is composite in character) may reflect an oral tradition which recited these passages as having been spoken by Jesus at this point. It is possible that Jesus did make such a claim, though the Lucan setting may not be the actual or only occasion. For the importance of this and other texts which proclaim the gift of the Spirit to Jesus, see W. C. van Unnik, 'Jesus the Christ', *NTS,* VIII (1961–2), 101–16. The author claims that the essential element in the Messiahship of Jesus for the early Christians was, not the outward activity of a king, but the person manifestly possessed by the Spirit. And he thinks this was not invented by the Church, but rested upon the life and actions of Jesus (p. 115). E. F. Scott, *The Spirit in the New Testament* (London, 1923) makes no reference to Luke 4: 18 in his chapter on the Gospels, yet he states (p. 77) 'it may be confidently inferred that the Holy Spirit was not a primary conception with Jesus'.

[4] Cf. E. F. Scott, *op. cit.* p. 69.

Jesus may be significant. Is its omission meant to suggest that Jesus did not require to grow 'in *the* spirit' since he already possessed it fully from his conception?[1] But if Luke had meant to describe John's growth in the Spirit (i.e. in the Holy Spirit) we should have expected to find ἐν τῷ πνεύματι. It therefore seems likely that we are dealing with the psychological use of πνεῦμα to denote the deeper-than-physical level of a man's being, the inner personality, the spring of feeling and emotion, and not with a reference to the Spirit of God, or the power of God imparted temporarily to man.[2] Now there is some evidence (A Θ Koine Peshitta Syr.) for πνεύματι at 2: 40. If this is original, it must have been misinterpreted as 'the Spirit' and omitted in order to avoid the suggestion that Jesus required to grow in the Spirit after his birth and baptism: most probably, however, the word was introduced from 1: 80. In the Magnificat (1: 47) τὸ πνεῦμα μου is parallel to ψυχή and is obviously used in the psychological sense to connote the seat of spiritual awareness.[3] At 9: 55 some manuscripts (D Θ Marc.) give as part of the content of Jesus' rebuke to his disciples the words 'you know not what spirit you are of', and here πνεῦμα connotes 'disposition or dominant attitude'.[4]

In addition to the twelve instances of πνεῦμα denoting the evil 'spirits' of illness, etc., the word is used by Luke in quotation from the LXX of Ps. 31: 6, 'Into thy hands I commend my spirit', where πνεῦμα (רוּחַ) means 'essential life-force', or simply 'life'. The same meaning appears at Luke 8: 55. In 24: 37, 39 πνεῦμα means 'a spirit' in the sense of a ghost.

[1] Cf. Lampe, *op. cit.* p. 168 and Schweizer, *The Spirit of God*, pp. 37–8.

[2] The Bauer–Arndt and Gingrich Lexicon lists Luke 1: 80 among the references to 'human spirit'.

[3] On this verse, Schweizer, *op. cit.* p. 38 note 1, says, 'Luke wishes to emphasise that it is not simply a human faculty which is the agent here, but the self which ultimately cannot be separated from God's Spirit and is bestowed on man'. However far we may agree with Schweizer's view that the spirit of man is dependent on and inspired by God, the interpretation here looks like forcing the plain meaning of an occurrence of πνεῦμα into a theological strait-jacket.

[4] If the connection with Elijah is to be stressed, a contrast may be implied between the spirit-inspiration of the prophet which could result in destructive action, and the Spirit of the new dispensation. But this explanation involves a strange use of πνεῦμα to mean the 'spirit of a period or time'.

2. *The Acts of the Apostles*

We have already seen that Luke's Gospel not only emphasises the relation of the Spirit to Jesus but also stresses its availability to the faithful in Jesus' church (Luke 11: 13, and the variant to 11: 2). This latter concern with the age of the Church is constantly evident in the Book of Acts. Of the fifty-three occasions on which the word πνεῦμα appears in Acts meaning 'Holy Spirit', forty-five are in some way related to the life of the Church: thirteen times in connection with individuals (Peter, Stephen, Paul, etc.), thirty-two times as promised to and experienced within the expanding community. Of the remaining occasions, three refer to the Spirit as the inspirer of Holy Scripture (1: 16; 4: 25; 28: 25), two to the Spirit resting on or guiding Jesus (1: 2; 10: 38), two to sinning against the Holy Spirit (5: 3, 9) and one to Israel resisting the Spirit (7: 51; cf. Isa. 63: 10).

Before looking at these passages in detail, we may mention that πνεῦμα is used eight times in Acts to denote 'evil spirits' of uncleanness or disease[1]—a use with which we are already familiar from the Synoptic Gospels, the Jewish Intertestamental literature and the writings of both Judaism and Hellenism. A few instances of the use of πνεῦμα to denote the 'human spirit' are also found. In Stephen's dying words (reminiscent of Jesus' utterance at Luke 23: 46), 'Lord Jesus, receive my spirit' (7: 59), the word πνεῦμα means the essential life-force or spirit given by God and returned to him at death. At 17: 16 πνεῦμα refers to the seat of emotional disturbance, and at 19: 21 to the seat of the will, although it is possible that the latter occurrence connotes the directing influence of the Spirit of God. Apollos is described at 18: 25 as 'fervent in spirit'. Some scholars wish to interpret this phrase as 'fervent in the Spirit'. But how could Apollos be fervent in the Spirit, if he knew only the baptism of John which was not a baptism in Spirit? The first view is more satisfactory. At 20: 22 we read that Paul went to Jerusalem 'bound in the spirit'. This may represent an attempt to describe a sense of inward compulsion deriving from Paul's own will, but it seems more likely that the reference is to a supernatural influence (i.e. the Holy Spirit) which controls the course of the Apostle's journey. Consequently, 20: 22 rightly belongs to the 'Holy Spirit' passages. Twice, at

---

[1] Acts 5: 16; 8: 7; 16: 16, 18; 19: 12, 13, 15, 16.

23: 8 and 9, we find the word πνεῦμα used to mean 'a spirit', that which enjoys some kind of existence subsequent to the death of the body (cf. Luke 24: 39).

We turn now to the use of πνεῦμα for the 'Holy Spirit', and, first of all, to the three passages in which it is regarded as the inspirer of Scripture (1: 16; 4: 25 and 28: 25). In these verses, the (prophetic) Holy Spirit is regarded as the real source of the authority of Scripture in expressing the divine will and purpose. This theme, common in the writings of Judaism, had its ultimate origin in the Old Testament understanding of 'spirit' as *charisma*.

Ananias and Sapphira are accused of trying to deceive the Holy Spirit (5: 3) and of agreeing to tempt or try the Spirit of the Lord (5: 9). However this story be understood—as a Christianising of the Achan story,[1] as an explanation of the incidence of death in the Christian community,[2] or as based on the tradition that the surrender of private property was the condition of progressing from a novitiate to full membership of the community (as in Qumran)[3]—it is clear that it assumes that the Spirit has so guided the Church's organisation and life that failure to abide by the community's rules is tantamount to transgression against the Holy Spirit. We may have here an illustration of Luke's understanding of the 'sin against the Spirit' (Luke 12: 10) as speech or action against the constitutive factor of the Church's life. E. Haenchen[4] suggests that the story illustrates the belief of primitive Christianity (cf. 1 Cor. 14: 14 ff.) that the spirit-filled man could predict and reveal the secrets of a man's being: in which case the original narrative may have concluded with the judgment. According to this interpretation, the 'Holy Spirit' and the 'Spirit of the Lord' must connote the spirit of prophecy and insight present in the Church, and particularly in Peter. In this connection we may recall that the 'vexing of the Holy Spirit' in Isa. 63: 10 means 'rejection of the prophet's witness'. This verse is alluded to in the speech of Stephen, 'Ye do always resist

[1] G. W. H. Lampe, in *New Peake, ad loc.* p. 892: ἐνοσφίσατο recalls Josh. 7: 1.

[2] P. H. Menoud, 'La Mort d'Ananias et de Saphira', *Aux Sources de la Tradition Chrétienne*, Mélanges offerts à M. Goguel (Paris, 1950), pp. 146–54.

[3] E. Trocmé, *Le Livre des Actes et l'histoire* (Paris, 1957), pp. 196 ff., and J. Schmitt, *Les Manuscrits de la Mer Morte* (Paris, 1957), pp. 93–109. But are the νεώτεροι (*v.* 6) the novices or simply 'youths'?

[4] *Die Apostelgeschichte* (Meyers Kommentar, 12 Auf., Göttingen, 1959), pp. 197–8.

the Holy Spirit' (7: 51) where the explanation in the following verse ('Which of the prophets have not your fathers persecuted...') reveals that the Holy Spirit is almost identified with the prophetic message of which it was the inspiration. 'Holy Spirit' and prophetic activity are equivalent means of expressing the active, directing presence of God in the nation's and in the church's life.

The two references to the Holy Spirit in relation to Jesus are 1: 2 and 10: 38. Whether the former passage be interpreted to mean that Jesus gave his commandment 'by the Holy Spirit' or that he chose his disciples 'by the Holy Spirit', the phrase illustrates the charismatic idea of the Spirit in connection with the ministry of Jesus. The kerygmatic summary of the ministry (10: 38) declares that 'God anointed Jesus of Nazareth with the Holy Spirit and with power'. Here the reference is to the Spirit as the specific endowment or possession of the Messiah, the Anointed One. This theme is familiar in the Synoptic Gospels and characteristic of Luke's Christology.

The story of the strange, revolutionary event of Pentecost presents many problems, both theological and historical.[1] With these we are not directly concerned here, save to say that, whatever the traditions behind Acts 2 and whatever their content, the narrative, *as it now stands*, is based upon, and intended to create in others, the conviction that the gift of the Spirit to the Church at Pentecost inaugurated a New Age, a new order of existence, a new Creation. What we are concerned to discover is the nature of the gift described, in the hope that this may help towards the solution of some of the problems of the story.

The opening verses of Acts 1 take the reader back to the closing verses of Luke's gospel, especially to 24: 49 where Jesus declares to his disciples, 'Behold, I send the *promise* of my Father upon you; but stay in the city until you are clothed with *power* from on high'. The idea of spirit-endowment which the word δύναμις suggests is made explicit in Acts 1: 4–5:

Wait for the *promise* of the Father, which, he said, you have heard of me: for John baptised with water, but before many days you shall be baptised with the *Holy Spirit*.

[1] See Haenchen, *op. cit.*, and C. S. C. Williams, *The Acts of the Apostles* (London, 1957). Valuable background material is assessed by W. L. Knox, *The Acts of the Apostles* (Cambridge, 1948), pp. 81 ff.

The two terms 'power' and 'spirit' are brought together in *v.* 8, where the Risen Christ is made to say:

You shall receive power after that the Holy Spirit has come upon you, and ye shall be my witnesses, in Jerusalem, in all Judaea...and unto the uttermost parts of the earth.

The power of the promised Spirit will enable the Apostles to witness. When the outpouring of Pentecost actually takes place the result is consistent with the expectation formed in chapter 1. 'They were all filled with the Holy Spirit and began to speak in other tongues, as the Spirit gave them utterance' (2: 4). Representatives from every part of the then known world who were gathered at Jerusalem heard the mighty deeds of God, each in his own dialect. Whatever allusions we find in this narrative (e.g. to the giving of the Law at Sinai) one thing is clear: the gift of the Spirit is understood as an endowment which enables the Apostles and other Christians to *communicate* with all people: it makes possible and effective the preaching of the word and works of God. As it had endowed the messianic ministry, so it endows those who continue and extend that ministry through the declaration of God's acts.[1]

This understanding of the Spirit reappears at 4: 31 (a verse which Harnack thought was the historical account of Pentecost): 'When they (the Church) had prayed, the place was shaken... and they were all filled with the Holy Spirit and spoke the word of God with boldness.' As G. W. H. Lampe puts it, 'The Spirit, as always, inspires and empowers the missionary enterprise'.[2] At this point, the inspiration of the Spirit for proclamation is experienced afresh in the face of Jewish opposition. When Peter declared God's actions in Christ before the Sanhedrin, the Spirit filled him (4: 8; cf. Luke 12: 11f.). Again, when we read that the wisdom and Spirit with which Stephen spoke to his disputants could not be withstood (6: 10), πνεῦμα probably denotes inspired prophetic endowment. Paul—'a chosen instrument to bear my name before the Gentiles, kings and the sons of Israel'—is filled with Holy Spirit to fulfil his task of proclamation (9: 17). After the essential facts of the life of Jesus and of the Gospel have been

---

[1] Notice the emphasis on prophesying in the outcome of the gift at 2: 17–18 (quoting Joel 2).

[2] Lampe, The Acts of the Apostles, in *New Peake*, p. 892.

declared to the Council, the apostles affirm that 'we are witnesses to these things, and so is the Holy Spirit which God has given to those who obey him' (5: 32). The gift of the Spirit is essentially concerned with the proclamation of the Good News.

The second Pentecostal endowment, that of the Gentiles, is recorded at 10: 44ff., and is of the same character as the first. While Peter was speaking, 'the Holy Spirit fell on all who heard the word'. The Jewish Christians were amazed that the gift had been poured out on the Gentiles, 'for they heard them speaking in tongues and extolling God'. That Luke is so careful to record the same signs of spirit-possession on these two great occasions demonstrates clearly that for him the 'prophetic' character of the gift is central. It is the equipment for Gospel proclamation, the new prophesying (cf. 11: 15, 16; 15: 8). When the disciples at Ephesus (who had known only John's baptism) received the Spirit after baptism, 'they spoke with tongues and prophesied'.[1] The traditional idea of prophetic spirit appears on a few occasions. Agabus foretold 'by the Spirit' that there would be a famine (11: 28). Paul, filled with the Holy Spirit, penetrated the hidden thoughts of Elymas and declared to him his own heart— a prophetic function (13: 9 and cf. also 5: 9). This aspect of the Spirit's power is found in those passages where its action provides a vision or forecast of the future (20: 23; 21: 4, 11).[2]

Several passages in Acts heighten the prophetic and missionary character of the Spirit by presenting it as the agent of God's purpose in the entire missionary enterprise. The Spirit gives direct instructions for concrete action in the expansion of the mission. For instance, it is the Spirit which tells Philip (8: 29) to go and join himself to the chariot of the Ethiopian, and this directive brings him the opportunity of declaring the Gospel and winning a convert.[3] The Spirit creates the opening for missionary

---

[1] The difference in the order of Spirit-endowment and baptism in 10: 44 ff. and 19: 6 will be discussed later.

[2] Ch. 7: 55 records that Stephen, 'full of the Holy Spirit' had a vision of heaven before his death. The vision has the character of a prophetic insight given to the witness (μάρτυς).

[3] 'The Spirit of the Lord snatched away Philip' (8: 39) is a strange statement. It resembles 2 Kings 2: 16 where the possibility of the Spirit having snatched away Elijah is mentioned. The Western text—'The Holy Spirit fell on the eunuch and the angel of the Lord snatched away Philip'— seems to be an attempt to resolve the difficulty. Perhaps the verse is not

service. Similarly at 10: 19, the Spirit reveals to Peter that the men who will conduct him to Cornelius have come and urges him to accompany them. This instruction marks the first stage in the extension to Gentiles of membership in the Church, a significant step in the evangelical cause (cf. 11: 12). The Holy Spirit gave direction for Paul and Barnabas to be set apart for special work, and they 'being sent out by the Holy Spirit' undertook the mission in Cyprus (13: 2, 4). Again the Holy Spirit is understood as the controlling agent in the missionary expansion. An interesting example of this theme is found at 16: 6–7 where it is recorded that the Spirit forbade the entry into Asia and Bithynia. This may imply a vision or prophetic message, but it is possible that it is an attempt to explain an unsuccessful venture. Missionary action was controlled by the Spirit: if, in any area, the enterprise was not received and forwarded, this could be regarded as a sign that the Spirit 'forbade' the proclamation there.[1]

Thus far we have been concerned to elucidate the primary emphasis in Luke's understanding of the Spirit, namely, its essentially prophetic character, as endowment and in action.[2] Just as Jesus' claim to have the Spirit's endowment stands at the beginning of the Gospel record of the messianic ministry (Luke 4: 18), so the event of the Pentecostal endowment of the Church for its ministry of proclamation stands at the beginning of Acts. And that which is given is the Spirit of prophecy, symbolised by the gift of tongues, for the inspired declaration of the mighty acts of the Gospel. Prophets no longer appear singly: all the Lord's people are prophets, preaching the Word. In short, the gift of the Spirit is the power for Gospel preaching. Since this activity is such an integral part of the expansion of the Church's mission, it naturally follows that the Spirit is regarded (in a personalised way, cf. 13: 2) as the controller of that mission, directing men to

more than an attempt to show that the 'missionary' Spirit had other preaching engagements for Philip elsewhere.

[1] Some think that missionary work was already in progress in Asia and that the Spirit, as directing agent, would not lead to territory which was being evangelised.

[2] Thus Luke does not regard the Spirit as the direct source of gifts of healing, nor as the secret of the Church's community life. The gift of the Spirit is scarcely related to miraculous acts or to moral renewal, but only to missionary enterprise.

opportunities, selecting them for special tasks. They, as they continue the messianic ministry, are Spirit-endowed, and the entire enterprise is Spirit-guided. When the Apostles say, 'It seemed good to the Holy Spirit and to us...' (15: 28), they acknowledge the directing role of the Spirit. In all this there is demonstrated a building upon the Old Testament idea of the 'spirit' as the endowment of man by God with power and a sense of divine presence for the carrying out of special (in this case 'prophetic') tasks.

The understanding of the gift of the Holy Spirit as being the power of missionary service, and in particular for the proclamation of the Gospel, may illumine the relation between the Spirit and Baptism. The pattern and meaning of Jesus' baptism is of importance here. The Synoptic writers (including Luke) interpret the Baptism of Jesus as his entry upon his messianic ministry: as equipment to fulfil this vocation, the Spirit comes upon him. Baptism (the act of self-surrender and identification with his people) and the gift of the Spirit (the accession of power) form the prelude to that ministry. The book of Acts takes over this pattern and applies it in the life of the Church. Baptism is not merely a cleansing rite, but the symbol of a man's willing self-identification with the community of believers, to which (and to whose members individually) is given the missionary task, the continuation of Christ's ministry. The equipment to fulfil this task in speech and in life is the same as that given to Jesus, the power of God's Spirit. Consequently it is normal to find baptism, as the sign of conversion, preceding the endowment with Spirit. On the day of Pentecost Peter declares to the people: 'Repent and be baptised in the name of Jesus...and ye shall receive the gift' (2: 38). In the case of the Ephesian disciples, who had experienced only John's baptism of repentance, there was no experience of the Spirit until they were baptised into the name of the Lord Jesus, until they were brought into the Community, and so were concerned in its mission (19: 6). At 10: 44-8 the endowment with the Spirit precedes baptism. But, as Lampe says, 'this episode is in no way typical; it is a major turning point in Luke's narrative, a second purely Gentile Pentecost',[1] and, as such, is described as parallel to the events of Acts 2.[2] The coming

---

[1] *The Seal of the Spirit* (London, 1951), p. 66.

[2] For the view that Acts 10: 44 ff. preserves the original order of Spirit-endowment and baptism—an order truer to the Gospel principle of God

of the Spirit is direct and unmediated. This does not make baptism superfluous, but indicates that those whom God has chosen must be immediately received into the Christian community. The Spirit has freedom and is not bound to or by institutional practice. The power for missionary service is the gift of God alone and he may give it to whom he will. This fact is emphasised by Luke in these accounts of the Jewish and Gentile Pentecosts, the key moments in the Church's expansion.

One question remains. Is there not evidence in 8: 14 ff. that the gift of the Spirit is dependent upon a 'laying on of hands' by the Apostles? Is the Spirit given only by the Apostolic ministry? Some writers have claimed that this is the case and suggest that prayer and laying on of hands is the ritual of ordination and confirmation. It is likely, however, that when we remember the dominance of the missionary motive throughout Acts and the missionary character of the Spirit's endowment, we shall see in the 'laying on of hands' simply the symbol of the Church's incorporation of the individual(s) into the missionary task, for which the Spirit is given, in special office and humble service alike, since *all* believers are witnesses.[1] Luke is concerned to delineate the progress of a *missionary*, not an institutionalised, Church, and therefore it is reasonable to interpret what appears to be a statement on order and ritual from within that context. 'Laying on of hands' does not mean the implanting of the Spirit; it symbolises incorporation into the community, and, on occasion, also the imparting of the right to undertake a special task. The Spirit is a gift from God of power to fulfil the duty and privilege of witnessing: it is not a substance controlled and imparted by the Apostles alone.

It is clear, then, that in Acts the Spirit is the power which makes possible and guides the missionary expansion of the Church. In this conception there is a real indebtedness to the

approaching sinners while they are yet sinners—see T. W. Manson, 'Entry into Membership of the Early Church', *JTS*, XLVIII (1947), 25–33. J. E. Yates, *The Spirit and the Kingdom*, takes over Manson's view of the originality of Acts 10: 44 and uses it in drawing his distinction between the Spirit as agent and as gift. It is possible that Manson has done less than justice to the desire of Luke to make this second Pentecost in all points parallel to the first.

[1] Cf. Lampe, *The Seal of the Spirit*, pp. 69 ff. and 306 ff.; also C. S. C. Williams, *The Acts of the Apostles*, pp. 291–3.

Old Testament and to Jewish tradition: the Spirit gives power to fulfil a task or express faith. In the new dispensation, however, it is not a few individuals, but the entire Church (continuing Christ's ministry) which is the bearer of the endowment, and the task is the prophetic proclamation of the Gospel of Christ.

There is little reference in Acts to the presence of the Spirit as the inner principle of the believer's life or as an abiding gift within the Church's life. The word 'spirit' is used to describe the Christian character of the deacons (in association with 'wisdom') at 6: 3, of Barnabas at 11: 24 and of Stephen at 6: 5: and its presence within the community is declared at 13: 52 and 9: 31. But the quality of *koinonia* within the Church is nowhere actually stated to be the creation of the Spirit. In Luke's view, *the* gift of the Spirit is the power for missionary enterprise, not church cohesion or a quality of Christian living. Nevertheless, it is probably legitimate to assume that the vitality of Christian experience and the unity manifested in the early days of the Church were, in fact, due to this experience and understanding of the Spirit. In declaring and spreading the Good News, in its involvement in missionary service, the Community was made one in purpose and action, and the faith of each member strengthened and enriched.

3. *The Writings of Paul*

In the writings of Paul, unlike the Synoptic Gospels and Acts, the word πνεῦμα is never used to denote the demons or spirits which cause disease or mental derangement. There is one instance of the word used to mean 'breath', when Isa. 11: 4 (LXX) is quoted at 2 Thess. 2: 8. The two main uses of the word in Paul are (i) with reference to the Holy Spirit, and (ii) with reference to the human spirit: almost all the occurrences belong to one or other of these two classes.

It is difficult to systematise Paul's use of πνεῦμα when it means 'the Spirit (of God)' or 'Holy Spirit'. A beginning may be made, however, from 1 Cor. 12–14 in which the Apostle criticises popular conceptions of the Spirit and attempts to bring some order into the Corinthians' confused understanding of its inspirational activity. Among the Corinthians the ability to speak in tongues (γλωσσολαλία) was regarded as the supreme, if not the only endowment of the Spirit. Here we are in touch with an aspect of Hellenistic religious thought, within which the 'speaking in tongues' was considered as a sign of intense spirituality and of possession by the god who inspired the utterance.[1] Now Paul rates this psychological gift below the moral gifts of the Spirit. He does not deny that it is a gift of the Spirit, but he wants it kept in its rightful place. Prophecy or preaching is the spiritual gift to be desired most. A person who speaks with tongues may be at one with the god himself, but he communicates nothing (except by an interpreter) to his audience: but anyone who prophesies (under the inspiration of the Spirit) builds up the Church by his preaching and strengthens his hearers (14: 2 ff.). The understanding of the Spirit here, as the inspiration for delivering God's message to men, is the same as that found in Acts, and the entire discussion of spiritual gifts is indebted to the Old Testament understanding of the Spirit as the source of any special endowment or ability.

From these chapters another important point emerges. The Corinthians probably believed in many spirits, giving many varied gifts: for Paul, there are many gifts, but only *one Spirit* (12: 4). The manifestations of the one inspiring Spirit are related to the functions of the various members within the Body. The gift may be a word of wisdom (probably moral teaching) or a word of knowledge, or a deep faith, or a gift of ability to heal or work miracles, to preach, to discern spirits, or—last in the list— to speak in tongues or interpret them. But all these have their origin in the one and the same Spirit. 'There is one Body and one Spirit' (Eph. 4: 4)[2] and participation in that Spirit should create unity, rather than individualism.[3]

A little may be said about the various gifts which are the Spirit's endowments (1 Cor. 12: 8–10). Account has been already

---

[1] The Corinthian *glossolalia* is one instance of a phenomenon common at all times; the gift or ability to utter noises when under deep emotional stress or under the influence of hypnosis.

[2] Even if Ephesians was not written by Paul, most of its theology is essentially Pauline.

[3] In some modern thinking, the Spirit stands for individual freedom against institutionalism; for Paul, the experience of the Spirit is essentially meaningless apart from the Church. The Corinthians believed that personal possession of the Spirit set men apart and justified individualism. This Paul rejected and insisted that the Spirit is one, and that all manifestations of it build up the Church.

taken of the gift of tongues. It is possible that Paul again alludes to it at 1 Thess. 5: 19–20 ('Quench not the Spirit: despise not prophesyings') if this passage is drawing attention to two manifestations of the Spirit (glossolalia and prophecy) rather than referring to the single gift of prophecy under two forms.[1] The ability to work cures and miracles (ἐνεργήματα δυνάμεων) is included among the gifts of the Spirit (1 Cor. 12: 9–10). That the charismatic activity of the Spirit attests itself in miracles is again implied at Gal. 3: 5,[2] and the working of signs and wonders forms part of Paul's ministry 'in the power of the Spirit' (Rom. 15: 19). The inclusion of πίστις in the list of the Spirit's gifts probably means that the word is to be understood as 'trust' in the miraculous power of God to perform signs through human agents, rather than as the personal relationship of faith in Christ (cf. 1 Cor. 13: 2). The gifts to which Paul gives priority in his list are 'a word of wisdom' and 'a word of knowledge'. While this particular passage suggests that the emphasis lies on 'word' as the Spirit-inspired *message* of wisdom and knowledge *declared within the Church*, other passages in Paul make it clear that the possession of 'wisdom' and 'knowledge' depends on the Spirit.[3] But this 'wisdom' and 'knowledge' are both *of God* and of the way of salvation, not worldly cleverness. Paul explains this wisdom of God (which the spiritually mature receive) as a wisdom which enables the Christian to know the purpose of God in the victory of Christ over all hostile powers (1 Cor. 2: 7 ff.).[4] It is revealed through the Spirit, which alone can know the things of God (*v.* 11), and is communicated only to those who possess the Spirit. The πνευματικοί here are not 'ecstatics'[5] but those who are

---

[1] Schweizer, *The Spirit of God*, p. 65, suggests that prophecy is one form under which the exceptional character of πνεῦμα is revealed.

[2] Cf. E. D. Burton, *Galatians* (ICC), p. 151.

[3] The association of 'Wisdom' with the Spirit is found in the Intertestamental literature, while the relation of divine Spirit to inspired knowledge is expressed by Philo (*Gig.* 22 ff.) and in the Old Testament, Exod. 31: 2 ff.

[4] The knowledge is of 'the deep things of God' (2: 10). The expression τὰ βάθη τοῦ θεοῦ is gnostic, but Paul uses it with Christian meaning to refer to the spiritual truths about the purpose of God in Christ.

[5] For a discussion and criticism of Reitzenstein's theory that this term and almost all Paul's uses of πνεῦμα are developed from Hellenistic mysticism, see H. A. A. Kennedy, *St Paul and the Mystery Religions* (London, 1913), and Davies, *Paul and Rabbinic Judaism*, pp. 191–200.

illumined by the revealing Spirit and so understand the spiritual truth of the Gospel of the Cross. The content of the Spirit-endowed knowledge is not restricted to the meaning of the victory of the Cross: it includes the apprehension of our Sonship. The Spirit enables the believer to say, 'Abba, Father': it bears witness that he is a son of God (Rom. 8: 15f.). Moreover, the presence and testimony of the Spirit reveal that the believers know God, or rather are known (γνωσθέντες ὑπὸ θεοῦ), i.e. are acknowledged by God as his own (Gal. 4: 6f.).

Paul's conception of the Spirit as the source and inspiration of special gifts—tongues, prophecy, miracles, wisdom and know-ledge—is essentially in harmony with Old Testament and Jewish ideas of charismatic endowment from God. There may be some Hellenistic influence present when the Apostle claims that revelation by the Spirit includes higher truth and understanding hidden from sense and reason: but in the main he avails himself of that view of the Spirit which was his inheritance from Hebrew thought. It is a view characteristic of the Gospels and especially of Acts, but in the writings of the Apostle an extension of reference and emphasis can be discovered. In Acts the super-natural endowment is pre-eminently the power to declare the Gospel message in missionary service, but in Paul, a greater range of actions and abilities is regarded as Spirit-inspired. There is also a greater emphasis on the Spirit's action within the life of the individual believer. To this we now turn, as we consider the function of the Spirit in the Christian life.

(a) *The Spirit in relation to initiation into Christian life.* In our earlier discussions we suggested that the baptism with *water and spirit* in Acts reflected the pattern and meaning of Jesus' baptism, and symbolised not only cleansing but also self-identification with the community which accepts the way of Jesus, *and* the equipment with power to carry on his ministry. Paul expresses the same basic idea in his own characteristic terminology: 'We were all baptised by (in) one Spirit (ἐν ἑνὶ πνεύματι) into one Body, and all were made to drink of one Spirit' (1 Cor. 12: 13). Incorporation into the Body of Christ—the instrument of Christ's continuing ministry—is ascribed to the power of the Spirit, communicated in baptism. Since inclusion in the Body by baptism and inclusion in the saving events of the Cross and Resurrection (i.e. justification) are ultimately the same thing, the latter can also be ascribed to the action of the Spirit: 'You were washed, you were sanctified, you are justified in the name of the Lord Jesus, and by the Spirit of our God' (1 Cor. 6: 11). That the reception of the Spirit marks the beginning of the Christian life is implied in Gal. 3: 2–3:

Did ye receive the Spirit[1] by works of law or by a hearing with faith (ἐξ ἀκοῆς πίστεως)? Are ye so foolish? Having begun (ἐναρξά-μενοι) with the Spirit, are ye now ending with the flesh?

Paul is here alluding to the Jewish belief that the Spirit is a reward acquired by an effort of perseverance in the law: but the Galatians did not receive the gift thus, but by accepting the Gospel and committing themselves to Christ in faith. Again, Gal. 3: 14 speaks of the receiving of the promise of the Spirit (the promised Spirit) *through faith*. In connection with these verses two important points may be noted. First, by declaring that the endowment of the Spirit can be and is a reality of experience, Paul is affirming that the era of the Spirit, the messianic era, has come. The active presence of the Spirit in power was to be a sign of the *Endzeit*, and therefore the advent of the power of the Age to come confirmed the messianic claims of Christ. Secondly, the experience of the Spirit's power is made dependent on 'faith', which, for Paul, meant a trusting in and total surrender to Christ in his death and resurrected life. By this self-committal the power of the Spirit is effectively experienced as the source and sustainer of new life.

(*b*) *The Spirit in relation to the character of Christian living.* For Paul the whole of the Christian life in its ethical aspects is the expression of the activity of the Holy Spirit. This is an emphasis which is not prominent in Acts where the Spirit is understood mainly in terms of endowment for mission, although (as we earlier suggested) that understanding of the Spirit must have affected the quality of Christian living, and so may be regarded as having some moral connotation. Consequently, when Paul directly insists upon the Spirit as the source of Christian morality, he is not necessarily at variance with the conception of the Spirit

---

[1] That Paul has in mind especially, though not exclusively, the charismatic manifestations of Spirit-endowment (evidenced by outward signs) is suggested by the reference to δυνάμεις in *v.* 5, which in effect repeats the question of *v.* 2.

in the primitive Church,[1] nor is he reversing the thought of rabbinic Judaism.[2] While it is true that in Judaism the Spirit was considered chiefly as the reward for achievement in works of obedience, rather than as the source of good works, this cannot be taken to mean that the rabbis would have denied that the Spirit itself was conducive to morality. The fact that this thought finds scarcely any expression in their writings is probably accounted for by their denial of the presence and action of the Spirit in their generation.[3] If there was only a very faint experience of the Spirit in the age, then morality could hardly be considered as spirit-inspired. Paul, on the other hand, was dominated by the conviction that the Age of the Spirit had come. Life 'in the Spirit' was both a possibility and a necessity for Christian believers, and therefore the ethical aspect of the Spirit's activity was given great prominence. It should be noted that already in Old Testament thought the Spirit had acquired ethical significance: the Spirit was to create in the revived Israel of Ezekiel's vision a new heart, and the heart was the centre of decision and motive: and the Spirit was to endow the messianic ruler with wisdom and righteousness. In ethicising the Spirit, Paul was not an innovator: he was emphasising what had been present in the Old Testament and what was implicit (though only rarely expressed) in later Jewish thought.

The clearest expression of the Spirit's relation to Christian living is at Gal. 5: 22. After affirming the mutual contrariety of life under the leading of the Spirit and life in obedience to the impulses of the flesh, Paul goes on to contrast the qualities which each principle produces: 'The fruit of the Spirit is love, joy, peace, long-suffering, kindness, goodness, faith (or faithfulness),[4] meekness, and self-control',[5] whereas 'the works of the flesh are

---

[1] H. Gunkel, *Die Wirkungen des Heiligen Geistes* (Göttingen, 1888), pp. 72 ff., regarded the Pauline teaching as a transformation of the idea of the Spirit in the early Church.

[2] This was the opinion of Lagrange, *Le Judaïsme avant Jésus-Christ* (Paris, 1931), p. 443.   [3] Cf. Davies, *op. cit.* pp. 219–20.

[4] In the list of the manifestations of the Spirit in 1 Cor. 12 πίστις means 'trust in God to work miracles', but here it means 'faithfulness (or fidelity) to another'.

[5] In our discussion of the Dead Sea Scrolls we mentioned the affinity between this list and the characteristics of the Spirit of truth in 1QS 4: 2 ff. The contexts also are similar, in that Paul (like the Manual) is discussing the principle or power by which life may be founded and controlled.

fornication, uncleanness . . .'. The fruits of the Spirit include moral qualities and spiritual experiences which were not popularly thought of as evidence of the Spirit's presence, but which, for Paul, were of as great, even greater value than the spectacular gifts of tongues and healing. The Christian can and must produce these fruits of the Spirit because he has died to the flesh, having shared in Christ's crucifixion (Gal. 2: 20), and thereby entered a new, risen life. Moreover, because the body is the 'temple of the indwelling Spirit' (1 Cor. 6: 19) the believer should seek to achieve ethical purity and holiness. The whole matter is succinctly stated in Gal. 5: 25: 'If we live in the Spirit, let us also walk in the Spirit.' This means that, since we have entered a new life in the Spirit and by its power, we must conduct ourselves according to the Spirit, which is both the standard and the source of power for Christian behaviour.[1] These verses from Galatians leave no doubt that Paul considered the 'spirit' to be a *power* working within men, influencing the will and producing conduct of a moral kind in which personal relationships are of crucial importance (5: 26). But the power is not an impersonal force: nor, as the norm of life and conduct, is it a cold impersonal ideal. Both the standard and the power[2] are grounded in something real and personal, because they are essentially related to Jesus Christ and men's continuing experience of him. We shall say more about this when we discuss the Spirit and Christ.

(c) *The Spirit as the 'earnest' of final salvation.* The view of the Spirit as 'the anticipation of the end in the present'[3] seems to have been introduced by Paul at 2 Cor. 1: 22. Both he and his converts (he says there) were made over to God through Christ, consecrated, marked with his seal (in baptism) and given the 'earnest of the Spirit'.[4] This word ἀρραβών means 'the down-payment or deposit' which was given as a guarantee that the remainder would be delivered later. The Spirit, then, is the first instalment of something to be consummated, an assurance that

[1] Cf. P. Bonnard, *L'Épître de St Paul aux Galates* (Commentaire du NT, Paris, 1953), p. 116.
[2] In this twofold understanding of the Spirit as standard and as power there is a certain likeness to what we found to be the content of the phrase 'holy spirit' (lit. 'spirit of holiness') in Ps. 51.
[3] O. Cullmann, *Christ and Time* (ET, London, 1951), p. 72.
[4] The genitive, τοῦ πνεύματος is epexegetic, not partitive: see J. Héring, *La Seconde Épître de St Paul aux Corinthiens* (CNT, Paris, 1958), p. 28.

God's promises (*v.* 20) would be fulfilled. Later in the same letter (5: 5) the term is used again and the context makes it clear that the presence of the Spirit is the guarantee of the resurrection state, the security that our longing for the 'heavenly covering' will be satisfied. Again, at Rom. 8: 23 the Spirit is declared to be ἀπαρχή—the 'first-fruits' of the harvest which assures the delivery of the whole; and the reference is to the present anticipation of the final salvation, the final acceptance into God's family and the redemption of the body in the New Creation of the future Age. Eph. 1: 13–14 reiterates this theme. The gift and present possession of the Spirit is the foretaste of future bliss and the assurance of our inheritance in the eschatological redemption, when God shall claim his own.

Having discovered the significance of the terms 'earnest' and 'first-fruits', we must go on to ask what it means to declare that *the Spirit* is a down-payment, and what understanding of the Spirit and its functions makes it possible to apply to it such terms? Does Paul mean that the *fact* of the Spirit's presence and action is itself a guarantee of something fuller? Is it possible to be more explicit?[1] It may be that the conception of the Spirit as 'guarantee' is based on the observed character of Christian living and on the Christian's experience of the Spirit's action in certain areas of his faith and hope. The life of man, even within the fellowship of Christian faith, is marked by its incompleteness, or rather, its unfulfilled character. Evidence of this unfulfilledness appears in relation to knowledge, communion with God, power and freedom in Christian living, and the desire for eternal life. It is on these four levels that the experience of the Spirit gives anticipation of completeness and fullness.

(i) Knowledge is partial now (1 Cor. 13: 8, 12) but will one day be complete. And an earnest of that future knowledge may be given by the Spirit. Eph. 1: 17–18 speaks of the gift of the Spirit of wisdom and revelation in the knowledge of Christ which will enlighten men's minds to know the hope of their calling and the riches of the glory of Christ's inheritance in the saints.[2]

---

[1] Sanday and Headlam (*Romans*, ICC, p. 209) suggested that the possession of the gifts of the Spirit (the moral and spiritual gifts, as well as the charismata) serves to quicken the sense of yet greater gifts to come.

[2] Cf. C. Masson, *L'Épître de St Paul aux Éphésiens* (CNT, Paris, 1953), p. 153, speaks of the Spirit here as a divine gift which will render men capable of spiritual knowledge which is of an eschatological kind.

Knowledge of the plan and scope of redemption is a gift of the Spirit. According to 1 Cor. 2: 7 the Spirit alone reveals the mystery of the victory of Christ's cross, and the revelation is discerned only by those who have received the Spirit. In short, man cannot know the things of God: the first stages of insight into his will and purpose depend solely on the illumination of the Spirit which gives a foretaste of the fuller revelation and understanding to come.

(ii) The Spirit's inspiration is the pledge of a deeper communion with God. 'We do not know how to pray as we ought: but the Spirit itself intercedes for us with wordless utterances' (Rom. 8: 26 ff.). In other words, the Spirit, by giving shape and value to our aspirations, leads to communion with God. It is the source of access to God in prayer (cf. Eph. 6: 18) and the inspirer of worship (Phil. 3: 3;[1] Eph. 5: 18). It is by (or in) the Spirit that we cry out (probably in worship), 'Abba, Father' (Rom. 8: 15); and that spirit-inspired activity is an assurance and anticipation of communion with God as adopted sons.

(iii) We have already mentioned the importance for Paul of the ethical aspect of the Spirit as the source and power for Christian living.[2] Love, joy, peace and 'every victory won' in the moral sphere are the fruits of the Spirit. But the Christian's achievement, in the power of the Spirit, has only begun. Righteousness is incomplete, but *through the Spirit*, by faith, we wait for the hope of righteousness' (Gal. 5: 5), where δικαιοσύνη refers to ethical character as well as to forensic standing. The Spirit's presence and power is the ground of the Christian's expectation of complete righteousness and final justification (cf. Phil. 3: 9).

(iv) According to Gal. 6: 8 the harvest of the Spirit is 'life eternal' and at 2 Cor. 5: 5 the presence of the Spirit is the guarantee of the eternal heavenly dwelling. The life of man, *when the Spirit of God is active and present in it*, is the first instalment of the life that is eternal. The gift of the Spirit here and now is, in fact, the substance of Paul's 'inaugurated eschatology'. Just as in the

---

[1] Reading οἱ πνεύματι θεοῦ λατρεύοντες.

[2] Rom. 8: 28 will also belong to this theme, if the verse is interpreted as 'with those who love God, the Spirit co-operates for good': see M. Black, 'The Interpretation of Rom. 8: 28', *Neotestamentica et Patristica* (Festschrift O. Cullmann, Leiden, 1962), pp. 166–72.

Synoptic Gospels, the Kingdom of God breaks into the present in the life and ministry of Jesus, so in Paul, the future age breaks into the present in the action of the Spirit.[1]

We turn now to the discussion of Paul's expressions 'being in the Spirit' and 'walking in the Spirit'. It has been claimed that these phrases reveal the influence of Stoic ideas upon the Apostle's thought. According to this view, Paul developed his conception of the Spirit in harmony with the Stoic idea of the world-soul (*anima mundi*) which is the cohesive principle of power in the universe, the spirit which permeates the whole world and infuses itself into the souls of men. If this is the background, the Spirit would require to be interpreted in materialistic terms, and J. Weiss actually described it as 'a fluid which surrounds us and also penetrates us'.[2] On the other hand, W. D. Davies has sought to show that the physical or material conception of the Spirit (which he thinks may be occasionally found in Paul, for example, I Cor. 15: 44) need not necessarily be due to Stoic influence: within rabbinic Judaism, he maintains, the Spirit is often conceived in material terms.[3] But it is doubtful if this can be considered as parallel to the materialistic conception of the Spirit attributed to Paul, since the materialistic terms used by the rabbis are attempts to describe, in metaphors, the Spirit's action, not definitions of its substance. In any case, a prior question must be raised. Does Paul actually present anywhere a materialistic conception of the Spirit? The expressions which are usually considered to contain such a conception are 'being in the Spirit', 'walking in the Spirit' and 'the indwelling Spirit': the first two (it is claimed) representing the Spirit in terms of an atmosphere in which we live, and the third in terms of a penetrating fluid. Is this the most likely explanation? Our interpretation of these phrases would begin from the Old Testament and Jewish view of the Spirit of God as power, as the personal and present action of God within the lives of individuals and in the community, creating righteousness and causing renewal. Now for Paul, the greatest manifestation of God's presence and action in history was the life, death and especially the resurrec-

[1] Cf. N. Q. Hamilton, *The Holy Spirit and Eschatology in Paul* (SJT Occasional Papers, no. 6, Edinburgh, 1957), ch. 2.

[2] *History of Primitive Christianity* (ET, London, 1937), II, 464.

[3] *Paul and Rabbinic Judaism*, pp. 182 ff.

tion of Jesus. The messianic ministry was the scene of the activity of God's Spirit, and through the Resurrection Christ himself has become 'life-giving Spirit' (1 Cor. 15: 45), that is, the power acting upon men which leads to true life, and which we might consider as the 'presentness' (through effective remembrance) of the person and work of Christ, which exerts a re-creating influence upon man's total life. We shall have more to say on this when we consider the relation of the Spirit to Christ, but already the direction in which we must seek the explanation of the phrases 'in the Spirit', 'according to the Spirit' is becoming apparent. 'Spirit' does not mean a rarefied atmosphere or pervasive fluid: it is the present, continuing and powerful impact on man of the total Christ-event, a transforming power which, when acknowledged and allowed to mould life, will produce the fruits of righteousness and moral renewal.[1] It is not a material substance, nor an impersonal force: it is intensely personal, because it is the power or influence of *a life lived* acting upon the lives of men and women. 'To live in, or by the Spirit' means to recognise that the experience of the Spirit—the power of Christ's life in the here and now—is the source and sustenance of true life: 'to walk according to the Spirit' means that the Spirit, or impact of Christ's life, is determinative of all conduct.

The most significant single passage in which these and related themes find expression is Rom. 8: 1–11. Freedom from the controlling power of sin which leads to death is achieved under the regulative influence[2] of the Spirit which leads to life (8: 1). To live with this authority as the norm and guide for all life is 'to walk according to the Spirit' (*v.* 4) or 'to have one's mind set on the Spirit', which will result in life and peace. In other words, to have one's whole life determined, not by the immediate and the physical (σάρξ), but by the Spirit, the power of Christ's life, brings life and peace, both within and with God. The Apostle goes on to affirm that life 'in the Spirit' means having the Spirit dwelling within, that is, the influence of Christ's life as the inward controlling power in all conduct. If the Spirit's power is not present and active, there is no possibility of Christian life:

[1] Our discussion of the Qumran material brought us to a similar conclusion concerning the character and function of the 'spirit of truth'. For Paul, the delineation of the Spirit was governed by the person of Jesus Christ.

[2] For this interpretation of νόμος see Sanday and Headlam, *op. cit.* p. 190.

where it is present, real *life* can come into being because there is a right relationship to God (*vv.* 9–10). The vistas of life in the Spirit extend beyond this mortal life.

If the Spirit of him who raised up Jesus from the dead dwells in you, then he who raised up Christ Jesus from the dead will quicken your mortal bodies through (διά) the Spirit that dwells within you (*v.* 11).

The genitive case after διά is the commonly accepted reading and stresses the active function of the Spirit in revivifying the believer. The accusative case, however, is well attested[1] and would imply that the presence of the Spirit controlling the believer's life is *the ground on which* God will give life to mortal bodies. The second alternative seems to be in harmony with the general content of the passage and may be correct. Both readings, however, lead to the same conclusion, that the experience of the Spirit is of decisive importance for the coming into existence and the sustaining of the future life.

The phrases κοινωνία πνεύματος at Phil. 2: 1 and κοινωνία τοῦ ἁγίου πνεύματος at 2 Cor. 13: 13 are subject to more than one interpretation. It is improbable that they mean 'fellowship with the Spirit'. The choice lies between 'participation in the Spirit' and 'fellowship created by the Holy Spirit', among those united in the one Body.[2] In either case, the idea of a material substance is incorrect: 'Spirit' connotes the present power (of Christ's life) which may be shared in by many, and which creates unity and fellowship among those whose lives are controlled by it.

The Spirit and Christ. By way of introduction to the discussion of the relation of the Spirit to Christ we may consider some further points from Rom. 8: 1–11. Paul's usage suggests that 'the Spirit of God within' (*v.* 9) means the same as 'Christ within' (*v.* 10); that the 'Spirit of God' and the 'Spirit of Christ' have no difference in meaning; and that 'to be in the Spirit' is equivalent to being 'in Christ'. The interchangeability of these expressions, however, does not mean that Paul is identifying Christ and the Spirit: the very phrase 'Spirit of Christ' (*v.* 9) would contradict

---

[1] See Sanday and Headlam, *op. cit.* pp. 198–9 for details.

[2] So Davies, *Paul and Rabbinic Judaism*, p. 178, and J. Héring, *La Seconde Épître de St Paul aux Corinthiens*, p. 105. The first interpretation is chosen by J. Y. Campbell, *JBL*, LI (1932), 378–80. Campbell's article is reprinted in *Three New Testament Studies* (Leiden, 1965).

such a view. What Paul is trying to express is the relation of Christ to the Spirit *in experience*. The experience of the Spirit as an inner power moulding and controlling life is virtually the same as the experience of the indwelling Christ, of having Christ at the very centre of the personality. If the function of the Spirit is indeed the making present and effective to the life of the believer of the power and influence of the living Christ, then to live under the control of the Spirit is certainly equivalent to having 'Christ within' as a living, guiding presence. The significance of this virtual identification of the experience of the Spirit with the experience of the indwelling Christ has been accurately stated by C. H. Dodd:

It saved Christian thought from falling into a non-moral, half-magical conception of the supernatural in human experience, and it brought all 'spiritual' experience to the test of the historical revelation of God in Christ.[1]

We turn now to those passages which directly relate the Spirit to Christ, and first we look at Gal. 4: 6, 'God has sent the Spirit of his Son into our hearts, crying, "Abba, Father"'. Paul has just declared (*v.* 4) that God sent[2] his Son that we might receive adoption. Now he affirms that the inward experience and expression of that adoption is given by the sending of the Spirit. In other words, the relationship of the believer to God which it was the purpose of the Incarnation to establish is made an experienced fact by the presence of the Spirit. While the function of the Spirit is thus made clear, the actual nature of the Spirit and its relation to Christ is not. Perhaps the most that can be said is that the Spirit of Christ is the presence and power of Christ inwardly experienced and active in the life of the believer.[3] Something similar may be said of Phil. 1: 19 where Paul assures his readers that, through their prayers and the equipment of the Spirit of Christ, the present state of affairs will turn out for his salvation. Although the reference may be to the Spirit promised by Jesus to those in need (Mark 13: 11), it seems more likely that

---

[1] *The Epistle to the Romans* (MNTC), p. 124.

[2] Only here and in *v.* 6 does Paul use the verb ἐξαποστέλλω.

[3] P. Bonnard, *L'Épître de St Paul aux Galates* (CNT, Paris, 1953), p. 87 note 2, speaks of the 'Son sent as the Spirit (comme Esprit)'; E. D. Burton, *Galatians* (ICC), *ad loc.*, speaks of the 'experiential identification of Son and Spirit'.

Paul has in mind the strength and inspiration of Christ himself who is made immediately and dynamically present to him in his situation *as the Spirit*.[1]

We now investigate the much-discussed statement at 2 Cor. 3: 17*a*, 'The Lord is the Spirit'. The context assists interpretation here. The epistle of Christ—which is the Corinthian church —has been written, not with ink, but 'with the Spirit of the living God' in the hearts of living people (*v.* 3). The Christian life of the Corinthians has been created by, and at the same time demonstrates the action of the Spirit. The verse suggests that the Spirit is the means by which God is active in his Church and that it is experienced within man as a power operative in his heart. Paul goes on to declare that his ministry is concerned with this new covenant of the Spirit which gives life (*v.* 6), and not with the old written code which kills. The verses which follow expound the superiority of the new over the old by comparing the splendour or glory (δόξα) which each can promise, and explain how the transfer from the old to the new may take place. The splendour of the old Covenant was fading, but the splendour of the dispensation of the Spirit is such as will transform its beholders into ever-increasing glory (18). It is the conviction of present and future glory that gives Paul boldness and confidence. This freedom is contrasted with the veil (κάλυμμα) of Moses (12–15), the symbol of the partial understanding and the partial revelation of the Law. To be freed from bondage to what is only partial one must turn to the Lord (*v.* 16, quoting Exod. 34: 34). In this context, the word 'Lord' must refer to Christ, since *v.* 14 clearly states that 'only in Christ is it (the veil) removed'. Verse 17 goes on to declare, 'Now the Lord is the Spirit', that is to say, the Lord to whom we can turn for illumination and for understanding is the Spirit, that Spirit which is experienced as life-giving, liberating power within, and which is the means by which Christ is operative in the Church. 'Wherever the Spirit of the Lord is, there is freedom' (17*b*). The passage ends with the declaration that the process of illumination and transformation into the likeness of the Lord is brought about as from (or by) the

[1] Cf. Hamilton, *The Holy Spirit and Eschatology in Paul*, p. 15: 'The Spirit mediates the presence of the Lord.' In connection with this idea of the Spirit's function, the place of memory, knowledge of the tradition concerning Jesus, and even of imagination, would make an interesting topic for study.

Spirit of the Lord, or the Lord who is experienced as Spirit (not, 'by the Lord of the Spirit').

By reason of the fact that 'turning to the Lord' achieves what only Christ can do, *v.* 17*a* presents us again with a virtual identification of Christ and the Spirit: but it is not an identification of essence or nature, but of function, in terms of Christian experience. The means by which we encounter or experience Christ here and now is through the Spirit, and to experience the Spirit is to be in effective relationship with Christ. In other words, the Spirit is Christ as he is active *in the present* in the lives of men and women: it is not an impersonal force, but a *personal* power drawing that character from him whom it makes present with all his benefits. The Spirit is the ever-present power and influence of the Christ-event, the impact on men of Christ freed from the confines of past history.[1] Using the term mentioned earlier in our Old Testament discussions on the Spirit, we might say that the 'Spirit' is the extension of Christ's personality.

This leads naturally to the consideration of the relation of the

---

[1] This interpretation substantially agrees with the view set forth by Ingo Hermann, *Kyrios und Pneuma: Studien zur Christologie der paulinischen Hauptbriefe* (Munich, 1961). This is not an entirely new understanding of the passage. N. Q. Hamilton, *op. cit.* p. 6, says, 'The Spirit brings the ascended Lord to earth again. The Spirit bridges the gap between transcendence and immanence. The identity here posited is not ontological, an identity of being, but dynamic, an identity which occurs in redemptive action'. Cf. also E. Schweizer, *The Spirit of God*, on 2 Cor. 3: 17*a*. Hermann reviews and rejects the other main interpretations of the verses. The hypostatic-Trinitarian view is found defective because it introduces terms and concepts which are posterior to Paul. The explanation of the identity of the Lord and the Spirit in terms of the revealing of the hidden meaning of Scripture (see A. Richardson, *An Introduction to the Theology of the New Testament*, London, 1958, pp. 121f.) cannot be carried through in *vv.* 17*b* and 18. W. Schmithals (*Evangelische Theologie*, XVIII [1958], 552f.) claims that 3: 17*a* is a Gnostic gloss: but the statement is too closely integrated with and necessary to the context to make this view at all likely. Hermann's monograph was discussed by B. Schneider (in *Biblica*, XLIV [1963], 358–69) and the criticisms there offered are not concerned with Hermann's exegesis of Paul, but with the functional interpretation of Paul's doctrine of the Spirit to which Hermann is led in his book. Schneider's desire to extract from Paul hints on the essence or nature of the Spirit are not likely to be fulfilled on the basis of honest exegesis. Paul was describing experience, not engaging in metaphysical discussion. Cf. Hamilton, *op. cit.* p. 3; O. Cullmann, *Christ and Time*, p. 26; F. Büchsel, *Der Geist Gottes im NT* (Gutersloh, 1926), p. 396.

Spirit to the resurrection of Christ. Two passages are important in this connection. At Rom. 1: 3–4 Paul makes use of what may be an early Christological formula describing the Son: 'born of the seed of David κατὰ σάρκα, appointed Son of God in power κατὰ πνεῦμα ἁγιωσύνης ἐξ ἀναστάσεως νεκρῶν.' Paul is not here contrasting two evaluations of the person of Christ, a fleshly (human) judgment and a spiritual judgment. The phrases κατὰ σάρκα and κατὰ πνεῦμα ἁγιωσύνης denote two spheres of existence: in the realm denoted by 'flesh' Jesus was a descendant of David: in the sphere denoted by 'Holy Spirit' (lit. 'spirit of holiness')[1] he was appointed[2] Son of God in power since (or, on the ground of) the resurrection of the dead.[3] It is probable that ἐν δυνάμει should be construed with 'Son of God': after the resurrection, Christ was appointed Son of God *in power*. This would not exclude his having been previously Son of God, though without the manifestation of power which took place in the Resurrection.[4] Consequently we may say that both before, but supremely *in power* after the resurrection, Christ is Son of God in

[1] The descriptive genitive is probably of Semitic origin, and this lends support to the claim that the formula is pre-Pauline.

[2] The word ὁρισθέντος is sometimes rendered 'defined' or 'declared to be', or 'manifested'. This translation avoids the charge of adoptionism which can be brought against 'appointed'. The New Testament usage, however, favours 'appointed' (cf. Acts 10: 42; 17: 31). The parallelism with γενομένου suggests that we should see in ὁρισθέντος the second phase of the career of the Son.

[3] The likelihood that the formula is pre-Pauline may account for the use of ἀνάστασις νεκρῶν rather than ἀνάστασις ἐκ νεκρῶν to refer to the Resurrection. S. H. Hooke, 'The Translation of Romans 1: 4', *NTS*, IX (1963), 370–1, thinks that we should translate literally 'the resurrection of dead persons', now made possible by the resurrection of Christ. In Hooke's opinion, it is his initiation of resurrection that marks out Christ as Son of God.

[4] The words κατὰ πνεῦμα ἁγιωσύνης may include a reference to the earthly ministry of Christ and the power with which he was endowed: see T. W. Manson, *The Beginning of the Gospel*, 1 (Oxford, 1950), 110; J. E. Yates, *The Spirit and the Kingdom*, p. 47, and W. C. van Unnik, 'Jesus the Christ', *NTS*, VIII (1961–2), 101–16. Van Unnik makes much of the idea of the possession of the Spirit as the essential element in the early Christian understanding of the Messiahship of Jesus. Manson claims that the Romans passage refers to three stages—the human side, the spiritual and divine side of Jesus' life and ministry, and his becoming *Kyrios* after the Resurrection. This requires a comma after ἁγιωσύνης. It is not necessary to adopt this expedient in order to keep alive in the phrase 'spirit of holiness' some connection with the ministry of the Lord.

relation to the spirit of holiness (κατὰ πνεῦμα ἁγιωσύνης). This accords with our understanding of 'Holy Spirit' up to this point. Divine spiritual power, with its source in God, was operative among men in the ministry: but after the Resurrection, that Spirit becomes the mode or manner of Jesus' existence as Lord: the limitations and infirmity of the flesh have given way to *power* in the Spirit. By the resurrection there has been brought into being the age of the Spirit, the age of power, in which the impact of the Christ becomes effective upon all believers.[1]

The most important passage connecting the Spirit and the Resurrection is 1 Cor. 15: 44–5. Paul here states that the last Adam (i.e. Christ) became 'life-giving Spirit' (πνεῦμα ζωο-ποιοῦν). The occasion of this becoming is not stated, but the context on chapter 15 requires that it be the time of the Resurrection. As the first-fruits of them that sleep Christ became equipped with Spirit, not for a temporary period, but in the same way as a man is equipped with life: thus it is the very essence of the post-Resurrection life. Here 'Spirit' and the life of the resurrected Lord are identified. Moreover, this life is communicable: it can make others alive, because Christ has become 'life-*giving* Spirit'. In all this we find expressed what we have been suggesting in this study concerning the relationship of the Spirit to Christ. We have attempted to understand the Spirit as the total impact of the Christ event (life, death and resurrection) upon man in the present, a power to guide and control conduct. This power or influence means the transcending by Christ of the limits of time and place, the making present of the meaning and power of a past event. Now we find Paul clearly relating this to the Resurrection as the 'event' which liberated the power of Christ's life from historical confines to be active and operative upon all who will acknowledge and obey him. The Resurrection is the occasion of the liberating of Christ to be 'life-giving Spirit'. This, in very personal terms, means that Christ is known to be alive because he is experienced today as a power influencing our lives, and this living and abiding impact is the Spirit.[2]

---

[1] Cf. Hamilton, *The Holy Spirit and Eschatology in Paul*, pp. 12 f.; C. K. Barrett, *The Epistle to the Romans*, pp. 18 ff.; F. J. Leenhardt, *The Epistle to the Romans*, pp. 36 ff., and I. Hermann, *Kyrios und Pneuma*, p. 61.

[2] There is no notion of materiality present here, no idea of a substance: what is in view is personal power originating in God. Hermann, *op. cit.*

Having thus interpreted 'life-giving Spirit', we must seek the meaning of 'spiritual body' (σῶμα πνευματικόν). In the first place, this term is contrasted with σῶμα ψυχικόν, the body which lives on the physical plane, marked by weakness, corruption and dishonour: the 'spiritual body' is what lives on a spiritual plane and it is characterised by incorruption, glory and power. Secondly, the physical body is transformed by the act of God ('it is raised') not by the working out of immanent evolutionary processes. Therefore, in σῶμα πνευματικόν the word πνεῦμα cannot be explained in terms of the Hellenistic idea of a spirit-substance which guarantees the continuance of life. In his resurrection Christ became 'Spirit' and as 'life-giving Spirit' is able to raise those who are his: in their resurrection, the form of existence shared with Adam will give way to a new mode of being, shared with the living Christ, a mode of being defined (by reason of its source) as 'Spirit', within which there is continuity of essential personality and individuality (σῶμα).[1]

We conclude our study of Paul's use of πνεῦμα (referring to divine Spirit) with a brief mention of the other occurrences of the adjective 'spiritual' (πνευματικός). In I Cor. 2: 13 ff. Paul states that the natural man is blind to the meaning of God's saving work, while the 'spiritual' people recognise it. It is clear that the term denotes persons who are illumined by the power of God's Spirit (cf. Jude 19). The things of God can only be interpreted 'spiritually' (v. 15) and that means 'under the guidance of the Spirit'. It follows that 'spiritual things' (1 Cor. 2: 13) are truths given by or relating to the Spirit of God, namely the Gospel. These can be contrasted with 'fleshly things', things concerned with natural life (1 Cor. 9: 11). The description of food and drink as 'spiritual' (1 Cor. 10: 3) connotes their divine origin and ability to communicate divine power. The foods are not 'bearers of the Spirit': that interpretation is excluded by the presence of the words 'spiritual rock' at 4b, where the meaning is

---

admits that there are a few traces of Hellenistic ideas and expressions in Paul's teaching on πνεῦμα (1 Cor. 1–3 and Rom. 5: 5) but these have little bearing on his fundamental conception, which is firmly rooted in the tradition of the Old Testament and rabbinic Judaism.

[1] Paul's use of σῶμα for the solidarity of man as a whole does not exclude its reference to the reality of individuality. Cf. J. A. T. Robinson, *The Body* (London, 1952), p. 79 note 1, and K. Grobel, 'Σῶμα as "Self, Person" in the LXX', *Neutestamentliche Studien* (für R. Bultmann, Berlin, 1954).

'of supernatural or divine origin'. At 1 Cor. 14: 1 πνευματικά connotes the totality of spiritual gifts, while at Rom. 7: 14 the law is described as 'spiritual' in order to make clear that it is a law which was given by God and possessed divine authority, not just the authority of man. At Eph. 6: 12 τὰ πνευματικὰ τῆς πονηρίας probably means 'the spiritual powers of evil' (cf. Eph. 2: 2).

In attempting to summarise our study of Paul to this point, we may begin by saying that Paul broke with the tendency to associate the Spirit exclusively with the abnormal. The Spirit is not an agent of division or of showy individualism. Although there are many manifestations of its power and presence, the Spirit should be the source of unity in the Church, and all the gifts of the Spirit should be judged by the extent to which they build up the Community. The endowment with the Spirit in baptism marks the commencement of Christian living. Throughout the Christian life, the Spirit is the source of moral virtue: it is radically ethical and the highest manifestation of its presence is 'love'. In view of the unfulfilled and incomplete nature of the life in this realm, the presence and inspiration of the Spirit are regarded as anticipations of a fuller possession and salvation in the future. For Paul, the Spirit does not have independent personality: it is spoken of in personal terms, because it is God's power in action, the means whereby God in Christ is operative in the life of the Church and in the hearts of individuals. The relation between the Spirit and the living Christ is described as an identity in terms of function: the power of the Spirit is the controlling, guiding impact on the lives of men of Christ, freed, by the Resurrection, from the confines of past history to become an ever-present reality. As far as the background of this usage is concerned, we may confidently assert that it is to be found, not in Hellenistic ideas of spirit as substance, but in Old Testament and Jewish thought about the Spirit of God as divine presence and power.

Paul employs the word πνεῦμα to denote 'human spirit' much less frequently than to denote 'divine spirit'. When it appears with this sense it bears (as in other New Testament writings) a psychological connotation and refers to the seat of the will and of emotions, and to the disposition or general attitude of a person. This use is in harmony with the Old Testament and Jewish use of רוּחַ/πνεῦμα as a psychological term.

At 2 Cor. 2: 13 Paul claims that at Troas he had no relief and rest in his 'spirit' because he had not found Titus: here 'spirit' connotes the seat of feeling and emotion, with some hint of the involvement of the will. What the Apostle means is not just that he had no physical rest (cf. 2 Cor. 7: 5), but that he experienced mental and emotional strain. Likewise, at 2 Cor. 7: 13, where we read that the 'spirit' of Titus was refreshed, just as Paul was restored, by the Corinthians' change of heart and attitude, the word 'spirit' refers to the inward depths of a man where emotions of anxiety, joy and encouragement are felt (cf. Philem. 7, 20). In the opening section of Romans (1 : 9) Paul declares that 'he serves God ἐν τῷ πνεύματί μου in the Gospel of his Son'. Schweizer claims that here πνεῦμα is 'the Spirit of God which is made available to the Apostle personally',[1] but it seems rather that what Paul means is that his service to God in the Gospel has become the dominating impulse in his life: it is no partial involvement, but has taken hold of him at the very core of his being. When the Apostle encourages the Philippian Christians to 'stand fast in one spirit' (1 : 27) he means, not unity in the Holy Spirit, but unity of will and purpose, parallel to μιᾷ ψυχῇ. The meaning 'disposition or attitude' belongs to 'spirit' at 2 Cor. 12: 18 and perhaps also Eph. 4: 23.

In Paul's final salutation at Gal. 6: 18; Phil. 4: 23 and Philem. 25—'The grace of the Lord Jesus Christ be with your spirit'— the word πνεῦμα is equivalent to 'you' (cf. 1 Thess. 5: 28). The phrase may have a liturgical origin, but it reflects also the Old Testament and Jewish use of רוּחַ to mean 'a person's self'. At 1 Cor. 2: 11 'spirit' connotes something like 'human consciousness', the organ of self-knowledge.[2] A similar use is evidenced at Rom. 8: 16—'The Spirit of God beareth witness to (or, with) our spirit that we are the children of God'—where the human spirit is considered as that part of man which receives spiritual knowledge. The greeting at 1 Thess. 5: 23 suggests that Paul accepted the popular tripartite psychology: 'May your whole spirit, soul and body be preserved blameless unto the coming of our Lord Jesus Christ.' The combination may be fortuitous (since Paul's use of these terms is rather fluid) or the salutation may be

---

[1] Schweizer, *The Spirit of God*, p. 85.

[2] Cf. R. Bultmann, *Theology of the New Testament*, I, 207: '*pneuma* approaches the modern idea of consciousness.'

a traditional liturgical expression which tells us really nothing about Pauline anthropology.[1] Paul wishes to stress the completeness of the preservation desired, and draws upon a traditional means of expressing the totality of a person. The idea of the entirety of a person is conveyed at 1 Cor. 7: 34 by 'holy, both in body and spirit', where 'spirit' perhaps suggests the inward aspect of a person and 'body' the outward.

At Col. 2: 5 and 1 Cor. 5: 3 we find 'absence in the body' contrasted with 'presence in the spirit'. The context suggests that 'spirit' means 'mind' or 'wish and will'. Though he is not physically present, Paul's 'mind' on the question is known to his correspondents, and his sympathies and interest will support them in their decision. It is possible, however, that there is included in the phrase the idea of presence in the power of the Holy Spirit. The spirit or mind of Paul is formed and dominated by the active influence of the Spirit, and so he brings to bear on the situation the mind or attitude of Christ (cf. *v.* 4 'I judge...in the name of the Lord Jesus'). In *v.* 5 of 1 Cor. 5 σάρξ and πνεῦμα are contrasted, the first requiring destruction, the second salvation. Here πνεῦμα refers to the real self, the real person, perhaps even the spirit of the Corinthian member in so far as it has already been regenerated by the Spirit of God and contains in germ the body of the resurrection in the inner man.[2]

Once, in Eph. 2: 2, πνεῦμα is used to refer to 'evil spirit', a use found frequently in the Synoptics. A somewhat similar suggestion is implied in the phrase 'the spirit of the world' (1 Cor. 2: 12) which has not been received by the Christian. It would seem that the idea expressed is of the temper or attitude of the world, the 'spirit' of human life alienated from God.

These are all the examples of Paul's use of πνεῦμα to mean 'human spirit': they bring us to the end of our survey of Paul's usage.

4. *The Gospel of John*

When we consider the Fourth Gospel we find that the use of the word πνεῦμα to denote a 'spirit' of uncleanness and disease is totally absent. The accounts of exorcisms, so characteristic of the

---

[1] Cf. Bultmann, *op. cit.* pp. 205–6, 'The formulation is to be explained as coming from liturgical-rhetorical (perhaps traditional) diction'.

[2] Cf. J. Héring, *The First Epistle of St Paul to the Corinthians* (ET, London, 1962), p. 36.

Synoptics, are wanting in John. The word is used once to denote 'wind':

The wind (τὸ πνεῦμα) blows where it wills, and thou hearest its sound, but knowest not whence it comes and whither it goes: so is everyone that is born of the Spirit (3: 8).

Since the author immediately passes to the use of the word to denote the agent of regeneration, it is obvious that he had in mind the Hebraic understanding of רוּחַ/πνεῦμα as 'wind' (the example of mysterious, superhuman power) and 'the Spirit of God'. In the phrase describing the death of Jesus, παρέδωκε τὸ πνεῦμα (19: 30), it is probable that πνεῦμα means the 'human spirit' or 'vital principle of life' which leaves a man at death.[1] Twice in the Gospel (11: 33 and 13: 21) the word is used in the psychological sense. That the phrases refer to disturbance of the human spirit of Jesus (the seat of emotion), and not to spasms brought on by the Spirit, is clear from the former passage where 'in the spirit' is synonymous with 'in himself'.

From our study of the Synoptic Gospels and Acts we found that the basic outline of Christian belief and teaching about the Spirit was as follows: John the Baptist had predicted a baptism 'with holy Spirit': Jesus was anointed to his messianic ministry by the Spirit: he promised the aid of the Holy Spirit to his disciples in times of need: the post-Resurrection promise of the endowment with the Spirit was fulfilled in the experience of the Church. In his Gospel John has reproduced these basic articles of Christian teaching.

(i) Chapter 1: 32f. records the descent of the Spirit on Jesus, the sign that he was the one who baptises 'with holy Spirit'.[2] Jesus receives the Spirit that others may share in it. Two points of interest may be observed here. Only when John is in immediate contact with the articles of the tradition (as here and at 20: 22) does he use the common early Christian term πνεῦμα ἅγιον. Secondly, just as in the Synoptics the endowment with the

---

[1] The words could be interpreted as 'He bequeathed the Spirit' (to the world): this is a common connotation of παραδίδωμι. Probably John is intentionally suggesting both ideas, since, in his view, it was precisely at this moment—the moment of glorification in death—that the gift of the Spirit became possible.

[2] For the interpretation of this phrase, see above, pp. 244–7.

Spirit in baptism (together with the conception by the Holy Spirit in Matthew and Luke) means the inauguration of the Messiahship, so too in John the descent of the Spirit is a confirmation of the messianic status.

(ii) John 3: 34—'For he does not give the Spirit by measure'. Since it is probably correct to assume that the subject of the verb is 'God', the statement refers to the completeness of the gift of the Spirit (the prophetic Spirit) by reason of which Jesus speaks the words of God.

(iii) 7: 39—'For the Spirit was not yet, for Jesus was not yet glorified'. This parenthetic statement does not mean that John denied the earlier existence and activity of the Spirit (cf. 1: 32 f.), but rather that 'the Holy Spirit was not given in the characteristically Christian manner and measure till the close of the ministry'.[1] In John's view, this depended on the completion of Jesus' work in the glorious denouement of the Cross.

(iv) John 14: 16–17 and other passages record the promise of the Paraclete, 'the Spirit of truth', to strengthen, guide and illumine believers.

(v) After his Resurrection Jesus appeared to the eleven disciples and breathed upon them (ἐνεφύσησεν) and said, 'Receive the holy Spirit' (20: 22). This Johannine Pentecost has no tongues of fire, no rushing mighty wind. Just as God breathed into Adam (ἐνεφύσησεν, LXX Gen. 2: 7) the breath of life and he became a living being, so the risen and glorified Lord breathes his Spirit upon the disciples and they become the 'new Creation'. The evidence of the endowment is not inspired utterance, but, as in Acts, authority for the continuation of the ministry of Christ. 'Whosoever sins ye remit, they are remitted, whosoever sins ye retain, they are retained.' The gift of the Spirit signifies power and authority to declare the gospel of redemption. The parallel with the Acts tradition is strengthened if we regard the eleven disciples as representatives of believers in general.[2] To all

---

[1] C. K. Barrett, *The Gospel according to St John*, p. 272.

[2] Schweizer, *The Spirit of God*, p. 95, and R. N. Flew, *Jesus and His Church* (London, 1938), pp. 242 ff. For the view that the Eleven receive the Spirit by reason of their special office, see J. H. Bernard, *St John* (ICC, Edinburgh, 1928), pp. 672, 676, and *The Apostolic Ministry*, ed. K. E. Kirk (London, 1946), pp. 108–9.

members of the Church is given the gift of the Spirit by which the ministry of its Lord is perpetuated.[1]

The author of the Fourth Gospel then has reproduced the framework of early Christian belief concerning the Spirit. The main points of the Synoptic and Acts tradition are retained, sometimes with their language (1: 33 and 20: 22). Jesus is endowed with the Spirit in his ministry: to a greater degree than in the Synoptics he is represented as the bestower of the Spirit, although the gift to men is integrated into John's general futuristic scheme: it is only in the future, after the death and resurrection, that the Spirit will be given. Indeed, except for the passages in which the Spirit is spoken of as resting on Jesus, all the Johannine statements about it relate to the period after Jesus' death. This is demonstrated by the use of the simple future tense (as in chs. 14–16) or by the association of the Spirit with aspects of later Church life—baptism (ch. 3), worship (ch. 4) and the Eucharist in 6: 63.

In 4: 23 ff. we have a general reference to worship 'in the Spirit'. Those who worship the Father must worship him 'in spirit and in truth'. This phrase is frequently interpreted as counselling sincerity and depth in worship, as against ritualism, but many recent commentators consider that the meaning is more far-reaching. For one thing, the association of πνεῦμα καὶ ἀλήθεια recalls that one of the characteristic Johannine titles of the Holy Spirit is 'the Spirit of truth'. Secondly, the single 'in (ἐν)' suggests that 'spirit and truth' are to be considered as one entity. Thirdly, the meaning of the phrase 'in spirit...' must depend on the force of the same word in the next verse: 'God is spirit'. To translate this as 'God is a spirit' suggests that God is one of the class of 'spirits'—a use of πνεῦμα which is not found anywhere in John. Verbally, the phrase might seem to echo the Stoic definition of God as πνεῦμα διῆκον δι' ὅλου τοῦ κόσμου, that is, a very tenuous form of air suffused through the whole universe and appearing in living beings as the soul.[2] It is difficult to imagine that John's usage is giving support to this form of

[1] 'The authority implied conveys an extension of the ministry of Jesus through that of the Holy Spirit', C. K. Barrett, *The Gospel according to St John*, p. 475.

[2] The materialism of this definition was never completely transcended even by the writers who tried to maintain, by using πνεῦμα, a non-material, Platonic conception of deity.

semi-materialistic idea of God, especially when we recall that his characteristic understanding and use of πνεῦμα is grounded firmly in Hebraic thinking. 'God is spirit', like the expressions 'God is light' and 'God is love', is not a definition of the being of God, but an attempt to describe the nature of his relation to the world and his activity within it. 'Spirit' is to be understood here, as in the Old Testament, of the personal power of the Divine manifested purposefully in the world and in the lives of men. When John says that God is 'spirit' he is asserting his nature as creative life-giving power in relation to his people. To worship 'in spirit' is therefore to worship in the sphere of this divine activity, which was supremely manifested in Christ who is 'truth', the faithful fulfilment of God's purpose. The verse reinforces the teaching implicit in the narrative of the Cleansing of the Temple, and there is much to be said for the idea which Bultmann notes in his commentary that 'in spirit and in truth' is equivalent to the Pauline formula 'in Christ'.[1] Neither on Gerizim, nor in Zion, but in Christ—the manifestation of truth and power—is true worship realised.

In John's Gospel, the Spirit is closely connected with the Sacraments. The statement, 'Unless a man is born of water and spirit (ἐξ ὕδατος καὶ πνεύματος) he cannot enter the kingdom of God' (3:5) is a definition of Christian regeneration, equivalent to 'the begetting from above (again)'. It is baptismal regeneration through the Spirit. The importance of 'spirit' in John's teaching here is demonstrated by its repetition at v. 6 and vv. 8 ff.: it was the addition of 'spirit' which transformed John the Baptist's baptism into Christian baptism (Acts 19: 1–7). In discussing the Matthean and Lucan stories about the miraculous conception by the Holy Spirit, we suggested that the Spirit should be understood as the creating power and activity of God inaugurating the New Creation in the birth of the messianic redeemer. Is there not a parallel theme in John's doctrine of regeneration? The Spirit is brought into relation to baptismal regeneration as the originator, or begetter, not of physical life, but of *new* life (v. 6). The Spirit is the life-giving power which makes men and women anew. 'Birth from above, or, from the Spirit' hardly differs in substance from Paul's conception of

[1] *Das Evangelium des Johannes* (2 Abt., 16 Auf., Göttingen, 1959), p. 140, note 3.

'New Creation'. By understanding John's reference to the Spirit in baptism in this way we do justice to the emphasis which he lays upon it in this chapter, and we give a greater unity to the whole passage. The Spirit brings about the New Creation: it is the source of new life: baptism is the symbol and the occasion of the re-birth.

The life-creating power of the Spirit is again emphasised at 6: 63, a verse which explains the discourse on the Bread of life:

What then, if you should behold the Son of Man ascending where he was before? It is the Spirit which is life-giving: the flesh profiteth nothing. The words which I have spoken to you, they are spirit, they are life.

The teaching about the Bread of Life must be viewed in the light of two facts which John can introduce from his own later standpoint; namely the Ascension and the work of the Spirit which the Ascension makes possible (cf. 7: 39). Life (which is for John the content of salvation) is conveyed not by 'flesh', but by the Spirit which is life-giving. Since this discourse was composed with reference to the Eucharist, it seems likely that John intends to imply a connection between that rite and the Spirit. The sacramental meal, if it is to give life, must be a vehicle of the Spirit; and such indeed it is, not in itself, but in its witness to the historic act of revelation and redemption in Jesus.[1] But the Eucharist is not the only life-giving agency. The words of Jesus are 'spirit and life'. If the standpoint of John is correctly taken to be that of the age of the Church, 'words' need not refer exclusively to the preceding discourse: all the teaching of the Incarnate Christ is productive of life, because it is 'spirit'. Just as the sacramental rite brings out of the past into the present the redeeming act of Christ and is therefore a vehicle of the Spirit, so knowledge of his words keeps alive and effectual the historical teaching: sacrament and Scripture convey life by bringing men into vital touch with the historic Christ.[2] If this is what is implied in John's doctrine, then his characteristic understanding of the Spirit is close to what we discovered in Paul. Moreover, the

---

[1] In a context concerned with the Eucharist, ἡ σάρξ may have a reference to the symbols or elements of the sacrament. The material symbols of Jesus' body and blood do not in themselves convey life: they have value only as vehicles of the life-giving Spirit.

[2] Cf. C. H. Dodd, *The Interpretation of the Fourth Gospel*, p. 342 note 3.

fact that (for John) the activity of the Spirit could only follow the glorification of Christ in resurrection and ascension is parallel to Paul's teaching on the Spirit as the post-Resurrection power of Christ's life.

At 7: 38ff. the Holy Spirit is likened to 'living water'. When the verse is interpreted in the way adopted earlier in this work,[1] the declaration is as follows: living water, the gift which creates and maintains life, comes from Christ: the living water is the Spirit and the Spirit comes from the glorified Christ. Now 'living water' is used in the Old Testament as a metaphor for the divine activity in quickening men to life, and appears in Judaism as a symbol of the Holy Spirit. So John declares that that which quickens men to life is the Spirit (cf. 6: 63), the power and presence of the exalted Christ active in the hearts of believers to create and sustain new life.

The phrase 'the spirit of truth' (τὸ πνεῦμα τῆς ἀληθείας) occurs three times in John's Gospel. According to 14: 17, the Paraclete is the Spirit of truth whom the world cannot receive, but who dwells with the disciples and will be in them, the divine presence with them continually after the ascension; 15: 26 affirms that the Paraclete is the spirit of truth who proceeds from God and who will bear witness (as the disciples also testify) to Jesus; and 16: 13 declares that the spirit of truth will guide into all truth; he will not speak on his own authority; he will glorify Christ and take what is Christ's and declare it. In 14: 26 the Paraclete is described as the Holy Spirit (τὸ πνεῦμα τὸ ἅγιον) who will teach the disciples all things and bring to their remembrance all that Jesus said. From these verses it is clear that 'Paraclete', 'Holy Spirit' and the 'Spirit of truth' are synonymous expressions. The coming of the Spirit or Paraclete depends on the completion of Christ's work and his departure from earth (16: 7): it proceeds from the Father in the name of Christ, that is, to act in relation to Christ, in his place and with his authority. The Spirit does not act independently of Christ, as if taking up a task which Christ had commenced and relinquished. It declares to the world the truth of the mission and being of Christ (16: 14): it operates on the consciences of men to convince of sin (in themselves), righteousness (in Christ) and of judgment:[2] it is not

---

[1] See pp. 199–200.

[2] Barrett, *The Gospel according to St John*, pp. 405–6.

received by the world, but dwells with and in the disciples, that is to say, it is experienced in and mediated through the Church. It is through the witness which the Church bears to Christ, its preaching, worship and sacraments, that the conscience of the world is touched and men are judged. What Christ in his ministry had effected is made continually operative by the presence of the Spirit.

It is of interest to note the link between this teaching and Synoptic tradition. The promise that Christians who bore witness (μαρτύριον) to Christ before courts of justice would receive the help of Christ (Luke 21: 13–15) or of the Holy Spirit is deeply rooted in the Synoptic tradition (Mark 13: 9–11; Matt. 10: 17–19; Luke 12: 11–12). And the same ideas find expression again in John. For those who are hated and persecuted (15: 18 ff.) the Spirit will speak and give instruction (16: 13). The discourse includes the themes of martyrdom and excommunication and these lie close to the themes of witnessing and the Spirit in the tradition. The Johannine themes are worked out in his own characteristic way and the title 'Paraclete' is given to the Spirit. The functions of the Spirit, as described in the Synoptic passages mentioned, may be the clue to understanding the Johannine title as 'vindicator' or 'advocate'.[1] When Christians undergo trial for their faith, they are supported, strengthened and vindicated by the Spirit:[2] he is counsel for the defence (of believers) and at the same time prosecuting counsel (against unbelievers).

From this summary of the *functions* of the Paraclete (or Spirit) we proceed to the discussion of the meaning of the words 'the spirit of truth'. It is doubtful if 'of truth' is simply a defining genitive: already in the chapter (*v.* 6) Jesus is declared to be 'the truth', so that the expression may mean 'the Spirit of the Truth', that is, of Jesus. Barrett prefers to explain the phrase as

[1] See Dodd, *Historical Tradition and the Fourth Gospel*, pp. 410–12.

[2] Barrett thinks that the Paraclete is the Spirit of the Christian *paraclesis*, the Spirit who is operative in the Christian proclamation of the redemption effected in Jesus (*op. cit.* pp. 385–6 and also in *JTS* (n.s.), 1 (1950), 1–15, and esp. pp. 7 ff.). That more than one sense is present in John's use of the word is quite possible: the continuation of Christ's work and his judging and saving power are certainly related to the proclamation of the kerygma in the Church: but the emphasis, we think, is on the notion of 'vindication'.

'the Spirit who communicates truth',[1] but even in that definition 'truth' must refer to Christ himself and the revelation in him. It seems best to understand the phrase as 'the Spirit which mediates the truth as it is in Jesus'. The fact that its activity is to witness to Jesus within the Church and to convict of sin, righteousness and judgment suggests that the Johannine understanding of the Spirit is essentially the same as the Pauline: the Spirit is the powerful impact of the person, work and teaching of Jesus upon the hearts and lives of believers in every generation.[2] The departure of Jesus is the necessary precondition of this prolongation of the ministry through the Spirit. The glorification of the Son of Man, which, for John, is the hour of Jesus' death which precedes the giving of the Spirit, makes possible his continuing presence with, and transforming power in, all who believe: to experience this power and presence is to experience the Spirit.

In all this, we may observe, we are in touch with the central Hebraic idea of the Spirit of God as divine power and activity entering into the world to recreate and inspire men. The power is the power of God's revelation in Christ and therefore personal.

John's characteristic teaching on the Spirit, then, relates its activity to the life of the Church and particularly to Christian worship. In baptism the power of the Spirit in recreating life is symbolised: both the Eucharist and Scripture are vehicles of the life-giving Spirit. The activity of the Spirit is the making present to the lives of men of the power and influence of the historical life of Jesus, the bridging of the gap between the events of nearly two thousand years ago and the life of believers in every new generation. The power of the Spirit is the present power of the living Lord.

---

[1] *Op. cit.* p. 386.

[2] In our discussion of the Dead Sea Scrolls we interpreted the 'spirit of truth' in the Manual (which is parallel to the 'holy spirit' in the Hymns) in terms of a power—with perhaps some cosmic dimension—which is inwardly experienced and brings about right conduct. At Test. Jud. 20 'the spirit of truth' has the same functions as the Johannine Paraclete, but in John the actions are governed by their reference to Christ. In Test. Jud. the spirit is equivalent to the good inclination, the inward disposition towards righteousness.

CHAPTER VII

CONCLUSION

The purpose of this concluding chapter is to relate the findings of the word-studies and the principles of investigation to the issues raised for biblical theology by Professor Barr's recent work.

The discussions of this work have little to say to the controversy of Barr and Boman on the theory that the nature of Hebrew thought is revealed in the Hebrew verb-system. There are two reasons for this: first, we have not been concerned to construct a picture of Hebrew thinking and culture and to distinguish this from Greek and Hellenistic thought; and secondly, we have not concentrated attention on the verb and its forms to the exclusion of other parts of speech. We have sought to discover the meanings of certain words in the Greek of the New Testament, and neither these words nor the surveys of their background and usage in Hebrew and extra-biblical material provide evidence from which we may argue to general modes of thinking. However, on the problem of which the Barr–Boman controversy is a reflection, namely, the problem of the relation between language and thought, we have some contribution to make. We have already indicated agreement with those linguists who maintain that the difference between the thought and culture of peoples is reflected in the vocabulary stocks of their languages. We may now go further and say that the difference may also be illumined at the level of semantic studies. Greek thought, for instance, had no idea of the 'righteousness of God' as a divine activity bringing about salvation: the phrase δικαιοσύνη θεοῦ (with that meaning) entered Greek only as a translation of the Hebrew צִדְקַת יהוה. Again, Greek thought did not operate with the notion of the 'two Ages'—this Age and the Age to come: the adjective αἰώνιος meant to a Greek simply 'very long lasting': it was its use to render the developed meaning of the Hebrew עוֹלָם which gave to it in the New Testament the Hebraic significance. The usage of the word πνεῦμα in Greek literature reveals nothing comparable to the Hebrew use of רוּחַ for 'human spirit' and for the powerful and active presence of God. The word πνεῦμα in

Greek stands essentially for a substance, *fluidum*, refined and ethereal, penetrating the entire cosmos, the substance of which God and the human soul are composed—a meaning which may have given direction, at a later date, to a certain kind of Trinitarian theology. The strongly theological character of Hebraic thinking is witnessed to in the vocabulary stocks of the Greek Bible and also in the meanings of some New Testament terms which are deeply indebted, for their overtones of meaning, to Hebrew thought and language. This said, we must add that the attempt to base the contrast between Greek and Hebrew thought on grammatical, morphological and syntactical differences remains a most precarious undertaking,[1] especially when these differences are interpreted without proper consideration of general linguistic theory and without systematic study of the relevant languages in their entirety.

On the matter of dependence on etymologies, we indicated in the first chapter a substantial measure of agreement with Barr's position. In so far as our studies have considered the etymologies of the words discussed, this has been for the sake of gaining illumination on meaning from parallels, not for the purpose of establishing an essential meaning which must be considered applicable in all subsequent usage.

We must take up again the points at issue between Barr and the Kittel *Wörterbuch*. Barr maintains that at the basis of this work there lies a totally wrong idea of the relation between concept and word, and that this is a fruitful source of error in its lexicographical method. Contributors (in Barr's opinion) constantly confuse 'concept' and 'linguistic entity' and so waver between discussing words and discussing the theological realities signified by the words. Now the problem of the relation between 'word' and 'concept' belongs to the philosophy of language and to the realm of psychology, and Barr does not clearly indicate what position he takes on these matters. Because of this lack of clarity he can occasionally suggest that a word may refer to or indicate an idea or concept, but, in general, his work gives the impression that he is opposed to everything that savours of Idealist thought and suspicious of the application of psychology to linguistic science. But he cannot hold both positions at

---

[1] For a cautious acceptance of the view, see M. Hadas, *Hellenistic Culture* (New York and Oxford, 1959), ch. 5, esp. pp. 51–2.

once. Either a word indicates (in some way) a concept or it does not. The *Wörterbuch* is built upon the view that it does: is this erroneous, as Barr for the most part maintains? It must be said, in the first place, that because the question at issue here touches on the realm of philosophy and, more particularly, on the realm of the philosophy of language, the proponents of one viewpoint cannot say that they are right and all others wrong: it is rather a case of two *different* starting-points, two *different* philosophical approaches. Barr and the *Wörterbuch* build up their methodologies on *different* grounds or bases. In the second place, when an attempt is made to judge the relative merits of two different standpoints, the element of personal preference is always present: and our preference, when discussing words, and particularly when discussing theological words, is to retain an idealist framework. The word 'symbolises' the 'thought' or 'reference' which in its turn 'refers' to the feature or event about which we are speaking.[1] According to this widely-held view, the meaning of a word, as a socially accepted symbol, cannot be gauged by simply investigating how it is used or its relation to other words, or solely on the basis of contextual analysis: it can be arrived at, in its totality, only as the aspect of experience which the word symbolises or to which it points is clarified and understood. On the Barr–Kittel controversy on the basic philosophy of language, we are inclined to support the *Wörterbuch* rather than the viewpoint implied in Barr's work.

This, however, does not mean that everything said and done in the *Wörterbuch* calls forth our approval. Although its basic approach to the study of theological terms is preferred, we admit that that approach has dangers, both in the methodology it

---

[1] Cf. G. Stern, *Meaning and Change of Meaning* (Gothenburg, 1931), p. 85: 'There is no getting away from the fact that single words have more or less permanent meanings, that they actually do refer to certain referents, and not to others, and that this characteristic is the indispensable basis of all communication.' In the same vein, Ullmann writes in *Semantics: An Introduction to the Science of Meaning* (p. 48), 'Statements like "the word exists only through the context and is nothing in itself" (A. Rosetti, *Le Mot: Esquisse d'une théorie générale*, 2me ed., Copenhagen, 1947, p. 38) which are frequently heard nowadays, are neither accurate nor realistic'. Ullmann notes (p. 49) that a series of tests designed to study the influence of context has shown that there is usually in each word a hard core of meaning which is relatively stable and can only be modified by the context within certain limits.

produces and in the conclusions it reaches. These Barr has pointed out very clearly. Indeed the main contribution of his book to the study of biblical language is just here: it demonstrates the pit-falls which exist for the unwary lexicographer who proceeds by Kittel's method. One does not need to share Barr's philosophical standpoint on language to appreciate and to avoid these dangers. In the end, two things only are required. First of all, one must possess some knowledge of language-structure and semantics (such as Barr provides) and a willingness to apply this knowledge to biblical interpretation. In this way, such errors as the root-fallacy and the adding to significances will be made impossible. It is of interest to note that when Barr rightly pays tribute to the rather traditional type of biblical philology—which has never, he says, been deceived by the kind of arguments from linguistic evidence which he has criticised—the only real inadequacy he can find in it is that it just did not study language structure and the problems of semantics.[1] Yet it was never deceived by false methods of interpretation! Why? Because it possessed in great measure something which Barr does not mention, but which we think is the second means of avoiding pit-falls, namely, sound common sense. The application of common sense would certainly have outlawed many of the arguments of those biblical theologians whom Barr so trenchantly criticises on linguistic grounds. For instance, how would Torrance's attempt to link Christ's ascension and the idea of sacrificial offering by referring to the Hebrew root עלה[2] stand up to the light of cool common sense? It is true that the lexicographical studies of theological words in Kittel's *Wörterbuch* are sometimes characterised by a lack of common sense as well as by a disregard for linguistic science, but the whole method of approach is not thereby invalidated. This approach may be used, or used again, provided we use common sense and proceed with that knowledge of linguistics which avoids the errors in interpretation which the root-fallacy, neglect of context, etc., have produced. While following the Kittel method—which we think Barr has not proved wrong—we must gratefully learn from Barr to proceed more cautiously. This we have tried to do in the foregoing studies. We have paid attention to context in the explication of word-meanings, both the strictly verbal context of

[1] *Semantics*, pp. 295–6.   [2] See *Semantics*, pp. 151–2.

sentence, paragraph or chapter, and the wider context of situation or cultural background: the role of 'context' is to provide precision or determinateness to the meaning of the word.[1]

We must now look again at Barr's claim that the impress of the Old Testament–Jewish tradition on New Testament language and meanings is borne by the things said (the formulations, sentences, etc.) and not by the words used, since these often retained the semantic value which they normally had in the usage of Hellenistic speakers. Of many words this is undoubtedly true. The pronoun ἐγώ, for instance, does not acquire in New Testament Greek a semantic value that is new and specific as compared with Hellenistic Greek: nor do such words as θύρα, πόλις and ἱμάτιον. But these are words which denote physical entities. What about connotative words, the words which are pointers to abstract ideas? The word ἀπολύτρωσις, for instance, does not have in New Testament Greek a meaning which is completely different from that which it has in Hellenistic Greek, but it does have a dimension of reference with relation to the Old Testament idea of deliverance (channelled to the word through the LXX translation) which it did not have in Classical or Hellenistic Greek. Likewise, the word ἀλήθεια did not have in the New Testament a sense that is altogether different from that in spoken Greek of the first century; but it did gain, and expresses often, overtones of meaning which are traceable to the association of the Hebrew word for 'truth' with God, and these overtones come to the Greek word through the LXX. The same is true of words like πίστις, δικαιοσύνη and πνεῦμα, and indeed of every significant theological word. We simply cannot claim to have understood the meaning of New Testament theological words if we have missed the overtones of meaning, the extra or

[1] In this connection, we would repeat our conviction that Barr has failed to distinguish between the aims and intentions of the *Wörterbuch* and the use made of it by writers of biblical theology. The *Wörterbuch* provides a guide to the material and a synthesis (often, too neat) of main themes: it lists the semantic variations which accompany the appearances of words in different contexts and situations of thought: but it is not right for the users of the *Wörterbuch* to assume (and the editors never meant them to assume) that every occurrence of a particular word carries all the associations worked out in the relevant article. The possibilities for interpretation are listed, but this does not relieve the interpreter of making the decision as to which *precise* meaning is required by the context with which he is dealing.

special content which comes to them (in our opinion) out of the biblical tradition, and is related especially to the language of the Septuagint, the locus of that extension (or change) of meaning which is due to their Hebrew background. At this point in our discussion a remark of N. W. Porteous on Barr's work is relevant: we should not be blind, he says, to 'the likelihood that in the course of their usage certain words became so loaded with theological meaning that a hearer or reader of utterances or passages in which these words occurred would often catch, and was perhaps intended to catch, overtones of meaning. Much of the beauty and significance of poetry depends on the suggestive-ness of the words employed, and to come with too dry a logic to great literature may sometimes be almost as serious a fault as indulgence in linguistic fallacies and indeed may result in the impoverishment of one's own understanding.'[1] But, concerning those words which, in our opinion, possess Hebraic emphasis or overtones of meaning Barr might say that they were covered by his declaration that semantic change has to be related to the extent to which words had a specialised use and were on their way to becoming technical terms.[2] But, surely then, almost every New Testament word which is significant theologically will have to be regarded as 'technical', and therefore open to the possi-bility of having its meaning altered or enriched, and that with reference to its Old Testament background.

The discussion of a special biblical content for New Testament meanings leads naturally to the question of the impact of Christianity itself upon language. Barr dismisses as 'romanticism' the contention that Christian faith had a creative and trans-forming influence on the language used in the New Testament, and favours Deissmann's contention that Christianity had little or no effect on language. Now it is certainly true that too much has been made in the past of the 'language-moulding power' of the Christian faith, but surely Barr has overstated his arguments. The essential Christ-reference of theological terms, which is born out of the Christian faith, has influenced the *total meaning* of New Testament terms. The Pauline use of the word πνεῦμα is indebted to the Old Testament–Jewish understanding of the

---

[1] N. W. Porteous, 'Second Thoughts—II: The Present State of Old Testament Theology', *ET*, LXXV (Dec. 1963), 70–4: quotation from pp. 71–2.
[2] *Semantics*, p. 263.

'spirit of Yahweh', but the relation to Christ which the term bears and the experience to which it points as a symbol in Paul's writing and thought are surely added dimensions within the total meaning of the word in the Apostle's usage, dimensions which ought not to be missed if our understanding of the word is to be adequate. The same might be said about the word λύτρον, as part of the New Testament atonement vocabulary. Perhaps even more can be said concerning the term δικαιοσύνη. Here Paul's distinctive understanding of the word (as 'justification') is related to an aspect of the Old Testament meaning (namely, the divine activity which brings about salvation): this was channelled to the Greek word through the Septuagint translation; but, in his use of the word, Paul so relates its meaning and significance to the work of Christ that, in his hands, δικαιοσύνη has a Christianised content radically different from anything it possessed in Hellenistic thought and usage and linked only with one strand of the Hebraic tradition. The central figure or event in Christian faith has had an influence on the total meaning of the theological words whose semantics we have been investigating.

The final topic to which we wish to relate our methods and studies is that of the activity of writing biblical theology. It ought to be remembered that Barr's book is not an attack on biblical theology itself, many of the insights of which he appreciates: he is concerned to criticise the linguistic methods on which many of the statements of biblical theologians have been content to rest. In our lexicographical studies we have tried to avoid these erroneous methods and presuppositions, but it has not been our intention to write essays in biblical theology. We have endeavoured to investigate some soteriological terms and to understand their meanings as used by various New Testament authors. This type of survey must be undertaken before any attempt is made to construct a biblical theology or theologies. The development and variations in the use and meaning of biblical terms must be presented and examined before any synthesising theological statement can be offered.

BIBLIOGRAPHY

Abelson, J. *The Immanence of God in Rabbinical Literature* (London, 1912).

Abrahams, I. *Studies in Pharisaism and the Gospels* (Cambridge, 1917–24).

Anderson, A. A. 'The Use of "Ruaḥ" in 1QS, 1QH and 1QM', *JSS*, VII (1962), 293–303.

Arndt, W. F. and Gingrich, F. W. *A Greek–English Lexicon of the New Testament and other early Christian Literature* (Cambridge, 1957).

Bacon, B. W. 'The Festival of Lives given for the Nation in Jewish and Christian Faith', *Hibbert Journal*, XV (1917), 256–78.

Bammel, E. 'Zum jüdischen Märtyrerkult', *TLZ*, LXXVIII (1953), 119–26.

Barr, J. *The Semantics of Biblical Language* (Oxford, 1961).

—— *Biblical Words for Time* (London, 1962).

—— 'Hypostasization of Linguistic Phenomena in Modern Theological Interpretation', *JSS*, VII (1962), 85–94.

Barrett, C. K. *The Holy Spirit and the Gospel Tradition* (London, 1947).

—— 'The Place of Eschatology in the Fourth Gospel', *ET*, LIX (1947–8), 302–5.

—— 'The Holy Spirit in the Fourth Gospel', *JTS*, I (1950), 1–15.

—— *The Gospel according to St John* (London, 1955).

—— *The Epistle to the Romans* (London, 1957).

—— 'The Background of Mark x. 45', in *New Testament Essays*, ed. A. J. B. Higgins, pp. 1–18 (Manchester, 1959).

Basilius, H. 'Neo-Humboldtian Ethnolinguistics', *Word*, VIII (1952), 95–105.

Beare, F. W. *The First Epistle of Peter* (Oxford, 1947).

—— *The Epistle to the Philippians* (London, 1959).

Bernard, J. H. *The Gospel according to St John* (Edinburgh, 1928).

Best, E. 'Spirit-Baptism', *NT*, IV (1960), 236–43.

—— 'Matthew v. 3', *NTS*, VII (1960–1), 255–8.

Beyer, K. *Semitische Syntax im Neuen Testament*, Band I (Göttingen, 1961).

Birkeland, H. 'The Belief in the Resurrection of the Dead in the Old Testament', *ST*, III (1950), 60–78.

Black, M. 'The Eschatology of the Similitudes of Enoch', *JTS*, III (1952), 1–10.

—— *An Aramaic Approach to the Gospels and Acts*[2] (Oxford, 1954).

Black, M. *The Scrolls and Christian Origins* (Edinburgh, 1961).
—— 'The Interpretation of Romans viii. 28', in *Neotestamentica et Patristica*, pp. 166–72 (Leiden, 1962).
—— 'The Semitic Element in the New Testament', *ET*, LXXVII (1965), 20–3.
—— and Rowley, H. H. (eds.). *Peake's Commentary on the Bible* (Edinburgh, 1962).
Boman, Th. *Hebrew Thought compared with Greek*, Eng. trans. J. L. Moreau (London, 1960).
—— 'Hebrew and Greek Thought-forms in the New Testament', in *Current Issues in New Testament Interpretation*, ed. W. Klassen and G. F. Snyder, pp. 1–22 (London, 1962).
Bonnard, P. *L'Épître de St Paul aux Galates* (Paris, 1953).
—— *L'Évangile selon St Matthieu* (Paris, 1963).
Bonsirven, J. *Le Judaïsme Palestinien au temps de Jésus-Christ* (Paris, 1934–5).
Bornkamm, G., Barth, G. and Held, H. J. *Tradition and Interpretation in Matthew* (London, 1963).
Braun, F. M. (ed.). *L'Évangile de Jean* (Paris, 1958).
Browne, L. E. (ed.). *From Babylon to Bethlehem²* (Cambridge, 1951).
Bruce, F. F. *The Epistle to the Ephesians* (London, 1962).
Büchler, A. *Studies in Sin and Atonement in the Rabbinic Literature of the First Century* (London, 1928).
Büchsel, F. *Der Geist Gottes im Neuen Testament* (Gütersloh, 1926).
Bultmann, R. *Theology of the New Testament*, Eng. trans. K. Grobel. (London, 1952–5).
—— *Das Evangelium des Johannes* (16te Auf., Göttingen, 1959).
—— *et al. Life and Death* (Bible Key Words Series, London, 1965).
Burrows, M. *The Dead Sea Scrolls* (New York, 1955).
Burton, E. D. *Spirit, Soul and Flesh* (Chicago, 1918).
—— *The Epistle to the Galatians* (Edinburgh, 1921).
Carmignac, J. *La Règle de la Guerre des fils de lumière contre les fils de ténèbres* (Paris, 1958).
Charles, R. H. *The Testaments of the Twelve Patriarchs* (Oxford, 1908).
—— (ed.). *The Apocrypha and Pseudepigrapha of the Old Testament*, 2 vols. (Oxford, 1913).
Chevallier, M. A. *L'Esprit et le Messie dans le bas-Judaïsme et le Nouveau Testament* (Paris, 1958).
Colwell, E. C. 'The Greek Language' (*Interpreter's Dictionary of the Bible*, II, pp. 479–87) (New York and Nashville, 1962).
Cross, F. M. *The Ancient Library of Qumran* (London, 1958).
Cullmann, O. *The Earliest Christian Confessions*, Eng. trans. J. K. S. Reid (London, 1949).

Cullmann, O. *Baptism in the New Testament*, Eng. trans. J. K. S. Reid (London, 1950).
—— *Christ and Time*, Eng. trans. F. V. Filson (London, 1951).
Dalglish, E. R. *Psalm Fifty-One in the Light of Ancient and Near Eastern Patternism* (Leiden, 1962).
Dalman, G. *The Words of Jesus*, Eng. trans. D. M. Kay (Edinburgh, 1902).
Danby, H. (ed.). *The Mishnah* (Oxford, 1933).
Daube, D. *Studies in Biblical Law* (Cambridge, 1947).
—— *The New Testament and Rabbinic Judaism* (London, 1956).
—— *The Exodus Pattern in the Bible* (London, 1964).
Davidson, A. B. *The Theology of the Old Testament* (Edinburgh, 1904).
Davies, W. D. *Paul and Rabbinic Judaism*² (London, 1955).
—— 'Paul and the Dead Sea Scrolls: Flesh and Spirit', in *The Scrolls and the New Testament*, ed. K. Stendahl (London, 1958).
—— *The Setting of the Sermon on the Mount* (Cambridge, 1964).
—— and Daube, D. (eds.). *The Background of the New Testament and its Eschatology* (Cambridge, 1956).
Deissmann, A. *Bible Studies* (Edinburgh, 1901).
—— *Light from the Ancient East* (London, 1927).
Descamps, A. *Les Justes et la Justice dans les évangiles et le christianisme primitif* (Louvain, 1950).
Dodd, C. H. ''Ιλάσκεσθαι, its cognates, derivatives and synonyms in the Septuagint', *JTS*, xxxii (1931), 352–60.
—— *The Epistle to the Romans* (London, 1932).
—— *The Bible and the Greeks* (London, 1935).
—— *The Johannine Epistles* (London, 1946).
—— *The Interpretation of the Fourth Gospel* (Cambridge, 1953).
—— *Historical Tradition and the Fourth Gospel* (Cambridge, 1964).
Downing, J. 'Jesus and Martyrdom', *JTS*, xiv (1963), 279–93.
Driver, G. R. *Canaanite Myths and Legends* (Edinburgh, 1956).
Driver, S. R. *Deuteronomy* (ICC, Edinburgh, 1896).
Drummond, J. *Philo Judaeus* (London and Edinburgh, 1888).
Duncan, G. S. *The Epistle of Paul to the Galatians* (London, 1934).
Dupont-Somner, A. *The Dead Sea Scrolls* (Oxford, 1952).
Ebeling, G. 'The Meaning of "Biblical Theology"', *JTS*, vi (1955), 210–25.
Eichrodt, W. *Theology of the Old Testament*, vol. i, Eng. trans. J. A. Baker (London, 1961).
Fahlgren, K. H. *Sedaka: nahestehende und entgegengesetzte Begriffe im Alten Testament* (Uppsala, 1932).
Feuillet, A. 'La citation d'Hab. ii. 4 et les huit premiers chapitres de l'épître aux Romains', *NTS*, vi (1959–60), 52–80.
—— *Études Johanniques* (Bruges, 1962).

Firth, J. R. *Papers in Linguistics* (Oxford, 1957).

Flusser, D. *Aspects of the Dead Sea Scrolls* (Scripta Hierosolymitana IV; Jerusalem, 1958).

Foerster, W. 'Der Heilige Geist im Spätjudentum', *NTS*, VIII (1961–2), 117–34.

Frend, W. H. C. *Martyrdom and Persecution in the Early Church* (Oxford, 1965).

Frey, J. B. 'La vie de l'au-delà dans les conceptions juives au temps de Jésus-Christ', *Biblica*, XIII (1932), 129–68.

Friedrich, G. 'Die Problematik eines theologischen Wörterbuchs zum neuen Testament', *Studia Evangelica* (ed. K. Aland, Berlin, 1959).

Funk, R. W. (trans.). *A Greek Grammar of the New Testament* (Chicago and Cambridge, 1961).

Gärtner, B. *The Temple and the Community in Qumran and the New Testament* (Cambridge, 1965).

Gehman, H. S. 'The Hebraic Character of Septuagint Greek', *VT*, I (1951), 81–90.

Gerleman, G. *Studies in the Septuagint: I. Job* (Lund, 1946); II. *Proverbs* (Lund, 1956).

Goodspeed, E. J. 'Some Greek Notes: III. Justification', *JBL*, LXXIII (1954), 86–91.

Gordon, C. H. *Ugaritic Literature* (Rome, 1949).

Gray, G. B. *Sacrifice in the Old Testament* (Oxford, 1925).

Gray, J. *The Legacy of Canaan* (Suppl. vol. V of *VT*) (Leiden, 1957).

Grelot, P. 'La Géographie Mythique d'Hénoch et ses Sources Orientales', *RB*, LXV (1958), 33–69.

Grundmann, W. 'Der Lehrer der Gerechtigkeit von Qumran und die Frage nach der Glaubensgerechtigkeit in der Theologie des Apostels Paulus', *RQ*, II (1959–60), 237–59.

Guillet, J. *Thèmes Bibliques* (Paris, 1950).

Gunkel, H. *Die Wirkungen des heiligen Geistes*[2] (Göttingen, 1899).

Hadas, M. (ed.). *The Third and Fourth Books of Maccabees* (New York, 1953).

—— *Hellenistic Culture* (New York and Oxford, 1959).

Haenchen, E. *Die Apostelgeschichte*[12] (Göttingen, 1959).

Hamilton, N. Q. *The Holy Spirit and Eschatology in Paul* (Occasional Papers *SJT*, VI; Edinburgh, 1957).

Hatch, E. *Essays in Biblical Greek* (Oxford, 1889).

Hatch, E. and Redpath, H. A. (eds.). *A Concordance to the Septuagint* (Oxford, 1897).

Hehn, J. 'Zum Problem des Geistes im Alten Orient und im Alten Testament', *ZAW*, XLIII (1925), 210–25.

Henle, P. (ed.). *Language, Thought and Culture* (Ann Arbor, 1958).

Héring, J. *La Seconde Épître de St Paul aux Corinthiens* (Paris, 1958).
—— *The First Epistle of St Paul to the Corinthians*, Eng. trans. A. W. Heathcote (London, 1962).
Hermann, I. *Kyrios und Pneuma: Studien zur Christologie der paulinischen Hauptbriefe* (Munich, 1961).
Hertz, J. H. (ed.). *The Authorised Daily Prayer Book with Commentary* (London 1959).
Higgins, A. J. B. (ed.). *New Testament Essays: In memory of T. W. Manson* (Manchester, 1959).
Hoijer, H. (ed.). *Language in Culture* (Chicago, 1954).
Holm-Nielsen, S. *Hodayot: Psalms from Qumran* (Aarhus, 1960).
Honeyman, A. M. 'Notes and Communications: Notes on a Teacher and a Book', *JJS*, IV (1953), 131 f.
Hooke, S. H. 'The Translation of Romans i. 4', *NTS*, IX (1962–3), 370 f.
Hooker, M. D. *Jesus and the Servant* (London, 1959).
Hoskyns, E. C. *The Fourth Gospel* (London, 1940).
—— and Davey, F. N. *The Riddle of the New Testament* (London, 1947).
Hyatt, J. P. 'The View of Man in the Qumran "Hodayot"', *NTS*, II (1955–6), 276–84.
van Imschoot, P. 'L'esprit de Yahvé, source de vie dans l'ancien Testament', *RB*, XLIV (1935), 481–501.
—— 'Sagesse et Esprit dans l'ancien Testament', *RB*, XLVII (1938), 23–49.
Jacob, E. *Theology of the Old Testament* (London, 1958).
Jastrow, M. *A Dictionary of the Targumim, the Talmud Babli and Yerushalmi, and the Midrashic Literature* (London, 1903).
Jenni, E. 'Das Wort *'olam* im Alten Testament', *ZAW*, LXIV (1952), 197–248; LXV (1953), 1–35.
Johnson, A. R. *The Vitality of the Individual in the Thought of Ancient Israel* (Cardiff, 1949).
—— 'The Primary Meaning of √גאל', *VT Suppl.* I (1953), 67–77.
—— *Sacral Kingship in Ancient Israel* (Cardiff, 1955).
—— *The One and the Many in the Israelite Conception of God*[2] (Cardiff, 1961).
Johnson, R. J. *Sacrifice and Penitence in Israel* (Leiden, 1964).
Johnson, S. E. 'Paul and the Manual of Discipline', *HTR*, XLVIII (1955), 157–65.
de Jonge, M. *The Testaments of the Twelve Patriarchs* (Assen, 1953).
—— 'Christian Influence in the Testaments of the Twelve Patriarchs', *NT*, IV (1960), 182–235.
Jongeling, B. *Le Rouleau de la Guerre des Manuscrits de Qumran* (Assen, 1962).

Käsemann, E. 'Gottesgerechtigkeit bei Paulus', *ZTK*, LVIII (1961), 367–78.

Kennedy, H. A. A. *St Paul and the Mystery Religions* (London, 1913).

Kennedy, H. A. A. *Philo's Contribution to Religion* (London, 1919).

Kilpatrick, G. D. 'A Theme of the Lucan Passion Story and Luke xxiii. 47', *JTS*, XLIII (1942), 34–6.

—— *The Origins of the Gospel according to St Matthew* (Oxford, 1946).

Klostermann, E. *Das Markusevangelium*² (Tübingen, 1926).

Knox, W. L. *The Acts of the Apostles* (Cambridge, 1948).

Koehler, L. *Old Testament Theology*, Eng. trans. A. S. Todd (London, 1957).

Kronasser, H. *Handbuch der Semasiologie* (Heidelberg, 1952).

Kuhn, K. G. 'Romans vi. 7', *ZNW*, XXX (1931), 305–10.

Lagrange, M.-J. *Épître aux Romains* (Paris, 1931).

—— *Le Judaïsme avant Jésus-Christ* (Paris, 1931).

—— *Évangile selon Saint Marc*⁶ (Paris, 1942).

Lampe, G. W. H. *The Seal of the Spirit* (London, 1951).

—— 'The Holy Spirit in the Writings of St Luke', in *Studies in the Gospels*, ed. D. E. Nineham, pp. 159–200 (Oxford, 1955).

Laurin, R. B. 'The Question of Immortality in the Qumran "Hodayot"', *JSS*, III (1958), 344–55.

Leaney, A. R. C. 'The Eschatological Significance of Human Suffering in the Old Testament and the Dead Sea Scrolls', *SJT*, XVI (1963), 286–96.

Leenhardt, F. J. *The Epistle to the Romans*, Eng. trans. H. Knight (London, 1961).

Légasse, S. 'Les Pauvres en esprit et les "Volontaires" de Qumran', *NTS*, VIII (1961–2), 336–45.

Löhse, E. *Märtyrer und Gottesknecht* (FRLANT, 46; Göttingen, 1955).

Lyonnet, S. 'De "Justitia Dei" in Epistula ad Romanos i. 17 et iii. 21, 22', *Verbum Domini*, XXV (1947), 23–34, 118–21, 129–34, 193–203, 257–63.

Lys, D. *Rûach: Le Souffle dans l'Ancien Testament* (Paris, 1962).

Manson, T. W. 'ΙΛΑΣΤΗΡΙΟΝ', *JTS*, XLVI (1945), 1–10.

—— 'Entry into Membership of the Early Church', *JTS*, XLVIII (1947), 25–33.

—— *The Sayings of Jesus* (London, 1949).

—— *Ethics and the Gospel* (London, 1960).

—— *On Paul and John* (London, 1963).

Marmorstein, A. *The Doctrine of Merits in the Old Rabbinical Literature* (London, 1920).

—— *Studies in Jewish Theology* (Cambridge, 1950).

Martin-Achard, R. *From Death to Life* (Edinburgh, 1960).

Masson, C. *L'Épître de St Paul aux Éphésiens* (Paris, 1953).

May, H. G. 'Cosmological Reference in the Qumran Doctrine of the Two Spirits and in Old Testament Imagery', *JBL*, LXXXII (1963), 1–14.

McNeile, A. H. *The Gospel according to St Matthew* (London, 1915).

Mendenhall, G. E. *Law and Covenant in Israel and the Ancient Near East* (Pittsburgh, 1955).

Menoud, P. H. 'La Mort d'Ananias et de Saphira', in *Aux Sources de la Tradition Chrétienne*, pp. 146–54 (Paris, 1950).

Metzger, B. M. 'The Language of the New Testament' (*Interpreter's Bible*, VII, 43–59; New York and Nashville, 1951).

Milik, J. T. 'Hénoch au pays des aromates', *RB*, LXV (1958), 70–7.

—— *Ten Years of Discovery in the Wilderness of Judaea* (London, 1959).

Moffatt, J. *The First Epistle of Paul to the Corinthians* (London, 1938).

Montefiore, C. G. and Loewe, H. (eds.). *A Rabbinic Anthology* (New York, 1938).

Moore, G. F. *Judaism in the First Three Centuries of the Christian Era*, 3 vols. (Cambridge, Mass., 1927–30).

Morris, L. *The Apostolic Preaching of the Cross* (London, 1955).

—— 'The Meaning of ἱλαστήριον in Romans iii. 25', *NTS*, II (1955–6), 33–43.

Moule, C. F. D. *An Idiom Book of New Testament Greek*² (Cambridge, 1959).

Mowinckel, S. 'The Spirit and the Word in the pre-exilic reforming Prophets', *JBL*, LIII (1934), 199–227.

Müssner, F. ΖΩΗ — *Die Anschauung von 'Leben' im vierten Evangelium* (Munich, 1952).

Nötscher, F. *Zur Theologischen Terminologie der Qumran-Texte* (Bonn, 1956).

Oepke, A. 'Δικαιοσύνη θεοῦ bei Paulus in neuer Beleuchtung', *TLZ*, LXXVIII (1953), 257–64.

Öhman, S. 'Theories of the "Linguistic Field"', *Word*, IX (1953), 123–34.

Orlinsky, H. M. 'The New Jewish Version of the Torah', *JBL*, LXXXII (1963), 249–64.

Parzen, H. 'The Ruaḥ Hakodesh in Tannaitic Literature', *JQR*, XX (1929–30), 51–76.

Peake, A. S. (ed.). *The People and the Book* (Oxford, 1925).

Pedersen, J. *Israel: its Life and Culture*, I–II (Oxford, 1926).

—— 'Wisdom and Immortality', *VT Suppl.* III (1955), 238–46.

Philonenko, M. *Les Interpolations chrétiennes des Testaments des Douze Patriarches et les Manuscrits de Qumran* (Paris, 1960).

Ploeg, J. van der 'L'Immortalité de l'homme d'après les Textes de la Mer Morte', *VT*, II (1952), 171–5.

Porteous, N. W. 'The Present State of Old Testament Theology', *ET*, LXXV (1963), 70–4.

Porzig, W. *Das Wunder der Sprache* (Bern, 1950).

Rad, G. von *Theology of the Old Testament*, I, Eng. trans. D. M. Stalker (Edinburgh, 1962).

Rashdall, H. *The Idea of the Atonement in Christian Theology* (London, 1919).

Richardson, A. *An Introduction to the Theology of the New Testament* (London, 1958).

Roberts, B. J. *The Old Testament Texts and Versions* (Cardiff, 1951).

Robinson, H. W. *The Cross of the Servant* (London, 1926).

—— *Inspiration and Revelation in the Old Testament* (Oxford, 1946).

Robinson, J. A. T. *The Body* (London, 1952).

—— 'The Baptism of John and the Qumran Community', *HTR*, L (1957), 175–91.

—— *Twelve New Testament Studies* (London, 1962).

Ropes, J. H. '"Righteousness" and "The Righteousness of God" in the Old Testament and in St Paul', *JBL*, XXII (1903), 211–27.

Rowley, H. H. (ed.). *The Old Testament and Modern Study* (Oxford, 1951).

Sanday, W. and Headlam, A. C. *The Epistle to the Romans*[5] (Edinburgh, 1902).

Sandmann, M. *Subject and Predicate* (Edinburgh, 1954).

Schechter, S. *Some Aspects of Rabbinic Theology* (London, 1909).

Schlatter, A. *Der Evangelist Johannes* (Stuttgart, 1948).

—— *Der Evangelist Matthäus*[4] (Stuttgart, 1957).

Schoeps, H. J. *Paul: The Theology of the Apostle in the Light of Jewish Religious History*, Eng. trans. H. Knight (London, 1961).

Schrenk, G. *et al. Righteousness* (Bible Key Words Series, London, 1951).

Schulz, S. 'Zur Rechtfertigung aus Gnaden in Qumran und bei Paulus', *ZTK*, LVI (1959), 155–85.

Schweitzer, A. *The Mysticism of Paul the Apostle* (London, 1931).

Schweizer, E. 'Gegenwart des Geistes und Eschatologische Hoffnung bei Zarathustra, spätjüdischen Gruppen, Gnostikern und den Zeugen des Neuen Testaments', in *The Background of the New Testament and its Eschatology*, eds. W. D. Davies and D. Daube (Cambridge, 1956).

—— *Lordship and Discipleship* (London, 1960).

—— *The Spirit of God* (Bible Key Words Series, London, 1960).

Scott, C. A. A. *Christianity according to St Paul* (Cambridge, 1927).

Scott, E. F. *The Spirit in the New Testament* (London, 1923).

Scroggs, R. 'Romans vi. 7', *NTS*, X (1963–4), 104–8.

Selwyn, E. G. *The First Epistle of Peter* (London, 1946).
Simpson, E. K. *Words Worth Weighing in the Greek New Testament* (London, 1946).
Skinner, J. *Isaiah*, I–II (Cambridge Bible for Schools and Colleges: Cambridge, 1896–8).
Smith, W. R. *The Prophets of Israel*[2] (London, 1897).
Snaith, N. H. *The Distinctive Ideas of the Old Testament* (London, 1944).
Spicq, C. *L'Épître aux Hébreux*, I–II (Paris, 1952–3).
Stendahl, K. 'Implications of Form-Criticism and Tradition-Criticism for Biblical Interpretation', *JBL*, LXXVII (1958), 33–8.
—— (ed.). *The Scrolls and the New Testament* (London, 1958).
Stern, G. *Meaning and Change of Meaning* (Gothenburg, 1931).
Stevens, W. A. 'On the Forensic Meaning of Δικαιοσύνη', *AJT*, I (1897), 443–50.
Strecker, G. *Der Weg der Gerechtigkeit* (Göttingen, 1962).
Swanson, J. W. 'Linguistic Relativity and Translation', *Philosophy and Phenomenological Research*, XXII (1961), 185–92.
Taylor, V. *Behind the Third Gospel* (Oxford, 1926).
—— *Jesus and His Sacrifice* (London, 1937).
—— *The Gospel according to St Mark* (London, 1952).
Teicher, J. L. 'The Dead Sea Scrolls: Documents of the Jewish Christian Sect of Ebionites', *JJS*, II (1951), 67–99.
Thackeray, H. St J. *The Relation of St Paul to Contemporary Jewish Thought* (London, 1900).
Turner, N. 'The Unique Character of Biblical Greek', *VT*, V (1955), 208–13.
—— 'The Language of the New Testament', in *Peake's Commentary on the Bible*, eds. M. Black and H. H. Rowley, pp. 659–62 (Edinburgh, 1962).
—— *Syntax*, vol. III of J. H. Moulton's *A Grammar of New Testament Greek* (Edinbrugh, 1963).
—— 'Papyrus Finds', *ET*, LXXVI (1964), 44–8.
Ullmann, S. *The Principles of Semantics*[2] (Oxford, 1957).
—— *Semantics: An Introduction to the Science of Meaning* (Oxford, 1962).
van Unnik, W. C. 'Jesus the Christ', *NTS*, VIII (1961–2), 101–16.
Urban, W. M. *Language and Reality* (London, 1939).
de Vaux, R. *Ancient Israel: Its Life and Institutions*, Eng. trans. J. McHugh (London, 1961).
Vermès, G. *Discovery in the Judaean Desert* (New York, 1956).
—— *Scripture and Tradition in Judaism* (Leiden, 1961).
Volz, P. *Der Geist Gottes* (Tübingen, 1910).
Vriezen, Th. *An Outline of Old Testament Theology* (Oxford, 1958).
Wallace, D. H. 'Biblical Theology: Past and Future', *TZ*, XIX (1963), 88–105.

Warfield, B. B. 'The New Testament Terminology of Redemption', *PTR*, xv (1917), 201–49.

Watson, N. M. 'Some Observations on the Use of Δικαιόω in the Septuagint', *JBL*, lxxix (1960), 255–66.

Watson, P. S. 'The Nature and Function of Biblical Theology', *ET*, lxxiii (1962), 195–200.

Weingreen, J. 'The Title "Moreh Sedek"', *JSS*, vi (1961), 162–74.

Weiser, A. *The Psalms* (London, 1962).

Wernberg-Møller, P. 'A Reconsideration of the Two Spirits in the Rule of the Community, 1QS 3. 13–4. 26', *RQ*, iii (1961), 413–41.

Whorf, B. L. *Four Articles on Metalinguistics* (Washington, 1952).

—— *Language, Thought and Reality* (New York, 1956).

Wilcox, M. *The Semitisms of Acts* (Oxford, 1965).

Wilkinson, J. *Interpretation and Community* (London, 1963).

Williams, C. S. C. *The Acts of the Apostles* (London, 1957).

Willoughby, H. R. (ed.). *The Study of the Bible Today and Tomorrow* (Chicago, 1947).

Wolfson, H. A. *Philo*, i–ii (Cambridge, Mass., 1947).

Woude, A. S. van der *Die Messianischen Vorstellungen der Gemeinde von Qumran* (Assen, 1957).

Wright, G. E. *The Old Testament against its Environment* (London, 1950).

Yates, J. E. *The Spirit and the Kingdom* (London, 1963).

Zahn, Th. *Römerbrief* (Leipzig, 1910).

INDEX OF AUTHORS

INDEX OF PASSAGES CITED

A. THE OLD TESTAMENT

B. THE APOCRYPHA AND PSEUDEPIGRAPHA OF THE OLD TESTAMENT

321

21-2

D. THE DEAD SEA SCROLLS

E. RABBINICAL LITERATURE

(Tractates are alphabetically arranged)

(i) The Mishnah

(ii) The Babylonian Talmud

F. CLASSICAL AND HELLENISTIC AUTHORS
AND EXTRA-CANONICAL
CHRISTIAN WRITINGS